A literature of restitution

MANCHESTER
1824
Manchester University Press

A literature of restitution

Critical essays on W. G. Sebald

Edited by
Jeannette Baxter, Valerie Henitiuk and Ben Hutchinson

Manchester University Press

Published by Manchester University Press
Altrincham Street, Manchester M1 7JA, UK
www.manchesteruniversitypress.co.uk

British Library Cataloguing-in-Publication Data is available

Library of Congress Cataloging-in-Publication Data is available

ISBN 978 1 7849 9350 4 *paperback*

First published by Manchester University Press in hardback 2013

This edition first published 2016

Printed by Lightning Source

CONTENTS

LIST OF ILLUSTRATIONS

NOTES ON CONTRIBUTORS

Jeannette Baxter is Senior Lecturer in English Literature at Anglia Ruskin University, Cambridge. She is the author of *J. G. Ballard's Surrealist Imagination: Spectacular Authorship* (Ashgate 2009) and numerous articles and book chapters in the areas of literary modernism, postmodernism and contemporary British fiction. She is the editor of *J. G. Ballard: Contemporary Critical Perspectives* (Continuum 2008) and co-editor (with Rowland Wymer) of *Visions and Revisions: Essays on J. G. Ballard* (Palgrave 2011).

Anthea Bell is a translator from German and French. Her translations from German include modern and classic fiction by authors including E. T. A. Hoffmann, Kafka and Stefan Zweig. Her translation awards include the 2003 Austrian State Prize for Literary Translation, and in 2002, for the translation of W. G. Sebald's *Austerlitz*, the Schlegel-Tieck Prize, the Helen and Kurt Wolff Prize (USA), and with the author the Independent Foreign Fiction Prize. She also translated W. G. Sebald's *On the Natural History of Destruction* and his posthumous *Campo Santo*.

David Darby is Associate Professor of German and Comparative Literature at the University of Western Ontario. His recent publications include essays on German and Austrian literature of the nineteenth and twentieth centuries, focusing primarily on the imaginative depiction of urban environments and the experience of modern city life. His current research focuses on the (mis-)reading, and the role that memory plays therein, of changing landscapes in literary and visual representations of cities and their environs since the late eighteenth century.

Peter Filkins is the translator of H. G. Adler's novels *The Journey* (2008) and *Panorama* (2011). A recipient of a Berlin Prize, a Fulbright and an Outstanding Translation Award from the American Literary Translators Association, he is also the translator of Ingeborg Bachmann's collected poems, *Darkness Spoken* (2006). His translations, reviews and poems have appeared in numerous publications, including the *N.Y. Times Book Review*, *Partisan Review*, *The New Criterion*, *Paris Review*, and *The New Republic*. He teaches writing, literature and translation at Bard College.

Helen Finch is Academic Fellow in German at the University of Leeds. Her publications include *Sebald's Bachelors: Queer Resistance and the Unconforming Life* (Legenda, 2013), 'Günter Grass's Account of German Wartime Suffering in Beim Häuten der Zwiebel: Mind in Mourning or Boy Adventurer?' in *'Germans as Victims' in The Literary Fiction of the Berlin Republic*, ed. Karina Berger and Stuart Taberner (2009), and 'Die irdische Erfüllung: Inherited Guilt, Elective Affinities and Poetic Utopias in W. G. Sebald's Work', in *W. G. Sebald and the Writing of History*, eds Anne Fuchs, J. J. Long (2007). She is working on a major project on canon-formation in German Holocaust literature.

Graeme Gilloch is Reader in Sociology at Lancaster University; a former Alexander von Humboldt Research Fellow at the J. W. Goethe University, Frankfurt am Main; and a recent Research Fellow at Pusan National University, Korea. He is author of two books (*Myth and Metropolis: Walter Benjamin and the City* (1996) and *Walter Benjamin: Critical Constellations* (2002) both published with Polity Press, Cambridge) and has written numerous articles and essays on critical cultural theory, film, photography and contemporary literature (including essays on Paul Auster and Orhan Pamuk). He is presently writing a monograph on the works of Siegfried Kracauer.

Valerie Henitiuk is Director, Faculty Commons at Grant MacEwan University in Edmonton, Canada, where she also holds an academic appointment in English. Until March 2013, she was Senior Lecturer in Literature and Translation and Director of the British Centre for Literary Translation (founded by W. G. Sebald in 1989) at the University of East Anglia. Her work has appeared in the *Canadian Review of Comparative Literature, Comparative Literature Studies, META, Translation Studies* and *TTR*, and in *Teaching World Literature* (MLA 2009), *Thinking through Translation with Metaphors* (St. Jerome 2010), and *Translating Women* (University of Ottawa Press 2011). She has also published *Embodied Boundaries: Images of Liminality in a Selection of Woman-Authored Courtship Narratives* (Gateway 2007), *One Step towards the Sun: Short Stories by Women of Orissa* (co-edited for Rupantar 2010), and *Worlding Sei Shônagon:* The Pillow Book *in Translation* (University of Ottawa 2012).

Graley Herren is a Professor of English at Xavier University in Cincinnati, Ohio, USA. He is the author of numerous articles and reviews on twentieth-century literature, with a special emphasis upon the work of Samuel Beckett. His book *Samuel Beckett's Plays on Film and Television* was published by Palgrave Macmillan in 2007. He serves on the executive boards of the Comparative Drama Conference and the Samuel Beckett Society, and he edits the Society's newsletter, *The Beckett Circle*.

Ben Hutchinson is Professor of European Literature at the University of Kent. Alongside numerous essays on German, English and French literature, he has notably published one of the first monographs to make use of Sebald's annotated library, *W. G. Sebald. Die dialektische Imagination* (2009), as well as a chapter in the catalogue of the Marbach exhibition *Wandernde Schatten. W. G. Sebalds Unterwelt* (2008). He is also the author of the monographs *Rilke's Poetics of Becoming* (2006) and *Modernism and Style* (2011), the editor of an English edition of *Rainer Maria Rilke's The Book of Hours* (2008, tr. Susan Ranson), and the co-editor (with Shane Weller) of *Archive: Comparative Critical Studies 8: 2–3* (2011). In 2011, he was awarded a Philip Leverhulme Prize.

Russell Kilbourn is Associate Professor in English and Film Studies at Wilfrid Laurier University, specializing in film theory and memory studies. In addition to several essays on Sebald, he has published on film, cultural studies and comparative literature. His book, *Cinema, Memory, Modernity: The Representation of Memory from the Art Film to Transnational Cinema*, was published by Routledge in 2010. He is also a series editor for the Film and Media Studies series at WLU Press, and is co-editor, with Eleanor Ty, of *The Memory Effect: The Remediation of Memory in Literature and Film* (WLU Press, forthcoming summer 2013).

Simon Murray is Senior Lecturer in Theatre Studies at the University of Glasgow. He was recently Director of Theatre at Dartington College of Arts and has been a professional performer and director working particularly in devised physical or visual theatre. He trained with Philippe Gaulier and Monika Pagneux in Paris in the late 1980s, and is author of *Jacques Lecoq* (Routledge 2003). He is joint author / editor (with John Keefe) of *Physical Theatres: A Critical Introduction* and *Physical Theatres: A Critical Reader* (both Routledge 2007). He is co-founder and co-editor (with Jonathan Pitches) of the journal *Theatre, Dance and Performance Training*.

Dora Osborne is Leverhulme Early Career Fellow in German at the University of Edinburgh. She completed her PhD at the University of Cambridge in 2008, with a thesis on trauma and visuality in the prose of W. G. Sebald and Christoph Ransmayr. Her current research looks at archive and memory in recent German literature and visual culture.

Clive Scott is Professor Emeritus of European Literature at the University of East Anglia, and a Fellow of the British Academy. His principal research interests lie in French and comparative poetics (*The Poetics of French Verse: Studies in Reading* (1998); *Channel Crossings: French and English Poetry in Dialogue 1550–2000* (2002) (awarded the R. H. Gapper Book Prize, 2004)); in literary translation, and in particular the experimental translation of poetry (*Literary Translation and the Rediscovery of Reading*,

2012; *Translating the Perception of Text: Literary Translation and Phenomenology*, 2012); and in photography's relationship with writing (*The Spoken Image: Photography and Language*, 1999; *Street Photography: From Atget to Cartier-Bresson*, 2007). He is at present preparing a study on translation's contribution to comparative literature.

George Szirtes was born in Budapest in 1948 and came to England as a refugee in 1956. His poems began appearing in national magazines in 1973 and his first book, *The Slant Door*, was published in 1979. It won the Faber Memorial prize the following year. Since then he has published several books and won various other prizes, including the T. S. Eliot Prize for *Reel* in 2005. Beside his work in poetry and translation he has written *Exercise of Power*, a study of the artist Ana Maria Pacheco, and, together with Penelope Lively, edited *New Writing 10*, published by Picador in 2001.

Shane Weller is Professor of Comparative Literature, Co-Director of the Centre for Modern European Literature and Head of the School of European Culture and Languages at the University of Kent. His publications include *A Taste for the Negative: Beckett and Nihilism* (2005), *Beckett, Literature, and the Ethics of Alterity* (2006), *Literature, Philosophy, Nihilism: The Uncanniest of Guests* (2008), *Modernism and Nihilism* (2011), and (with Dirk Van Hulle) *The Making of Samuel Beckett's 'L'Innommable'/'The Unnamable'* (2013). Edited volumes include (with Ben Hutchinson) *Archive: Comparative Critical Studies 8: 2–3* (2011) and (with Anna Katharina Schaffner) *Modernist Eroticisms: European Literature after Sexology* (2012).

Arthur Williams held a Personal Chair in Contemporary German Studies at the University of Bradford. He was Head of German and of Modern Languages and chaired the University's Advisory Committee on the Arts (Music, Theatre, Visual Arts). He had a strong teaching interest in translation and interpreting. He is particularly associated with the Bradford Biennial International Colloquium on Contemporary German-Language Literature (now the Leeds-Swansea Colloquium).

ACKNOWLEDGEMENTS

Special thanks are due to the contributors to this volume for their tireless commitment and patience during its long preparation. The editors are also grateful to the following people and organizations: the Estate of W. G. Sebald for permission to quote from and reproduce Sebald's works throughout the volume; Julie de Chazal at the Wylie Agency for her invaluable advice in securing permissions; English Heritage for permission to reproduce 'Bomb damage at Holland House'; and Kim Walker and Matthew Frost at Manchester University Press for their help with editorial queries. Jeannette Baxter would like to thank her parents and K and W for their continued love and support, and she would like to remember her brother, Tony, who died before this project was fully completed. Ben Hutchinson gratefully acknowledges Richard Sheppard for his continuing advice on all matters Sebaldian, as well as Shane Weller for the many fruitful hours of discussion. Throughout this project, Valerie Henitiuk has been particularly inspired by both of her co-editors, as well as by the old letter-tray sitting in her office, with its faded label that reads 'Prof. Sebald'.

Some of the ideas in this volume started life at the 'W. G. Sebald: An International and Interdisciplinary Conference' held at the University of East Anglia in 2008. The editors would like to thank the organizers and all participants of that conference for the thoughtful reflection and on-going discussion it has engendered.

PERMISSIONS

For granting permissions to quote, reproduce pages and/or images from the works of W. G. Sebald, the editors and Manchester University Press would like to thank: the Estate of W. G. Sebald; Eichborn Verlag; Carl Hanser Verlag; Penguin Books; Random House (UK); Random House (US); Knopf Press; and Berg Press.

From *For Years Now*

From *Logis im einem Landhaus*

Über Gottfried Keller, Johann Peter Hebel, Robert Walser und andere

From *Luftkrieg und Literatur (On the Natural History of Destruction)*

From *Nach der Natur (After Nature)*

From *A Radical Stage*

From *Die Ringe des Saturn (The Rings of Saturn)*

INTRODUCTION: 'À QUOI BON LA LITTÉRATURE?'

What good is literature? This question surfaces throughout 'Ein Versuch der Restitution' ('An Attempt at Restitution'), an essay first delivered by W. G. Sebald in the form of a speech to mark the opening of a House of Literature in Stuttgart in 2001.[1] In characteristic fashion, the author resists all pressure to give a straightforward assessment of what the function, value or responsibility of literature might be at the dawn of a millennium haunted by the catastrophic legacy of the recent past. Instead, Sebald responds in tentative mood: 'Einzig vielleicht dazu, daß wir uns erinnern und daß wir begreifen lernen, daß es sonderbare, von keiner Kausallogik zu ergründende Zusammenhänge gibt' ('Perhaps only to help us to remember, and teach us to understand that some strange connections cannot be explained by causal logic' (2003b: 247; 2005a: 213–14)). Putting his theory of literature to the test, Sebald proceeds by making a series of associative links between the host city of Stuttgart and the French town of Tulle, which the poet Friedrich Hölderlin visited whilst traveling (on foot) from Stuttgart to Bordeaux, and which was the site of an SS massacre 'am 9. Juni 1944, gerade drei Wochen nachdem ich im Seefelder-Haus in Wertach das sogenannte Licht der Welt erblickte, und fast auf den Tag genau einhundert Jahre und eines nach Hölderlins Tod' ('on 9 June 1944, exactly three weeks after I first saw the light of day in the Seefeld house in Wertach, and almost exactly a hundred and one years after Hölderlin's death' (2003b: 247; 2005a: 214)).

Illustrated in crystallized form here are some of the recurring concerns of, and tensions in, Sebald's writing: the interanimation of historical and literary discourses; the clash of individual and collective memories; the coincidence of life and death; the collision of documentary evidence with the contingent powers of the imagination. As the author goes on to note, 'Es gibt viele Formen des Schreibens; einzig aber in der literarischen geht us, über die Registrierung der Tatsachen und über die Wissenschaft hinaus, um einen Versuch der Restitution' ('There are many forms of writing; only in literature, however, can there be an attempt at restitution over and above the mere recital of facts and over and above scholarship' (2003b: 248; 2005a: 215)).

But what, precisely, does a literature of restitution look like? What forms, styles and techniques might it employ? And what are the aesthetic and ethical possibilities and limitations of such a project? If, as Russell J. A. Kilbourn suggests in concluding the volume, restitution is to be distinguished from 'the more loaded concepts' of retribution or redemption,[2] it is because it attempts to restore agency to marginalized historical subjects without seeking to intervene either physically or metaphysically, without prejudicing their alterity. And if Sebald argues for a *literature* of restitution, rather than pursuing it through historical testimony, it is because 'die Berichte einzelner Augenzeugen [...] nur von bedingtem Wert [sind] und bedürfen der Ergänzung durch das, was sich erschliesst unter einem synoptischen, künstlichen Blick' ('the accounts of individual eyewitnesses [...] are of only qualified value, and need to be supplemented by what a synoptic and artificial view reveals' (1999e: 33; 2004b: 25–6)). For Sebald, it is literature's ability to worry away at claims of historical veracity, to imagine alternative, and often elliptical, expressions of historical experience, and to pose unnerving questions about the relationship between, and representation of, the past and the present that might just facilitate a project of restitution.

Written by a range of scholars from fields as various as translation studies, English, German and comparative literature, photography, critical theory, psychoanalysis, poetry and art theory, the essays collected in this volume endeavour to explore these questions. Although the aim of each critical perspective is to offer individual and differentiated readings of Sebald's literary and critical writings, each response is also written out of a shared awareness of the ambiguities inherent in Sebald's project of literary restitution: 'Der synoptische Blick [...], ist verschattet und illuminiert doch zugleich das Andenken derer, denen das grösste Unrecht widerfuhr' ('The synoptic view [...] is overshadowed and illuminated, however, by the memory of those to whom the greatest injustice was done' (2003b: 248; 2005a: 215)). In the context of the volume, this passage has a double significance. First, the modulation from the passive 'verschattet' to the active 'illuminiert' in the original German, which produces the double effect of overshadowing *and* illuminating, gestures to a productive ambiguity at the heart of Sebald's project; one that is alive to the inevitable shortcomings of literary representation, but which nevertheless strives to recuperate that which has been lost. Second, the way in which the English translation contains the active nature of the original formulation in a passive construction and thereby transforms, albeit subtly and unwittingly, its potential meanings, opens up a necessary set of questions about the formal and substantive differences between the German and the English versions of Sebald's literature of restitution.

Indeed, the question of whether Sebald's work is read in German or English should not be misunderstood as a sign of scholarly pedantry or, for that matter, territorialism. This is because very specific interpretations of the author and his work have emerged out of language-specific contexts. Anne Fuchs and J. J Long note, for instance, how: 'Anglophone critics and readers are particularly fascinated by a mode of writing which appears to give literary expression to history's unfolding catastrophes, above all to the Holocaust as a defining caesura of 20th-century history' (Fuchs and Long 2007: 7). Certainly, Sebald's work does engage, albeit from predominantly oblique angles, with the Holocaust, and each essay in this collection is alive to the ways in which the Holocaust and its legacies haunt his literary imagination. But if Sebald's writings constitute a project of literary restitution, as this volume proposes, it would be erroneous to limit its restorative ambitions to the atrocities of the recent past.

Just one example of the way in which Sebald's project of restitution engages with a much longer history of European modernity manifests itself in the centrality of the German poet Friedrich Hölderlin to 'Ein Versuch der Restitution'. For the question – *A quoi bon la littérature?* – preoccupied the Romantic poet long before it concerned the late twentieth-century author. It is also worth noting that, rather than simply reciting Hölderlin's original formulation – 'Wozu Dichter in dürftiger Zeit?' (What use are poets in destitute times?) – Sebald offers a playful translation that not only demands of the reader that s/he read French (Sebald presumably turns to French at this moment in the text because he is recalling Hölderlin's travels in France), but also that s/he understand the embedded literary reference. Championed by influential commentators in the English-speaking world such as Susan Sontag and James Wood, Sebald in English was perceived as a striking new voice, yet what emerges even from this brief analysis is that his saturation in the Germanic tradition arguably makes him a less singular figure in his native language. This does not make Sebald's literary achievement any less remarkable; indeed, it is only in returning to the original German texts, as this volume attempts to do, that the full subtlety of his elusive, allusive prose becomes apparent, and that the composite and comparative nature of his project of literary restitution can begin to be fully appreciated.

The publication history of Sebald's work can be rapidly established. Having fled what he saw as the repressive, conformist atmosphere of post-war West German higher education, Sebald taught and studied at the universities of Manchester and, from 1970 onwards, East Anglia. During the 1980s, he became increasingly disenchanted with the Thatcherite reforms of the university system and began to take refuge in what he called the 'inner exile' of creative writing. His first 'creative' book, the long poem *Nach der Natur (After Nature*, 2002), emerged in 1988, followed two years later, in 1990, by the first prose work, *Schwindel. Gefühle (Vertigo*, 1999),[3] which Hans Magnus Enzensberger, the prominent German author and intellectual, published in his series 'Die andere Bibliothek' ('The Other Library') for Eichborn.[4] In 1992, Sebald published what was perhaps his breakthrough work, *Die Ausgewanderten (The Emigrants*, 1996); his growing international reputation was consolidated by the publication, in 1995, of *Die Ringe des Saturn. Eine englische*

Wallfahrt (*The Rings of Saturn*, 1998). Six years later, in 2001, emerged what would prove to be Sebald's final work, *Austerlitz* (*Austerlitz*, 2001); as the almost unanimous acclaim was growing, he died in December of the same year, after suffering a heart attack whilst driving. Posthumously published works include the collection of fragments and essays *Campo Santo* (2003), a selection of his poems, *Über das Land und das Wasser. Ausgewählte Gedichte 1964–2001* (2008), and the fragments of his so-called 'Corsica Project' published in the catalogue to the Marbach exhibition *Wandernde Schatten. W. G. Sebalds Unterwelt* (2008).

Alongside this body of prose work, Sebald was also active as a literary critic over the course of some three decades. Starting with the publication of his MA dissertation on the German playwright Carl Sternheim in 1969 (*Carl Sternheim. Kritiker und Opfer der Wilhelminischen Ära*), followed by his doctoral dissertation on Alfred Döblin in 1980 (*Der Mythus der Zerstörung im Werk Döblins*), Sebald published a series of books and essays – mainly, but not exclusively, on his specialist subject of Austrian and Swiss literature.[5] Somewhat marginalized in the English-speaking world, owing to the nature of their focus, the essays collected in *Die Beschreibung des Unglücks* (1985), *Unheimliche Heimat* (1991), and *Logis in einem Landhaus* (1998 (translated by Jo Catling as *A Place in the Country*, 2013)), as well as in the edited volume *A Radical Stage: Theatre in Germany in the 1970s and 1980s* (1988), provide important insight into Sebald's intellectual heritage and idiosyncratic prose style. The only critical work of Sebald's to have gained any substantial attention in the English-speaking world was his Zürich lecture series *Luftkrieg und Literatur* (1999, published in English as *On the Natural History of Destruction*, 2003), where the perceived interest to an English-language audience of Sebald's controversial thesis – namely, that German writers failed in their duty to document the full atrocity of the allied bombing raids during the Second World War – was felt to be of a largely historical rather than literary nature (as Anthea Bell notes in her foreword to this volume).

Sebald's rapid rise to prominence has been accompanied by the equally rapid establishment of a substantial body of secondary literature in several languages.[6] German-language criticism (or at least criticism written by professional Germanists) has benefited, of course, from the fact that it can engage with the original texts; some of the more frustrating aspects of Anglo-Saxon criticism derive from this basic inability, or perhaps disinclination, to engage with not only Sebald's German prose, but also the German secondary literature. The initial phase of English-language reception, which began in earnest after the translation of *The Emigrants* in 1996, involved establishing the basic tenets of Sebald's technique (the use of photographs, the blending of narrative and reportage, the interest in repressed traumatic experiences, etc.). After his death in 2001, there followed a phase of consolidation: the whole published oeuvre was now available for scrutiny *sub specie aeternitatis*. Since 2004, meanwhile, a third, on-going phase of reception has been opened up by the deposition of Sebald's annotated library in the

Deutsches Literaturarchiv Marbach, whilst a fourth phase, centred on Sebald's influence on visual art, arguably began around the same time.

What have been the main critical axes of interest? In his *Forschungsbericht* of 2009, Richard Sheppard gives a helpful summary:

> The staple topics of Sebald 'research' include 'the poetics of memory', the text/picture relationship, 'nature, travel, exile and "Heimat"', 'intertextuality and intermediality', 'illness as a metaphor for social repression, messianism and realism in literature, and nature as the destruction of the environment by capitalism', the 'unhappiness caused by the alienating conditions of modernity', and 'Sebald's relationship to the Holocaust', especially among 'anglophone critics'.[7]

Whilst the essays contained in this volume touch on all these subjects, they attempt to bring new impetus to the established lines of enquiry by tackling some of the implicit critical problems head on. One particular focus of the essays, in the spirit of viewing Sebald's project of literary restitution as collective and comparative in nature, is the relationship between the original German text and its English translation. What resonances are lost, what analytical insights gained, by transferring Sebald's carefully stylized prose from one language into another? Clearly it is no slight on the excellent work of the translators Michael Hulse, Michael Hamburger and Anthea Bell to state that the German and English versions of his texts are not the same, nor do they – nor *can* they – resonate in the same way with their respective readers. That this is true not only at the level of individual words and idioms, but also at that of syntactical construction and intertextual allusion, is one of the abiding lessons of Sebald's translation history. In a writer as careful of language, as attentive to the historical and metaphysical resonances of style as Sebald, readers of him in English must be wary of the linguistic 'vertigo' occasioned by translation.

The volume accordingly begins with a section of essays devoted to issues of translation and style. The foreword by Anthea Bell, the translator of *Austerlitz*, *On the Natural History of Destruction* and *Campo Santo* (which includes the essay 'An Attempt at Restitution'), gives a valuable insight into the process of working with Sebald on the English translations. How to preserve Sebald's Germanic style in English? How to avoid the temptation to 'jazz it up a little'? Despite Sebald's claim to have 'grave doubts about the book', *Austerlitz* works so triumphantly, precisely because of its delicate style, not in spite of it. Reproducing this voice in the different cadences of English was one of the great challenges of the translation process, recalls Bell; echoing it and, indeed, the critical voices at work in *Campo Santo* without his input became the great challenge after his death. Nonetheless, drawing on real and imagined conversations with Sebald, Bell reflects on how she was able to maintain the 'illusion' of authorial presence and, in so doing, not only contribute more broadly to the 'transmission of literature' but also, in her own way, collaborate more specifically in Sebald's project of literary restitution.

Taking up Bell's understanding of translation as a process of co-operation that ensures the continued reading/reception of a piece of work, Arthur Williams explores the revisionist potential of translation, noting how Sebald continued to amend the English versions of his work even after publication. Going on to pay particular attention to some of the more elusive aspects of the English and German texts, Williams explores how the titles, subtitles and epigraphs, which shift across editions, pose particular problems to the translator. At the same time that these textual amendments afford Sebald the opportunity to modify, and in some instances moderate, the tone and reach of his historical critique, they also belie a 'body of work marked as much by unity of ethos as by variety of form and content'. A close reading of the translations, Williams argues, illustrates just how closely Sebald came to see his various works as a multilayered but consistent attempt to give voice to European history and its victims.

George Szirtes pursues the question of translation into Sebald's poetry. His discussion of Sebald the poet is in fact a discussion of 'Sebald–Hamburger', he asserts, inasmuch as an analysis of Sebald's poetry in English must also be an analysis of Michael Hamburger's choices in translation. Szirtes enquires into how we are to distinguish between the poetic and prose elements in Sebald's work. The 'business of the Sebaldian imagination', argues Szirtes, is 'encounter, cry and naming': Sebald's famously stylized prose is in fact a kind of poetry, 'with the expectations of prose as counterpoint'. What implications does this have for our understanding of the formal energies and dimensions at work in Sebald's 'literature of restitution'? Szirtes suggests that the prosody of *After Nature* (written before all the major prose works, but published in English only after them) underpins the prose work; the real distinction in Sebald's oeuvre is thus not between poetry and fiction, he insists, but between verse and prose.

Shane Weller concludes the first section of the volume with an investigation into Sebald's 'writing of the negative'. If, as Kafka observed, 'doing the negative is imposed on us', Weller draws on a term of Samuel Beckett's in order to argue that Sebald seeks to follow Kafka's stricture through the strategic deployment of 'unwords'. The frequency with which such unwords recur – terms examined include 'Unglück', 'unruhig', 'unsicher' and 'ungut', as well as related syntactical structures – suggests not only the manner in which Sebald's project of restitution draws on 'an entire literary tradition' in order to articulate the catastrophe of recent European history, but also the 'irreducible doubleness of that negativity'. In refusing to make any kind of 'compromise' with a history that he regards as 'obscene', Sebald's 'tarrying' within the negative, Weller argues, is necessarily dialectical: it seeks to resist both unremitting nihilism and any facile attempt to overcome it, since, in the words of Adorno, 'acts of overcoming – even of nihilism [...] – are always worse than what they overcome'.

The central section of the volume, comprising a series of close readings of

Sebald's main prose works, begins with Jeannette Baxter's reading of *Vertigo* as an exercise in Surrealist literary historiography. Tracing, in particular, echoes of the writings of Roger Caillois, Georges Bataille and André Masson, Baxter associates the leitmotif of vertigo with 'the domain of play', 'chance' and the 'anti-architecture' of the labyrinth, as well as with the 'double vertigo' of the uncanny. Opening Sebald's text up to its dissident and desublimatory energies, Baxter argues (following André Breton) that *Vertigo* oscillates 'between oppositional poles: illumination and darkening; conscious and unconscious; sublimation and desublimation'. The famously untranslatable pun in the German title – the play on feelings both of dizziness and of being swindled – typifies this oscillation; if *Vertigo* resists any sense of an ending, this is part of its aesthetic strategy to articulate the uncertainties and risks inherent in a literary project of historical retrieval.

Where *Vertigo* oscillates between the Surrealist poles of the conscious and the unconscious, Dora Osborne suggests that *The Emigrants* can be read as a contest between vision and obscurity. Drawing on Jacques Derrida's *Memoirs of the Blind* (1993), Osborne argues that Sebald's text attempts 'to mourn and remember the losses experienced by the emigrants' and at the same time 'to supplement the gaps which these losses leave'. If the four 'portraits' collected in the book all in some sense concern vision and blindness, the term 'memoirs of the blind' makes use of a double genitive: at once *about* and *by* the blind, *The Emigrants* relates the visual impairment of both the protagonists and the Sebaldian narrator. The narrator's vision paradoxically works to obscure the portraits of the emigrants; the blind spots that emerge come to characterize what Osborne calls Sebald's technique of 'effacement in exhibition', an authorial technique which is inevitably, and ineluctably, marked by the blind spots of Sebald's own 'belatedness and failed witness'.

Helen Finch pursues the implications of historical blind spots in her reading of Anglo-Irish themes in *The Rings of Saturn*. Tracing Sebald's literary preoccupations with Ireland to the short stories of Jorge Luis Borges, Finch argues that Sebald (following Borges) appropriates an Anglo-Irish history of exile, colonialism, hybridity and deterritorialization as a potential foil, or pretext, for discussing 'his wider prosodics of the negative effects of Enlightenment'. Sebald embellishes source materials, Finch suggests, in a way that forces, rather than forges, particular historical connections. Exploring the aesthetic and ethical dimensions of Sebald's literature of historical recovery, Finch asks not only whether Sebald's 'hagiographic' depiction of the Anglo-Irish diaspora elides, amongst other things, the complexity of Anglo-Irish relations, but also whether Sebald's project of restitution 'falls prey to a wilfully blinkered exoticism' that deals in large 'clichés' of Irish history in its attempt to champion the minor and local.

Written shortly after the completion of *The Rings of Saturn* in the mid-1990s, the various fragments of Sebald's aborted 'Corsica Project' offer a precious glimpse into a work-in-progress. Graeme Gilloch suggests that the work is to Sebald what

The Arcades Project is to Walter Benjamin, compelling the reader's attention precisely through its haunting, fragmentary nature. Both, notes Gilloch, are 'panoramic historical-archaeological projects preoccupied with the ruinous residues of the nineteenth century'; both, importantly, were used as quarries for other works. Gilloch compares Benjamin's motif of the 'arcade' with Sebald's image of the 'arca': from the cemetery in Piana to the echoes of the Mexican 'Day of the Dead', from the 'dream-hunters' of the Corsican forests to the 'dream-world' of the Napoleonic Empire, Sebald's unwritten 'Arca Project' evokes at every turn 'the future of the past', just as Benjamin's *Arcades Project* attempts to archive the ephemera of nineteenth-century capitalism. The fact that it was left unfinished, argues Gilloch, offers an appropriate formal parallel to its thematic preoccupation with 'fragility and contingency', whilst suggesting, at the same time, that Sebald's project of restitution is unavoidably partial and open ended.

The first of two essays on *Austerlitz* explores the 'entwined narratives' of Sebald and H. G. Adler. Peter Filkins investigates not only the extent to which Adler's work functions as a key intertext for *Austerlitz*, but also the extent to which Adler's fiction helped determine Sebald's 'role and identity as a writer attempting to render aspects of the Holocaust'. Whilst Adler's most famous work, *Theresienstadt 1941– 1945*, is cited explicitly in *Austerlitz*, his approach to the Holocaust informs Sebald's technique more broadly, argues Filkins. In a 1986 interview, Adler remembered how he determined upon arrival at Theresienstadt that, should he survive the camps, he would respond to his experiences both as historian and as artist; whilst Sebald's trademark blending of fact and fiction can be said to follow this lead, the methodology is not wholly unproblematic. Alongside Sebald's explicit responses to Adler's documentary work, Filkins explores the largely unacknowledged presence of Adler's fiction in the detail and plot structure of *Austerlitz*. As a writer at several removes from the Holocaust, Sebald is careful, notes Filkins, to suggest the difference in status between his 'literary' text and Adler's quasi-documentary perspective: through his various narrative clues Sebald points the reader towards Adler, but he does so in a deliberately 'circumspect manner'. How are we to interpret these authorial manoeuvres? Sebald's ambiguous textual appropriations of Adler's writings, which include deliberate modifications of source materials, together with his conspicuous epitextual silence on Adler, should be read, Filkins suggests, less in the spirit of willful misappropriation than as an expression of the inevitable limitations, and ultimately failings, of a project that attempts to reconstruct 'a past that, like Austerlitz', Sebald 'can only begin to glimpse through Adler'. Sebald is ultimately ensnared in 'a bind from which he cannot extricate himself, namely that of having to remain a witness to a witness'.

In the second essay on *Austerlitz*, David Darby also holds up to scrutiny the recuperative and revelatory possibilities of Sebald's literary project. Turning his attention to the series of train stations that recur through the course of *Austerlitz* –

the Centraal Station in Antwerp, Liverpool Street Station in London, the Wilson Station in Prague, and the Gare d'Austerlitz in Paris – Darby suggests that all function as turning-points both in the protagonist Austerlitz's story and in his encounters with the narrator. Following Walter Benjamin's notion of the 'Schwelle', Darby interprets these train stations as 'threshold zones': in analogy with photographic images, Darby sees them as 'Sebald's metaphoric darkrooms, dark zones of transition between the visible and invisible, the remembered and the forgotten'. Such locations are ultimately ambiguous, argues Darby, since on the one hand they are complicit in the capitalist catastrophe of modernity, whilst on the other hand they offer the possibility of mediating between inauthentic and 'authentic' life. Yet these moments of mediation, of recollection and construction, Darby insists, are not without pain or trauma; at the same time that they may allow for a confrontation of despair, they do not, contra Adorno, defy it.

The final section of the volume explores the status of what are arguably the two key aspects of Sebald's aesthetic technique, namely 'prose' and photography. Simon Murray begins by exploring an under-researched area of Sebald's prose, namely its resonance for contemporary performance practices. If Sebald's critical writings suggest his view that Brechtian dramatic conventions are now unable to 'deal with our traumatised consciousness', what kind of theatre would represent an adequate response to his own prose? Murray offers the examples of a range of contemporary dramatists, such as the 'Volcano Group' and their appropriation of Sebald's 'hopscotching', or Goat Island's representations of post-war attempts at 'repair', all of which are alive to, and attempt dialogue with, the 'ethical and ideological imperatives for restitution' that propel Sebald's writings. Specifically, Sebald's poetics of digression resonate repeatedly in contemporary theatre, argues Murray: his quest for 'lightness' to oppose to the gravity of the twentieth century, his rejection of classical notions of a 'contract' between author-dramatist and reader-spectator, and his attempts to blur the boundaries between the fictional and the real, find renewed forms of expression and a new range of significance as they make the transition from prose to performance, from page to stage.

Clive Scott opens up the visual dimensions of Sebald's literature of restitution by revisiting the better-documented area of Sebald's relationship with photography. Between the poles of still life and portrait, Scott constructs a quasi-dialectical understanding of Sebald's photographs: since his portrait photographs 'attempt to re-inhabit' the world of the still life, the still life photographs have conversely 'appropriated the power of the portraits which the portraits have themselves surrendered'. Scott locates a paradox at work in 'An Attempt at Restitution', namely in Sebald's claim that his work, following that of his friend Jan Peter Tripp, proceeds by means of a certain methodology: 'im Einhalten einer genauen historischen Perspektive, im geduldigen Gravieren und in der Vernetzung, in der Manier der *nature morte*, anscheinend weit auseinander liegender Dinge' ('in adhering to an exact historical perspective, in patiently engraving and linking together apparently disparate things in the manner of a still life' (2003b: 243–4; 2005a: 210)). In response to this paradox, Scott proposes a distinction between the 'archaeology' and the 'teleology' of the photograph, arguing that Sebald follows Tripp's paintings in tending to the latter, where the still life functions not as an index of chronological history, but as a projection of a history of encounters with subsequent spectators. Scott's phenomenological view of Sebald's use of images – photographs are said to 'constitute Merleau-Ponty's "pre-human gaze"' – extends to his discussion of the 'metaphysicalization' of Sebald's photo-portraits. Sebald spoke in an interview of how black-and-white photographs 'stand for this territory that is located between death and life', and Scott accordingly argues that, in its 'dissemination', the photograph 'has the capacity constantly to rejoin history, to be part of all histories subsequent to it'.

Graley Herren pursues the relationship between photography, history and spectatorship in his discussion of the topos of the repressed mother as silent and complicit witness in Sebald's work. Herren turns the customary critical concern to distinguish carefully between Sebald the author and Sebald the narrator on its head, arguing that 'the narrator himself is frequently held up for critique'. The narrator's 'closeted Catholicism' causes him either to 'idolize women as divine Mothers or revile them as carnal predators', observes Herren; the maternal is accordingly figured as the 'uncannily familiar'. Using examples from *Vertigo* and *The Emigrants*, Herren argues that Sebald's anxieties about the mother are often related to anxieties about the Holocaust; indeed, Sebald's 'literature of reparation' may be 'rooted in large part in the troubled paternal legacy as the son of a soldier in the *Wehrmacht*', but it is also rooted in a troubling maternal legacy of conspiracy and collusion. If Sebald's narratives at times display an oedipal complex, suggests Herren, it is '*Oedipus Rex* refracted through Kafka and Beckett': by the end of *The Emigrants*, the narrator 'effectively chooses to blind himself rather than face the full implications of his family crisis head on'. Yet the reader is meant to see beyond the narrator's 'averted gaze', and thus to reach the very conclusions that the narrator seeks to avoid.

The various intellectual and ethical demands that the Sebaldian text makes on the reader inform the closing essay in this volume, Russell J. A. Kilbourn's investigation of Sebald's understanding of 'genre'. Sebald's 'blending of genres' is a critical cliché that is more often stated than argued. In an attempt to move beyond the 'two-part truism' that Sebald preferred the term 'prose' to 'novels', and that his texts display extraordinary generic 'hybridity', Kilbourn surveys previous critical discussions on the subject in order to argue that Sebald's texts must be viewed 'as self-reflexive meta-critiques of genre; as, in effect, aestheticized works of genre theory'. In a grant application held in his *Nachlass*, Sebald himself writes of the 'semi-documentary prose fiction for which I have become known';[8] Kilbourn suggests that it is Sebald's self-conscious understanding of genre as a system of literary classification founded on 'pre-existing and predictable categories' of meaning that conditions not only his aesthetic, but also his ethical strategies. Indeed, the 'obliteration' of any 'stable frame of reference', Kilbourn argues, results in a 'highly productive negativity' in Sebald's work, a 'negativity' that founds a new genre, namely 'the literature of restitution' with all of its ethical-aesthetic possibilities and limitations.

Can Sebald's work ultimately be understood as an attempt to interrogate the very possibility, indeed the desirability, of such a literature? Is the critic necessarily complicit in this 'attempt at restitution'? When considering the range of perspectives collected in this volume, it is striking that Sebald seems to have anticipated the various different critical approaches at every step of the way. If Sebald has elicited such an overwhelming critical reaction in the last decade, it is in part because he himself laid down the tracks, building into his aesthetic technique the possibility of informed response. It is not only that Sebald's extensive critical writings suggest angles of approach to his fiction, but also that he constructs his prose in such a way that it *requires* critical engagement in order to be understood. The strategy of using a narrator as an intermediary between author and protagonist is clearly a major aspect of this, since the narrator functions as an ersatz reader, inviting the reader not only to identify, but in some sense also to assume a role within the Sebaldian drama. To use Hans-Georg Gadamer's terminology, Sebald 'fuses the horizons' of protagonist, narrator, author and reader, conflating them into a composite perspective whilst at the same time taking care to differentiate between them. Whilst much critical work[9] has been done on the notion of 'Familienähnlichkeiten' (family resemblances) between Sebald's protagonists, the model needs to be extended to include the reader, the implied critic. Carolin Duttlinger has suggested that Sebald requires 'the reader to adopt a non-directed openness of the kind which is also displayed by the protagonists' (2010: 108); arguably the whole project of 'restitution' can be understood as an attempt to close this circle, as an attempt to invite the reader, via the mediation of the narrator/author, to adopt the protagonists' perspective. For if Sebald's work seeks to explore the convergences between an aesthetic and ethical response to historical events, this project in turn calls for an equally sensitive response from the reader. Sebald's hermeneutics presuppose an informed critical engagement with his texts; restitution is contingent on reception.

The recurring themes identified in this collection of essays – from Sebald's carefully calibrated syntax to his self-consciousness about 'genre', from his interest in liminal spaces to his literal and metaphorical preoccupation with blindness and vision – all suggest that the 'attempt at restitution' goes further than mere narrative technique. Sebald's enduring challenge to his readers consists in taking them seriously enough to invite, to require, their criticism; the anticipated critical response becomes a constituent part of his aesthetic project. If Sebald shows his readers such respect, it is to be hoped that these essays repay the compliment.

NOTES

1 The text was first published under the title: 'Zerstreute Reminiszenzen: Gedanken zur Eröffnung eines Stuttgarter Hauses' in the *Stuttgarter Zeitung*, 18 November 2001.

2 See p. 247–64 in this volume.

3 These earlier works were not translated in the order in which they were published in German: *Nach der Natur* (1988) appeared only in 2002, *Schwindel. Gefühle* (1990) in 1999.

4 'Die andere Bibliothek' is a prestigious and niche series of new commissions and reprints which Enzensberger began in 1985. According to Alisdair King, 'The Other Library' is to be understood as 'a series of distinctive publications which would build into a coherent yet diverse collection, with a new title, chosen and edited by Enzensberger, appearing each month at a fixed price of 25DM'. See King (2007: 297).

5 For a comprehensive list of both Sebald's criticism and fiction, see Richard Sheppard's 'An analytical bibliography of the works of W. G. Sebald', in *Saturn's Moons: W. G. Sebald – A Handbook*, ed. Jo Catling and Richard Hibbitt (Oxford: Legenda, 2011), pp. 446–96.

6 For a full bibliography, see *Saturn's Moons*, pp. 497–547.

7 Sheppard (2009): 81.

8 Quoted in von Bülow (2011: 254–6).

9 See, for instance, Ceuppens (2006: 256–7): 'the four stories which make up *The Emigrants* could be said to function like Galton's composite photographs: by superposing a number of stories describing similar fates, one could expect a typical emigrant story to appear – which, on the other hand, would be as neutral and vague as most of Galton's results'.

FOREWORD

Translating W. G. Sebald, with and without the author

Anthea Bell

I am told, by a German friend, that in the German-speaking countries translators tend to specialize in a particular genre more than we do in the English-speaking world. As we all know, however, more translations are published in other languages, so I suppose translators into those languages can afford to specialize. I prefer to switch happily between genres, even between books for adults and books for the young. And when I am sent a text with a suggestion that I might translate it, I have never entirely lost the thrill I felt as a child at the arrival of a new, still unread book. What joys may it contain? I do, of course, read a book that I am asked to translate before agreeing to do it, although I know two translators who prefer not to. But of course I already knew the work of W. G. Sebald (always known as Max) when I was asked to translate two of his books, *Austerlitz* and *Luftkrieg und Literatur*, so you can easily imagine how happy I was to say yes.

A brief parenthesis: I sometimes feel that translators ought to apologize for existing at all. We are notoriously insular in the English-speaking countries as far as the reception of literature in other languages is concerned, and there have been various pieces in the press recently about the redundancy of literary translators and their translations. In the *Times*, first David Baddiel and then Michael Gove wondered what is the point of literature in translation. Gove was induced to retract at least in part by Tony Briggs, the distinguished translator of *War and Peace*; then along came Matthew Parris saying no, Michael Gove was right in the first place, why bother with translation at all. There was a little sequel to this saga: some months later Gove – then Opposition spokesman on schools and families, since the 2010 general election secretary of state for education – could be read lavishing praise, also in the *Times*, on Jonathan Littell's long Prix Goncourt winner, *The Kindly Ones*, translated by Charlotte Mandell, so he had probably changed his mind. Why bother, then? One answer was given in the *Independent*: 'The most influential author to come out of the UK in recent years wrote not in English but in German' (The Literator 2008: n.p.). I am sure those of us who knew Max have often been asked why he didn't in fact write in English, or translate himself into English. I think I can see the answer to the first question: it lies in the great affinity of his thinking with his native language. As for the second, up to the time of his death Max of course worked closely with his translators.

And I definitely feel that I ought to explain how I came to be one of them. When I was first approached, I had no idea that I might be involved as a translator with his new novel, or as some would prefer to put it his new narrative, since Max Sebald's narratives were often some way from our usual ideas of fiction. In fact *Austerlitz* has always seemed to me more of a novel as we usually understand the term than its predecessors. It is even a double novel, with the framework chapters in which the typically Sebaldian narrator describes his acquaintanceship with the protagonist, Jacques Austerlitz, and the inner core of the book, Austerlitz's own account of his life.

However, it was about another book that I first heard: in the summer of 1999 Max Sebald's then publishers, Harvill, were – or so I was given to understand – thinking of forging ahead in some haste with the English publication of his lectures, delivered in Zürich and published as *Luftkrieg und Literatur*, together with his reflections on the reactions and the correspondence that they had called forth. To make the material up to book length, he had added an essay on Alfred Andersch. The rationale at the time for the sudden wish to bring the book's translation forward, again so I understood, was its topical relevance; it was felt that the Allied fire-bombing of German cities in the Second World War, so graphically described by the eye-witnesses of the time whose words Max Sebald quotes, had a modern echo in the NATO bombing campaign in Kosovo in the first half of 1999. Topicality can of course be a short-lived phenomenon, and in this case it was. The bombing campaign that began in Kosovo and spread to Serbia as a whole lasted some six months, and, despite after-effects, there was no way that *Luftkrieg und Literatur* could have been translated and published in English quickly enough to appear still topical at the time of publication. However, I was told that a translation was needed urgently, and that Max's regular translator was too busy to do it. Translators do not, as a matter of principle, try to poach authors from other translators, and I needed the reassurance. Michael Hulse is the translator of *The Emigrants*, *Vertigo* and the beautiful English version of *Die Ringe des Saturn*, my favourite of Max Sebald's works after *Austerlitz*. I knew *The Rings of Saturn* well, having read it in both English and German, and it had particularly attracted me because I grew up in its East Anglian setting.

I was one of three translators invited by Harvill to submit sample translations from *Luftkrieg und Literatur*. I heard afterwards, from Max himself, that another three had been commissioned by the editor of an architectural magazine. After that no more was heard for months, and anyway the topical factor had presumably evaporated with the end of NATO operations in midsummer that year. I was therefore taken by surprise in November 1999, when Max's agent got in touch to ask me to translate not just *Luftkrieg und Literatur* but also the next novel, *Austerlitz*, not yet completed. I was in fact placed in what I felt then, and still do, was an awkward situation in relation to Michael Hulse, and I am glad to have the opportunity of clearing it up here, but you do not say no to translating an author like Max, especially when you have already submitted a sample, even if it was from a different book.

Max had just moved to a new literary agent, the Wylie Agency, and as his side of our correspondence is, I understand, part of Max's literary estate, I will take the opportunity of thanking Andrew Wylie for permission to quote from it here. I heard from Max personally in late November 1999, and he set out the situation: 'My agents will now seek offers from publishers for the Air War essay (the English edition will probably also include three shorter pieces on Andersch, Améry and Weiss) [...] and for a prose fiction book called *Austerlitz* which I am currently working on and about which I still have misgivings.'

A week later I had my first sight of some of the book so far. Max wrote: 'Enclosed are pp. 105–135 of the *Austerlitz* project.' He referred to his MS pages, each of 30 lines. 'The pages,' he went on, 'come at the point where Austerlitz recalls the times, after the death of his foster-parents, which he spent with the Fitzpatricks at their house Andromeda Lodge on the Welsh coast.' This is the section of the book that I always think of as the Welsh idyll in the troubled life of Max's protagonist, Jacques Austerlitz, and it remains a favourite with me. I returned the translation as soon as I could, and in February 2000 the two books were ensconced on the publishing programmes of Hamish Hamilton at Penguin UK, and Random House in the United States.

I received the complete manuscript of *Austerlitz* in June, sat in my garden reading it all one warm summer's day, and was bowled over by it – even though, when I wrote to say so, Max replied, 'I fear I still have grave doubts about the book.' The MS was typed on a genuine old-fashioned typewriter – Max was computer resistant, and at the reading and interview with Maya Jaggi of the *Guardian* that he gave in the autumn of 2001, soon after the English publication of *Austerlitz*, claimed that although a computer had been delivered to his room at the University of East Anglia (UEA), it still stood there in its pristine packaging. Those 30-line pages had indications of where the pictures were to come. These pictures – photographs that had taken Max's fancy, reproductions of works of art, diagrams, architectural views of both interiors and exteriors – cannot properly be called illustrations to *Austerlitz*; as with the similar pictures in its predecessors, I consider them more of a gloss on the text. There are not many containing human figures, but those among them that do include such photographs are especially haunting. I think in particular of the group with a parrot on one man's shoulder, occupying pages 120 and 121 of the English edition of *Austerlitz* (2001d), placed in that Welsh idyll, where the amiably eccentric Fitzpatrick family have cockatoos in their garden, introduced long ago by a forebear. Then there is the little girl sitting with her dog on her lap in the village of Vyrnwy before it was drowned by a reservoir; and of course the five-year-old boy in fancy dress as a pageboy who has featured on the cover of the majority of editions of *Austerlitz* in all languages. Because of the almost simultaneous publication of the novel in both German and English, I had not seen this jacket before the arrival in February 2001 of Hanser's German edition, although I had read and translated its description in the main text; this one is definitely to be taken as illustrating the figure of Austerlitz himself as a child. I think that the design team at Penguin and at Random House worked miracles, faced with the task of inserting the pictures where, as in the German original, they are relevant to the text, if only tangentially.

During the first months of 2000, while Max was still working on *Austerlitz*, I had been drafting the material in *Luftkrieg und Literatur*. As the passage from his letter above indicates, Max was still referring to it in English as *Air War and Literature*, but the title in English was a problem. There was no way of reproducing the alliteration of the German. The ultimate English title was *On the Natural History of Destruction*, and it was Max's own idea. The subtitle of 'Air War and Literature' was retained within the book for that part of it comprising the text of the two lectures on the subject delivered by Max in Zürich, with a third essay in which he considers the mixed reactions to them. Towards the end of the first lecture he mentions Solly Zuckermann's plan to write an account of his visit to the bombed-out city of Cologne directly after the Second World War; although never written, it was to have been called 'On the Natural History of Destruction'. The phrase became Max's choice for the overall title of the English version. When I first saw the posthumous collection of Max's works previously unpublished in book form, *Campo Santo* (no title difficulties there, any more than there were with *Austerlitz*), and found that one of the essays in literary criticism, first published in 1982 in the journal *Orbis literarum*, 'Zwischen Geschichte und Naturgeschichte' [Between History and Natural History] bore the subtitle 'Über die literarische Beschreibung totaler Zerstörung' [On the literary description of total destruction], I saw why Max had fixed upon it, because the essay covers some of the material to which he referred in the Zürich lectures.

There is a postscript to the history of this title; only a few months ago, as I write this in 2010, I was called in to arbitrate in a little dispute between academics. Academic A had said, in print, that *On the Natural History of Destruction* was entirely the wrong English title for the book, and not one that Max Sebald would ever have allowed if he had been alive at the time of publication. Academic B was not so sure, and it occurred to him to adopt the simple expedient of asking me about it, as Academic A could have done if he had thought of it. I was, of course, able to confirm that the title was certainly Max's own; I would never have ventured on a title so far from the German original, I told my correspondent, and I doubted whether, without Max's authority, the English-language publishers would have done so either.

In the summer of 2000 a translation workshop was held at the UEA, under the aegis of Peter Bush, the eminent translator from Spanish and Catalan who at the time was Director of the British Centre for Literary Translation, founded in 1989 by Max Sebald himself at the university. Indeed, as I live only sixty miles from Norwich, before I came to translate anything by Max we had met at some of the workshops on translation periodically held at the UEA while Peter was professor of literary translation there. On this occasion Max and I were discussing the English version of the second Zürich lecture (opening, in English, 'How ought such a natural history of destruction to begin?'). I remember a well-meant suggestion by one of the younger participants in the workshop that perhaps Max's style should be jazzed up a little in English . . . which, as anyone who knew Max will readily be able to imagine, did not go down especially well with him. Or indeed with me, for it is the job of a translator to reflect the original voice of the author as closely as possible, in so far as that is compatible with a faithful rendering of the *spirit* of the work. Sometimes there is a clash that obliges the translator to be free with the letter in order to preserve the spirit of a text, but not in this case. For a translator of modern German literature, it was an interesting experience to render Max Sebald's unique style, which preserves the special affinity of earlier German writers with long, intricate sentences made up of many interlinking subordinate clauses. *Austerlitz* contains the famous – or should I say notorious? – nine-page sentence about the camp regime at Terezín (Theresienstadt), to which Austerlitz has found out that his mother Agáta was taken. It would have been conventional English to break up that sentence, but Max would not have liked it, and it would not have done justice to his style.

The core of the book, Austerlitz's account of his own life set inside the first-person framework of the anonymous narrator, is punctuated by the recurrence of the words 'said Austerlitz'. Professor Jean Boase-Beier of the UEA, herself a former colleague of Max Sebald, has suggested to me that by using direct narrative punctuated by 'said Austerlitz', Max was avoiding German indirect speech, which is indicated by the use of the subjunctive, and that he did so with an eye to the English version. For we don't have this neat way of flagging up indirect speech in English, and I sometimes wish we did; given a long passage of reporting, one can go on for a certain time without interpolating a reminder in the form of 'he said', 'she continued', or the like, but not indefinitely. Jean's is an interesting theory; we can only wish that Max were alive to confirm it or otherwise. It has also been suggested to me by one of the editors of this book that the use of the indirect-speech method may arise from Max's admiration, expressed in an interview, for Thomas Bernhard and what he called Bernhard's 'periscopic' narrative style. Whatever its rationale, I like the rhythm of the recurrent 'said Austerlitz'. Once Max had completed *Austerlitz*, I moved back to it, leaving *On the Natural History of Destruction* until later, because the publishers on both sides of the Atlantic wanted to bring out the novel first. In the latter half of 2000, therefore, I concentrated on its translation. I would send Max a chunk of draft passages, and he would go through them, answering my questions and making his own changes, often marked on the draft English MS, while I drafted the next chunk. I quote, from my own side of the correspondence, a couple of the matters raised, or comments on comments (page numbers are of Max's MS):

> p. 2: it's a pity we don't have a word in English which contains the 'washing' idea for *Waschbär* [racoon], but there it is, we don't . . .

> p. 88, about the repetition 'breathing/breath'; I feel that the pronunciation of the two words is so different in English, with one long vowel and one short vowel, one disyllabic and one monosyllabic word, that there is no difficulty here.

(Such, by the way, are the fiddly little questions to which translators constantly put their minds – one is always listening to the sound of the text, trying to avoid clumsy repetition.)

Max had said, in sending me the sample with the Welsh idyll from the still unfinished book in late 1999: 'There is a fair bit of botanical/entomological stuff in this, which I know can be troublesome. I don't think it is necessary to find the exact English equivalents of, e.g., all the moths mentioned. The same goes for plants [. . .] etc.' We had a good deal of correspondence on plant names. Most of the plants that he mentioned in German do have familiar English vernacular names, but other matters arose – considerations of English style and of euphony, for instance. 'Botany again,' I wrote in the closing stages of the work on *Austerlitz*, 'the *Anemone nemorosa* . . . *feingefiedert* would technically translate as "pinnulate", but I feel that is a bit pedantic in this context. My copy of Mrs Grieve's *Modern Herbal* calls the leaves "deeply-cut"; I have tried "finely-cut". If we call these flowers not "wood anemones" [. . .] but the alternative and rather pretty "windflowers", then we can have "woodland floor" in the same sentence without clumsy repetition.' 'I much like "windflowers",' Max replied, and in it went. He had already been charmed to find out that one of the vernacular English names for the wild clematis, *Clematis vitalba*, is traveller's joy.

Once I had the finished German edition complete with its pictures, I was able to print out the translation, arranging the layout to indicate the positions for pictures in the English version, and I sent off printouts to all concerned. This, again, was clearly before the practice of sending long texts by email attachment had become as widespread as it is now, and it would have been no use to the computer-averse Max anyway. Then we turned back to *On the Natural History of Destruction*. This too contained some problems – any text worth translating does. One concerned a quotation. In a passage on the role of music in the Third Reich, Max quotes Alexander Kluge on a radio broadcast of Verdi's *Aida* the night before the air raid on Halberstadt, claiming that at the end the lovers are strangled in their tomb; they aren't, of course, they are walled up in it alive, admittedly using up what little air is left in singing passionately about their love. With Max's approval, I fudged this as (translating the quotation from Kluge's account), 'Around one a.m. the lovers go to their death in the tomb.' The three essays connected with the Zürich lectures went off to Max in the summer of 2001, and came back to me with his annotations a little later.

Max had already added his essay on Alfred Andersch to the German edition of the book, and, as he had indicated to me in late 1999, he also included his essays on Jean Améry and Peter Weiss, previously published in journals but not in book form. That could have made for complications in *Campo Santo*, the posthumous collection of Max's essays, since the German edition printed the Améry and Weiss pieces. Fortunately, it is quite an extensive book, and even when docked of Weiss and Améry, there was still plenty of material left for the English edition.

But before then, of course, came Max's tragically early death in a car crash. *Austerlitz* had appeared, to wide acclaim, in early autumn 2001. I do feel its reception must have set to rest Max's early doubts of its merits. I had sent him the draft translations of the Andersch, Améry and Weiss essays in early December 2001, and was waiting for his comments. Indeed, I wondered if we would have crossed in the post. Not quite, but his notes on the Andersch draft, found on his desk after his death, were returned to me early in the New Year. I worked through them with great concentration. It was a strange feeling, like a personal farewell. And that, of course, was, strictly speaking, the end of our co-operation. I revised the Améry and Weiss essays myself, doing my best to guess at Max's probable reactions to this or that phrase. I was immensely grateful to Irène Heidelberger-Leonard, a personal friend of Max and an expert on the life and works of Jean Améry, war-time Resistance worker, philosopher and essayist, whose biography she was then writing, when she got in touch with me out of the blue to say that she approved of my translation of Max's Améry essay. Since then, I have translated Irène's fine biography of Améry, published by I. B. Tauris in 2010 as *The Philosopher of Auschwitz*, and enjoyed my correspondence with her over the book very much.

Finally, then, came *Campo Santo*. The critical essays included in the book are fascinating in themselves, although of course they presented some problems to me and to the editors on both sides of the Atlantic, and this time we could none of us turn to Max for answers. I particularly enjoyed translating some of the shorter, occasional pieces, for instance on Bruce Chatwin, Nabokov, Kafka's impressions of the early cinema, Max's friend the artist Jan Peter Tripp. But most fascinating of all were the passages from the book about Corsica that was begun in the 1990s but never completed – I believe Max set it aside in order to concentrate on *Austerlitz*.[1]

These passages in *Campo Santo* on aspects of Corsica and its customs are very much Max in his later mood of melancholy, reflective narrative, with touches of the dry humour that was also typical of him, both in writing and in real life. As I looked at other sources containing Corsican folklore of the kind on which he drew, I was fascinated to find connections with *Austerlitz*. Readers of the novel will remember the theme of 'little people' in it; they feature in the ghost stories told by Evan the cobbler to the boy Austerlitz in his Welsh childhood, and are strangely echoed by 'some ten or a dozen small people' seen by Austerlitz and his friend Marie de Verneuil in Marienbad, 'the sort of visitors sent to the spa by some Czech enterprise or other ... strikingly short, almost dwarfish figures' (Sebald 2001d: 305). The little people in Evan's Welsh stories are ghosts trying to return to life. 'If you had an eye for them they were to be seen quite often, said Evan. At first glance they seemed to be normal people, but when you looked more closely their faces would blur or flicker slightly at the edges' (Sebald 2001d: 75). Seen by Evan's grandfather, they were 'beings of dwarfish stature who strode on at a fast pace, leaning forward slightly and talking to each other in reedy voices' (Sebald 2001d: 75). Legends of little people, and of the plaintive, unreconciled dead, abound all over the world, but these could easily have emigrated to Wales from Corsica, where the spirits of the dead are described by Max thus: 'About a foot shorter than they had been in life, they went around in bands and groups, or sometimes followed a banner along the road, drawn up in regiments. They were heard talking and whispering in their strange piping voices, but nothing they said to each other could be understood, except for the name of whoever they intended to come for next' (Sebald 2005a: 29–30). In reflecting on the funeral customs of Corsica, and with his empathy for Sir Thomas Browne's melancholic approach to mortality, might Max Sebald, had he returned to the project, have given us a latter-day *Urn Burial*? We shall never know because, as Sir Thomas himself resonantly says, 'the iniquity of oblivion blindly scattereth her poppy'.

Translating *Campo Santo* was a farewell to a part of my professional life that I had valued greatly. This entire volume refers, in its title of *A Literature of Restitution*, to one of the occasional pieces in that posthumous collection, Max's speech made at the opening of a House of Literature in Stuttgart in 2001, 'An Attempt at Restitution'. Taking the city of Stuttgart, naturally, as his starting-point, and his first encounter with it on a pictorial card in a children's game, featuring the notable sights of a pre-war Germany still undivided and intact, he crams a remarkable number of ideas into the ten pages of this essay. Its translation called for the closest attention, so condensed is the thinking in it. The reader finds Max, as ever, acutely and painfully aware of the disastrous history of modern Germany in the middle of the twentieth century, a theme that is interwoven with reflections on the poet Hölderlin, brought up near Stuttgart and in his own time facing 'an epoch of violence, and [...] personal misfortune' (2005a: 212), his unhappy love story and the mental illness that he suffered for most of his adult life. 'What,' Max asks through Hölderlin, 'is literature good for?'

A difficult question indeed in the face of injustice and suffering, specifically the horrors of the Nazi regime. It is not quite fair to quote, out of its context, Adorno's remark of 1949 that 'to write a poem after Auschwitz is barbaric', but none the less it has become a truism, and by extension is applied to literature in general. Max answers his own rhetorical question in welcoming the new Stuttgart House of Literature thus: 'Only in literature [. . .] can there be an attempt at restitution over and above the mere recital of facts and over and above scholarship' (2005a: 214). It could also be said that his own work is, in itself, a fine refutation of Adorno's bleak dictum.

I would very much have liked to be able to talk or write to Max about the translation of the Stuttgart essay, and indeed the whole of *Campo Santo*. I kept doing so in my head, for a translator is always trying to get inside the mind of the author of the original text. It is impossible to inhabit an author's mind entirely, but it is up to translators to make that effort at least seem reasonably convincing. Translation, as I have said elsewhere, is a matter of illusion, the illusion being that the words before the reader are the author's own. In trying to create that illusion, translators have their own small contribution to make to the transmission of literature, and perhaps in the case of a writer like Max Sebald even to the work of restitution of which he speaks. It was not just a pleasure but a great privilege to be associated with him for the brief period of my translation of those three books of his.

NOTES

1 For further fragments (in German) from this abandoned Corsican project, see Sebald (2008d); for a detailed critical analysis of the Corsican project, see Gilloch's essay in this volume.

Part I

TRANSLATION AND STYLE

1

W. G. SEBALD'S THREE-LETTER WORD: ON THE PARALLEL WORLD OF THE ENGLISH TRANSLATIONS

Arthur Williams

INTRODUCTION

One of the most poignant moments in W. G. Sebald's oeuvre comes at the point in *Austerlitz* when Jacques, having returned to Prague to rediscover his roots, dares to ring the bell at his parents' last-known address, where he hopes to find the friend who had been his much-loved baby-sitter. Věra opens the door and greets him immediately with: 'Jacquot, [. . .], est-ce que c'est vraiment toi?' (Sebald 2001b: 220). The English translation, remarkably, has an additional word, and it speaks volumes: 'Jacquot, [. . .], *dis*, est-ce que c'est vraiment toi?' (Sebald 2001c: 216; my italics). Věra, with Sebald, is inviting Austerlitz to find his voice, to re-own and tell his story for himself.

Throughout *Austerlitz*, Sebald uses a formulaic repetition around 'X said, said Y' and even 'X said, said Y, said Z' to remind his reader that neither he, the author, nor his narrator, nor often his narrator's informants or sources, own directly the story they are passing on. They are intermediaries, often themselves readers or interpreters of texts left behind by those whose story is being resurrected. Although it is debatable whether the addition of the three-letter word 'dis' in the translation of *Austerlitz* makes the French more authentic, it does pinpoint Sebald's concern to give a voice to some of the victims of European history, including the victims, direct and indirect, of the Holocaust, and epitomizes his fundamental narrative strategy as a facilitator of other narratives within his overarching vision. However, because it emerges only in the translation, at a late stage in the text's production, it also indicates how he retained ownership of his texts and exploited every opportunity to advance a project of restitution only possible through literature (cf. *Campo Santo*: 'Ein Versuch der Restitution'; Sebald 2003b: 240–8, esp. 248; Williams, 2007b, esp. 55). In passing from German to English, Sebald inserts a third language, French; the refugee Austerlitz is given voice in the interstices between languages.

As Michael Hamburger's intriguing 'Translator's Note' to *Unerzählt* (*Unrecounted*), tells us, Max (as we all knew him) was scrupulous in all his dealings and so meticulous over the editing of his writings that he spent hundreds of hours on the checking of their English versions – and even the finished copy of the English *Austerlitz* he inscribed and gave to my wife [. . .] contains emendations in his hand, after the book's publication. (Sebald and Tripp 2004a: 1)

The process of translation offered Sebald an opportunity to identify significant traits in his work, and to hone the literary aspects of his originals as well as change a number of names. This essay examines the translations of his work, from *Schwindel. Gefühle* to *Austerlitz*, in order to demonstrate that the later work increasingly evidences Sebald's concern with the integrity and integration of his oeuvre as a whole: in particular, it will be seen that he modified some of the early portraits of his compatriots and also adjusted various epigraphs and structural devices.

While this essay sets out the evidence of amendments to the texts that only Sebald could have authorized, it also betrays its own origins in an initial curiosity about the rendering in English of some moments where Sebald's German seemed 'difficult' (either highly determined or uncommonly open). The present context, obviously, limits the number of examples that can be adduced. However, what is here is not merely the tip of the iceberg; the sample is substantial and, it is hoped, provides an insight into a process that was clearly of importance to the author, as his understanding grew of his oeuvre as a body of work marked as much by unity of ethos as by variety of form and content.

THE ELUSIVE NATURE OF THE TASK: SOME REMARKS ON SEBALD'S LANGUAGE

Read in juxtaposition with the originals, the translations offer a parallel world that prompts both questions and discursive contemplation – processes of crucial importance for Sebald and his unrelenting resistance to hegemonic systems of power and knowledge (see Williams 2000: 109; 2004b: 187; 2007b: 54; and 2007a). In two short letters to me, Max made two simple points that speak of his central concerns. In July 1997 he claimed that 'I write pour ceux qui savent lire' (15 July, 1997); one year later, he stated that he was increasingly preoccupied with the 'Presence of the Dead' (1 July, 1998). The former statement is in all likelihood a reference to *Monsieur le Marquis de Custine en 1844* by Eugène de Breza (1845), the seventh letter of which records that the Marquis 'ne sait écrire que pour ceux qui savent lire' (de Breza 1845: 98). When combined with his stated preoccupation with the 'Dead', this suggests that Sebald's work aims at defying the most radical of hegemonic systems: he writes in order to resist the grip of received historiography (cf. *Nach der Natur*, where the first three cantos address, *inter alia*, the dubious nature of the written record), he writes for those who know how to read the past.

In Sebald's work, reliance on language is axiomatic. No matter how deeply rooted in the Germanist's culture is a sense of 'Sprachskepsis', Sebald nonetheless invested deeply in language's magical ability to cut through inflexible boundaries and dominant discourses to suggest elusive new dimensions. His literary and intellectual world displays a compelling unity: it is a world where Mandelbrotian fractal geometry (here understood as recurrent patterns in nature that defy definition and yet share a fundamental identity not encapsulated by simple rules)[1] and the butterfly effect of chaos theory are the reader's constant companions. Indeed, butterflies (and moths) often flutter a message of kinship from one volume to another as well as between Sebald and two of the many literary presences in his work, Kafka and Nabokov. Since the German language is the instrument and vehicle for this, any transposition to a different language can pose a threat to immediate and delayed resonances within his oeuvre.

The translations are not read here to illustrate points of translation theory, nor to identify and expose weaknesses in the translators – indeed, all three achieve admirable levels of excellence. However, the works from *After Nature* through to *Austerlitz* represent a prodigiously consistent vision – the beginning cries out for review in the light of the end. Hamburger's remarks tend to confirm that Sebald's own awareness of this unity intensified as he worked at his later volumes. There is abundant textual evidence of the care taken to build links between and within individual works (such as the opening sections of *Die Ringe des Saturn* or *Austerlitz*). This fact alone places the work of Michael Hulse, Sebald's first translator, in a somewhat different category from that of Hamburger or Anthea Bell.

One word, used just once by Sebald, serves to bring home something of the elusive nature of his language: 'Masche'. It is a casual remark in *Schwindel. Gefühle*: 'Das Binden einer Masche habe ich übrigens auch von der Engelwirtin gelernt' (Sebald 1994d: 225). Hulse renders the immediate sense: 'It was also from her that I learned how to tie a bow' (Sebald 1999d: 199). Sebald's oeuvre can be read as a series of threads tied skilfully together, not so much as 'bow ties' (the Austrian diminutive: 'Mascherl') but rather as 'stitches' as in knitting or crotchet-work, or, in a work which draws on Kafka's story 'Der Jäger Gracchus', in a 'net' or 'mesh', possibly even a 'snare'. The self-conscious author-narrator-reader Max Sebald would have been aware of the vibrating threads of the English terms, and, given his subtle, often wry humour derived from word (and name) association, 'Masche' may also be a 'trick of the trade', linguistic sleight of hand.

One late image, in particular, has its own 'Maschen'. The quincunx at the beginning of *Die Ringe des Saturn* describes a lattice of interconnected lines that link the whole of creation (Sebald 1997b: 31; 1999a: 20). These are lines that stir under the most distant of influences and, unlike lines of perspective in traditional landscape painting that lead to a vanishing point, suggest a vertiginous pattern in which the two-dimensional diamonds of the quincunx become three-dimensional fractals across the universe. This long passage at the end of the 'Erster Teil' can be read almost as a 'mission statement' (Sebald 1997b: 29; 1999a: 18). Thomas Browne seems to have anticipated Mandelbrot's geometry of nature 'mit welch eleganter Hand die Natur geometrisiert' (Sebald 1997b: 32); 'the elegant geometrical designs of Nature' (Sebald 1999a: 21), as he espouses the unity of all nature – and, finding the words to express this, he is already an answer to Hofmannsthal's Lord Chandos, who was overwhelmed by the task and whose presence Sebald will later signal more directly with the beetle in Michael Hamburger's well (Sebald 1997b: 228; 1999a: 190), foreshadowed by the 'Entenpaar' (Sebald 1997b: 110) which, in the translation, becomes 'a solitary mallard' (Sebald 1999a: 89) – the narrator can see 'even the pores in the lid closed over its eye' (Sebald 1999a: 89). In the introduction, an unnamed Jean Paul rubs shoulders with a named Borges, a named Grimmelshausen with *Nature Watch* and *Survival* (Sebald 1997b: 33; 1999a: 22): the telescope and the magnifying glass will be employed to scrutinize the real and the imaginary world, a constantly changing nature with its miracles of survival and its monstrous aberrations. Browne sought isomorphic lines to link them all and knew that his only recourse was to attempt 'ein[en] gefahrvoll[en] Höhenflug der Sprache' (Sebald 1997b: 30); Hulse departs somewhat from the original image: 'a parlous loftiness in his language' (Sebald 1999a: 19); Sebald, again unlike Lord Chandos, is attempting a similarly risky feat that challenges his every reader.

In *Vertigo*, the first-person narrator (as ever, all but identical with Sebald), describes his work as 'drawing connections between events that lay far apart but which seemed to me to be of the same order' (Sebald 1999d: 94); 'und zog Verbindungslinien zwischen weit auseinanderliegenden Ereignissen, die mir derselben Ordnung anzugehören schienen' (Sebald 1994d: 112). Even this part-sentence indicates the precision of Sebald's expression: he is the one who is drawing lines that bestow belonging on apparently unrelated events. Sebald's German challenges his translators as much with its diamond-hard precision as with its slippery suggestiveness.

Another expression, clearly intended to give German readers pause, might warn us that Sebald's use of language is never innocent. Addressing the difficulty of gaining an uncompromised vision of recent German history, he takes the colloquial expression for 'opening someone's eyes to the truth': 'jemandem den Star stechen' and adds the adjective 'grau'. 'Grauer Star' is the medical term for cataracts ('grüner Star': 'glaucoma'), but it would be naïve to believe that Sebald was guilty of a lapse of concentration; he intended the combination of 'grau' and 'Star' ('starr') in relation to views of German history clouded by a fixation with its grey-uniformed militarism:

> Ja, sagte der Lukas, es sei wirklich eine eigenartige Sache mit der Erinnerung. Er habe [...] oft das Gefühl, als müsse ihm nun endlich der graue Star gestochen werden. (Sebald 1994d: 244)

(Yes, said Lukas, there was something strange about remembering. When he [...] thought back, it all became blurred as if he was out in a fog. (Sebald 1999d: 215))

The linkage is underlined in 'Paul Bereyter' (*Die Ausgewanderten*) when Paul has had an operation 'am grauen Star' (Sebald 1994a: 76; 1997a: 51); when a second operation is ruled out, he is left with a 'mausgrauen Prospekt' for the future (Sebald 1994a: 88; 1997a: 59). 'Grey', now coupled with the central theme of vision and perception, is one early example of the poetic 'Nervatur' (Sebald 1995a: 71; 2002b: 81) that Sebald traced through to *Austerlitz* and exploited comprehensively in *Die Ausgewanderten*, above all in association with ashes and dust. No degree of ingenuity in English can fully capture the resonances of 'grauer Star'.[2]

ON SEBALD'S TITLES, SUB-TITLES AND EPIGRAPHS

Two of Sebald's titles in particular defy the translator's best efforts: *Schwindel. Gefühle* and *Die Ausgewanderten*. In the first, Sebald has deliberately split a word one might use for 'vertigo' and emphasized the division by adding full stops and making 'Gefühl' plural. Any sense of 'swindle' that the German might carry as a result of the isolation of this element is lost in English – and, while Sebald never uses 'Schwindel' in that sense, his works always rely on the author's sleight of hand with his levels of narration, the identity of his narrators and the authenticity of his sources. For Sebald, any gain in (historical) perspective, particularly from a height, comes at a cost; real 'feelings' are involved in the vertigo that ensues. Perhaps the earliest reference can be found in *Nach der Natur* ('Die Dunckle Nacht Fahrt Aus'): 'Ich seh hinab in das Tal,/ und mir schwindelte die Seele' (Sebald 1995a: 91), which Hamburger translates brilliantly as 'I gaze down into the valley/ and my soul is sent reeling' (Sebald 2002b: 104). Since this was the last translation Sebald oversaw (see Hamburger's 'Translator's Note', Sebald 2002b: 2), he must have been happy to lose the superficial link between two early works for the fundamental disorientation he intended.

The translation of 'emigrants' back into German ('Rückübersetzung') is unlikely to result in 'die Ausgewanderten'. Notwithstanding a possible gain in literary status through the intertextual reference to Goethe's Boccaccio-inspired 'Unterhaltungen deutscher Ausgewanderten' (published anonymously in 1795), it is also possible that Sebald's fascination with the suggestive power of words influenced his choice of a substantive which would not otherwise spring readily to mind. He hints at a subliminal line of meaning, a force field, triggered by a substantival adjective drawn from the past participle of the verb. The root verb may be intransitive, but the resulting substantive hints at the outcome of a deliberate act. Sebald's 'emigrated ones' have been variously forced out, they are victims of historical processes and attitudes which robbed them of a homeland and left them disenfranchised. Unlike the post-war situation of the German groups hinted at in these descriptors

('Heimatvertriebene', 'Entrechtete'), they had no semblance of representation. Sebald's linguistic choice allows us to see his literary act of restitution against the background of a Germany that made him uneasy.

Unerzählt also challenges the translator's skill with equivalences. Hamburger's masterly translation, analysed with deft clarity in his 'Note' (Sebald 2004a: 7), both meets the challenge and echoes the argument of the present essay: *Unrecounted*. The teller of tales is also the accountant of the truth, a link that Sebald made more than once. *Schwindel. Gefühle* (Sebald 1994d: 286; 1999d: 252) offers the obvious example. At the beginning of a long passage in which Sebald makes his feelings about the new Germany brutally clear, he introduces (not without a hint at Kafka's Gregor Samsa; see Sebald 1997b: 13; 1999a: 5) that symbol of the 'Wirtschaftswunder', the commercial traveller. He chooses the term 'Handlungsreisender' (reflecting, perhaps, the older use of 'Handlung' as 'business'), rather than 'Handelsreisender' or 'Handlungsvertreter'. There is wickedly self-deprecating humour in the hint that Max discovered so much of his content ('Handlung' – plot) on journeys both real and imaginary and that his role was not that of 'deputy' or 'representative' ('Vertreter'), but that of the observant traveller ('Reisender'). It is, perhaps, ironic that the English omits a clause which underwrites Sebald's search for distant connections. Like the commercial travellers, he bends over his papers and, like them, 'only now and again lets his gaze wander absently into the distance' ('und gleich ihnen [ließ ich] nur zwischenhinein einen gedankenverlorenen Blick in die Ferne schweifen'). However, the omission does bring the English text more smoothly to the point that his appearance betrays a more dubious calling ('zweifelhafteres Metier'). While they calculate their 'Prozent- und Provisionssätze' ('percentages and rates of commission') and enter them up in their accounts to close the business of the day, he implies that he frames 'sentences' that involve 'recounting' the elusive truths that resist the closure of inclusion in the ledgers of history.

The translation of titles is always a particularly thorny issue, and Sebald seems to have been much more concerned about his epigraphs, which he modified for the translations. In the story of the first emigrant, 'Dr Henry Selwyn', the source text exhortation, 'Zerstöret das Letzte/ die Erinnerung nicht' (roughly: 'Do not destroy the last thing, memory'), shifts to a target text that seems to signal a complete loss of hope: 'And the last remnants/ memory destroys'.[3] It is an interesting change in the light of Sebald's project of literary restitution. The original German itself involves a misquotation of Hölderlin. His poem 'Elegie' turns on the rhetorical question of a poet sinking into despair at the loss of inspiration: 'Danken möcht' ich, aber wofür? Verzehret das Letzte/ Selbst die Erinnerung nicht?' (ll. 55/56; roughly: 'I'd like to be grateful, but why? Does not the last thing, memory itself, fade away?'). The poet goes on to rediscover his inspiration in a positive conclusion. Sebald, always the melancholic, has set himself the insecure task of leaving the outcomes of his work to his readers. His act of restitution quietly gives the lie to the English epigraph, with the original German perhaps read as a less than modest declaration of intent. However, the book does open with the word 'Ende' (echoing the end of *Schwindel. Gefühle*; both lost in the translations) and ends with an indelible image that lives on in the reader – a poetic *tour de force* in both versions.

The changes made in *Die Ringe des Saturn* are even more intriguing. The original sub-title is suppressed: 'eine englische Wallfahrt' ('an English pilgrimage') might have given the impression that a German writer was setting out to do penance for the recent past, or regarded England as some sort of holy land. The 'englisch' may also have suggested 'angelic' (as in 'der Englische Gruß' – 'the Angelic Salutation'), a pun the Germans have long enjoyed and one which easily finds its place in Sebald's oeuvre, peopled as it is with saints and angels (cf. for example, the opening of *Nach der Natur*), but it is not one that could survive in translation. And Sebald no longer cites *Paradise Lost* in his epigraphs, in its place extending the simple 'et' in the quotation from Joseph Conrad's French correspondence with Marguerite Poradowska by a few words, thereby highlighting a fundamental concern (my italics):

> Il faut surtout pardonner à ces âmes malheureuses qui ont élu de faire le pèlerinage à pied, qui côtoient le rivage et regardent sans comprendre l'horreur de la lutte, *la joie de vaincre ni* le profond désespoir des vaincus.

The relationship between good and evil gives way to that between the conqueror and the conquered. Sebald thus aligns *The Rings of Saturn* more clearly with his constant preoccupation with the victims of history, a preoccupation which goes back at least as far as a letter of 14 December 1968 to Adorno, in which Sebald speaks of his interest in the playwright Carl Sternheim as being 'du côté des vaincus' (Atze and Loquai 2005: 15).

SCHWINDEL. GEFÜHLE: A TEXT FOR A GERMAN READERSHIP?

One of the underlying themes of *Schwindel. Gefühle* is that of the 'ugly German', the post-war opportunist who has not changed, but merely erected a neat façade of prosperity. It is a sentiment that persists in *Die Ausgewanderten* as a background presence associated with the 'furniture' inherited from the past (symbolized by the 'altdeutsche Kredenz' – properly 'German Renaissance' sideboard). By the time of *Die Ringe des Saturn*, the ugliness has transferred to Belgians, in so far as they represent the dark side of colonialism (and have their own 'Kredenz'; Sebald 1997b: 149), while the Nazi past is depicted through a more precise presentation of practices and propaganda. By the time of *Austerlitz*, while no punches are pulled in respect of the Nazi period, Sebald seems to indicate a change for the better in the German style of life and attitudes. These citizens of the Federal Republic are no longer like the Germans of 1936 (a point subtly emphasized by Sebald); they differ also from their brash compatriots as depicted in *Schwindel. Gefühle.* Indeed, it seems possible that the prospect of a readership beyond his homeland, realized through the translations, perhaps caused Sebald to moderate somewhat the image of his contemporaries in his first prose work.

Vertigo was translated after *The Emigrants* and *The Rings of Saturn.* Sebald may have felt that this somewhat harsh depiction of his compatriots had been better framed in the one and superseded by the other, and so modified the first in translation accordingly. My italics indicate where the German seems stronger than the somewhat understated English:

> Von der Terrasse herauf drang [...] das Stimmengewirr der *großteils schon angetrunkenen Gäste*, bei denen es sich, wie ich *zu meinem Leidwesen* feststellen mußte, *fast ausnahmslos* um meine *ehemaligen* Landsleute handelte. Schwaben, Franken und Bayern hörte ich die *unsäglichsten* Dinge untereinander reden, und waren mir diese *auf das ungenierteste sich breitmachenden* Dialekte schon zuwider, so war es mir geradezu eine Peine, die lauthals vorgebrachten Meinungen und witzigen Aussprüche einer Gruppe junger Männer aus meiner unmittelbaren Heimat mit anhören zu müssen. (Sebald 1994d: 111)

> (From the terrace came [...] the confused blathering of the revellers, most of whom, as I realised with some dismay, were compatriots of mine. I heard Swabians, Franconians and Bavarians saying the most unsavoury things, and, if I found their broad, uninhibited dialects repellent, it was a veritable torment to have to listen to the loud-mouthed opinions and witticisms of a group of young men who clearly came from my home town. (Sebald 1999d: 93))

There is, in the original, more than a hint of the irritable German academic venting his spleen on his less cultured, younger compatriots.[4] Then again, these children of the Economic Miracle on their travels are close to familiar caricatures of German tourists[5] and not too distantly related to Sebald's commercial travellers. As we examine other passages in the text, it becomes clear that he is also bridling at an unhealthy relationship to the past. Commercial success is essentially a palliative. These uncouth blatherers do not echo his own childhood associations with his village on All Saints' Day, but are of a piece with the fashionable décor and furnishings of the renovated Engelwirt – which irk Sebald just as much as the 'altdeutsche Kredenz':

> auch der Engelwirt [...] war von den Grundmauern bis hinauf zum Dachstuhl um- und ausgebaut worden, von der *Innenausstattung* natürlich ganz zu schweigen. Was sich jetzt *sauber herausgeputzt* in dem über die gesamte Republik verbreiteten *neudeutsch*-alpenländischen Stil als eine *sogenannte Stätte* gepflegter Gastlichkeit darbot, war *seinerzeit* ein übel beleumundetes Wirthaus gewesen, in dem die Bauern bis tief in die Nacht hinein hockten und, vor allem im Winter, oft bis zur Besinnungslosigkeit tranken. (Sebald 1994d: 212)

(here too [. . .] the whole house had been rebuilt and converted from the foundations up to the rafters, not to mention the changes to the furnishings and fittings. What now presented itself, in the pseudo-Alpine style which has become the new vernacular throughout the Federal Republic, as a house offering refined hospitality to its patrons, in *those distant days* was a hostelry of disrepute where the village peasants sat around until deep in the night and, particularly in winter, often drank themselves senseless. (Sebald 1999d: 186))

The style in the Engelwirt is not just 'pseudo-Alpine', it is 'neudeutsch', a distinctly negative term, supported by the Bernhardian *sogenannte* Stätte' ('so-called site', where 'Stätte' is normally reserved for a place of some historic or religious importance). The force of 'sauber herausgeputzt' suggests not just 'freshly and neatly turned out', it smacks also of 'made to look decent, unsullied, faultless, unpolluted' (a child is 'sauber' if it is toilet trained). 'Those distant days' gain definition a few pages later (Sebald 1994d: 232; 1999b: 204), when the locals, whom our narrator recognizes, almost merge into a painting by the Nazi favourite Hengge, which still hangs in the renovated Engelwirt.

The contrast of the new with the old, the substitution of one kind of uniformity for another, is brought to the fore again later when our narrator grows uneasy at the suspicious glances of the commercial travellers (see above) and the approach of the new tourist season. He decides to leave for England and does not mince his words about the Germany through which he travels. One man he sees, for instance, has 'grown beyond all reasonable measure' and wears the fashionable folksy gear that passes for smart decency (the 'Masche' of the day), but only sacrifices individuality for uniform conformity. One wonders how far his aspirations differ from those of the pre-war Sebalds and their generation (Sebald 1994d: 219; 1999d: 193) – his 'Trachtenanzug' sounds echoes in Sebald from a Nazi past. This caricature marks the beginning of a long, significant passage which shows many changes between the two versions.

[N]ichts ist mir davon erinnerlich als die groteske Gestalt eines *viel zu groß geratenen, wahrhaft überdimensionalen* Menschen, der zu einem häßlichen modischen Trachtenanzug eine breite Krawatte mit aufgenähten vielfarbigen Vogelfedern trug, in denen der Wind sich zu schaffen machte. (Sebald 1994d: 287)

(I cannot remember anything about this journey other than the grotesque figure of *a middleaged chap of gigantic proportions* who was wearing a hideous, modishly styled Trachten suit and a broad tie with multi-coloured bird feathers sewn onto it, which were ruffled by the wind. (Sebald 1999d: 253))

As the text continues, the urge to create a new order of utter cleanliness is projected onto the countryside, and human beings disappear in their cars – trust has been lost in humanity and invested in technology. Sebald's German in the train to Hoek van Holland is both loaded and deliberately placed, for example, in the first

extended adjectival adjunct: '[ich] fuhr durch das *mir von jeher unbegreifliche, bis in den letzten Winkel aufgeräumte und begradigte deutsche* Land. Auf eine ungute Art befriedet und betäubt schien mir alles, und das Gefühl der Betäubung erfaßte bald auch mich' (1994d: 287 my italics). Sebald locates his opening descriptors within the framework of 'das [...] deutsche Land', only a hair's breadth away from 'Deutschland' itself and sounding peculiarly stilted, as if from an earlier political register. The whole country ('bis in den letzten Winkel', 'into the furthermost corner') has been 'aufgeräumt' ('cleared up'), 'begradigt' ('straightened out'), 'befriedet' ('pacified'), and 'betäubt' ('numbed', perhaps suggesting 'narcosis') – all in a manner that is 'ungut' ('makes one uneasy').[6] The agents of this process are not specified, but the repeated inseparable prefix 'be-', most often used to create transitive verbs, underlines the situation of 'das deutsche Land' as the direct object of these processes. We could be in the world of a defeated Germany swept clean and medicated by the victors after the war. In less dexterous linguistic hands than those of Max Sebald, these echoes from the past might have taken on a different tenor, for he flies perilously close to crypto-nationalist sentiment. In passing, it is worth noting how Sebald echoes something of this passage in the scene where the young Max Aurach waits to be flown out of Nazi Germany 'enclosed' in an 'Einfriedung' consisting of a 'Ligusterhecke' ('privet hedge') (1994a: 280 – in which context his motif of the cemetery, 'Friedhof', also comes into play). It soon becomes clear in *Schwindel. Gefühle*, however, that the post-war Germans themselves have initiated and prosecuted this process.

The English version, deliberately pruned towards the end, could never recapture the rhythms of the original, which suggest those of the train and underpin the repetitive geometry of a landscape shaped solely by the needs of the economy:

> I sat in the Hook of Holland express travelling through the German countryside, which has always been alien to me, straightened out and tidied up as it is to the last square inch and corner. Everything appeared to be appeased and numbed in some sinister way, and this sense of numbness soon came over me also. [...] Stretches of grassland swept past on either side and ploughed fields in which the pale green winter wheat had emerged according to schedule; *neatly delineated* fir-tree plantations, gravel pits, football pitches, industrial estates, and the ever-expanding colonies of family homes behind their rustic fences and privet hedges, *all of them painted in that slightly greyish shade of white which has become the preferred colour of the nation.* [...] It was as if mankind had already made way for another species, or had fallen under a kind of curfew. The silence of my fellow passengers sitting motionless in the air-conditioned express carriage did nothing to dispel such conjectures, but as I looked out at the passing landscape which had been so thoroughly parcelled up and segmented, the words 'south-west Germany', 'south-west Germany' were running over and over in my mind, till after a couple of hours of mounting irritation I came to the conclusion that something like an eclipse of my mental faculties was about to occur. (Sebald 1999d: 253–4)[7]

The translator has had to opt for a free rendering, and Sebald has reduced the focus on the narrator, but between them they have also made some additions: 'neatly delineated' can be seen as helping out the translation of 'vorschriftsmäßig' ('according to schedule', when the German is strong enough to suggest 'prescription'), while the 'greyish shade of white' that is the 'preferred colour of the nation' not only compensates in some way for the loss of 'grauer Star' (see above), but also points strongly towards other motifs developed centrally in *Die Ausgewanderten* – the translation of which Sebald could now also draw on (there is an intriguing reference to Procul Harum's 'A whiter shade of pale' in *Die Ausgewanderten* (1994a: 179); the group's name is suppressed in the translation (Sebald 1997a: 121)).

The original German of *Schwindel. Gefühle* has a quite vicious edge that seems to indicate something of Sebald's discomfort at the way his compatriots had dealt with their recent history (the grim humour of the post-war 'Persilschein' – that 'certified' that people were clean to proceed in public life – comes to mind). The English version may be seen to reflect a reduced hyperaesthesia as well as a different readership. A comparison of this train journey with the later one in *Austerlitz* (Sebald 2001b: 316) underlines the change in Sebald's attitudes to Germany and the Germans (see Williams 2003: 194) as he detects change in them.

SEBALD'S LINGUISTIC EMPOWERMENT OF THE PAST

In Sebald's German, the past often seems more real than it appears in the translations. In the first example, from *Schwindel. Gefühle*, the word order facilitates a typically Sebaldian emphasis: it is the past which returns, making it a serious agent of unforeseen and unforeseeable events. In the English, the past seems to be a less potent force, affecting only Clara:

und auf dem ganzen Weg dorthin und den ganzen Abend hindurch konnte sie sich nicht beruhigen über die unversehene *Wiederkunft der Vergangenheit*. (Sebald 1994d: 55)

(and neither on the way there nor that entire evening did she regain her composure following this unexpected *encounter with her past*. (Sebald 1999d: 45))

In *Die Ausgewanderten*, Dr Selwyn and his friend show the narrator slides of themselves when younger, in which they have 'returned out of their past' (rather like returning exiles) to confront their present selves and remind them of their mortality, while 'their past selves' of the English seems only a nostalgic interlude:

Ich spürte, daß sie beide *ihrer Rückkehr aus der Vergangenheit* nicht ohne eine gewisse Rührung beiwohnten. (Sebald 1994a: 28)

(I sensed that, for both of them, *this return of their past selves* was an occasion for some emotion. (Sebald 1997a: 16))

35

In *Die Ringe des Saturn*, when the Ashburys show their home movies, Sebald's word order projects the emphasis onto 'die stummen Bilder der Vergangenheit', while the English seems to focus more on their poor quality:

Ich nahm neben ihr Platz unter dem Papiertütenhimmel, das Licht ging aus, der Apparat fing an zu rattern, und auf der kahlen Wand über dem Kaminsims erschienen, manchmal in nahezu bewegungslosen Einstellungen, manchmal ruckartig aneinandergereiht, überstürzt oder durch dichtes Gestrichel undeutlich gemacht, die stummen Bilder der Vergangenheit. (Sebald 1997b: 253)

(I sat down beside her under the paper-bag heavens, the light went out, the projector began to whirr, and on the bare wall above the mantle-piece the mute images of the past appeared, at times quite still and then again following jerkily one upon another, headlong, and rendered unclear by the projection scratches. (Sebald 1999a: 213))

In *Austerlitz*, our view of the past is unsettled from the start. The central theme of 'Time' enters the book with its eponymous central figure, in the 'salle des pas perdus'. When, towards the end of the book, Sebald launches an extended attack on the new French Bibliothèque Nationale, the diametric opposite of his beloved Sailors' Reading Room in Southwold (Sebald 1997b: 114), its compartmentalism and inaccessibility are shown as inimical to the past. At this point, there is again a slight weakening of the presence of the past in the English version. It arises with Sebald's use of the preposition 'an' (my italics). In a whispered conversation, the spectral Lemoine talks about:

die im Gleichmaß mit der Proliferation des Informationswesens fortschreitende Auflösung unserer Erinnerungsfähigkeit und über den bereits sich vollziehenden Zusammenbruch, l'effondrement, wie Lemoine sich ausdrückte, de la Bibliothèque Nationale. Das neue Bibliotheksgebäude, das durch seine ganze Anlage ebenso wie durch seine ans Absurde grenzende innere Regulierung den Leser als einen potentiellen Feind auszuschließen suche, sei, so sagte Austerlitz, sagte Lemoine, quasi die offizielle Manifestation des immer dringender sich anmeldenden Bedürfnisses, mit all dem ein Ende zu machen, was noch ein Leben habe *an* der Vergangenheit. (Sebald 2001b: 400)

(the dissolution, in line with the inexorable spread of processed data, of our capacity to remember, and about the collapse, l'effondrement, as Lemoine put it, of the Bibliothèque Nationale which is already under way. The new library building, which in both its entire layout and its near-ludicrous internal regulation seeks to exclude the reader as a potential enemy, might be described, so Lemoine thought, said Austerlitz, as the official manifestation of the increasingly importunate urge to break with everything which still has some living connection to the past. (Sebald 2001c: 398))

Anthea Bell's elegant solution suggests a selection process to be implemented to the disadvantage of the living: 'to break with everything which still has some living connection to the past' (Sebald 2001c: 398). The German seems to suggest: to 'put an end to anything about the past that still has life' and, implying the opposite of 'sterben an' ('to die of'), that 'the past as a life is terminated and buried'. These solutions are as ugly as the thought, which would condemn to failure Sebald's project of restitution.

The structure of *Austerlitz* has drawn much comment, particularly the very long sentence on Theresienstadt / Terezín, which Bell renders with characteristic fidelity and subtlety (Sebald 2001b: 335; Sebald 2001c: 331), but also the lack of paragraph divisions. Sebald uses asterisks to mark off the book's main sections, and em-dashes to mark shifts in the levels of the narrative, the identity of the narrator, or the location. One em-dash is substituted by the remark that Austerlitz makes a long pause in his narration (Sebald 2001b: 366; Sebald 2001c: 363). These clear, albeit somewhat unconventional, divisions in the original are not all retained in the English version.

All em-dashes have been suppressed in the first section, which already differs from the rest of the volume by having the only footnote in Sebald's literary works. This is the preamble which sets the scene, establishes links with previous works and puts in place a series of symbols and ideas that will underpin and inform what is to follow. Austerlitz becomes central only at the end, rather like St George on the wing of the Lindenhardt Altarpiece in the opening lines of *Nach der Natur* (Sebald 1995a: 7). A peripheral figure we might not have noticed is brought into focus. Only when his story begins does Sebald re-introduce his em-dashes in the English version. Indeed, the first is reserved for the powerful moment (borrowed from Susi Bechhöfer's autobiography *Rosa's Child*: 40; see also Williams 2004b: 127, 139 n.21) when Austerlitz learns his true name for the first time (Sebald 2001b: 96; 2001c: 93). Sebald has used the opportunity of the translation to bring home to his reader that these sub-divisions are highly meaningful.

In the suspended time of Iver Grove, a superficially lugubrious addition to the English version forges kinships with earlier works that tell us they are all part of the same long story. The ledger in which meticulous accounts of the games of billiards had been recorded (a motif underpinned by the 'uncounted souls' just evinced) now has 'the rubric Ashman vs. Ashman' (Sebald 2001b: 156; 2001c: 152). The name Ashman is thus doubly emphasized; the reader must make the link back to *Die Ringe des Saturn*, to Ashburnham and Ashbury, to the central role of ash and dust in the story of Max Aurach in *Die Ausgewanderten* as well as to its important intertexts of Thomas Mann's *Der Tod in Venedig* (Aschenbach) and Paul Celan's seminal poem 'Todesfuge' ('schwarze Milch' and 'aschenes Haar'; see Williams 2007b: 66).[8]

We are reminded, too, of the impossibility of reproducing in the English versions all the echoes of the names that Sebald revels in: not just 'Asche' and

'Bach', or 'Au' and 'Ache', but also 'Wiesen' and 'Grund' (see Williams 1998: 104; and Williams 2007b: 71), to say nothing of the names he conjures in the course of the book (e.g. Fahnstock, Braunmühl, Lanzberg, Lindwurm). In *Nach der Natur*, many (Grünewald, Riemenschneider, Altdorfer, Hölderlin, Haller, Brueghel – to take examples from early and late in the text) are cited to enhance the intellectual, somewhat archaic, tone of the poem, but others already testify to his interest in the quirky nature of names that add *couleur locale*: the Irk and the Irwell, and Liston's Music Hall (Sebald 1995a: 83, 85; 2002b: 95, 98). Already, in this first literary work, Sebald includes a list of magical Jewish names (1995a: 86; 2002b: 99) which he later transforms with the glorious roll-calls in *Die Ausgewanderten*, especially in the cemetery at Bad Kissingen. His memorable words remind us, in the German, that these Jewish names live *in the language*:

> das gab mir den Gedanken ein, daß die Deutschen den Juden vielleicht nichts so mißgönnt haben als ihre schönen, mit dem Land und *der Sprache, in der* sie lebten, so sehr verbundenen Namen. (Sebald 1994a: 335)

> (made me think that perhaps there was nothing the Germans begrudged the Jews so much as their beautiful names, so intimately bound up with the country they lived in and with its language. (Sebald 1997a: 224))

These names live in the German in which they were created. Similarly, in the case of Austerlitz and, for example, Selwyn, the change of name resulted from a change of language, emphasizing a lost homeland. This becomes a pivotal element in *Austerlitz* (Sebald 2001b: 97; 2001c: 220), yet neither moment is recorded in German (nor in Austerlitz's native Czech): the first is in English, the second in French. All of Sebald's non-German expressions, even his mischievous use of Welsh, are retained in the English version, and this raises an interesting point about the visibility, and thus force, of his English interventions in the new context.

The stations of Austerlitz's life, in Bala, London, Prague and Paris, allow Sebald to exploit the four languages (although principally French and English). As befits the movement of the narrative, the use of English is restricted to the first half of the book, where it is again reserved for key moments and the highlighting of themes. Sebald, through his narrator, creates a stitch back to the Snow on the Alps of *Nach der Natur* by both using the term directly and then quoting a line of verse on snow in London. Texts chosen by Old Elias for his hell-fire sermons are quoted in English (when he would probably have used Welsh) to establish the motifs of stars, lost homelands, rivers and deserts, and his last disastrous sermon, after Gwendolyn's last words, is conveyed in English, as is the comment on his failing mental state: 'he's not a full shilling, you know' (Sebald 2001c: 96). And the transition in Austerlitz's life from his false Welsh identity to his new mystery identity is completed when Penrith-Smith informs him of his real name. The happy interlude with Gerald's family closes on a 'Good night, gentlemen' in the Great Eastern

Hotel, and the decision to seek his roots in Prague is heralded by a moment of misunderstanding between Austerlitz and Penelope Peacefull. She is completing a crossword puzzle as their words cross without correspondence. It is a case of gentle 'aneinander vorbeireden', but it signals Austerlitz's distancing from English and his imminent return to the Czech that the Eliases had stripped from him (Sebald uses English elsewhere, in particular in *Die Ausgewanderten* and *Die Ringe des Saturn*, to mark moments of change in his narrative).

As the symmetry of the book demands, Austerlitz slips away after the last em-dash:

> Ich weiß nicht, sagte Austerlitz, was das alles bedeutet, und werde also weitersuchen nach meinem Vater und auch nach Marie de Verneuil. Es ging auf zwölf Uhr, als wir uns verabschiedeten, vor der Métrostation Glacière. (Sebald 2001b: 410)

> (I don't know, said Austerlitz, what all this means, and so I am going to continue looking for my father, and for Marie de Verneuil as well. It was nearly twelve o'clock when we took leave of each other outside the Glacière Métro station. (Sebald 2001c: 408))

Our narrator is left to close his account, since time is running out, but the name of the station reminds us of the skaters in *Die Ausgewanderten* (and of others) who leave traces in the ice (Sebald 1994a: 327; 1997a: 218). As in *Die Ausgewanderten*, the narrator needs to seek out a Jewish cemetery, and Austerlitz has given him the key to his home where he will find the latter's photographs, which '*one day*', as the English adds, 'would be all that is left of his life' (Sebald 2001c: 408; 'die als einziges übrigbleiben würden von seinem Leben' (Sebald 2001b: 410)). These 'last remnants', we can be sure, the narrator will not allow 'memory' to destroy. This Ashkenazi cemetery, Austerlitz opines, was the source, only belatedly discovered, of the moths that flew into his house. These moths continued to tremble, like Sebald's isomorphic lines, even after death, as if speaking to us from some parallel world beyond the range of our present knowledge. Their wings, as Bell memorably suggests, 'might have been woven out of some immaterial fabric' (Sebald 2001c: 233). It is an image close to oxymoron that demands contemplation, while the original German: 'aus einem man weiß nicht wie gewobenem Stoff' (Sebald 2001b: 237) – 'a material, woven we know not how' does less than justice to Sebald's haunting act of restitution.

CONCLUDING NOTE

When we embark on an examination of a text in translation, we are obliged to engage intimately with the original. In the case of Max Sebald, this brings us face to face with the absolute rootedness of his works in the language in which they live. His German is meticulous in both its precision and, when he so determines, its unclinchable elusiveness. There is structural and semantic poetry and potency in

Sebald's German that can be captured but rarely in the foreign language. However, the translations reveal more about Sebald than his masterly use of language. We discover a writer polishing his expertise with his literary medium and understanding his oeuvre increasingly as one long story, with many varied parts and individual messages, but with a constant underlying ethos. We can chart how he used the opportunity afforded by the translations to refine structures, to create clarity, to moderate early moments which he, perhaps, later regretted (as in, for instance, the quite brutal caricatures of his fellow West Germans in *Schwindel. Gefühle*). And we also discover the Sebald who does not exist in the lives he re-invests with dignity and worth, but who does exist in every detail of the vehicle he provides for them. As the translations take us back to the originals, we may discover a detail previously missed about Jacques Austerlitz or Paul Bereyter; what we cannot escape is the presence of the author, so often hidden behind a narrator or an informant. This author follows the dictates of his multi-faceted task of restitution with unswerving integrity; since it is achievable only through literary means, he seeks constant improvement in the legacy he is creating. Much of Sebald's fundamental vision and ethos is encapsulated in his first work, the long, elemental poem *Nach der Natur*. It is perhaps fitting that this was also, by dint of its late translation, the last work he authorized. It thus enables us to close the circle, to look back on his daring, high-altitude flight of the imagination and of language, and it brings into view the isomorphic lines created by his poetic devices. In 'Dark Night Sallies Forth', we begin to uncover the 'Nervatur/ des vergangenen Lebens [. . .]/ in einem Bild', and perhaps we can say with Sebald, as he continues: 'dann denk ich immer,/ es hätte dies etwas mit der Wahrheit/ zu tun' (Sebald 1995a: 77) – 'But if I see before me/ the nervature of past life/ in one image, I always think/ that this has something to do/ with truth' (Sebald 2002b: 81).

NOTES

1 For a differently oriented discussion of fractals in Sebald see Beck (2004, esp. p. 85).

2 See also the abandoned project on Corsica, where Sebald writes that in one of his dreams he could suddenly see with unprecedented clarity, 'als habe der Schleier der Atmosphäre sich gehoben oder als sei der Star gestochen worden' (Sebald 2008a: 188).

3 Simon Ward mentions the ambiguity of this epigraph in Ward (2001, here p. 64).

4 Possibly there is also an echo of one of Sebald's favourite authors, the Austrian essayist and Auschwitz-survivor Jean Améry, who writes in a chapter entitled 'Wieviel Heimat braucht der Mensch' of how startled he was when, in exile in Brussels during the war, he heard an SS officer bark at him 'im Dialekt meiner engeren Heimat' ('in the dialect of my homeland'). See Améry (2002: 99).

5 For a discussion of Sebald's relationship to tourism, see Long (2010).

6 For a discussion of Sebald's use of 'unwords', see Shane Weller's contribution to the present volume.

7 It is worth noting in passing that the narrator's repetition of the phrase 'south-west Germany' as he looks out of the train window seems to echo a passage from Adalbert Stifter's autobiographical fragment 'Mein Leben', where Stifter sits looking out of the window repeating to himself 'Da geht ein Mann nach Schwarzbach, da fährt ein Mann nach Schwarzbach' ('There is a man walking to Schwarzbach, there is a man driving to Schwarzbach'). Sebald quotes this passage in an essay on Stifter and Peter Handke ('Helle Bilder und dunkle. Zur Dialektik der Eschatologie bei Stifter und Handke', (Sebald 1994a: 165–86, here p. 167)), where he cites Hans Blumenberg's understanding of 'die ordnende, ja fast gesetzgebende Funktion des Namens [als] die erstmals absehbar werdende Hoffnung, aus der Enge des Eingesperrtseins hinauszugelangen' (the ordering, perhaps even law-making function of names as the first time that the hope of escaping the constriction of being locked-up becomes apparent). See also Neil Christian Pages (2010, esp. p. 231).

8 For a discussion of Sebald's use of names, see Denneler (2001: 133–58).

2

ENCOUNTER AND CRY: W. G. SEBALD AS POET

George Szirtes

To clear one important matter out of the way, I do not read German, so this chapter is about W. G. Sebald's poetry – that is to say *For Years Now* (2001), *After Nature* (2002) and *Unrecounted* (2004) – as it has been translated into English.[1] In other words it is about Sebald–Hamburger, except in the case of *For Years Now*, where Sebald wrote the poems directly in English (the only example of this in all his oeuvre).

For Years Now is an interesting place to begin, since the cover of the book distinctly says 'Poems by W. G. Sebald', while the publisher's blurb on the relevant Amazon page talks of '23 short stories by W. G. Sebald'. This immediately raises a fascinating question about the nature of Sebald's writing, not only in the work that he himself called poems, but also in the prose. The book appeared in 2001, the year of *Austerlitz*, at the acme of Sebald's work and reputation, which was also the year of his death. Part of my endeavour here, then, will be to sound the elements of poetry in the prose, as well as the elements of prose narrative in the verse. I shall not keep reminding myself that all the work (except *For Years Now*) is translated, so that must be assumed, though, no doubt, the matter will raise its head now and then.

How, one might ask at the very beginning, should we distinguish the poetic and prose elements in Sebald? How to distinguish it in any work? How did the blurb writer on Amazon come to refer to the work in *For Years Now* as short stories? What definition can we offer of either poetry or prose that might be useful?

We might suggest that – while we are in no position to know whether in antiquity the poem or the story came first, and in even less of a position to know whether those who employed them thought about them as distinct categories – the origins of the two ancient practices might be different. My own sense of it is that the poem is the development of the cry, whereas the story is the development of action. The cry is then associated with encounter, naming, condition and meaning, the story with action, reaction, consequence and lesson. The poem says: 'Look! Tiger!' The story says: 'Run! What next?' Roland Barthes said the lyric poem was a single indivisible signifier; the great Hungarian poet Ágnes Nemes Nagy regarded the poem as the naming of a single complex experience. Auden famously claimed that poetry was a way of happening, a mouth. In other words, definition is at the heart of poetry, narrative is at the heart of story.

Whilst it is best not to think of these as comprehensive definitions of poetry subsuming all the various kinds of poems – since the existence of epics and ballads would immediately prove them inadequate – they might be useful as definitions of the poetic *principle*, at work even in epics and ballads. This is partly because the resources of narrative poems exceed the demands of narrative, exceeding them precisely in their use of poetic form. It was Edgar Allan Poe who suggested that long poems were short poems tied together:

> Were we bidden to say how the highest genius could be most advantageously employed for the best display of its own powers, we should answer, without hesitation – in the composition of a rhymed poem, not to exceed in length what might be perused in an hour. Within this limit alone can the highest order of true poetry exist. We need only here say, upon this topic, that, in almost all classes of composition, the unity of effect or impression is a point of the greatest importance. It is clear, moreover, that this unity cannot be thoroughly preserved in productions whose perusal cannot be completed at one sitting. We may continue the reading of a prose composition, from the very nature of prose itself, much longer than we can persevere, to any good purpose, in the perusal of a poem. This latter, if truly fulfilling the demands of the poetic sentiment, induces an exaltation of the soul which cannot be long sustained. All high excitements are necessarily transient. Thus a long poem is a paradox. And, without unity of impression, the deepest effects cannot be brought about. Epics were the offspring of an imperfect sense of Art, and their reign is no more. (Poe 1842: 298–300)

One needn't follow Poe all the way, but that 'exaltation of the soul which cannot be long sustained' is not beside the point. There are *longueurs* in almost all long poems. There are memorable passages where the pulse races, and dutiful parts that serve as string to tie the narrative together.

And what is it that makes the memorable memorable, the exaltation exalting? It is, I suggest, a quality of language – not in the sense that the language is prettier or more jewel like, but that the language holds the attention and directs it back into itself rather than towards a point beyond it. The narrative dynamic in a story is suspense and resolution. In a strong narrative, the dynamic is towards conclusion. No one, however, has ever raced through a poem to find out what the last line might be. We know the poem is not that kind of construction. The point of the poem is not 'And so he died' or 'Reader, I married him', but what the poem defines as state. Language in a poem is less vehicle than metaphor. I don't mean that the poem employs metaphors as a device, though it often does, but that it is an attempted transformation of the phenomenon into language.

How does this idea, or, if you like, just a shadow of an idea, a suggestion, inform a reading of Sebald? In various and complex ways. Sebald's first published literary work was *Nach der Natur* (1988). Translated by Michael Hamburger, it was published in English only in 2002, after the author's death, under the title *After Nature*. The critic John Taylor wrote of it:

> The title itself is intriguing. *Nach der Natur* suggests 'after (the end of) Nature' or even 'after Nature's place (in a row)'; also 'toward Nature'; and if the etymology of *nach* is taken into account, then 'near Nature' is likewise imaginable. Considered as an expression, the title signifies '(painted) from life', and this additional sense crops up in an important passage of this unusual book. Regretfully, the obliquely provocative German subtitle, *Ein Elementargedicht*, is missing from this American edition of *After Nature* (as Michael Hamburger has rightly entitled his accurate and engaging version). With this subtitle, the author stresses the unity of his tripartite project and ironically likens it to a 'primer'. (Taylor 2010: 259–261)

The primer is a nice idea. For the Anglophone reader, of course, the Sebald oeuvre begins with *The Emigrants*, moves to *The Rings of Saturn*, then *Vertigo*, then *Austerlitz* and *For Years Now*, followed by *After Nature*, then *On the Natural History of Destruction*, *Unrecounted* and *Campo Santo*. That's not the order of writing. In German *After Nature* comes first, so it might be regarded as a venture in the deployment of material.

The book begins with an epigraph from Canto II of Dante's *Inferno*, at the point where Dante sets off with Virgil down 'the steep wild-wooded way', then presents us with three long poems, each in several parts. Taylor refers to this group of three as a triptych, each section – 'As the Snow on the Alps', 'And if I Remained by the Outermost Sea', and 'Dark Night Sallies Forth' – being 'a life study', which 'resembles a classical Vita in that a man's essence is distilled from a series of telling anecdotes' (Taylor 2010: 259). The life studies are those of the painter Matthias Grünewald, the eighteenth-century botanist Georg Steller and the authorial figure 'Sebald' himself. Although the book was awarded the Fedor-Malchov Prize for lyric poetry, it did not make Sebald a household name in Germany. Importantly, though, it won the support and praise of Hans Magnus Enzensberger. Enzensberger had long been recognized as a major literary figure by that time and it is possible to see why he might have been taken by Sebald's poetry.

Enzensberger's own long poem in thirty-three cantos, *The Sinking of the Titanic* (*Der Untergang der Titanic*, 1978) had been published ten years earlier, and while the poem was clearly allegorical – the Titanic disaster offering a Marxist critique of society – its manner of telling had borne some resemblance to that of *After Nature*. Both long poems are concerned with real historical events, both employ anecdote, both deploy a variety of strategies, including passages very close to prose, complete with evidential details, numbers and metatextual interludes. In other words, their angle to the material is similar. Both reject the rhetorical voice of lyric poetry, both draw on Modernist verse techniques in terms of lineation and distancing. This doesn't mean that Sebald's poetics is derived directly from Enzensberger, only that they share certain common ground and that Enzensberger might throw useful light on Sebald.

In talking about verse translation, as we must when exploring the nature of the text more closely, we may probably assume that while, line by line, the character of the voice – that is to say, the poem's peculiar and specific handling of poetic devices and its positioning in the language of speech, literature and other poetry as echo chamber – must be heard as response and not as cry, when it comes to the organization of material, what we might regard as the architecture of the longer poem, we are reading Sebald's design rather than Hamburger's.

The architecture is one part of the key, the line-by-line development and character of the poem is the other. In view of Poe's strictures about the long poem, it is worth pointing out that both *The Sinking of the Titanic* and *After Nature* are episodic, consisting of passages short enough to be comprehended in Poe's terms as something capable of being comprehended at a single sitting. The episodes themselves carry the consciousness of being fragments of a greater narrative whole, of course, and behave as such. So there are passages such as the beginning of Part IV of 'As the Snow on the Alps' that sail consciously close to prose:

> In the Chicago Art Institute
> hangs the self-portrait of an unknown
> young painter which in 1929
> passed into the Frankfurt art trade
> from Sweden. (Sebald 2003a: 17)[2]

It is interesting to compare passages such as this not only with the prose to be found particularly in, say, *Austerlitz*, but also with the titles of the three poems in *After Nature*. The contrast is fascinating. All three titles sound like self-conscious quotations from Romantic literature. All three set high rhetorical stakes. We are, in other words, made aware fairly early on of the polarities between which the poems will move. This establishes a certain literary space that the discourse of the poem can occupy. Sebald associates himself with the Romantic, and therefore, by association, a concept of the tragic, that his drier mode of writing can comment on, as a form of melancholy. In other words, it opens up the space of the melancholy without melodrama.

'As the Snow on the Alps' begins with a hypothetical figure, presumably the attendant, closing the wings of the Lindenhardt Fourteen Saint Altarpiece of 1503. On closing and locking up the altar this person, we are told, will be met by the figure of St George. Here I am in Hamburger's hands entirely, because telling us that the figure *will* be met, rather than, say, *must* be met, by the figure of St George implies an encounter yet to come, one that even the attendant must discover at some time in the future.[3] It is perhaps a minor point but it stresses naming (it names) and condition (the description that follows) rather than consequence. Nothing is going to happen to the attendant, or whoever is in a position to close the altarpiece as a result of his or her action, in fact the figure is only a way of focusing the sense of encounter.

The description that follows is a faithful rendering of the appearance of the martial saint, among many others (for example, saints Barbara, Catherine) in the painting, but the saint is not the point. Through the saint we pass to other works by Grünewald, arriving finally at his self-portrait at Erlangen. The probe moves from this work, through other works, to the man whose attitude and expression is seen in terms of the eyes 'veiled / and sliding sideways down into loneliness' (Sebald 2003a: 6).[4] I am not sure that the drawing does show the eyes in the portrait sliding down (the figure is looking up), nor that the 'crowned female saint' (6)[5] by Holbein in Basel that follows is certain to be based on the features of Grünewald, but that is what the art historian William Fraenger ('whose books were burned by the fascists' (6))[6] wrote. So, beside the present of the poem and the period of Grünewald's life, we now have a third term, Fascism. At this point we return to the Lendenhardt altarpiece and almost immediately come face to face with the author, as he had met himself, many years ago. We have traced a full circle of some sort, back to the description of the altarpiece, complete with the naming of saint, moving on to the problem of the separation of the sexes, the importance of which is as yet unexplained.

I am undertaking this brief close reading of the poem simply to follow the narrative trajectory, which is circular or spiral rather than linear. Part II continues in apparently straightforward but in fact mannered (if Hamburger is to be trusted), scholarly fashion. Phrases such as 'a written or oral / testimony of that praiseworthy hand' (9)[7] and 'limned by him in watercolours, especially / one cloud of wondrous beauty, wherein / above the Apostles convulsed / with awe, Moses and Elijah appear, / a marvel surpassed' (9–10)[8] suggest either quotation, from the Baroque period art historian, Joachim von Sandrart, or historical pastiche based on a reading of Sandrart. The whole section is a balance between plain, business-like description and such pastiche (it is like reading Browning). It is Sandrart's view of Grünewald that we are interested in here. The world so far is books and art, with the glimpsed face of the author as a ghostly presence. Through the art we are pointed at violence and sainthood, with Grünewald as a gentle, melancholy witness. It is a kind of beating about the burning bush; the sense, anyhow, of both the fire of sainthood and of destruction. And so we pass, by a characteristic Sebaldian leap, to the history of Jews in Frankfurt in Part III. Persecutions, slaughter, massacres and fire are the fate of the Jews, the fire itself introducing another prospect. 'Again, the chronicles tell that the Jews / burned themselves and that / after the fire there was a clear view from / the Cathedral Hill over to

Sachsenhausen' (12).[9] So the constant Sebaldian theme of the Holocaust is glimpsed – much like Sebald's own face earlier – as a significant incidental. As with the prose, there is a sense that the speaking voice could at any moment – at a glimpse – mutate into another's voice, so the passages become peopled with apparitions, including apparitions of the writer's presence. The writing here is matter of fact and, but for the shortness of the sentences (poems, Robert Frost suggested, work as a kind of counterpoint between sentence and line), we might imagine ourselves within the thickets of Sebald's prose of the *Austerlitz* period. After a quibble about Grünewald's name ('greenwood'), we are soon back with another book on Grünewald, this time by a certain 'Dr. W. K. Zülch', produced in 'ancient Schwabach type' (14),[10] a detail that suggests the book has been handled by Sebald. The book is hot property in historical terms because it was published in 1938 for Hitler's birthday and therefore could make no mention of the fact that Grünewald had married a Jew, albeit one who forsook her religion. We follow the early days of the marriage in close documented detail, recognizing Sebald's constant reference to the specific in both time and place. We recognize it, but we may not necessarily place our complete confidence in it. A little personal digression here might fill out the relevant material and propose the way such a deliberately positioned lack of confidence might work.

The first time I met Sebald to sit and talk to was when my wife, Clarissa, and I were invited to dinner by Anne and Anthony Thwaite, along with the novelist Rose Tremain and her partner, the biographer Richard Holmes (you will see I want to proceed in Sebaldian manner). I was seated next to Sebald, whom everyone knew as Max, and asked him about a detail in *The Emigrants*. The book, as is generally known, consists of four parts, each part named for the person about whose life we are to learn something significant. The first part concerns Dr Henry Selwyn, who turns out to be a Lithuanian *Kindertransport* child called Hersch Seweryn. Interestingly, by way of Sebaldian coincidence, a dinner party is at the heart of the story. The story begins:

> At the end of September 1970, shortly before I took up my position in Norwich, I drove out to Hingham with Clara in search of somewhere to live. (Sebald 1997a: 3)[11]

It is in Hingham where Dr Selwyn and his wife Elli live (Elli is Swiss by birth but is called Elaine in England), in a house called, we discover four pages in, Prior's Gate. Since we ourselves were fairly recent arrivals in Norfolk, I asked Max where Prior's Gate was, because we had visited Hingham and hadn't seen a house that might have fitted the description – a description complete with photographs in the book (photographs in the Sebaldian sense, that is). Max smiled and said he would let me into a secret. The house, he said, was not in Hingham, but where we lived, not too far away, in fact in the next street but one behind us. Afterwards, when we looked at the photographs and read through the description again, we thought it did indeed resemble the house so close to us. But why change the details, or, rather, why change the details, substituting a fictional place for the real one, but one so densely furnished with specifics that a witness might well stand up in court and convince the jury that s/he had lived precisely there. Was it part of a literary strategy that suffused the whole world of Sebaldiana? Was it simply common sense and tact to protect the new owner of the house from intrusion, especially in view of the death of Dr Selwyn as described at the end of the section? Certainly the new owner of the house, who, when I asked her, confirmed that hers was the property mentioned in *The Emigrants*, was not pleased to have the story clinging to the house and was worried that, despite the fact that Max had relocated and renamed it, the house might still be identifiable to the curious. Whatever the reason, however pragmatic, for the shifting of location in the book, the shift is so much a Sebaldian trope that it is fascinating to see a specific, quite concrete, example of it.

Almost inevitably one slips into pastiche of Sebald in indulging such a digression, but the invitation exists throughout Sebald's work, and the careful positioning of evidential material in the poetry serves the invitational function, much as it does in the prose. It is, I suspect, a key element in what makes Sebald, despite the stories, more a poet than a novelist.

To return to the poem, we discover at the end of the section that Grünewald might have been a repressed homosexual, leaving his wife, Anna, grown 'shrewish, ill, a victim / to perverse reason, to brain fevers / and to madness' (16).[12]

Part IV begins with the 'prosaic' passage I quoted earlier, about the Chicago Art Institute. It is a natural move in Sebald to move from a position of intimacy (the death of Grünewald, his wife still living on, 'infirm / in body and mind' (16)) to the cooler, more distant tones of scholarship. Here we are introduced to what the catalogue describes as: 'South German: Portrait of Young Artist, c.1500, Oil on Panel'. Once again we get the ekphrastic description of the painting, or rather what the painting shows. The speculation here, following Zülch, is that this is a self-portrait of Grünewald. As the poem tells us, 'And indeed the person of Mathis Nithart / in documents of the time so flows into / the person of Grünewald that one / seems to have been the life, / then the death, too, of the other' (18).[13] This identification of apparently two people as one person, as in Henry Selwyn and Hersch Seweryn, one being the life and death of the other, is one of Sebald's key poetic preoccupations. The most basic structural example of this is the blurred border of the relationship between narrator and quoted speaker, between, for instance, the narrator figure in *Austerlitz* and Jacques Austerlitz himself. The question of dual identity, and, beneath it, the illusion or persistence of identity, certainly runs through the first section of *After Nature*. Beneath another Grünewald work, the St Sebastian wing of the Isenheim altarpiece – St Sebastian taken to be a potential likeness of Grünewald – X-rays reveal another face, the face in the Nithart painting; so the poem continues to explore Nithart, emerging with other Sebaldian motifs along the way, such as 'jet fountains driven / by a most complicated system of scoop / wheels and pipes like that on the Main / at Aschaffenburg' (20)[14] (one thinks of the fascination with eyes and domes at the beginning of *Austerlitz*) and others like 'the glory of a unique / store of paints: lead white and albus, / Paris red, cinnabar, slate green, / mountain green, alchemy green, blue / vitreous pastes and minerals / from the Orient' (21),[15] in which the love of exotic lists both assures and astonishes the imagination with the sheer multiplicity – with the sensation of what Louis MacNeice in his poem 'Snow' called the 'incorrigibly plural' and 'the drunkenness of things being various'.

We are back with names and naming here, which I suggested was one of the essential functions of poetry. Encounter, cry, naming and exploration of meaning and condition: this is the business of *After Nature*, or, rather, the business of the Sebaldian imagination.

Naturally enough, in Part V, we do eventually arrive in Isenheim, complete with Sebald's version of a historical Blue Guide. We note the brief early appearance of fire – St Anthony's fire – and the pursuit of all things Antonine, specifically Antonine hospitals and their treatments. We pick up the 'death manifested / in madness' (24)[16] foreshadowed (everything is either foreshadowing or haunting) by the account of Grünewald's wife, Anna, and return directly to Grünewald by way of that hint. We have the historical quotation or pastiche again 'executed in beauteous and harrowing / colours' (24–5),[17] discover 'the manners in which a human being / creeps into himself, herself or / seeks to get out, was assembled' (25),[18] learning that Grünewald, 'who, in any case must have tended / towards an extremist view of the world, / will have come to see the redemption of the / living as one from life itself' (25).[19] So we creep ever closer to the vital enigma of identity and freedom from identity. The Temptation inevitably follows, arising with another hint of androgyny. We are given more ekphrastic passages. Grünewald, to whom 'this is creation' (26),[20] the poem tells us, rendered a scream as 'a pathological spectacle / to which he and his art, as he must have known, / themselves belong' (27).[21] The insertion of a phrase such as 'as he must have known' serves as a rare overt piece of metatext here. The narrator – possibly the prose writer intruding into the poem – is not given to speculations of that sort. He is still the glimpsed self-portrait of Part I of the poem. The section ends with an apocalyptic scene conjured out of the Temptation of St Antony.

And because it does so, because once again the verse has been enticed from its pretence of scholarly distance into the midst of action, it is necessary to retreat again: back to art history, back to commentary in Part VI, the 'I' disappearing into the 'we' of the lecturer or tour guide. Now it is the Basel Crucifixion of 1505 that takes our attention. We approach the Passion. There is the Garden of Gethsemane, there the kneeling figure of Christ. This is then associated with the slightly earlier event of the eclipse of the sun, which serves as a figure for encounter with the apocalypse described at the end of the previous section. Now, with only two sections remaining, the ends are beginning to tie up. We are back with the miracle of the snow in Rome.

But first the poem must widen its scope. As meticulous with detail as ever, Sebald shows us Grünewald on a journey to Windsheim in April 1525, falling into conversation with the etcher/draughtsmen Barthel and Sebald Beham (so we do meet Sebald again, if only by coincidence of name!). What do they talk about? It is of Thomas Münzer and his insurrection. This comes complete with astronomical omens. Münzer's mission, as one of the leaders of the Peasants' War of 1524, was the relief of the poor, which, as Grünewald mentions, was also the aim of 'the kettle drummer of Niklashausen' (33)[22] who was 'roasted in Würzburg' (34).[23] Grünewald's conversation continues on the way to Windsheim. In the following month there is the 'curious battle of Frankenhausen' (34),[24] where the horseback army massacres an army of peasants, as a result of which Grünewald wears 'a dark bandage over his face' (35).[25]

In the very last part of the poem we see Grünewald and his nine-year-old son riding along. It is September 1527. His work proceeds, but then his son suddenly dies at the age of fourteen. The dates here are slightly confused, since Grünewald dies in 1528 and the poem has him dying shortly after his son. The poem ends:

> The forest recedes, truly,
> so far that one cannot tell
> where it once lay, and the ice-house
> opens, and rime, on to the field, traces
> a colourless image of Earth.
> So, when the optic nerve
> tears, in the still space of the air
> all turns as white as
> the snow on the Alps. (37)[26]

So we end with blindness and vanishings. Nature is as arbitrary as man is violent. The colours go, the child dies, the utopian visionary is tortured and beheaded, the identity of Grünewald/Neithard/Nithard shifts and hides, as does that of the narrator, Sebald, glimpsed now as image, now as voice. Identity is phantasmal. We seek it with X-rays, with evidence, through artefact and echo, through history and pastiche, but it eludes us. The journey we have made to get here, to the end of Part VIII, has managed to work its way through time, but time only moves about an enigmatic centre. And this would be a somewhat abstract piece of speculation or possibly a sentimental mystification, the conjuring of a melancholy that is more style than substance, were it not for the continuous tapping into at least a sense of life, some kind of trace, in which the apparatus of melancholy is suddenly cheered and illuminated by the brilliant relief of the drunkenness of things being various, in other words of the intimations, and all too many evidences, of mortality saved by the haunting presence of the world of phenomena.

The salient point is that what Sebald explores in *After Nature* as verse, complete with line breaks (Hamburger's line breaks), moves in the subsequent work, perfectly naturally, into prose. The distinction offered here, then, is not that between poetry and fiction but between verse and prose, and, at this point, I want to look at Sebald's verse in *After Nature* in terms of prosody and poetic device.

I have tried to draw some parallels between Sebald and Enzensberger's use of verse, that is to say a technique employing Modernist form – uneven line length, avoidance of regularity, avoidance of comfortable or predictable rhetorical forms unless by way of quotation or reference, the deployment of modes transferred from other contexts. In the case of Enzensberger, this manifests itself for instance in itemized lists; in Sebald, in the conscious adoption of the procedures of the period guide book.

For all the subtle and conscious hybridity of *After Nature*, distinctions between genres and modes remain. Poetry, when set out as poetry, cannot exist independently of the cumulative expectations of poetry, including regularity of metre, repetition and reiteration, the expectation of embodiment through rhythm, breath, onomatopoeia, alliteration and so forth, the apprehension of metaphor even when the language itself seems bare and functional. So, when we begin to read verse as line, we cannot help but be aware of the negotiation of the idea of line with the idea of sentence. John Taylor, in his review, talked about 'suspenseful enjambments' and 'carefully constructed free-verse narratives', claiming that *After Nature* was 'no Prosagedicht'. The lines of *After Nature* are fairly gentle in their suspenseful enjambments. It is rare for them to be abrupt. We have to move more than half way down the second page before we find a line that ends on a conjunction ('men had revered each other like brothers, and' (6))[27] or, four lines later, on a preposition ('Hence, too, at the centre of' (6)).[28] The section also contains a line ending on the definite article as detached from its noun ('with the scant company of the' (7)).[29] Reading the work as verse, these things draw the reader's attention as weak endings generally do, without a strong sense of strategy behind them. Maybe they are simply signifiers of a certain deliberate casualness of manner, warning us against the formality of verse, verse's neatness and potential assertiveness. Maybe they are simply what Michael Hamburger has chosen to do with Sebald's verse. The actual words are Hamburger's of course, and it is he who has chosen a particular kind of English-language versification to represent Sebald's German. Here and there you get noticeably short lines ('and to madness', 'in body and mind'). The shorter lines can, at the end of a sentence, suggest a prose paragraph, but more generally, when absorbed into a sentence, serve to remind us that line is important, that a decision to end the line has been taken, that, in short, it is a poem, not an account, we are reading. Like Enzensberger, Sebald will, if we go by Hamburger (Enzensberger translated his own verse in *The Sinking of the Titanic*), avail himself of the options of free verse to avoid getting hemmed in by too grand a style. But there is no great difficulty in trusting Hamburger. Quite apart from Hamburger's own record in translating German poetry, it seems fairly obvious that Sebald makes no great formal demands on his translator. The verse is not characterized by density or ambiguity. There may be varieties in degree but there is little or no use of simile or metaphor as device. The function of simile is fulfilled by juxtaposition or quotation. It is simply a kind of commentary.

In other words, Sebald's poetic isn't primarily evidenced as texture. The poems are open weave and appear to move forward in the way prose does. It is just that its purpose is not prosaic, not primarily logical, forward moving. The anecdotal detail that forms the pulse of the poem does not lead us towards any particular conclusion, not even as detective story (Who Killed Roger Ackroyd? Who Is Matthias Grünewald?), but moves round and round a hunch about life that is furnished in terms of documents that look like prose. There is no consequence that matters. There is no suspense as such, there are only Taylor's 'suspenseful enjambments'.

And indeed it is much the same set of devices and tones that we find in the great books of hard-to-classify prose, or Sebaldian prose as we might call it. The air of slightly dusty portentousness that some detect in the vast halls of *Austerlitz* is the product of the engines of poetry humming away in the cellar. The prose reader demands that the text get on with it, that there should be a certain crispness and momentum to the reader's passage through events, but the book resists that. It offers itself as a series of densities with false walls and floors. It may be that what irritates some people about Sebald is what – ironically, in view of Sebald's dislike of Rilke – might also irritate them about Rilke: the poetry of desire and metaphysics, or, rather, the articulation of feeling about these things can strike some English-language readers as a little precious. Who, after all, they will complain, wants to hear any more about the Holocaust, the War, or about the Sense of History? Yes, we might argue back, but the dust glistens. It is the atoms of the universe, the drunkenness of things being various, mingling with the atoms of the dead. That is the tension that produces the poetry.

That poetry was most fully realized not as verse but as prose. Sebald too realized that the function of verse was bound to change for him, and the short notational texts that we find in *For Years Now* and *Unrecounted* are what remain in the form of verse. It is the poetics of the residue. Some are like memos ('Apparently // the red spots / on Jupiter are / centuries old / hurricanes' (2001h: 18) – this also appears in *Unrecounted*, without the first line (Sebald and Tripp 2004b: 21)), some like found postcards ('My love // I am sending you / this picturesque / view of the river / Rhine as I will / be leaving today / by the six o' / clock steamer' (2001h: 21)), some like dreams ('Last night // a Polish / mechanic / came & for / a thousand / florins made / me a new / perfectly / functioning / head' (2001h: 30) – this too appears in

Unrecounted (Sebald and Tripp 2004b: 41)). The poems in *For Years Now* are all centred, as they generally are in *Unrecounted*. They seem almost whimsical but spacious, and airy, sometimes with just one word per line. In terms of poetics they are the opposite of the prose, where paragraphs have disappeared altogether. Each short line is dropped into the quiet pond of the page. The relationship of the poems to the images is clear but tangential. Jaray's visual work is entirely abstract: Sebald picks up suggestions of event and voice from the colour and the arrangement of the small white rectangle and square that break up the coloured surface. This isolating of the brief text implies both casualness (just a few odd words, nothing much) and portentousness (but every word must be important, given the attention it demands). As shown above, *Unrecounted*, the posthumous volume, replicates some of the poems from *For Years Now*. The collaboration was begun in 2001, the year in which *For Years Now* was published. It is a book of eyes, as drawn in lithograph by the artist Jan Peter Tripp, to which Sebald has added more small texts, working in much the same way as a poetics of residue, that is to say of pathos, or loss. The book, which contains an essay on Tripp by Andrea Köhler, is much more consciously a memorial, and probably draws more attention to Tripp's work than it does to Sebald's.

But it is interesting to end with eyes. *After Nature* is full of looking, beginning with those eyes, 'veiled / and sliding sideways down into loneliness' (6).[30] So the work of the imagination ends with two visual artists, artists who seem to have little in common except for Sebald and a Polish mechanic or two. The penultimate poem in *Unrecounted* is in fact 'Unrecounted'. Centred as before, it runs: 'Unrecounted / / always it will remain / the story of the averted / faces' (Sebald and Tripp 2004b: 81).[31]

These are in fact the residues and vestiges of the poetry in the prose: as if *The Emigrants*, or *Vertigo* or *The Rings of Saturn* or *Austerlitz* could be concentrated in a haiku or in a chance remark jotted down in a notebook or on a menu in a restaurant.

Clearly, *Austerlitz* is a far more substantial work, in every sense, than *For Years Now* or *Unrecounted*. Equally clearly, *After Nature* is the seed for the forest that is *Austerlitz*. But that doesn't mean that poetry is simply where things began and ended. I think it has been poetry all the way through, but poetry expanded as a melding of voices that plays itself out through the medium of prose, with the expectations of prose as counterpoint. It seems to be all sentence and no line, but it is all encounter too, and naming and condition, and cry.

NOTES

1 The posthumous collection *Über das Land und das Wasser* (2008) has not been translated into English.

2 'Im Chicagoer Art Institute / hängt das Selbstbildnis eines unbekannten / jungen Malers, das im Jahre 1929 aus Schweden / in den Frankfurter Kunsthandel kam' (Sebald 2008c: 16).

3 In the German, this is recounted in a neutral present tense: 'Wer die Flügel des Altars / der Pfarrkirche von Lindenhardt / zumacht und die geschnitzten Figuren / in ihrem Gehäuse verschließt, / dem kommt auf der linken / Tafel der hl. Georg entgegen' (7).

4 'verhängt / und versunken seitwärts ins Einsame hin' (7–8).

5 'eine gekrönte Heilige' (8).

6 'dessen Bücher die Faschisten verbrannten' (8).

7 'über die ruhmwürdige Hand eine Schrift / oder mündliche Nachricht' (10).

8 'die von ihm / mit Wasserfarben gebildete Verklärung / Christi auf dem Berg Thabor, insonders / eine verwunderlich schöne Wolcke, / darinnen, über die in Furcht ganz verzuckte / Apostel, Moyses und Elias erscheinen, / selzamkeit halber von nichts übertroffen' (10).

9 'Wieder / besagen die Berichte, daß die Juden / sich selber verbrannt hätten / und es nach der Feuersbrunst / möglich gewesen sei, vom Domhügel / bis nach Sachsenhausen zu sehen' (12).

10 'das große Buch über den historischen / Grünewald, das Dr. Phil. W. K. Zülch / im Jahr 38 zu Hitlers Geburtstag / in alter Schwabacher Type vorlegte' (13).

11 'Ende September 1970, kurz vor Antritt meiner Stellung in der ostenglischen Stadt Norwich, fuhr ich mit Clara auf Wohnungssuche nach Hingham hinaus' (Sebald 2008b: 7).

12 'händelsüchtig, krank, ein Opfer / der bösen Vernunft, des Kopffiebers / und des Wahnsinns geworden' (Sebald 2008c: 15).

13 'Und in der Tat geht die Figur des Mathis Nithart / in den Dokumenten der Zeit in einem Maß / in die Grünewalds über, daß man meint, / der eine habe wirklich das Leben / und zuletzt gar den Tod / des anderen ausgemacht' (17).

14 'ein hochkompliziertes Mühlen- und / Röhrensystem so wie das am Main / zu Aschaffenburg, das ein herrliches / Räderwerk war und Schaustück' (18).

15 'Pracht eines einzigartigen / Farbenlagers: blywyß und albus, / parißrot, cinober, schyfergrün, / berkgrün, alchemy grün, blauen / Glasflüssen und Mineralien / aus dem Morgenland' (19).

16 'die im Wahnsinn / sich herstellende Präsenz des Todes' (22).

17 'in den schönsten / und schauerlichsten Farben' (22).

18 'wie der Mensch / in sich hineinkriecht oder aus sich / heraus will' (22).

19 ' wird Grünewald, / der ohnehin zu einer extremistischen Auffassung / der Welt geneigt haben muß, die Erlösung / des Lebens als eine vom Leben verstanden haben' (22).

20 'Dieses ist ihm, dem Maler, die Schöpfung' (23).

21 'das Geraune eines pathologischen Schauspiels, / zu dem er, und seine Kunst, wie er wohl wußte, / selber gehörten' (24).

22 'der Pauker / von Niklashausen' (30).

23 'in Würzburg geröstet' (30).

24 'in der sonderbaren Schlacht von Frankenhausen' (31).

25 'eine dunkle Binde / vor dem Gesicht' (31).

26 'Der Wald weicht zurück, wahrlich, / in solcher Weite, daß man nicht kennt, / wo er einmal gelegen, und das Eishaus / geht auf, und der Reif zeichnet ins Feld / ein farbloses Bild der Erde. / So wird, wenn der Sehnerv / zerreißt, im stillen Luftraum / es weiß wie der Schnee / auf den Alpen' (33).

27 'die Männer einander verehrt wie Brüder, / einander dort oft ein Denkmal gesetzt' (8).

28 'Darum wohl / auch in der Mitte ...' (8).

29 This is not the case in the German, although the 'scant company of the fourteen auxiliary saints' is still given force by the break after 'Genossenschaft' (company): 'Das ist die Vorschrift, weiß der Maler, / der sich einreiht auf dem Altar / in die viel zu geringe Genossenschaft / der vierzehn Nothelfer' (8).

30 'verhängt / und versunken seitwärts ins Einsame hin' (7–8).

31 'Unerzählt / bleibt die Geschichte / der abgewandten / Gesichter' (Sebald and Tripp 2003: 69).

3

UNQUIET PROSE: W. G. SEBALD AND THE WRITING
OF THE NEGATIVE

Shane Weller

As the critical literature on W. G. Sebald grows, it is becoming increasingly clear just how haunted his oeuvre is by the works of other modern European writers. This intertextual haunting – which includes Hugo von Hofmannsthal, Franz Kafka, Jean Améry and Thomas Bernhard – renders Sebald's prose decidedly unquiet, and arguably lies at the heart of what Ben Hutchinson has described as his 'late style' (Hutchinson 2009b: 170). What is it, though, that distinguishes the literary tradition into which Sebald inscribes himself in his lateness? As I shall seek to demonstrate in this chapter, Sebald conceives of that tradition largely in terms of its *writing of the negative*; that is, a writing which seeks to resist the dark forces of modernity, as iden-tified by Horkheimer and Adorno in *Dialectic of Enlightenment* (1947), not through anything positive, but, rather, through a tarrying within the negative that accords with Adorno's conception of 'radically darkened art' (Adorno 1997: 19).

For Adorno, it is above all Kafka and Beckett who achieve such a radical darkening in the literary sphere. As he puts it in his 1953 essay on Kafka: 'in a world caught in its own toils, everything positive [...] helps increase that entanglement'. In support of this claim, Adorno cites one of Kafka's 'Zürau' aphorisms: 'Our task is to do the negative [Das Negative zu tun, ist uns noch auferlegt] – the positive has already been given us' (1981: 271). How is one to understand such a doing of the negative? According to Adorno, Kafka's own works supply the answer, in what he sees as their ambiguous alliance with death: on the one hand, Kafka articulates the dream of an end to 'the half-uselessness of a life which does not live'; on the other hand, the very failure of the attempt to reach this end, which is to say a failure of the negative or even a non-dialectical negation of the negative, is the sole source of hope: 'the fact that the mutilated creature cannot die any more is the sole promise of immortality which the rationalist Kafka permits to survive the ban on images' (1981: 270–1). In other words, there is a doubleness at the heart of the attempt to 'do the negative', and this is to be seen, according to Adorno, at the level of the literary work's content. As for the implications of this obligation to do the negative at the level of literary style, they remain unaddressed in Adorno's essay, his only comment on Kafka's style being that 'There is nothing mad about his prose, unlike the writer from whom he learned decisively, Robert Walser' (1981: 253).

That Sebald's aim is to join this tradition in which the writer's ethico-aesthetic obligation is 'das Negative zu tun' is nowhere more forcefully suggested than in his 1988 essay on Jean Améry, where he argues that Améry's works are distinguished by their refusal to make any 'Kompromiß mit der Geschichte' ('compromise with history'), their denunciation of 'die Obszönitat einer psychisch und sozial deformierten Sozietät' ('the obscenity of a psychologically and socially deformed society'), and their commitment to a writing that, like that of Georges Bataille and E. M. Cioran in France, is 'bedingungslos negativ' ('uncompromisingly negative' (2003b: 157–8; 2004b: 154)). If Sebald commits himself to such uncompromising negativity, he does so most obviously at the level of content: his is a radically darkening world of ruins, loss, trauma and isolation, refracted in a melancholic prism that, at times, is so exaggerated as to produce comic effects – and, arguably, not always intentionally so. Crucially, however, like that of Kafka, Beckett and Bernhard before him, Sebald's writing of the negative is always also *enacted* in his language – in his deployment of particular words and phrases, in his syntax, and in the rhythm of his prose.

First and foremost, Sebald aims to achieve this enactment of the negative through what – drawing on a term used by Beckett in a July 1937 letter to Axel Kaun – may be called 'Unworte' (unwords) (Beckett 2009a: 515). Arguably, the most important of these unwords in Sebald's oeuvre is 'Unglück', with others including 'unheimlich', 'ungeheuer', 'unruhig', 'unsicher', 'unversehens', 'ungut', 'unmöglich', 'unfähig', 'unbegreiflich' and 'unförmig'. One of the questions to be addressed in this chapter is how such unwords fare in translation. In addition to these unwords, Sebald also regularly deploys words with the prefixes 'aus-', 'ver-' and 'zer-', and with the suffix '-los'. As for phrases, among the most important is 'aus dem Nichts', which marks the moment when the negative appears to become productive. At the rhythmic level, he relies principally on anaphora, with 'kein … kein …', 'nicht … nicht …' and 'nirgends … nirgends …' being the most recurrent forms. Sebald also makes considerable – and increasingly frequent – use of the 'je mehr … desto weniger' construction, which, as Hutchinson argues, enacts at the syntactical level a 'Fortschrittskritik' ('critique of progress') akin to the one articulated by Horkheimer and Adorno (see Hutchinson 2009b: 120). Each of Sebald's four completed prose works also contains extended passages exhibiting a more general syntactical negativity, these passages helping to establish the overall rhythm of each work.

As soon as one begins to pay attention to this enactment of the negative, it becomes apparent that particular words, phrases and syntactical forms play a key role in a given work. For instance, while the word 'unheimlich' predominates in *Schwindel. Gefühle* (1990), where the very experience of 'Schwindel' ('vertigo') is directly related to that of the uncanny, the phrase 'aus dem Nichts' comes to the fore in *Austerlitz* (2001), where it is the return of memories that is central. Focusing on the specific ways in which the negative is written in Sebald's prose works can thus help to clarify the differences between them, and to counter any easy homogenization of his oeuvre. It can also help to reveal the manner in which the language of Sebald's primary narrators comes to resemble that of his protagonists, through a stylistic contagion that marks these narrators' ethico-aesthetic identifications. That this stylistic contagion is particularly evident in *Austerlitz* suggests that Hutchinson is arguably right to find a new, Giorgio Bassani-influenced conception of the narrator as his protagonist's 'Schutzengel' (guardian angel) in that work (see Hutchinson 2007). It also suggests, however, that the space of any potential irony is reduced, the implications of this impacting directly upon the function of the negative.

Although there is space here to focus on only a few of the ways in which Sebald enacts the negative, I shall seek to highlight the differences in this enactment in his four prose works and, above all, to consider the extent to which he achieves the principal aim that he sets for post-war German literature: to resist any compromise with a history that he sees as 'obscene'. The principal question underlying my analysis will be whether Sebald manages to avoid, on the one hand, the nihilism that he criticizes in his 1983 essay on Günter Grass and Wolfgang Hildersheimer (Sebald 2003b: 125; 2006: 127), and, on the other hand, any movement out of the negative of the kind condemned by Adorno in *Negative Dialectics* (1966), where he argues that 'Acts of overcoming [*Überwindungen*] – even of nihilism [. . .] – are always worse than what they overcome' (Adorno 1973: 380). This will then lead on to the question of whether Sebald locates what, in his 2001 essay 'Ein Versuch der Restitution' ('An Attempt at Restitution' (2003b: 248; 2006a: 215)), he identifies as the restitutive power of literature as lying above all in a writing of the negative that occurs not only in the matter but also in the very manner of his works.

'UNGLÜCK'

Not only does the word 'Unglück' recur throughout Sebald's critical writings, but it also plays a significant role in each of his prose works. Its importance is evident as early as 1969, in the foreword to his monograph on Carl Sternheim, which ends with a quotation from Kafka's diaries on the Jewish actor Jizchak Löwy: 'Auch sollen wir, wenn wir schon nicht ergriffen sind, seine Ergriffenheit anerkennen und ihm die Möglichkeit des beschriebenen *Unglücks* erklären' ('And we are supposed, even if we are not gripped, to acknowledge that he is gripped and to explain to him how the misfortune which has been described was possible' (quoted in Sebald 1969: 11; Kafka 1990: 359; 1964: 172))[1]. It is, of course, from this aesthetic imperative that Sebald derives the title for his 1985 collection of essays on Austrian literature, *Die*

Beschreibung des Unglücks (1994b). In the foreword to that volume, he states that a central concern of the essays will be 'das *Unglück* des schreibenden Subjekts' ('the misfortune of the writing subject' (1994b: 11)). Austrian literature's preoccupation with 'Unglück' is, he argues, so pronounced that one may characterize that literature as driven by a 'quasi naturgemäß negative Inklination' ('as it were natural negative inclination' (1994b: 12)). Crucially, however, this 'negative inclination' is not a weakness, but rather 'eine Form des Widerstands' ('a form of resistance'), its function 'alles andere als bloß reaktiv oder reaktionär' ('anything but reactive or reactionary' (1994b: 12)).

In his foreword to *Die Beschreibung des Unglücks*, then, Sebald sets out in the clearest terms his conviction that a writing of the negative, as he conceives it, is both politically radical and ethically grounded. No less crucially, he slips from a conception of literature as a form of 'Widerstand' to a thinking of it in terms of 'Überwindung', declaring that the description of 'Unglück' in the literary work 'schließt in sich die Möglichkeit zu seiner Überwindung ein' ('includes the possibility of its overcoming' (1994b: 12)). With this claim, Sebald might seem to depart from Adorno's conception of 'radically darkened art'. As we shall see, however, Sebald's own writing of the negative tends to accord more fully with a conception of the literary as a form of resistance, with this resistance lying in a certain tarrying with the negative.

In English versions of Sebald, 'Unglück' has most often been translated as 'misfortune', with other translations including 'unhappiness', 'disaster', and 'tragedy', although Sebald himself matches 'unglücklich' with 'calamitous' in the German and English versions of his 1976 essay on Kafka (1995b: 98; 1972: 52). Understood as calamity, 'Unglück' inhabits a liminal space, pointing in two directions simultaneously, challenging the reader to resist any simple answer to the question of why modernity should be a 'historia calamitatum' (1994b: 12). Sebald's 'Unglück' is at once personal – as he observes of Friedrich Hölderlin's in the essay 'Ein Versuch der Restitution' (2003b: 245; 2006a: 212) – and collective, at once natural and historical, and it has, above all, to be understood in dialectical relation to 'Glück', as suggested by Sebald's own marking of the following sentence in his copy of *Dialectic of Enlightenment*: 'Alle Geburt wird mit dem Tod bezahlt, *jedes Glück durch Unglück*' ('Every birth is paid for with death, every fortune with misfortune' (Horkheimer and Adorno 1997: 16)). This view is articulated in Sebald's essay on Robert Walser, in *Logis in einem Landhaus* (1998): 'Langsam habe ich seither begreifen gelernt, wie über den Raum und die Zeiten hinweg alles miteinander verbunden ist, [...] *das Glück mit dem Unglück*, die Geschichte der Natur mit der unserer Industrie, die der Heimat mit der des Exils' ('I have since slowly learned to understand that across space and time everything is connected, [...] fortune with misfortune, natural history with that of our industry, the history of the homeland with that of exile' (2000a: 163; my translation)). It is for this reason that any interruption of the dialectic of Enlightenment, which is to say the dialectic of 'Glück' and 'Unglück', will take the form not of 'Glück', but rather of 'Trost' ('consolation' (1994b: 13; my translation), Sebald's use of this word suggesting that he sees art in Schopenauerian terms as possessing a consoling power (see Schopenhauer 1966: i. 267). In order to grasp what it might mean to think 'Unglück' dialectically, however, one has to turn to Sebald's own poetry and prose, where a clear trajectory in the word's deployment becomes apparent.

In *Nach der Natur* (1988), Sebald twice addresses the question of art's relation to 'Unglück', first in the work of Matthias Grünewald and then in that of Brueghel the Elder (1995a: 9, 91; 2002a: 7–8, 104), and this relation is again addressed explicitly in the second part of *Schwindel. Gefühle*, when the narrator sees the Giotto frescoes in Padua (2001l: 96; 2002g: 84). It is, however, in the third part of *Schwindel. Gefühle*, 'Dr. K.s Badereise nach Riva', that the word comes to dominate Sebald's writing for the first time. This is hardly surprising, given that 'Unglück' is arguably thought first and foremost by Sebald in relation to Kafka. The narrator's remarks on Kafka's 'Jäger Gracchus' fragment conclude with the statement: '*Ungeklärt* bleibt die Frage, wer die Schuld trägt an diesem zweifellos großen *Unglück*, ja selbst die Frage, worin die Schuld, die offensichtliche Ursache des *Unglücks*, überhaupt besteht' ('The question of who is to blame for this undoubtedly great misfortune remains unresolved, as indeed does the matter of what his guilt, the cause of his misfortune, consists in' (2001l: 180; 2002g: 165)). Together with K. in *Das Schloß*, Gracchus is the principal textual paradigm for Sebald's travellers, inhabiting as he does the space of 'Unglück', the reason for this 'Unglück' remaining 'ungeklärt', beyond the power of any 'Aufklärung' precisely because the responsibility for that 'Unglück' lies, for Sebald, in the Enlightenment project itself.

In the final part of *Schwindel. Gefühle*, the narrator is himself marked by this 'Unglück' when he dreams of another Gracchus-like figure out of Kafka: an old tailor's dummy, dressed in the uniform of an Austrian *chasseur*. At the narrator's touch, this dummy crumbles into dust, and the narrator goes on to record that he now dreams repeatedly of the figure holding out its hand to him: 'Und jedesmal habe ich dann die von der Berührung staubig, ja Schwarz gewordenen Finger meiner Rechten wie das Zeichen für ein durch *nichts auf der Welt mehr auszugleichendes Unglück* vor Augen' ('And every time, I then see before me the fingers of my right hand, dusty and even blackened from that one touch, like the token of some great woe that nothing in the world will ever put right' (2001l: 249–50; 2002g: 228–9)). Wherein lies the narrator's guilt here? While it may seem to relate to some failure on the narrator's part to protect the other, it arguably remains as '*ungeklärt*' – that is, under the sign of the negative – as that of Kafka's Josef K. or the Jäger Gracchus.

Whereas 'Unglück' plays a decisive role in the final two parts of *Schwindel. Gefühle*, in Sebald's next prose work, *Die Ausgewanderten* (1992), there is a considerably less clearly defined arrangement, the word being used in all four narratives but not dominating any one of them. The dialectic of 'Glück' and 'Unglück' is touched upon in the second narrative, 'Paul Bereyter', when the narrator describes his former schoolteacher as the *'aus dem Glück ins Unglück* verstoßene Paul' ('a Paul who had plunged [...] from happiness to misfortune' (2001a: 73; 2002e: 49)), the 'Unglück' into which Paul is 'verstoßen' being not simply personal, as becomes clear when the narrator states that he sees Paul's Märklin model railway as 'das Sinn- und Abbild von Pauls *deutschem Unglück*' ('the very image and symbol of Paul's German tragedy' (2001a: 90–1; 2002e: 61)). In 'Ambros Adelwarth', the movement is again towards a terminal 'Unglück', the institutional frame for this being the sanatorium in Ithaca, New York, where Ambros dies. In Adornian fashion, the only hope for any redemption from this 'Unglück' appears to lie in another negation: the disintegration of the building itself through the activities of the 'Mäusevolk' ('mice') and various beetles, the intertextual link to Kafka being obvious (2001a: 161, 165; 2002e: 110, 112; cf. Hutchinson 2009b: 83–4). In 'Max Ferber' (originally 'Max Aurach'), although the word 'Unglück' appears in Luisa Lanzberg's manuscript autobiography (2001a: 285, 297, 322) – translated as 'tragedy', 'misery', and again 'tragedy' (2002e: 191, 198, 215) – it is more notable for its rarity. This can be explained by the very nature of the autobiographical text, which recounts a life before the catastrophe that was to befall the German Jews.

In *Die Ringe des Saturn* (1995), Sebald deploys the word in ways that extend from the personal to the historical, bringing the two into intimate relation. In chapter V, Joseph Korzeniowski (later, Conrad) is described as his father's 'von so viel *Unglück* bedrückten Sohnes' (2001k: 136), reduced in the English translation to 'troubled son' (2002f: 107). And, in chapter IX, Chateaubriand describes his affair with Charlotte Ives as 'unsere *unglückliche* Geschichte' ('our unhappy story' (2001k: 316; 2002f: 254)). The word 'Geschichte' can, of course, signify both 'story' and 'history', and other uses of 'Unglück' in *Die Ringe des Saturn* place the emphasis squarely upon the latter: the photographic history of the First World War is an '*Unglückschronik*' ('chronicle of disasters' (2001k: 122; 2002f: 95)); the Dowager Empress of China comes to the conclusion that 'die Geschichte aus nichts bestehe als aus dem *Unglück* und den Anfechtungen, die über uns hereinbrechen' ('history consists of nothing but misfortune and the troubles that afflict us' (2001k: 193; 2002f: 153)); and, reflecting on Chateaubriand's *Mémoires d'outre-tombe* (1848), the narrator concludes that, ironically, but in complete accordance with a darkened view of modern European history, the Vicomte's 'farbenprächtige Schilderungen von militärischen Schauspielen und Staatsaktionen bilden ... sozusagen die Hohepunkte der blindlings von einem *Unglück* zum nächsten taumelnden Geschichte' ('colourful accounts of military spectacles and large-scale operations form what might be called the highlights of history which staggers blindly from one disaster to the next' (2001k: 319; 2002f: 256)).

It is just such an imbrication of personal and historical 'Unglück' that characterizes Sebald's last prose work, *Austerlitz*. This is anticipated in striking fashion in a passage from his abandoned 'Korsika-Projekt', where Sebald returns to what is arguably the key principle underlying his critical views and his own practice as a writer: that art is privileged above all other cultural forms for its capacity to enact a 'restitution' for the 'Unglück' it describes. In a short text first published in 1996 under the title 'Kleine Exkursion nach Ajaccio', the narrator recounts his visit to the Musée Fesch, where he comes upon a double portrait by the seventeenth-century Italian painter Pietro Paolini. In the 12 September 1995 diary entry, which is the earliest surviving draft of this passage, the narrator's reaction to this painting is not recorded (see 2008a: 151). In the published version, however, the following sentence is added: 'Lange habe ich vor diesem Doppelporträt gestanden und in ihm, wie ich damals glaubte, das ganze *unergründliche Unglück* des Lebens *aufgehoben* gesehen' ('I stood in front of this double portrait for a long time, seeing in it, as I thought at that time, an annulment of all the unfathomable misfortune of life' (2003b: 9; 2006a: 5)). Here, the narrator reveals what he takes to be the essential capacity of art in its relation to 'Unglück' – the latter is 'aufgehoben', the Hegelian word signifying not only annulment but also preservation. This sense of art's power is radically modified, however, by the phrase 'wie ich damals glaubte'. The question thus becomes whether the narrator's view has changed on this crucial question, and in search of an answer one has to turn to Sebald's final prose work.

Early in *Austerlitz*, 'Unglück' is again used in relation to painting, on this occasion in Austerlitz's reflections on a work by Lucas van Valckenborch depicting the frozen river Schelde with the city of Antwerp in the background (2001b: 19; 2002c: 15; cf. Fuchs 2004: 181–2). The element in this painting that particularly attracts Austerlitz's gaze is located, appropriately, on the margins: 'Im Vordergrund, gegen den rechten Bildrand zu, ist eine Dame zu Fall gekommen' ('In the foreground, close to the right-hand edge of the picture, a woman has fallen' (2001b: 20; 2002c: 15)). Just as the 'Unglück' of Icarus in Brueghel's painting is not even noticed by the other figures depicted therein, so here, too, the woman's fall goes unnoticed – except, of course, by the artist and by Austerlitz. For the latter, it is '*als* geschähe das kleine, von den meisten Betrachtern gewiß übersehene *Unglück* immer wieder von neuem, *als höre es nie mehr auf und als sei es durch nichts und von niemandem mehr gutzumachen*' ('as if the little accident, which no doubt goes unnoticed by most viewers, were always happening over and over again, and nothing and no one could ever remedy it' (2001b: 20; 2002c: 16)). Everything in *Austerlitz* will depend upon the space that is opened here by the anaphoric 'als' ('as if'). Can art be the exception to the rule of the 'durch nichts und von niemandem mehr gutzumachen', the exception to the rule that there are certain forms of 'Unglück' for which no restitution can be made?

The words 'Unglück' and 'unglücklich' occur considerably more often in

Austerlitz than in any of Sebald's earlier works, supporting Richard Sheppard's claim for a distinct trajectory in Sebald's oeuvre (see Sheppard 2005: 441). There is space here for only a few key examples. Austerlitz considers the railway stations of Paris to be '*Glücks- und Unglücksorte zugleich*' ('places marked by both blissful happiness and profound misfortune' (2001b: 49; 2002c: 45)). Just as in the earlier prose works, so here the emphasis falls upon the dialectical relation – articulated by the word 'zugleich' – of 'Glück' and 'Unglück', and, as in 'Paul Bereyter', precisely through that apparent symbol of Enlightenment 'progress': the railway. On the Nazis' coming to power in Germany, Austerlitz's father is reported by his former neighbour Věra Ryšanová as not believing 'daß das deutsche Volk in sein *Unglück* getrieben worden sei' ('that the German people had been driven into their misfortune' (2001b: 240; 2002c: 236)). Recounting his reaction on examining with a magnifying glass the February 1929 photograph of himself, Austerlitz remarks upon 'das ihm bevorstehende *Unglück*' ('the misfortune lying ahead of him' (2001b: 264; 2002c: 260)). During his visit to Terezín, he comes upon a porcelain statuette representing a figure on horseback saving a girl from 'einem [...] grauenvollen *Unglück*' (a cruel fate' (2001b: 281; 2002c: 276)). If Austerlitz asks himself what the significance of this statuette might be, his description connects it for the reader with the motif of art's power to counter, even to lift one out of, 'Unglück'.

'UNRUHE'

Although the Freudian and Kafkan unwords 'unheimlich' and 'ungeheuer' play important roles in Sebald's prose, other, less obvious unwords are also decisive. Among these, one of the most significant is the series 'Unruhe', 'unruhig', 'beunruhigen'. The experience of 'Unruhe' is a frequent one in Sebald's prose works, and often accompanies the act of recollection. One of these forms of recollection is intertextual in nature, the word 'Unruhe' having, like 'ungeheuer', an important function in Kafka: the opening sentence of *Die Verwandlung* (1916), for instance, famously describes Gregor Samsa as awakening 'aus *unruhigen* Träumen' to find himself transformed into an '*ungeheurere[s] Ungeziefer*' (Kafka 1994: 115). That Sebald thinks the word 'unruhig' in relation to Kafka is suggested not least by its appearance in the opening paragraph of 'Dr. K.s Badereise nach Riva', in *Schwindel. Gefühle*: the narrator reports Dr K. coming upon a statement in a newspaper concerning the treatment of '*Unglücksfälle*', and adds: 'Dieser Satz *beunruhigt* Dr. K.' ('Dr K. finds this statement [...] disquieting' (2001l: 157; 2002g: 141)). Sebald returns to the experience of 'Unruhe' at the end of part three, when reflecting on Kafka's story of the Jäger Gracchus. The symmetry is clear, since Gracchus' is an 'Unglücksfall' of the most severe kind. As Sebald's narrator puts it, in unwording terms: since an 'Augenblick der *Unaufmerksamkeit* des Führers' ('moment of inattention on the part of the helmsman'), Gracchus has been '*ruhelos*' ('without respite' (2001b: 180; 2002c: 165)). As so often, a negative experience associated with Kafka's name goes on to become the experience of the narrator himself. In part four, the narrator reports that for him there is 'etwas äußerst *Beunruhigendes*' ('something most unsettling') about Hengge's paintings (2001b: 225; 2002c: 206). Although the precise reason for their disquieting effect is not made explicit, it is presumably their depiction of heroic worker types of the kind to be found in Nazi art. Experiences described as 'beunruhigend' are generally associated with the foreboding either of death or of that no man's land between life and death inhabited by Kafka's Gracchus.

Such moments also punctuate both *Die Ausgewanderten* and *Die Ringe des Saturn*. At the end of 'Paul Bereyter', Mme Landau says that her failure to grasp the 'landläufig[e] Bedeutung' ('innocent meaning') of Paul's uncle's expression 'bei der Eisenbahn enden' ('end up on the railways') caused her '*Beunruhigung*' ('disquiet') (2001a: 92; 2002e: 63). 'Ambros Adelwarth' contains numerous instances of 'Unruhe'. Cosmo's second nervous breakdown is seemingly prompted by his seeing a German film – unnamed in the text, but evidently Fritz Lang's *Dr Mabuse, der Spieler* (1922): 'Insbesondere *beunruhigt* haben muß ihn eine Episode gegen Ende des Films, wo ein einarmiger Schausteller und Hypnotiseur namens Sandor Weltmann eine Art von kollektiver Halluzination unter seinem Publikum hervorruft' ('He was particularly disturbed by an episode towards the end of the film in which a one-armed showman and hypnotist by the name of Sandor Weltmann induced a sort of collective hallucination in his audience' (2001a: 141; 2002e: 97)). In *Die Ringe des Saturn*, the narrator points out that in Borges's story 'Tlön, Uqbar, Orbis Tertius' a mirror produces 'eine Art *Beunruhigung*' ('a somewhat disquieting effect') in the story's narrator (2001k: 92; 2002f: 70). And in the 'Korsika-Projekt' material, the 12 September 1995 entry in which the narrator records his visit to the Musée Fesch includes the remark: 'Wie immer, wenn ich ein Museum besuche, bin ich voller *Unruhe*' (2008a: 150). These examples suggest that 'Unruhe' is prompted by the experience of the double, the past and the modern city, with death and the dead being the key uniting factor.

While the experience of 'Unruhe' punctuates Sebald's first three prose works, it is in *Austerlitz* that it comes to play its most decisive role, and to be associated not only with deathly motifs (fire, doubles etc.), but also explicitly with the feeling of guilt. Early on, the narrator experiences 'etwas *Beunruhigendes*' ('an uneasy, anxious feeling' (2001b: 16; 2002c: 11–12)) when he sees newspaper photographs of the Lucerne Station fire, and this feeling is transformed into the idea that he is responsible for the destruction. And, in December 1996, the narrator finds himself 'in einiger *Unruhe*' ('in some anxiety') when he discovers that he has suddenly lost the sight in his right eye (2001b: 50; 2002c: 47). Photographs, eyesight – the continuity here is reinforced when Austerlitz in his turn says that he must have been '*beunruhigt*' throughout his childhood by the fact that the house in Bala in which he grew up had a window on the outside for which there was no corresponding window on the inside (2001b: 67; 2002c: 63). Of the faces that he would see in train stations, Austerlitz says: 'sie verfolgten und *beunruhigten* mich' ('they would haunt and disturb me' (2001b: 183; 2002c: 179)). During his time in Prague with Věra, she recalls his 'stets von neuem [...] *beunruhigende* Frage' ('question which constantly troubled') concerning how squirrels find their buried nuts once the snow has covered the ground (2001b: 291; 2002c: 287). The 'Unruhe' here relates, then, to the difficulty of recovering the past.

'Unruhe' is prompted in Austerlitz not only by memory, but also by others' forgetting. The architecture of Nuremberg, for instance, provokes 'Unruhe' precisely because it marks the erasure of the past (2001b: 318; 2002c: 314). While Nuremberg is striking for being so highly populated, both Terezín and the Gare d'Austerlitz are completely unpopulated, signalling the disappearance of all those who were murdered by the Nazis, including Austerlitz's own parents. This absence, too, produces 'Unruhe' in him (2001b: 408; 2002c: 406). These experiences of topological 'Unruhe' recur in the narrator, who, of his return to Breendonk, recounts: 'Ich verbrachte eine *unruhige* Nacht in einem Hotel am Astridsplein' ('I spent a disturbed night in a hotel on the Astridsplein' (2001b: 412; 2002c: 410)).

Like the relation between 'Unglück' and 'Glück', that between 'Unruhe' and 'Ruhe' is presented by Sebald in dialectical terms. This is clear from the recurrent association of both 'Ruhe' and 'Unruhe' with death. In the first of his two essays on *Das Schloß*, Sebald argues that Kafka's world is one in which the only 'unabänderliche Ruhe' lies in death, and that it is towards this death that K.'s longing is directed (1994b: 92; 1972: 34). Sebald is, of course, fully aware of Adorno's verdict on the possibility of any such 'unabänderliche Ruhe'. As the latter puts it in his 1953 essay on Kafka: 'In the concentration camps, the boundary between life and death was eradicated ... Gracchus is the consummate refutation of the possibility banished from the world: to die after a long and full life' (Adorno 1981: 273). Like Kafka's figures, and in accordance with Freud's conception of the 'Todestrieb' (death drive), Sebald's travellers seek that *'unentdeckte[s]* Land' ('undiscovered country') in which *'unabänderliche* Ruhe' is to be found. As Sebald puts it on the dustjacket of his copy of Proust's *A la recherche du temps perdu*, however: 'Der Augenblick der Ruhe in der Vollendung der Zeit kann nicht bleiben; es geht weiter' ('In the fullness of time the moment of calm cannot endure; it goes on'). With biting irony, the narrator in *Austerlitz* remarks that what the Nazis put on at Theresienstadt for the Red Cross visitors in 1944 was 'ein alles in allem *beruhigendes* Schauspiel' ('a most reassuring spectacle' (2001b: 341; 2002c: 345)). In such a world, it seems that there can be hope only where there is 'Unruhe', the Adornian inflection here being evident: hope of restitution lies only in the negative.

'UNSICHER'

While Sebald's debt to Kafka's unwording is not difficult to detect, there are other, considerably less obvious intertextual relations in his writing of the negative. Among these, the relation to Samuel Beckett has remained largely unexplored in the secondary literature. That Sebald follows Adorno's lead here is suggested not least by the fact that he often mentions Beckett and Kafka together, as, for instance, when commenting on the style of 'exemplarisch moderner Autoren' ('exemplary modern authors') in his book on Alfred Döblin (Sebald 1980: 136). It is in the Döblin monograph that Sebald undertakes what is by far his most extensive analysis of Beckett, commenting on what he terms Beckett's 'ironische[r] Stil' ('ironic style'). Quoting from the English translation of *Molloy*, Sebald argues that Beckett explodes the 'Mythus des Todes' ('myth of death') – that is, death conceived as salvation (or 'Ruhe') – by imagining that, as Molloy puts it, there might be 'a state of being even worse than life' (quoted in Sebald 1980: 116). The 'kritische[r] Sinn' ('critical meaning') of Beckett's oeuvre lies, according to Sebald, in its showing that 'Regression' offers no genuine refuge; rather, it is simply the dialectical counterpart of 'Fortschritt' – just as 'Glück' is the dialectical counterpart of 'Unglück, and 'Ruhe' of 'Unruhe'. It is for this reason that when Sebald refers to Beckett, he generally does so in relation to mobility and immobility. In his 1972 essay on Kafka, for instance, Sebald compares the treatment of the 'stiff and helpless bodies' of Amalia's parents in *The Castle* to the treatment of Nagg and Nell in *Endgame* (1972: 27). This theme haunts Sebald's prose, as evidenced by the frequent recurrence of the unwords 'bewegungslos', 'unfähig' and 'unmöglich', out of which his acts of narration emerge.

The possible impact of Beckett on Sebald's writing of the negative is also to be detected in the relation between the passage from *Molloy* cited as an epigraph to the 1972 essay on Kafka and various moments in Sebald's prose works. The passage in question concerns a travelling figure whom Molloy names 'C'. Shortly before the lines cited by Sebald, Molloy says of this traveller that 'he went with *uncertain step*' (Beckett 2009b: 5). Turning to part three of *Schwindel. Gefühle*, one finds the departure of the Italian girl with whom Dr K. has fallen in love being described in the following terms: 'und sie mit *unsicheren Schritten* über die kleine Gangway an Bord des Schiffes hinüberging' ('and she mounted the little gangplank to board the ship, with an unsteady step' (2001l: 174; 2002g: 159)). At the beginning of *Austerlitz*, Sebald's narrator remarks: 'Ich entsinne mich noch, mit welch *unsicheren Schritten* ich kreuz und quer durch den inneren Bezirk gegangen bin' ('I still remember the uncertainty of my footsteps as I walked all round the inner city' (2001b: 5; 2002c: 1)). Later in the same work, when Austerlitz begins to count in Czech, he describes himself as feeling 'wie einer, der mit *unsicheren Schritten* hinausgeht aufs Eis' ('like someone taking uncertain steps out on to the ice' (2001b: 230; 2002c: 226)). For all the obvious stylistic differences between the two writers – not least Beckett's Mauthner-influenced pursuit of a minimalist literary language that would be the most radical form of 'Sprachkritik' ('language critique') – Sebald's writing of the negative arguably shares with Beckett's an insistence that these 'uncertain steps' are those of figures for whom there is no possibility of genuine 'Ruhe' and for whom, as Sebald writes (in decidedly Beckettian fashion) on the dustjacket of his copy of *A la recherche du temps perdu*: 'Es geht weiter'.

'AUS DEM NICHTS'

In addition to the unwords considered above, Sebald deploys a number of other unwords in his prose works, including 'ungut' – described by J. J. Long as a 'typically Sebaldian epithet' (Long 2010: 73) – 'unversehens', 'unselig', 'unbegreiflich', 'unentdeckt' and 'unendlich'. Some of these play a particularly important role in a specific work, and also often form part of a longer unwording sequence. In some cases, too, an unword can function in two, diametrically opposed ways. This is the case with 'unversehens', which occurs repeatedly in both *Schwindel. Gefühle* and *Austerlitz*, where it concerns the disconcerting nature of memory. In the former, the narrator recalls that, on a trip to Klosterneuburg to see her grandmother, Clara / Olga visits the school she attended as a child, and 'auf dem ganzen Weg dorthin und den ganzen Abend hindurch konnte sie sich *nicht beruhigen* über die *unversehene* Wiederkunft der Vergangenheit' ('and neither on the way there nor that entire evening did she regain her composure following this unexpected return of the past' (2001l: 52; 2002g: 45, translation modified)). In *Austerlitz*, after numerous occurrences of the word, Austerlitz tells of how, wandering in the thirteenth arrondissement of Paris, he is 'immer in der gegen jede Vernunft gerichteten Hoffnung, der Vater könne mir *unversehens* entgegenkommen' ('always thinking, against all reason, that I might suddenly see my father appear out of nowhere' (2001b: 360; 2002c: 358)). These two examples indicate that memory in Sebald has to be thought in terms of negation – and doubly so. The *negation of memory* is to be understood grammatically as both a subjective and an objective genitive. Memories are destroyed, but their return is also by way of the negative: memories return 'unversehens' and are 'unberuhigend'. They erupt into the Benjaminian 'Jetztzeit'.

This eruption is even more clearly marked by one of the most important expressions in Sebald's writing of the negative: 'aus dem Nichts'. The translation of 'unversehens' as 'out of nowhere' in *Austerlitz* is unfortunate, since it blurs the distinction between these two related but distinct forms of the negative. Sebald's use of the expression 'aus dem Nichts' is striking, not least for the fact that it comes to play a particularly important role in his later work. The expression (or a slight variant thereof) appears in *Die Ausgewanderten*, in the description of Paul Bereyter's ability to teach (2001a: 83; 2002e: 56), and is also to be found in *Die Ringe des Saturn*, when, in chapter IV, the narrator recalls an occasion in The Hague when an American limousine driven by a pimp appears 'als sei sie aufgetaucht *aus dem Nichts*' ('as if it had come out of nowhere' (2001k: 105; 2002f: 82)). Juxtaposed with this negative version of the 'aus dem Nichts' is the remark in chapter VI that the poet Swinburne has been seen by his biographers as a 'gleichsam *aus dem Nichts entstandenes epigenetisches Phänomen*' ('an epigenetic phenomenon sprung from the void, as it were' (2001k: 203; 2002f: 162)). It is after the completion of *Die Ringe des Saturn*, however, that the expression comes to play a major – and double – role in Sebald's prose.

In the 'Zweite Fassung' of the 'Korsika-Projekt', the expression is used in the context of flight. Gerald Ashman recalls a recurrent dream concerning his cousin, Hamish Arbathnot, who went missing during a Second World War bombing mission, Gerald saying that the German fighter planes 'wie Haie auftauchten *aus dem Nichts*' (appeared like sharks out of nowhere) (2008a: 165–6). And, of one of the flights on which he accompanies 'Douglas X', the narrator recalls that the Thames estuary appears 'wie *aus dem Nichts*' (2008a: 168), this passage finding its way, in only slightly revised form, into *Austerlitz* (2001b: 166; 2002c: 162). In the majority of cases, 'aus dem Nichts' marks the manner of something's emergence into the visual field, and it is in this sense, too, that the expression is used in Sebald's essay on Jan Peter Tripp in *Logis in einem Landhaus* (1998) (see 2000a: 177).

In *Austerlitz*, this sense of the 'aus dem Nichts' is associated with the art of photography and the experience of memory: Austerlitz is struck by the moment when 'man auf dem belichteten Papier die Schatten der Wirklichkeit sozusagen *aus dem Nichts* hervorkommen sieht, genau wie Erinnerungen' ('[one sees] the shadows of reality, so to speak, emerge out of nothing on the exposed paper, as memories do' (2001b: 113; 2002c: 109)). Just as the expression 'aus dem Nichts' establishes the connection between photographic developing and memory, so it also binds these two processes to the moth motif, which in its turn connects with the flying motif taken up from the 'Korsika-Projekt': Austerlitz recalls his school friend Gerald Fitzpatrick's great-uncle Alphonso placing a lamp outside at Andromeda Lodge one night, and the moths appearing 'wie *aus dem Nichts*' ('as if from nowhere' (2001b: 131–2; 2002c: 128)). Although that which seems to come 'aus dem Nichts' is not always positive – Věra, for instance, recalls the arrival of German troops in Prague during a snowstorm, 'das sie gewissermaßen *aus dem Nichts* hervorzubringen schien' ('which seemed to make them appear out of nowhere' (2001b: 246; 2002c: 242)) – the emphasis generally falls upon the seemingly miraculous nature of such appearances, and, significantly, this is seen as characteristic of art. In addition to Austerlitz's remark upon the apparent 'aus dem Nichts' of the photographic image, he experiences a mysterious 'aus dem Nichts' effect when he sees the circus performers playing in their tent beyond the Gare d'Austerlitz: 'Was in mir selber vorging, als ich dieser von den Zirkusleuten mit ihren etwas verstimmten

Instrumenten sozusagen *aus dem Nichts* hervorgezauberten, ganz und gar fremdländischen Nachtmusik lauschte, das verstehe ich immer noch nicht' ('I still do not understand . . . what was happening within me as I listened to this extraordinarily foreign nocturnal music conjured out of thin air, so to speak, by the circus performers with their slightly out-of-tune instruments' (2001b: 385; 2002c: 383)). The translation 'out of thin air' unfortunately loses the connection between this experience and all the other 'aus dem Nichts' moments in *Austerlitz*.

In each instance of the 'aus dem Nichts' in his final prose work, Sebald qualifies it with 'wie', 'sozusagen', or 'gewissermaßen'. While it is idiomatic in German to use the expression 'wie aus dem Nichts', Sebald revitalizes this idiom, suggesting not only that there is something seemingly miraculous about art but also that it is only *apparently* out of nothing that phenomena emerge, be they psychological or historical. For instance, while it might seem to Věra that the German troops entering Prague appear 'gewissermaßen *aus dem Nichts*' (2001b: 246), they are of course there as a result of historical forces that, for Sebald, following Adorno, have to be understood within the context of the dialectic of Enlightenment. Furthermore, the 'aus dem Nichts' is a form of the negative in which both the saving and the destroying are possible: this expression incorporates a negativity that is generative (in art), destructive (in history) and both generative and destructive (in memory).

INTENSIVE UNWORDING

In addition to the use of particular words and phrases, each of Sebald's prose works is also marked in distinctive ways by extended passages of 'unwriting'. Such passages are crucial within the overall architecture of each work. In *Schwindel. Gefühle*, the first instance of such an extended writing of the negative occurs in 'Dr. K.s Badereise nach Riva'. On his way to Vienna Dr K. reads about '*Unglücksfälle*', and what he reads '*beunruhigt* Dr. K.'. On arrival, he takes a room in the Matschakerhof Hotel, 'aus Sympathie für Grillparzer' ('out of sympathy for Grillparzer'), but this gesture '[erweist] sich [. . .] als *unwirksam*' ('has no good effect'), since while there he is 'äußerst *unwohl*' ('extremely unwell') and the spectral figure of Grillparzer 'macht *ungute* Faxen' ('indulges in all sorts of tomfoolery' (2001l: 157–8; 2002g: 142)). The following night, Dr K. 'wälzt sich *nutzlos* im Bett herum' ('tosses and turns in bed to no avail'), and the next day he notes anaphorically that 'Es sei *unmöglich* [. . .] das einzige mögliche Leben zu führen, mit einer Frau beisammen zu leben, [. . .] *unmöglich*, den einzigen möglichen Schritt über die Männerfreundschaft hinaus zu tun' ('It is impossible [. . .] to lead the only possible life, to live together with a woman, [. . .] impossible to take the only possible step beyond a friendship with men' (2001l: 158; 2002g: 142–3)). He feels an aversion to Otto Pick on account of the latter's having 'eine kleine, *unangenehme*

Lücke in seinem Wesen' ('a small, unpleasant hole in his nature' (2001l: 159; 2002g: 143)). On the way to the Prater, he finds the company of Pick and Albert Ehrenstein to be an *'Ungeheuerlichkeit'* ('unnerving') (2001l: 159; 2002g: 143). Aside from the relief granted by the company of Lise Kaznelson, he suffers *'unaufhörlich'* ('constantly') from headaches (2001l: 161; 2002g: 144). This intense burst of unwording is interrupted, however, by a moment of simulated flight, when the group have their photograph taken as passengers in an aeroplane. This is an example of that experience of levitation which, as Hutchinson observes (see 2009b: 145–65), marks an escape (albeit temporary, or 'einstweilens', as Schopenhauer claims of the 'Trost' provided by art) from the process enacted in Sebald's writing of the negative.

Travelling on to Trieste, Dr K. imagines another kind of flight – the appearance of an angel, despite his own *'Unglauben'* ('little faith') – but this proves to be illusory (2001l: 161; 2002g: 146). Part three ends with Sebald's narrator reflecting on the fate of Kafka's Jäger Gracchus, and here, as we have seen when considering 'Unglück', the unwording arguably reaches its climax (2001l 180; 2002g: 165). Matching this writing of the negative are the final pages of *Schwindel. Gefühle*, where the narrator's vision of an all-consuming fire culminates in a description that works largely through anaphoric negation that privileges the negating word syntactically: '*Nirgends* war ein Baum zu sehen, *kein* Strauch, *kein* Krüppelholz, *kein* Büschelchen Gras, sondern es war alles nur Stein. [. . .] *Nichts* rührte sich sonst' ('Not a tree was there to be seen, not a bush, not even a stunted shrub or a tussock of grass: there was nothing but the ice-grey shale' (2001l: 286; 2002g: 262)). As so often in cases of Sebald's writing of the negative, the English translation here reduces the negativity, the sentence 'Nichts rührte sich sonst' being omitted from the English text.

As we have seen, Sebald's writing of the negative is almost always disquietened by intertextual ghosts, and this is nowhere more clearly the case than in the most sustained passage of unwording in *Austerlitz*: the account of Austerlitz's breakdown in 1992, which closely resembles that of Lord Chandos in Hugo von Hofmannsthal's 'Ein Brief' (1902). As he loses his power over language, Austerlitz is struck by 'die peinliche *Unwahrheit*' ('the awkward falsity') of his linguistic constructions, the *'Unangemessenheit'* ('inadequacy') of the words he uses and the *'Ungereimtheiten'* ('inconsistencies') of what he writes (2001b: 176; 2002c: 172). In addition to 'vernichten' and 'auslöschen', it is the word 'aushöhlen' that captures the nature of the negativity at work here: '*Keine* Wendung im Satz, die sich dann *nicht* als eine jämmerliche Krücke erwies, *kein* Wort, das *nicht ausgehöhlt* klang und verlogen' ('There was not an expression in the sentence but it proved to be a miserable crutch, not a word but it sounded false and hollow' (2001b: 177; 2002c: 173)). To Hutchinson's analysis of 'aushöhlen' (see 2009b: 83–4, 109, 170), one might add the observation that this hollowing out is enacted in the above sentence through the anaphoric double negative 'kein ... das nicht' construction. The recurrent use of '*nicht mehr*' in Austerlitz's description of his breakdown emphasizes that the negation taking place here is of the very constructions – psychological and linguistic – that were based on the repression of his early childhood in Prague.

The writing of the negative here articulates a process in which, on the one hand, negation threatens Austerlitz's very identity and existence, while, on the other hand, it renders possible the emergence of memories that will enable him to construct an identity that was itself subjected to a negation both historical and psychological. As Sebald puts it in his 1981 essay on Ernst Herbeck, the 'Disintegriertheit' ('disintegratedness') of language contains within itself the possibility of renewal: 'Nicht nur ästhetisch, sondern auch psychologisch gesehen, wirkt die sprachliche *Unordnung* als Reservoir regenerativer Energien' ('Not only from an aesthetic, but also from a psychological point of view, linguistic disorder functions as a reservoir of regenerative energies' (1994b: 132–3)). Austerlitz's 'sprachliche Unordnung' makes possible the reconstruction of his identity based upon his experiences on his return to Prague.

'EIN AUSSICHTSLOSES UNTERFANGEN'

In his 2001 essay 'Ein Versuch der Restitution', which would prove to be his last public articulation of his conception of the literary, Sebald might seem to present the privilege of the literary in terms that are at odds with the writing of the negative outlined above. In that essay, Sebald states that: 'Es gibt viele Formen des Schreibens; einzig aber in der literarischen geht es, über die Registrierung der Tatsachen und über die Wissenschaft hinaus, um einen Versuch der Restitution' ('There are many forms of writing; only in literature, however, can there be an attempt at restitution over and above the mere recital of facts and over and above scholarship' (2003b: 248; 2006a: 215)). The essay's argument is shaped, however, by a series of unwords that establish a connection between Sebald's writing of the negative and that of two other German-language writers, Friedrich Hölderlin and Paul Celan.

Unlike the game 'Städtequartett' ('Cities Quartet'), which Sebald recalls playing as a child and in which Germany is pictured as 'noch *ungeteilt*, und nicht nur *ungeteilt* ist es gewesen, sondern auch *unzerstört*' ('still undivided [. . .] and not only undivided but intact' (2003b: 241; 2006a: 207)), post-war literary writing as Sebald conceives it must insist upon division and destruction, not least in order to chart – in the manner of the 'meridian' in Paul Celan's 1960 speech on the occasion of his being awarded the Georg Büchner Prize – '*unsichtbare* Beziehungen, die unser Leben bestimmen' ('the invisible connections that determine our lives' (2003b: 244; 2006a: 210)). One of the lives that Sebald has in mind here is Hölderlin's, shaped as it was by '*Unglück*' ('misfortune') (2003b: 245, 246; 2006a: 212, 213) and a sense of the '*Unmöglichkeit*' ('impossibility') of love (2003b: 246; 2006a: 212). It is Hölderlin

71

who, in the elegy 'Bread and Wine' (1802), asks the question that would so preoccupy Martin Heidegger during the Second World War: 'wozu Dichter in dürftiger Zeit' ('what are poets for in a destitute time'), a question that is asked again, this time in French, by Sebald in his 2001 essay: 'A quoi bon la littérature?' (2003b: 247; 2006a: 213). By translating Hölderlin's epochal question into French, Sebald not only reminds us of Hölderlin's time in Bordeaux, but also marks his own distance from a Heideggerian conception of *Dichtung*. In Sebald's essay, Hölderlin's 'Dichter' becomes 'la littérature', not 'le poète' or 'la poésie'. Moreover, whereas Heidegger's answer to Hölderlin's question is that *Dichtung* recalls *Sein* (Being), Sebald's response is that *literature's* 'good' as a form of restitution lies in its helping us to remember and in its teaching us that there are 'sonderbare, von keiner Kausallogik zu ergründende Zusammenhänge' ('strange connections [that] cannot be explained by causal logic'), connections between, for instance, German industry and the murder of a French town's entire male population by an SS division (2003b: 247; 2006a: 213–14). For Sebald, the kind of remembering that literature can achieve requires a tarrying with the negative, this negativity always being double: it is both the negativity of a 'historia calamitatum' and the negativity of a 'Widerstand' ('resistance') to any false 'Überwindung' ('overcoming') of the kind against which Adorno warns readers of *Negative Dialectics*.

That Sebald thinks the negativity of literature in these terms is suggested not least by his claim in his 1983 essay on Hildesheimer that the latter's novel *Tynset* (1965) has 'mit Nihilismus *im landläufigen Sinne*, nichts gemein' ('nothing in common with nihilism *in the usual sense of the word*' (2003b: 125; 2006a: 127, translation modified and emphasis added)). This claim suggests that there might just be another form of nihilism to consider in relation to the literary, and it is precisely to this other form of nihilism that Adorno directs us in his remarks on Beckett at the end of the section on nihilism in *Negative Dialectics*: 'Thought honours itself by defending what is damned as nihilism' (Adorno 1973: 381). In his essay on Hildesheimer, in which he quotes from Adorno's *Aesthetic Theory*, Sebald declares that the 'Ideal der absoluten Lichtlosigkeit' ('ideal of absolute lightlessness') in art remains 'ein aussichtsloses Unterfangen' ('a hopeless undertaking' (2003b: 125; 2006a: 127)). If Sebald is successful in his writing of the negative, then it is to the extent that he resists not only what he takes to be the negativity of modernity, but also the negativity of any 'Überwindung' of that modernity, and tarries instead within the negativity of this 'aussichtsloses Unterfangen'. Thus, if the moments of levitation in Sebald's prose interrupt the dialectic of modernity as forms of 'Trost' ('consolation'), the recurrent fall back into the 'Dialektik der Melancholie' ('dialectic of melancholy' (2003b: 123; 2006a: 126)) is necessary if those moments of levitation are not to be reified into myth. Just as for the Adorno of *Aesthetic Theory*, so for Sebald, only from the perspective of a writing that is 'bedingungslos negativ' can restitution be achieved, and the possibility of redemption from an 'obscene' history be glimpsed.

Sebald's commitment to a writing of the negative, which takes the form of a sustained engagement with an entire literary tradition, insists, then, upon the irreducible doubleness of that negativity. If, as we have seen, his writing of the negative reaches its most extreme enactment in *Austerlitz*, that work, in its very openness (with Austerlitz continuing the search for information about his father), is also, arguably, the most hopeful, the most committed to the power of writing: it ends, after all, with the narrator recording what he has read in another's text (Dan Jacobson's *Heshel's Kingdom*, 1998) regarding those victims of the Nazis who left a written trace, the last of these traces being a name, a place, and a date: 'Max Stern, Paris, 18.5.44' (2001b: 417; 2002c: 415). The date is, of course, 'Max' Sebald's own date of birth. As for 'Stern', it stands no doubt as a symbol of the Jewish people, and has to be seen in relation to an unword that appears only once in all of Sebald's prose works, and that in *Austerlitz*, the unword in question being 'Unstern' (2001b: 89). The English translation of this singular unword – 'unlucky star' (2002c: 85) – inevitably obscures its relation to the name 'Stern' and everything that name stands for in Sebald's work. While *Austerlitz* charts the movement from 'Unstern' to 'Stern', it nonetheless tarries within the negative, since for Sebald, as for Adorno, the only hope lies in an art that is uncompromisingly 'aus-sichts-los'. This is revealed nowhere more tellingly than in the final sentences of Austerlitz: like Hegel's owl of Minerva, the 'Stern' becomes visible only when evening falls.

NOTES

1 Unless otherwise indicated, all italics in quotations from the German are my own.

Part II

TEXTS AND CONTEXTS

4

SURREALIST VERTIGO IN *SCHWINDEL. GEFÜHLE*

Jeannette Baxter

It's like looking down a well shaft. Looking in the past has always given me that vertiginous sense. It's the desire, almost, or the temptation that you might throw yourself into it, as it were, over the parapets and down. There is something terribly alluring to me about the past. (Sebald in conversation with Wachtel 2007: 57)

W. G. Sebald's observations on the vertiginous nature of historical enquiry provide a useful starting point for this reading of *Schwindel. Gefühle* (1990). As motif and metaphor, vertigo repeats conspicuously across the counter-historical writings of the French Surrealists. In the second 'Manifesto of Surrealism' (1930), André Breton characterizes their project as: 'nothing other than the dizzying descent into ourselves, the systematic illumination of hidden places and the progressive darkening of other places, the perpetual excursion into the midst of forbidden territory' (2007: 137). For the Surrealists, vertigo, whether experienced involuntarily or induced actively, sets in train a series of productive tensions which, resisting any move towards a single state of resolution, remain in process in order to negotiate difficult and exigent questions pertaining to historical representation, memory and subjectivity. By tracing differentiated and tension-ridden manifestations of vertigo throughout Sebald's narrative, I want to make a case for reading *Schwindel. Gefühle* as an exercise in late twentieth-century literary historiography that is identifiably Surrealist in impulse.

To date, discussions of Sebald and Surrealism have focused exclusively on the transcendental potential of Surrealist aesthetics for Sebald's literary project. Richard Sheppard comments, for instance, on Sebald's initial faith in objective chance (*hasard objectif*) and 'bricolage' as aleatory techniques 'capable of generating auratic art' (2005: 424).[1] Yet this faith was, according to Sheppard, short lived, and Sebald's confidence in the transforming powers of juxtaposition gradually dissolved: 'art might have been able to create a network of actual, historical and intertextual connections, but it had ceased to be a channel for transcendent experience' (2005: 424–5). It is around this perceived failure of Surrealist aesthetics to initiate moments of insight that Judith Ryan constructs her reading of *Austerlitz* and Breton's *Nadja* (1928). Noting Sebald's familiarity with Surrealist texts such as Louis

Aragon's *Paris Peasant* (*Le Paysan de Paris*, 1926), Ryan suggests that it is through the works of Walter Benjamin, notably 'Surrealism: The Last Snapshot of the European Intelligentsia' (1929) and *The Arcades Project* (*Das Passagen-Werk*), that Sebald's understanding of French Surrealism is mediated. Collapsing Benjamin's concept of 'profane illumination' onto Sebald's variant, 'fulguration',[2] Ryan argues that *Austerlitz* is replete with moments of failed illumination, moments which do not 'point forward to an empowering revision of reality as in Aragon [and Breton], but back to terrible memories whose import *Austerlitz* cannot yet grasp' (2007: 233). In Ryan's estimation, Surrealism is ultimately revealed to be a limited aesthetic and political model for Sebald: the weight of his historical narratives is such that they simply ground any move towards transcendence.

Yet, Sebald's engagement with Surrealism is considerably more complex than these readings suggest, and it calls, in turn, for a more nuanced understanding of the Surrealist project; one that does not conceive it narrowly as being bound to transcendence, but which sees it oscillating dizzyingly, to follow Breton, between oppositional poles: illumination *and* darkening; conscious *and* unconscious; sublimation *and* desublimation.[3] It is precisely Sebald's interest in, and elaboration of, the complex and vertiginous trajectories of Surrealist enquiry that concerns me here. Specifically, I want to open *Schwindel. Gefühle* up to its desublimatory contexts and intertexts by tracing the writings of three dissident Surrealists – Georges Bataille, Roger Caillois and André Masson – across Sebald's narrative. Georges Bataille emerges as an important figure in this reassessment of Sebald's relationship with Surrealism. In his critical discussions of Bataille, for instance, Sebald is unequivocal in his appreciation of the dissident Surrealist's 'bedingunglos negativ' ('uncompromisingly negative' (2003b: 157–8; 2004b: 154)) attitude towards history, subjectivity, language, and desire.[4] Whilst Breton's recuperation of trauma or subversive desire tends to encourage the transformation of matter into metaphor in an ascending movement of sublimation, Bataille, the dark 'surrealist of catastrophe', always encourages a descent into a world without hope, a world that is 'vilest, most discouraging and most corrupted' (2007: 181).[5] Bataille's willingness to follow the uncertain and frequently unsettling path of desublimation, combined with his unwavering belief that writing 'should be thrown down as a challenge to the reader; it should be a deliberate provocation' (Richardson 1994a: 16), resonates suggestively with the contextual and aesthetic challenges of Sebald's post-war, post-Holocaust texts.

Sebald's relationship with the dissident Surrealism of Caillois and Masson is less straightforward to establish, however. To my knowledge, there is no suggestion in either his critical writings or annotated library that Sebald was familiar with the works of either author (not that this necessarily precludes the possibility that he *had* read them). Judith Ryan's observation that Sebald's knowledge of French Surrealism is largely mediated through his knowledge of Walter Benjamin might be helpful in this regard, then. Benjamin was involved briefly with the Collège de Sociologie (1937–39), a Paris-based group of intellectuals, including Masson and Caillois (the latter co-founded the group with Bataille and Michel Leiris), that concerned itself with, amongst other things, the ascendancy of Fascism across Europe and the efficacy of Surrealism as a form of aesthetic and political response.[6] The value of Caillois's writings for Benjamin can also be traced across numerous citations (mainly from Caillois's essay 'Paris, mythe moderne', published in *Nouvelle Revue française* (1937)) in *The Arcades Project*, the text which Benjamin entrusted to Bataille (he hid Benjamin's notebooks in the Bibliothèque Nationale de France during the Second World War) and which Sebald went on to study so meticulously.[7] Furthermore, Benjamin's involvement with Acéphale, the para-religious organization of the Collège de Sociologie, would have brought him into contact with the various written and visual expressions of Masson's dissident Surrealism across the interwar period. Masson illustrated the Group's publication *Acéphale: Religion, Sociologie, Philosophie* (1936), for example, and his numerous illustrations and texts for the dissident Surrealist publications *Documents* and *Minotaur* would have also been known to Benjamin.[8]

Of course, this form of literary detective work does not bring me any closer to establishing a firm line of influence between Sebald, Caillois and Masson, but it does allow me to posit an intertextual relationship between Sebald and the dissident Surrealists that I am terming 'discursive haunting'. At the same time that this model of discursive haunting follows a basic intertextual model which identifies multiple and complex relations – on conscious and unconscious levels – existing between texts, it also recognizes an unsettling vacuity at the heart of discursive plenitude. In 'Ein Versuch der Restitution' ('An Attempt at Restitution'), for example, Sebald echoes Friedrich Hölderlin's question – 'A quoi bon la littérature?' ('What good is literature?') – in order to gesture to the collective and collaborative nature of his project of literary restitution. Whilst this allusive methodology encourages a form of literary historiography that accommodates numerous and contingent 'kinds of history lessons … [ones] not in the history books' (Sebald in conversation with Cuomo 2007: 106), it also produces a form of literary historiography that is alive to the insufficiencies of language, and to the consequences of this for understanding and articulating subjectivity, history and memory: 'Der synoptische Blick … ist verschattet und illuminert doch zugleich das Andenken derer, denen das größte Unrecht widerfuhr' ('The synoptic view … is overshadowed and yet simultaneously illuminates the memory of those to whom the greatest injustice was done' (Sebald 2003b: 248; my translation)). What aligns Sebald's literature of restitution with the dissident Surrealist writings of Bataille, Caillois and Masson, I suggest, is its very willingness to recognize and give itself (and its reader) up to the dizzying energies of recovery and loss, memory and forgetting, light and darkness, life and death.

In what follows, I trace the oscillating tensions at work in *Schwindel. Gefühle* by exploring the significance of three Surrealist models of vertigo across Sebald's narrative.[9] Firstly, I explore the relationship between vertigo and play. Following Caillois's thinking in *Man, Play and Games* (*Les Jeux et les hommes* 1958), Sebald's narrative enacts 'a vertigo of a moral order' (2001: 24), which, in contrast to the ludic nature of postmodern textual play, initiates playful yet ethically charged moments that work hard to destabilize fixed historical perspectives. The game playing that interests Caillois and Sebald has less to do with discipline and self-improvement, and more to do with an opening up of the individual and the text to destructive and desublimatory impulses. Next, I examine the relationship between vertigo, chance and the labyrinth. Following Sigmund Freud's delineation of the unconscious as a labyrinthine space of repetition and trauma, the Surrealists frequently adopted the labyrinth motif in their visual and literary investigations into the unconscious. It is Bataille's version of the labyrinth, as set out in his interwar essay, 'The Labyrinth' (1936), that I want to focus on here, however. A Surrealist meditation on the vertiginous relationship between language, Being and chance, 'The Labyrinth' raises urgent questions pertaining to Sebald's own enquiries into post-war history and memory, and the relationship between subjectivity and the limits of language. Lastly, with reference to Masson's *Mémoire du Monde* (1974), a literary recollection of the artist-soldier's horrific experiences of trench warfare during the First World War, I explore (following David Lomas) the dissident Surrealist concept of 'double vertigo' (a fear of falling downwards *and* upwards) in order to explore its significance for Sebald's narrative. Linked inextricably to Freud's concept of the uncanny, Sebald's 'double vertigo' initiates a number of disorientating and disturbing coincidences between Eros and Thanatos in order to forge a desublimatory critique that is politically and historically motivated.

VERTIGO AND PLAY

Throughout Sebald's narrative, vertigo is inextricably linked to the domain of play. This is nowhere more evident than in the German title, *Schwindel. Gefühle*, which is itself a play on words. As Mark McCulloh observes, *Schwindel. Gefühle* is a 'punctuated pun' which recombines and divides the compound word 'Schwindelgefühle' ('feelings of dizziness') in order to destabilise its meaning' (2003: 87). Whilst 'Schwindel' means 'giddiness' or 'dizziness', for instance, it also translates as 'swindle', 'lie' or 'fraud'. Is the German title announcing a 'Gefühl' or 'sense' of play? Echoing Walter Benjamin's characterization of Surrealist writing as 'bluffs, forgeries' (Benjamin 1979: 227), Sebald also saw writing as a form of deception: 'you make something out of nothing. It is a con trick' (Sebald in conversation with Cuomo 2007: 108). Implicit in these comments is an understanding of 'swindle', and by extension 'vertigo', as forms of creative and critical intervention that challenge realist modes of representation and initiate new ways of seeing. It is precisely this destabilizing role that Roger Caillois, in *Man, Play and Games*, assigns to vertigo in the activity of play: 'The last kind of game includes those which are based on the pursuit of vertigo and which consist of an attempt to momentarily destroy the stability of perception' (2001: 23). Oscillating between two poles, vertigo induces surrender to 'a kind of spasm, seizure, or shock which destroys reality'. This vertigo is 'readily linked to the desire for disorder and destruction, a drive which is normally repressed' (Caillois 2001: 24), but which manifests itself in play.

Sebald's vertigo-inducing game gathers momentum on the very first page with an unreferenced and poorly produced black-and-white photograph of an image of a line of men snaking up a formidable mountain path. The magnitude of this physical undertaking is implied in a gross inequality of pictorial scale: almost indistinct human forms are dwarfed by an Alpine landscape extending into the sky and beyond the frame. Upon detailed inspection, a process of looking which requires the reader to get physically closer to the blurred image, we recognize the men as soldiers. With our noses up against the page, we must, if we are to bring the written text into focus, proceed by pulling up and back from the image. This movement of zooming out takes place in the moment in which we scan down the page to locate the first words of the text: 'Mitte Mai' ('mid-May' (Sebald 2009: 7; 2002g: 3)). Is it coincidental that the first word, used here to denote a moment in time, also possesses a spatial connotation; namely that of a mid-point between the visual image above and the text below? That 'Mitte' is not a stable linguistic platform (it is only half of a compound noun) is also noteworthy. From here, we are propelled forward and down into a brief narrative account of the image above, which, the text implies, is a visual representation of Napoleon Bonaparte's crossing of the Great St Bernard Pass in 1800. Whilst the repeating preposition 'über' ('over') works hard to articulate the sheer physical effort involved in this unprecedented Alpine ascent, it also works hard to represent a trajectory of ascent which is ideological in impulse. Looking away from the text and back up at the image, we are encouraged to see it as a visual representation of physical and political ascent: the 'rise' of Napoleon I, the soon-to-be Emperor of France, as he advances on Austrian-occupied Italy.

So why does Sebald plunge his readers into a narrative of imperialist ascendancy by means of such an unassuming image? For Deane Blackler, the photograph's resonance lies in its playful subversion of readerly knowledge: 'In the informed reader's mind, the most famous painting of the transalpine crossing is that of Napoleon in full uniform on a rearing horse in which Jacques-Louis David has captured a sense of the historical grandeur of this "next to impossible" undertaking' (2007b: 151). Although David actually produced a series of official paintings, *Napoleon Crossing the Alps* (1801–5), to commemorate this historical event, each one is a 'glorifying falsification of reality – a dusty and travel-weary Napoleon crossed the Alps on a mule' (Blackler 2007b: 151). Yet, even this latter version of events, one reproduced by Paul Delarouche in *Bonaparte Crossing the Alps* (1848–50), bears very little resemblance to Sebald's image. This is because *Schwindel. Gefühle* opens with a desublimatory form of representation, a dissident Surrealist manoeuvre that challenges realist accounts by replacing, as Hal Foster puts it, an 'imperative of resemblance' with 'a play of altération' (1993: 113). In other words, the formation of an image within an aesthetic of desublimation is its '*de*formation, or the defor-mation of its model' (Foster 1993: 113). Sebald's image is desublimatory, in as much as it deforms traditional models of history painting: indeed, any sense of histori-cal idealism, which is so replete in formal historicist narratives, is conspicuously absent. Furthermore, deformation resides in the very construction, or, rather, *de*struction, of the black-and-white image; for this undersized and out-of-focus photograph is an *altered* image, the status of which is never entirely clear (is it a photograph of a painting or a sketch?). A comparison with the opening photo-graph from the English edition, *Vertigo*, which is considerably larger and sharper in tone and contrast, also reveals the extent of Sebald's deforming practice. A double-edged process of intervention is at work here, then. Firstly, this deformed image enacts a visual critique of the 'rise' of Napoleonic Imperialism, a decisive moment, for Sebald, in the decline of European civilization.[10] Secondly, the reader's negotiations of the text's visual and verbal dimensions interrupt linear reading processes in order to refuse the kind of 'top-down' historical perspective that 'obliterates the emotional experience of history in the lives of its victims' (Fuchs 2006: 169).[11]

VERTIGO, CHANCE AND THE LABYRINTH

Sebald first connects vertigo and the labyrinth in an image of bodily corruption. Beyle, who by this time has transformed himself into Stendhal, is riddled with the symptoms of syphilis: 'Schlingbeschwerden, Schwellungen unter den Achseln und Schmerzen in seinen schrumpfenden Hoden ... seine Schlaflosigkeit, die Schwindelgefühle, *das Ohrensausen*' ('Difficulties in swallowing, swellings in his armpits, and pains in his atrophying testicles ... sleeplessness, his giddiness, the *roaring in his ears*' (Sebald 2009: 34; 2002g: 29, emphases mine)). As David Lomas notes, it is 'of more than a passing interest that vertigo is attributable to a disturbance of the vestibule or labyrinth, the name given to the canals and chambers of the inner ear that are responsible for balance' (2006: 83–4). Here, vertigo manifests itself pathologically: Beyle's infected, pustular body is unable to maintain a sense of balance – he records meticulously 'die Schwankungen seines Gesundheitszustands' ('his fluctuating state of health' (Sebald 2009: 34; 2002g: 29)) – and, ultimately, death ensues from an 'Anfall' ('fall' (Sebald 2009: 35–6; 2002g: 30)) to the pavement.

From this point on, however, Sebald connects vertigo and the labyrinth within a counter-historical investigation into what resides beneath neat and coherent surface narratives of history and culture. In this context, *Schwindel. Gefühle*'s subtle transition from pathological to metaphysical vertigo resonates with dissident Surrealism's own transformation of medical discourse into metaphysical enquiry. George Bataille's reading in the early 1930s included the neuro-psychiatric study, *Les Vertiges* (*Vertigo*, 1926) by J. Lévy-Velansi and E. Halphan, a text which went on to inform his interwar writings, including 'The Psychological Structures of Fascism' (1933) and 'The Labyrinth'. Indeed, the latter, an account of interwar Europe as a nightmarish labyrinth in which identity, structure and space are radically dislocated, has suggestive intertextual resonances for this reading of *Schwindel. Gefühle*. An 'anti-architecture' that resists order, stability and coherency, the Surrealist labyrinth is a space of radical contingency in which any claim to an orientated, unified self repeatedly comes undone: 'being ... is spasmodically shaken by the idea of the ground giving way beneath its feet' (Bataille 1994c: 177). Furthermore, in the absence of structure or certainty, being is opened up to a form of vertigo that is born specifically out of the 'extreme instability of connections' and the 'universal play' of 'unforeseeable chance' (Bataille 1994c: 174).

In 'All'estero', the narrator's endless wanderings through the labyrinthine streets of Vienna's 'Innere Stadt' trigger a series of vertigo-inducing chance encounters. The narrator's descent into the historical unconscious is signalled by his purported vision of the exiled poet, Dante, who weaves in and out of the narrow streets until he is: '*nirgends* mehr zu sehen' ('*nowhere* to be seen' (Sebald 2009: 43; 2002g: 35, emphases mine)). For the narrator, the effects of this chance encounter are striking: 'Nach dergleichen Anwandlungen begann in mir eine undeutliche Besorgnis aufzuquellen, die sich äußerte als ein Gefühl der Übelkeit und des Schwindels. Die Konturen von Bildern, die ich festzuhalten suchte, lösten sich auf, und die Gedanken zerfielen mir' ('After one or two turns of this kind I began to sense in me a vague apprehension, which manifested itself as a feeling of vertigo. The outlines on which I tried to focus dissolved, and my thoughts disintegrated' (Sebald 2009: 42; 2002g: 35–6)). The narrator's disorientation manifests itself linguistically in verbs that move up and down a vertical axis – 'aufquellen' ('to swell up'); 'zerfallen' ('to disintegrate'); and 'auflösen' ('to dissolve' *and* 'to (re)solve'). Visual and cognitive stability stand no chance in such moments of oscillation.

Significantly, though, Sebald's narrator also experiences the very 'nausea' (Übelkeit) [this is collapsed into the 'feeling of vertigo' in Hulse's translation]) which besets all who enter into Bataille's labyrinth: 'at each detour, with a kind of nausea, men discover their solitude ... being is in fact found NOWHERE' (Bataille 1994c: 172–3). A meditation on the composition and decomposition of communities between the wars, Bataille's negative toponym is freighted with meaning. Written in the face of Fascist ascendancy, 'The Labyrinth' not only engages with historical narratives of exile and dislocation between the wars, but it also indicts the totalizing and deracinating forces of Fascism as they swept across the physical and psychological landscapes of Europe. Building on 'The Psychological Structures of Fascism', a polemical analysis of the economies of homogeneity (Gesellschaft) and heterogeneity (Gemeinschaft) in relation to the (de)composition of communities, Bataille imagines Fascism as a monstrous 'UNIVERSAL', which, 'abandoned to the secret paleness of death', manifests itself as a brutal homogenizing force intent on reducing a multiplicity of European nations to a 'state of empty shadows' (Bataille 1994c: 176–7).

Although written out of a post-war, post-Holocaust perspective, *Schwindel. Gefühle* engages with Bataille's interwar critique in a number of ways. Not only is Sebald's text preoccupied with narratives of loss, exile and the anxieties of isolation, but it also concerns itself with the physical and psychological effects of persistent forces of homogenization in post-war culture, forces which are predicated on the 'aufräumen' ('clearing up') of heterogeneous presences.[12] These concerns come together in the following passage:

> ich weiß nicht, ob ich aus diesem Niedergang herausgekommen wäre, hätte mich nicht eines Nachts … der Anblick meines inwendig schon gänzlich in Fetzen aufgelösten Schuhwerks geradezu entsetzt. Es würgte mich im Hals … Im ersten Stock des Gebäudes … standen die Fenster des jüdischen Gemeindezentrums weit offen … und die unsichtbaren Kinder darinnen sangen in englischer Sprache selt-samerweise *Jingle Bells* und *Silent Night, Holy Night*. Die singenden Kinder und jetzt die zerfetzten und, wie mir vorkam, herrenlosen Schuhe. Schnee und Schuhe zuhauf – mit diesen Worten im Sinn legte ich mich nieder. (Sebald 2009: 44)

> (I cannot say whether I would have come out of this decline if one night … I had not been shocked by the sight of my shoes which were literally falling apart. I felt queasy … The windows of the Jewish community centre, on the first floor of the building … were wide open … and there were children within singing, unaccountably, 'Jingle Bells' and 'Silent Night' in English. The voices of singing children, and now in front of me my tattered and, as it seemed, ownerless shoes. Heaps of shoes and snow piled high – with these words in my head I lay down. (Sebald 2002g: 37))

The narrator is jolted out of his depression by a nausea-inducing image of disinte-gration that triggers, in turn, a memory of a visit to the Stadttempel in Vienna's first district. Notably, the stress falls on community, which is not only represented by the physical architecture of the community centre, but evoked also in the 'wide open' windows and the sound of collective voices singing Christmas carols on a 'hochsommerlicher Herbsttag' ('summery Autumn day' (Sebald 2009: 44; 2002g: 37)). This passage is suffused with oscillatory tensions: the 'high' sun and the falling leaves of autumn; the sound of children's voices emerging above the narrator's head and the image of disintegrating and dispossessed shoes. In turn, this image triggers another, either remembered or imagined, in which the Holocaust is metonymically invoked: a heap of ownerless shoes covered in snow. Once more, the oscillating energies enacted in this image are noteworthy: shoes pile up as snow falls down, erasing gradually the heterogeneous traces of a community of people. The fact that the narrator's words remain unspoken gestures, perhaps, to an act of willed repression, a psychological movement of descent that is echoed physically in the narrator's decision to lie down and enter into a 'tiefen, traumlosen Schlaf' ('deep and dreamless sleep' (Sebald 2009: 44; 2002g: 37)). Evidence of a criminal history may be partly concealed by falling snow and by a willingness to forget, but snow will gradually melt, and the suggestion remains that the evidence will eventually reveal itself to force troubling encounters.

Sebald continues to explore connections between vertigo, chance and the labyrinth towards the end of 'All'estero', when the narrator's very being is called into question: he has lost his passport and needs to obtain a new one from the German consulate in Milan. Unusually, the narrator seeks to orientate himself with a map of the city, one which features a black-and-white image of a labyrinth on its front cover and a paratextual promise of secure guidance (this is surely ironic) around the city on its back: ('UNA GUIDA SICURA PER L'ORGANIZZAZIONE DEL VOSTRO LAVORO') (2009: 123; 2002g: 108).[13] For the reader of the German edition of the text, however, this promise comes after the reader's gaze is directed by a black arrow that points to the entrance of a multicursal labyrinth. Falling into this black-and-white spiral of dead ends and broken connections is dizzying and ultimately frustrating because, having traced a path to the centre, one realizes that the only way out is to retrace one's gaze and return to the initial point of entry: passage in and around the labyrinth is marked by uncanny repetition. The reader's feeling of disorientation manifests itself still further in the visually fragmented lines of text that appear (in the German version of the text, at least) immediately below the image of the labyrinth:

> auf der Rückseite aber die für jeden,
> der weiß,
> daß er viel auf Irrwegen geht,
>   vielversprechende,
>   geradezu verheißungsvolle Versicherung
> (on the back an affirmation that must seem promising and indeed auspicious for anyone who knows what it is to err on one's way. (Sebald 2009: 122; 2002g: 107–8))

The staccato sentences enact the hesitant, stop–start rhythm of physical movement in and around the labyrinth at the same time that they undercut the promise of smooth passage around Milan, which is printed in the tiniest of fonts on the map's back cover. Indeed, the narrator's immediate experience of the city is swiftly shown to be governed by chance rather than design. Losing his way and finding himself on 'die falsche Seite des Bahnhofs' ('the wrong side of the station' (Sebald 2009: 123; 2002g: 108)), he encounters chance, writ large, on an advertising board: 'LA PROSSIMA COINCIDENZA' ('THE NEXT COINCIDENCE' (Sebald 2009: 123; 2002g: 108, translation mine)).

The narrator's next coincidence is curious for at least two reasons: firstly, the two Kafkaesque assailants, who emerge as if out of nowhere only to vanish enigmatically, are reminiscent of the anonymous, shadowy pairs that the narrator repeatedly encounters in the labyrinthine streets of Venice; secondly, this latest chance encounter is shot through with uncertainty. The narrator observes, for instance, how 'Keiner von den Passanten hatte Notiz von dem Zwischenfall genommen' ('None of the passers-by had taken any notice of the incident' (Sebald 2009: 123–4; 2002g; 109)). In the absence of any witnesses, the suspicion emerges that this violent coincidence may not have taken place outside of the narrator's own paranoid imaginings. Indeed, this 'uncertainty of inside and outside, psychic and perceptual' is fundamental to the Surrealist concept of 'objective chance' (Foster 1993: 60). Furthermore, the narrator's immediate reconstruction of events to the taxi driver and the *signora* of the hostelry (Sebald 2009: 124; 2002g: 109–10) is met with silence; it is almost as if the narrator is not there. And, of course, on one level, he isn't; without official proof of his identity, the narrator's sense of self is under threat. Following Bataille, Sebald constructs labyrinths of chance encounters in which notions of autonomy or, what Bataille would term, sufficiency, are put at risk: 'Being in the world is so *uncertain*' (1994c: 171–3, emphases in original). Decentred and disorientated, Sebald's narrator is rendered radically insufficient.

Even the newly issued passport, which features a barred-through photograph of the narrator (the photograph is of Sebald), fails fully to establish his identity. And, with obfuscating papers in hand, he wanders through the city's streets, losing not only his way, but also all memory of where he is:

> An dieser Lähmung meines Errinerungsvermögens änderte sich auch dann nichts, als ich auf die oberste Galerie des Doms hinaufstieg und von dort aus unter immer wiederkehrenden Schwindelgefühlen das vom Dunst über der mir nun vollends fremd gewordenen Stadt verdüsterte Panorama in Augenschein nahm. Wo das wort Mailand hätte auftauchen sollen, rührte sich nichts als ein schmerzhafter Reflex des Unvermögens ... Ein starker Wind erhob sich, und ich mußte mich einhalten, um hinabschauen zu können, wo die Menschen sich in seltsamer Neigung über die Piazza bewegten, als stürze ein jeder einzelne von ihnen seinem Ende entgegen. Laufet eilends vor dem Wind, ging es mir durch den Kopf, und zugleich kam mir der rettende Gedanke, daß es sich bei den dort unten kreuz und quer über das Pflaster hastenden Gestalten um nichts anderes handeln konnte als um lauter Mailänder und Mailänderinnen. (Sebald 2009: 130–1)

> (Nor did this lapse of memory improve in the slightest after I climbed to the topmost gallery of the cathedral and from there, beset by recurring fits of vertigo, gazed out

upon the dusky, hazy panorama of a city now altogether alien to me. Where the word 'Milan' ought to have appeared in my mind there was nothing but a painful, inane reflex. A stiff wind came up, and I had to brace myself so that I could look down to where the people were crossing the piazza, their bodies inclined forwards at an odd angle, as though they were hastening towards their doom – a spectacle which brought back to me an epitaph I had seen years before on a tombstone in the Piedmont. And as I remembered the words *Se il vento s'alza, Correte, Correte! Se il vento s'alza, non v'arrestate!* [If the wind is up run, run! If the wind is up, don't stop! – my translation], so I knew, in that instant, the figures hurrying over the cobbles below were none other than the men and women of Milan. (Sebald 2002g: 116))

The narrator's move to rise above the labyrinthine city in the hope that it might trigger memories of the past few days is rendered futile. Just as the 'summit of [the] pyramid' (Bataille 1994c: 173) within Bataille's labyrinth affords no vantage point outside of the labyrinth, so Sebald's labyrinth cannot be suppressed, or indeed, exited, by means of sublimation: there simply is no way out. Instead, the narrator is seized by fits of vertigo that refuse any sense of epistemological and ontological certainty. Even his eventual claim to know his spatial location is shown to be a 'puerile but convenient illusion' (Bataille 1994c: 174). This is because the narrator's moment of recognition is triggered by a flurry of words – conspicuously omitted from the German text – that run through his head. In a striking echo of Bataille's essay, Sebald makes explicit the contingent relationship between being and language: 'Words spring forth in his head, laden with a host of human or superhuman lives in relation to which he privately exists . . . Being depends on the mediation of words which cannot merely present it arbitrarily as "autonomous being" but which must present it profoundly as "being in relation"' (Bataille 1994c: 173– 4). Through the mediation of portentous words, the narrator's existence is established in relation to the men and women of Milan. But this narrative of doom is, of course, a repetition in itself, recalling the moment when Beyle looks down on the battlefield at Marengo 'wie ein Untergehender' ('like one meeting his doom' (Sebald 2009: 22; 2002g: 18)). And this repetition recalls, in turn, another textual repetition; namely Thomas Bernhard's *Der Untergeher* (1983), the intertextual resonance of which can be felt throughout Sebald's narrative.

Certainly, *Schwindel. Gefühle* is a dizzying labyrinth of other people's words and stories – the works of Kafka, Hofmannsthal, Grillparzer and Stendhal (amongst others) coincide with Sebald's own intricately spun tales. At the same time that these (inter)textual connections forge alternative forms of narrative, however, it would be reductive to see this process as wholly sublimative. As John Zilcosky suggests, the narrator's inability to escape Sebald's labyrinthine cities, 'has devastating symbolic importance . . . it brings into relief the miserable limits of his mind (his "reason", "imagination" and "willpower") and of his writing (the "ink[ing] in" of his wanderings)' (2004: 105). Whereas Zilcosky equates this inability to escape with an inability to get lost, however, my reading contends the opposite; namely, that Sebald's narrator is damned to wander the Surrealist labyrinth in a permanent state of 'lostness'. As Bataille puts it: 'One need only follow, for a short time, the traces of repeated circuits of words to discover, in a disconcerting vision, the labyrinthine structure of the human being' (1994c: 174). For Sebald and Bataille, intertextuality is a process of discursive haunting that also reveals the haunted nature of the self. Indeed, there is no being beyond language: only words remain, while the self 'strangely loses its way' (Bataille 1994c: 173) in a linguistic labyrinth that simultaneously creates and contains it.

'DOUBLE VERTIGO' AND THE UNCANNY

The opening pages of 'Il ritorno in patria' are conspicuous for the trajectory of their energy. The natural world is in a state of collapse: the clouds are hanging low; rain is falling incessantly; mountainsides have slid into the valley; hay is rotting in the fields; potatoes are decomposing in the ground (2009: 190–1; 2002g: 175). The predominantly downward movement of the natural world is echoed not only in the trajectory of the narrator's physical journey (he is walking down the Alpine valley to his childhood home in the village, W.), but also in his psychological descent into the uncertain territories of the unconscious, memory and dream, or, rather, nightmare ('Alptraum' in the German). As the narrator climbs down the impossibly dark valley, he pauses, only to be overcome by a paradoxical feeling of vertigo:

> An einem der wenigen halbwegs offenen Plätze, wo man von einer Art Kanzel sowohl auf einen Wasserfall und Gumpen hinab- als auch hoch in den Himmel hinaufschauen konnte, ohne daß sich hätte sagen lassen, welche Blickrichtung die *unheimlichere* war, sah ich durch die, wie es schien, endlos hinaufragenden Bäume, daß in der bleigrauen Höhe ein Schneegestöber ausgebrochen war. (Sebald 2009: 194–5, emphasis mine)

> (At one of the few more open places, where a vantage-point afforded a view both down onto a waterfall and a deep rockpool and upwards into the sky, without my being able to say which was the more eerie, I saw through the apparent infinite loftiness of the trees, flurries of snow high up in the leaden greyness. (Sebald 2002g: 178))

This passage echoes a key moment in the literary and visual history of dissident Surrealism when André Masson underwent an uncanny experience in the mountains of Montserrat near Barcelona in 1935. Whilst sketching the setting sun, Masson and his wife were caught out by a storm that left them stranded on a precipice in the dark. Masson went on to describe his experience in *Mémoire du monde* (1974): '"[T]he sky itself appeared to me like an abyss, something which I had never felt before – the vertigo above and the vertigo below"' (Masson cited in Lomas 2006: 91). As Lomas observes, a striking feature of Masson's 'double vertigo'

– a fear of falling into the abyss and into the void of the sky – is that it repeats an earlier trauma. In 1917, Masson lay wounded in a trench piled high with corpses, and with little hope of rescue: he recorded this event in *Mémoire du monde*: '"Never having seen artillery fire whilst facing up at the sky, I was seized by a boundless terror"' (Masson cited in Lomas 2006: 91). Formal and contextual repetition informed by Freud's reading of the uncanny became a recurrent feature of Masson's dissident Surrealism. Is it purely coincidental, then, that in a text steeped with repetition and concealed traumas, the narrator of 'Il ritorno in patria' describes his own experience of the terrifying depths and heights of the Alpine landscape as 'unheimlicher'?

The uncanny occupies a central yet troubling position in the Surrealist project. Indeed, Surrealism is 'achieved and undone' in the realm of the uncanny: 'where pleasure and death principles appear to serve one another, where sexual and destructive drives appear identical' (Foster 1993: 11). It is precisely this overlapping tension between Eros and Thanatos which dissident Surrealists such as Masson and Bataille risked and which *Schwindel. Gefühle* also elaborates. Within the space of just a few pages, the reader is informed of the violent deaths of two sets of lovers: Lena and her husband – 'Anscheinend seien die beiden in ihrem neuem Oldsmobile . . . in die Tiefe gestürzt' ('It seemed that the two of them simply left the road in their Oldsmobile . . . plunged into the depths' (Sebald 2009: 230–1; 2002g: 211)). And the death of an anonymous couple in a portrait of suicide: 'Gleichzeitig strebte der Fuß des Mädchens und des Mannes in die Tiefe, und man fühlte aufatmend, wie beide schon von der Schwerkraft ergriffen waren' ('Together, the foot of the girl and that of the man were suspended over the dark waters, and one could sense with relief how both were now in the grip of gravity' (Sebald 2009: 238; 2002g: 218)).

Yet, it is in the death of the hunter Schlag that the uncanny coincidence of sex and death is most forcefully expressed. Following his illicit encounter with Romana (which the infatuated narrator witnesses as a boy), Schlag is found: 'auf dem Grund eines Tobels . . . offensichtlich sei er beim Überqueren des Tobels . . . zu Tode gestürzt' ('at the bottom of a ravine . . . he had evidently fallen while crossing by the narrow footbridge' (Sebald 2009: 268; 2002g: 247–8)). This death triggers a proliferation of uncanny textual and intertextual connections. One thinks of Kafka's hunter, Gracchus, who, following a fatal 'fall', is condemned to wander everywhere but rest *nowhere*: his restlessness is embodied in the various uncanny echoes of his tale throughout Sebald's narrative. Furthermore, on the level of language, the verb – *stürzen* – connects a network of desublimatory images across the text: the horses 'plunging' off the tracks of the Great St Bernard Pass; the rat that 'plunges' from the rubbish-laden barge into the black Venetian waters; the verses of Ehrenstein which have such resonance for the sexually repressed Dr K.: '*Ich will zur Tiefe. Stürzen, schmelzen, erblinden zu Eis*' ('I will go down to the deep. Plunge, thaw, go blind, become ice' (Sebald 2009: 159; 2002g: 143). Ehrenstein's image of frozen flesh triggers another series of uncanny associations, anticipating as it does Dr Piazolo's suspicion that Schlag survived the fall only to freeze to death. This image engages, in turn, with the boy-narrator's desire to commit suicide with the beautiful Romana by freezing to death in the ice store (Sebald 2009: 262; 2002g; 240); and it also brings to mind the image of the crystal-encrusted twig which Madame Gerhardi is gifted when she and Beyle emerge from the Hallein salt mines.

Within the Surrealist tradition, crystallized forms exemplify the 'érotique voilée' (veiled erotic), an element in the Surrealist notion of convulsive beauty in which ontological distinctions break down. In *L'Amour fou* (1937), Breton locates the veiled erotic in that moment when 'the inanimate is so close to the animate that the imagination is free to play infinitely with these apparently mineral forms' (1987: 11). Breton 'illustrates' his argument with a series of photographs, including Braissai's extreme close-ups of rock crystals (1987: 12), which, when magnified to such an extent, begin to resemble other objects: blocks of ice; glass jewels; ice sculptures; distorted mirrors; an alien landscape. For Breton, aesthetic and erotic pleasures do not lie in the unmasking of some essential quality or truth in a particular object; instead, the convulsive effect of the 'veiled erotic' manifests itself through ambiguity. And it is precisely in such moments of indistinctness, when the inanimate borders on the animate, and when death impinges upon life, that 'the veiled-erotic brushes up against the uncanny' (Foster 1993: 23).

Towards the end of 'Il ritorno in patria', the 'veiled erotic' brushes up against the uncanny when the narrator recalls how, as a delirious child sick with diphtheria, he saw himself going repeatedly down to the cellar:

> Ich faßte mit der Hand und dem Unterarm durch die kalkige Oberfläche des Wassers bis fast auf den Grund des Gefäßes, spürte aber zu meinem Entsetzten, das es sich bei dem, was in diesem Topf eingelegt worden war, nicht um sauber in ihrer Schale aufgehobene Eier, sondern um etwas weiches, den Fingern Entgleitendes handelte, von dem ich sogleich wußte, daß es nichts anderes als Augäpfel waren. (Sebald 2009: 273–4)

> (I put my hand and forearm through the chalky surface of the water almost to the bottom of the container, to my horror I felt that what was stored in this pot was not eggs safely sequestered, each one of them, in its shell, but something soft, something that slipped through my fingers and which I instantly knew could only be eyeballs gouged from their sockets. (Sebald 2002g: 250–1))

E. T. A. Hoffmann's, *Der Sandmann*, a text that links desire with death, and which is so central to Freud's reading of the uncanny, resonates intertexually here. Yet, Sebald's descent narrative also echoes a less obvious textual presence; namely, Bataille's *Story of the Eye* (1928), a dissident Surrealist tale of sex, violence and death which, structured around a series of coincidences, culminates in the image of a dead man's eye gazing at the horrified narrator from his lover's 'hairy vagina'

(2001: 67).[14] As Bataille reveals, in the section called 'Coincidences', a parody of linear biographical narrative, two particular objects held imaginative significance for him: 'The entire *Story of the Eye* was woven in my mind out of two ancient and closely associated obsessions, *eggs* and *eyes* (2001: 71, emphasis in original). That Sebald had read *Story of the Eye* is evidenced in an essay, first written in 1984, on Gerhard Roth's *Winterreise*, in which Sebald measures the limitations of Roth's pornographic imagination against that of Bataille: 'Neben der eisigen humoristischen Kälte, mit der sich Bataille sein gefrässiges Auge herausoperiert ... hätten die pornographischen Etüden der *Winterreise* wenig Bestand' ('Next to the icy humorous coldness with which Bataille surgically removes his own gluttonous eye ... *Winterreise*'s pornographic études could hardly last' (Sebald 2006b: 160, translation mine)). The secret (das Geheimnis) of the pornographic imagination, Sebald goes on to suggest '[besteht] nicht in der Sexualität ... sondern im Tode' ('is not to be found in sexuality but in death' (2001: 161, translation mine)).

It is this desublimatory attitude towards sex, one which initiates a '(re)erupting of the sexual' at the cost of the '(re)shattering of the subject and object' (Foster 1993: 110), which binds *Schwindel. Gefühle* to the dissident Surrealist tradition. From Beyle's syphilitic excesses, to the suicidal deaths of lovers and the fatal 'fall' of the hunter Schlag, Sebald immerses the reader in repeated and disturbing coincidences of Eros and Thanatos. On the one hand, Sebald's dissident Surrealism elaborates a disturbing relationship between eroticism and violence, one which recognizes the 'uncanny power of desublimation' (Foster 1993: 110), and one which Bataille went on to describe as disquietingly 'vertiginous' (1994b: 249).[15] At the same time, however, Sebald also follows Bataille on a downward trajectory in order to posit a specifically anti-Fascist critique: by shattering the sublime (Fascist) ideal of the pure and unified human body, Sebald opens the material body up to its heterogeneous energies and debased impulses. As Bataille observes in 'The Psychological Structure of Fascism', the heterogeneous 'consists of everything rejected by homogeneous society as waste ... Included are ... persons, words, or acts having a suggestive erotic value ... *violence, excess, delirium, madness*' (1994d: 142, emphases in original). Against the productive elements of homogeneous society – work, exchange, function, sexual repression, procreation and discipline – heterogeneous elements resist assimilation into the order of everyday life by allowing play, risk and even death to intervene.

It is telling that Sebald acknowledges Bataille's refusal to compromise with history (Sebald 2003b:157–8; 2004b: 154) in a critical move that registers the absence of such radical thinking in post-war German literature.[16] *Schwindel. Gefühle*, Sebald's first published prose work in German, should be seen as a response to this intellectual and aesthetic deficiency. When opened up to its dissident Surrealist contexts and intertexts, *Schwindel. Gefühle* emerges as an uncompromising exercise in post-war literary historiography. Specifically, the three differentiated and tension-ridden models of Surrealist vertigo that I have traced across the narrative – vertigo and play; vertigo, chance and the labyrinth; 'double vertigo' and the uncanny – immerse the reader in a series of disquieting and desublimatory confrontations with the limits and insufficiencies of historical representation, memory, language and subjectivity. Within Sebald's project of literary restitution, then, dissident Surrealism manifests itself as an ambiguous yet effective aesthetic and political model. For the counter-historical imagination is not brought into play in *Schwindel. Gefühle* in order to reach a point of resolution or consolation; rather, it is repeatedly and relentlessly in process, open to risk, ambiguity and the certain threat of uncertainty.

NOTES

1 A discussion of the influence of Surrealism on Claude Levi-Strauss's concept of 'bricolage' is beyond the scope of this paper. For a fascinating account of Levi-Strauss's relationship with the Surrealists in exile (including André Breton, André Masson and Wilfredo Lam), see Tythacott (2003).

2 In his copy of *Camera Lucida* by Roland Barthes, Sebald marked up a sentence about the punctum and studium and encircled the word 'fulguration'. See Hutchinson (2009b: 63).

3 For an in-depth discussion of Surrealism's sublimatory and desublimatory energies, see Foster (1993).

4 Shane Weller's essay in this volume also makes reference to the significance of Bataille's 'unbedingungslos negativ' thought for Sebald.

5 Much has been written on the ostensible rivalry between Breton and Bataille. For a more nuanced discussion of the many points of consonance across their respective literary and artistic projects see Michael Richardson's introduction to Bataille's collected writings (Bataille 1994a: 1–27).

6 For detailed studies of Benjamin's relationship with Collège de Sociologie, see Hollier (1988) and Kambas (1983: 178–81).

7 In *Das Passagen-Werk*, Benjamin also quotes from Caillois's essay, 'La Mante religieuse: recherches sur la nature et la signification du mythe' ('The Praying Mantis: Investigations into the Nature and Meaning of Myth'), published in *Mesures* 3.2: (15 April 1937).

8 Masson also famously illustrated Bataille's *Histoire de L'Oeil* (*Story of the Eye*, 1928). On Benjamin's involvement with Acéphale, see Witte (1997).

9 I am following David Lomas's excellent work on dissident Surrealism. See Lomas (2000) and Lomas (2006). For a broader reading of the motif of vertigo in Sebald's writing see Leone (2004).

10 See Sebald in interview with Uwe Pralle (Pralle 2001).

11 Anne Fuchs also provides an illuminating reading of the sublimatory potential of fine art paintings in Sebald's work. See Fuchs (2006).

12 For a close reading of the 'aufgeräumte' ('cleaned up') landscapes of post-war Germany in *Schwindel. Gefühle*, see Arthur Williams's essay in this volume.

13 I gratefully acknowledge Anna Mele's assistance with the Italian passages in *Schwindel. Gefühle*.

14 The second part of Bataille's tale, entitled 'Coincidences', begins: 'While composing this partly imaginary tale, I was struck by several coincidences and since they appeared indirectly to bring out the meaning of what I have written, I would like to describe them' (Bataille 2001: 69).

15 A footnote in Benjamin's *Das Passagen-Werk* is illuminating in this context: 'L'attrait du danger est au fond de toutes les grandes passions. Il n'y a pas de volupté sans vertige.' ('The fascination of danger is at the bottom of all passions. There is no fullness of pleasure unless the precipice is near'). The quotation is from Anatole France's *Le jardin de l'Epicure* (1894), pp. 15–18. See Benjamin (1999a: 498).

16 In conversation with Joseph Cuomo, Sebald gestures to the suppression and eventual loss of the German Surrealist Konrad Bayer to the post-war German literary landscape: 'I just happened to be going down to London and reading a book by a rather obscure German writer called Konrad Bayer, who was one of the young surrealists, as it were, postwar surrealists who'd been kept down by the famous Gruppe '47, and who subsequently took his own life' (Sebald in conversation with Cuomo (Cuomo 2007: 98–9). Bayer was in fact Austrian and a key member of the Wiener Gruppe (Vienna Group). The book to which Sebald refers is *Der Kopf des Vitus Bering* (*The Head of Vitus Bering*).

5

MEMOIRS OF THE BLIND: W. G. SEBALD'S *DIE AUSGEWANDERTEN*

Dora Osborne

INTRODUCTION

W. G. Sebald's literary project is bound to an attempt at restitution which both obscures and illuminates the past. Through the use of photography, in particular, it foregrounds the visual in trying to recollect the past or recuperate that which has been lost. Yet these gestures are marked by blind spots which persist as a reminder of the belated perspective from which Sebald writes: he was born too late to know directly the violence of the Second World War and the Holocaust, but these traumatic events still overshadow his work. Thus, Sebald's narratives might constitute an attempt at restitution, insofar as they want to repay the debt incurred by the *Nachgeborener*, a debt which, ultimately, amounts to the failure to bear witness to the crimes of National Socialism. Sebald's use of what Carolin Duttlinger has called 'traumatic photographs' (2004: 155) is key to understanding the work of memory and commemoration undertaken in narrative and, as such, has been subject to considerable analysis.[1] However, less critical investigation has been made into the links between the writerly practices of Sebald as author and the artistic techniques used in the production of the many images – not just photographs – featured in his texts, either as physical inserts or as narrative descriptions.[2] Both the similarities and differences between the textual and visual modes of representation are crucial to understanding Sebald's literature of restitution, that is, for tracing its double gestures of inscription and erasure, of illumination and overshadowing.

The ambivalent effects of Sebald's narrative movement between text and image, between inscription and erasure are shown in heightened form in *Die Ausgewanderten* (1992) (*The Emigrants*). Before the publication of the 'vier lange Erzählungen' ('four long stories') in composite form, some of these emigrant narratives in fact appeared individually elsewhere, suggesting how they might work as discrete portraits (Sebald 1988b, 1994c). However, by bringing them together under a shared title, Sebald has the four stories operate via certain similarities or likenesses, in particular, that of the common experience of emigration (and an attendant sense of cultural, psychological and emotional displacement). And where associations emerge between emigrants, their singular features become obscured, an effect produced not just at the level of the text, but also through the overlaying of various visual elements.[3] Indeed, *Die Ausgewanderten* makes use of a broad range of visual material, either included or cited in the text; the narrative is supplemented not just by photographs, but also by oil paintings, frescoes, postcards, scale-drawings and sketches. In the proliferation of visual elements, the reader as viewer seems to be denied access to a comprehensive image of the emigrants themselves and is drawn instead into a relay between partial images. For their movement between revelation and obscurity, Sebald's *Die Ausgewanderten* might also be called 'memoirs of the blind'. This supplementary sub-heading takes its cue from Derrida's *Memoirs of the Blind: The Self-Portrait and Other Ruins*, a text indebted to images and concerned, like *Die Ausgewanderten*, with questions of vision, memory and representation.[4] Whilst Sebald remained sceptical towards Derrida and decon-struction more generally, the dialectical movement of his writing between obscurity and illumination, restitution and renewed loss, reveals an affiliation with this kind of poststructuralism despite himself.[5]

Derrida's *Memoirs of the Blind* was written to accompany one in a series of exhi-bitions shown at the Louvre in the 1990s entitled *Partis Pris*, and as such also features predominantly drawings and sketches selected by Derrida for display. In his descrip-tion of modes of visuality and inscription, Derrida recalls memories for, and of, an exhibition about blindness.[6] His essay discusses the exclusion and occlusion involved in acts of looking, drawing and inscribing, that is, the moment of blindness which necessarily accompanies the attempt at representation. As Derrida writes, already at its production, an image is marked by the impossibility of seeing at once the artistic subject and (what will be) its representation: 'From the outset, percep-tion belongs to recollection' (Derrida 1993: 51). Thus, the execution and exhibition of portraiture work to displace our gaze from the now absent object onto other, substitute or surrogate objects. And, together with the artist, the viewer becomes complicit in a relay of gazes between surrogate objects. In showing how acts of representation betray and ultimately reproduce the absence of the original object, Derrida traces a double movement, where inscription, always subject to re-inscription, effaces that which came before. And in writing about drawing, he shows how both modes of representation, the textual and the visual, partake of this double gesture of inscription. He uses the notion of the *trait* to render visually the trope of *différance*, describing how the simultaneous redrawing and withdrawing of trace in the act of drawing always produces a disjuncture between the object and its representation: 'The trait joins and adjoins only in separating' (Derrida 1993: 54).

Crucially, *Memoirs of the Blind* brings together written and visual modes of repre-sentation where both are found wanting: memory and blindness are (failed) modes of knowing what is now past or lost. With his title, Derrida draws attention to the need for supplement in every act of representation, as well as to the potential for writing to supplement what is lacking in images and vice versa. Moreover, with the notion of the *trait* and its closeness to drawing, he shows inscription to be more than just an act of writing, whilst exposing the insufficiency of inscription as *only* an act of writing. Indeed, writing about images, Derrida describes a fraternal rivalry between the author and artist, which is played out in the struggle for representation: 'Drawing comes in the place of the name, which comes in the place of drawing' (Derrida 1993: 57). This struggle for supremacy is illustrated in the book itself: a form of exhibition catalogue displays the images which elsewhere speak for themselves, but here are made to speak through Derrida's text.

In *Die Ausgewanderten*, Sebald also shows how both visual and written modes of representation require the supplement of the other to make available that which has been lost from sight or receded from memory. Like Derrida, Sebald adopts a double position vis-à-vis his emigrant portraits, drawing on visual as well as textual paradigms and so questioning what it means for us to think of him principally as writer. Even as author, Sebald has a vested interest in artistic practices. His engagement with, particularly, drawing (as etching) is illustrated in the posthumous volume *Unerzählt*, produced by friend and colleague Jan Peter Tripp.[7] *Die Ausgewanderten* is also preoccupied with both the similarity and difference between written and visual modes, between authors and artists: the narrator (as putative author) asserts a kind of fraternity with the artist protagonist of the final story, Max Ferber, and he even feels an affinity or affiliation with another artist, Matthias Grünewald (Sebald 2008a: 248, 253; 2002e: 166, 170). The story about the emigrant painter asks further questions about its own composition: originally entitled 'Max Aurach', it seems to refer to the artist Frank Auerbach, an example of whose work was included in the first German editions. The subsequent (and presumably unforeseen) need to exclude the explicit references to Auerbach ironically comes to perform the same kind of production through erasure which characterizes Auerbach/Aurach/Ferber's artistic technique. Furthermore, the story of a painter who shares the same name as that of the author (Sebald famously called himself Max) sets up at once an opposition and interchangeability between artistic and authorial practices, between the inscription of identity through image and text. Sebald gives language to the images he includes in his texts; he names the pictures made of and by others and in so doing re-inscribes them as his own. Moreover, unlike the posthumous reciprocal project *Unerzählt*, in *Die Ausgewanderten* the artist figure is found only *in absentia* and it is Sebald who moves between writerly and artistic practices, a movement which in turn is split between restoring the agency of inscription to another and retrieving it again for his own acts of narrative.

Using the supplementary sub-heading 'memoirs of the blind' for *Die Ausgewanderten* functions in a double sense, referring to the visual dysfunction which affects all four eponymous protagonists and suggesting that the memories recounted are told by a narrator who, coming at a belated juncture, is himself affected by a kind of blindness. Following Derrida, it makes use of a double genitive (narratives at once *about* and *by* the blind (Derrida 1993: 2)): the blind spots marking Sebald's emigrant portraits are symptoms both of the traumatic encounters which mark the protagonists' lives and of the narrator's failure to know the four men in any integral sense. However, Derrida's hypothesis of vision makes blindness the very condition of seeing where sight relates not to the faculty of visual perception but to a vision of the truth. So, ultimately, the dual effects of illumination and obscurity surrounding *Die Ausgewanderten* ask the question: can the act of narrative restore vision to either perspective? Whilst the deconstructive mode employed by Sebald can certainly be understood in the terms identified by Doren Wohlleben as a 'Deporträtierung von Porträts' (de-portrayal of the portrait) (2007: 1–2 (my translation)), here I want to consider how it might, in fact, be instrumentalized in his project of restitution. This essay will use Derrida's text and its title to cast new light on the text–image relationship fundamental to Sebald's work. It will show how the blindness marking Sebald's work – that residue of belatedness and failed witness – at once obscures his narrative figures and reveals in them a potentially visionary power. With *Memoirs of the Blind*, it will read the attempt at restitution that Sebald ascribes to literature in visual terms as an attempt to restore vision to the blind.

Whilst the faculty of sight cannot be revived by the text, there are moments where narrative restores a kind of vision which wants to reveal the truth of the emigrants' experiences (i.e., a truth beyond the mere facts of what happened to them). This is performed on the model of vision set out in *Memoirs of the Blind*, where Derrida develops a dialectic of cutting and outline which makes vision contingent on occlusion: in order for sight to be restored to the blind, the eye must be cut or traumatized. Derrida turns to the biblical story of Tobit, whose blindness is healed by his son, Tobias, and specifically to a drawing attributed to Rembrandt which shows not the application of the fish-bile balm usually described in scripture, but some kind of eye surgery: 'This scene of hands, of maneuvering and manipulation, calls to mind a properly surgical operation, which I dare not, or not yet, call graphic' (Derrida 1993: 26). The cut made with a scalpel or stylus shows the sacrificial inscription of the *trait*, that is, a mark which cuts in order to make vision possible. In *Die Ausgewanderten*, the narrator performs a kind of surgery of the blind, but one which treats blindness by a renewed act of incision; which is to say, by inscribing their stories in their place, he makes them visible by a further act of mutilation at the level of the text. As I will show, whether or not the narrator is able to restore any kind of vision to the blind, his intervention is apparent in a series of traces marking the emigrant portraits.

My discussion will proceed in four sections: firstly, I will explain how the emigrants and the narrator are affected by different sorts of blindness; secondly, I will describe how Sebald uses screens and shades at once to direct the gaze towards and away from his emigrant protagonists; thirdly, I will develop this idea to outline a broader strategy of effacement in exhibition operative within the text; and finally, I will show how the narrator attempts an act of restitution by trying to restore sight (as vision) to his portraits of the blind.

FAILURE OF SIGHT

The four portraits which emerge from *Die Ausgewanderten* are all, in some sense, obscured. This functions primarily in terms of the visual metaphor of memory images: on the surface of things, it seems that the failure to see is bound inextricably to the inability to remember. However, we find that the relationship between vision and memory is more complex when moments of apparent forgetting are privileged with momentary illumination. Beyond the failure of memory, the blindness which marks Sebald's emigrants has to do with their ultimate unknowability. Since these are composite images, in the sense of an unclear mix of fact and fiction, of memory and fantasy, they cannot be made entirely visible to the reader, or indeed the narrator. Although the narrator, with the help of others and of other material, wants to recount the lives of the protagonists, a fundamental obscurity surrounds their past.

The protagonist of the first story, Henry Selwyn, is a Lithuanian Jew who came to England in 1899. His memories of emigration have remained inaccessible for decades, but he notes how recently they have been returning to him (Sebald 2008b: 31; 2002e: 18–19). By contrast, he describes the Second World War and the years which follow as 'eine blinde und böse Zeit, über die ich, selbst wenn ich wollte, nichts zu erzählen vermöchte' ('a blinding, bad time for me, about which I could not say a thing even if I wanted to' (2008b: 35; 2002e: 21)). Since childhood, the protagonist of the second story, Paul Bereyter, has been plagued by punctuated vision (so-called 'Mückensehen' (2008b: 88; 2002e; 60)). A 'Dreiviertelarier' ('three quarters an Aryan' (2008b: 74; 2002e: 74)) who is made to give up his teaching post, he does not want to go over 'die von blinden Flecken durchsetzte Vergangenheit' ('the past punctuated by blind spots' (2008b: 80; 2002e: 54, translation modified)). Yet he is obsessed by that very past and sits for hours scrutinizing archive material: '[t]rotz seines schwächer werdenden Augenlichts' ('[a]lthough he was losing his sight' (2008b: 80; 2002e: 54)). Visual disturbances and headaches are just some of the symptoms of Ambros Adelwarth's decline described in the third story, symptoms, we understand, of the repression to which his personal life was subject: Adelwarth's Jewish companion, Cosmo Solomon, is, the text implies, his lover. Adelwarth must endure Cosmo's early death seemingly from his overwhelming disorientation faced with the demands of modern life and the senseless violence of the First World War. Following this, he retreats into the service of the Solomon parents, who themselves spend the years of the Second World War in complete seclusion. Great Uncle Ambros (the only emigrant related to the narrator) closes his eyes to the electroconvulsive treatment which awaits him. And, as if to distract the gaze of others from the outwards signs of his internal decline, he insists on impeccable dress as an alternative spectacle to disguise his physical and mental deterioration (2008b: 162–3; 2002e: 111). The treatment effects an obliteration of memory, which is betrayed by his strangely fixed gaze; his eyes are open, but they do not see (2008b: 170; 2002e: 116). In the case of Max Ferber, who is sent to England ahead of his parents to escape the encroaching Nazi presence in Germany, the failure of memory and vision is configured in extreme bodily experience, that is, in pain or unconsciousness: a slipped disk produces pain so great: 'daß es mir beim Einatmen schwarz wurde vor den Augen' ('that everything went black before my eyes when I breathed' (2008b: 254; 2002e: 171, translation modified)). Via a series of associations, characteristic of Sebald's writing, the protagonist conflates memory, vision and consciousness with physical experience at the limit where attempts to remember or to see result in bodily collapse. After compulsively recalling a series of images, Ferber closes his eyes as he falls unconscious (2008b: 271; 2002e: 182), and where he does see/remember, the experience produces pain: 'all das sehe er in schmerzlichster Schärfe vor sich' ('all of this he saw before him with painful sharpness' (2008b: 280; 2002e: 187–8 translation modified)).

The blindness affecting the emigrants can be understood in two ways, and as such reflects the complexity of the trope as it figures in *Die Ausgewanderten*: on the one hand, it is the symptom of the traumatic encounters of their past and the failure to make sense of the circumstances which led to their emigration and which prohibit their return; and on the other, it can be understood as the symptom of the narrator's (and by extension, the author's) inability to make sense of the experiences he came too late to know himself. Thus, the visual dysfunction affecting the emigrants might be understood in terms of the blindness which, following Derrida, is necessarily implied in the act of drawing. Sebald's compositions are made belatedly and bear the mark of having been produced in mediated fashion. In this sense, then, their blindness functions as an effect (paradoxically, an after-effect) of the narrator's or author's own blindness projected onto and inscribed into the image produced.

SHADES AND SCREENS

Describing his chosen images for *Memoirs of the Blind*, Derrida explains how the artist deflects the gaze from the blind spot marking these portraits through the use of other, supplementary objects in the composition. Where so often such adjunct objects seem to give composition to the real object, Derrida shows how our gaze is drawn away from the gaze of the sitter (Derrida 1993: 72). Using a series of visual examples which shade or distract the gaze of the model, he describes the 'ruse of an oblique or indirect gaze [which] consists in sidestepping rather than meeting head-on the death that comes through the eyes' (Derrida 1993: 87). The impossibility of looking the sitter in the eye whilst looking to the reproduction of that eye is represented through different kinds of shade or screen. These devices deflect the gaze from the traumatic encounter with the now-lost object of representation, which is to say, with the realization that the representation has no real or originary object which precedes it. In *Memoirs of the Blind*, Derrida shows how, perhaps in disavowal of this fact, the principle of the portrait image, that is, the production of physiognomic likeness, is deflected, variously, by the shading out of the eye, or else by glasses or an eyeshade.

In *Die Ausgewanderten*, shades and screens direct visual relations between emigrants. Sebald uses a green shade or veil as a mediating object between gazes both within and across stories; yet with its obscuring or deflecting function, it does not facilitate a direct exchange between emigrants, but, rather, trains the gaze to now unavailable images of past objects or places. At Henry Selwyn's slide show, the translucent images are covered by a green veil: 'Wie unter einem hellgrünen Schleier breitete vor uns die Insellandschaft sich aus' ('The landscape of the island seemed veiled in bright green as it lay before us' (2008b: 26; 2002e: 15)). The preceding two sentences describe the play of dust started by the projector fan and tell the reader that the journey documented in the slides was undertaken in the spring. Thus, the effect of the green veil could be attributed either to the slides themselves (capturing the spring atmosphere) or to the present viewing (the layer of dust stirred by the projector). Such a device distracts from the image itself and draws attention to the distance, both temporal and spatial, between object and viewing subject, which is to say, the unavailability of the past. In 'Paul Bereyter', the gunsmith Corradi wears a green eyeshade, which allows him to focus on his work (2008b: 58; 2002e: 38). He leads an introverted existence, making the shade characteristic of his desire to avoid the gaze of others (a behaviour shared by others in *Die Ausgewanderten*). The focus of the gunsmith, who is routinely found bent over complicated pieces of equipment, seems to replicate the gaze of the protagonist, who fixes melancholically on past images. Furthermore, it might refigure the story's opening image which shows (or symbolizes) the railway tracks where Paul commits suicide, but equally evokes the view down the barrel of a gun. The opening, singular view of Paul comes to be shared by the gunsmith (and also by the narrator in his attempt to imagine himself in Paul's position), thereby directing the gaze away from the moment of his death.

Ambros Adelwarth wears a green eyeshade to alleviate his symptoms: 'like someone who works in a gambling saloon' (Sebald 2008b: 169; 2002e: 115). The visor seems to be a remnant, perhaps even a souvenir, from Cosmo's gambling days and functions now as a sign of Ambros's complete withdrawal from the scrutiny of others. The narrator returns to Deauville, where Cosmo and Ambros played, and finds the casino moved to another hall, covered by green screens: 'Der Roulettetisch befand sich übrigens in einer offenbar vor kurzem renovierten, von jadegrünen Glasparavents abgeschirmten Innenhalle und also nicht an dem Ort, an dem früher in Deauville gespielt worden ist' ('The roulette table, screened off with jade-green glass *paravents*, was in a recently refurbished inner hall – not, in other words, where players had gambled at Deauville in former times' (2008b: 177; 2002e: 120)). This motif of the green shade produces a deflection from human physiognomy to architectural structures which at once obscures and draws attention to the temporal displacement in the narrative. The recent renovation suggests a return to past forms and structures, but this is resisted by the emphatic explanation of a change in location. It is as though the shaded gaze deflects our attention from some kind of imminent swindle. Like the green veil above, these two gambling shades, the physiognomic and architectural one, are a shared feature of the narrator's experiences and those of his great uncle, and thus blur the distinction between the two. In the memoirs of the protagonist's mother featured in 'Max Ferber', Luisa Lanzberg recalls a strange incident in her childhood village where a scene of domestic unrest is screened from the young onlookers: 'Anderntags bleiben die grünen Läden ihrer Wohnung geschlossen, und wir Kinder ... fragen uns, was dort drinnen vorgefallen sein mag' ('The next day, the green shutters at their windows remain shut, and we children ... wonder what can be going on in there' (2008b: 295; 2002e: 197)). The green blinds screen what is happening in the home, but they attract the curious gaze of others. They stand in for, and in front of, the events which are ostensibly represented in the different layers of *Die Ausgewanderten*. The motivic recurrence of the green veil, visor, screen or blind exemplifies Sebald's portraiture: it not only deflects the reader's gaze within each story, it also shades the gaze of the emigrants across the four stories. With its re-emergence, the green shade produces the effect of a relayed deflection which prevents, repeatedly, any of the four portraits from appearing with any clarity or integrity. This effect does, however, reveal or expose to the reader the blind spots marking each figure, underlining that each representation is precisely a mediated image in composite form.

Using visual elements, Sebald develops a double strategy of deflecting or displacing the gaze whilst inviting scrutiny. This is given emblematic form in the Rembrandt image mentioned by his narrator in 'Max Ferber'. In *Man with a Magnifying Glass*, the optical prosthesis can be found in the right-hand corner, but is ultimately somewhat obscure. Thus, in searching for the adjunct object promised by the title, the viewer looks away from the sitter. Moreover, this is one of the images evoked, but not inserted, in the text. So, if a curious reader wanted to look for the magnifying glass, they would have to look away from the text in order to find a reproduction. In the narrative, the painting is used as a means of distraction from the passage of time: 'Aren't we all getting on! ... Only he [Rembrandt's man with a magnifying glass] doesn't seem to get any older' (2001a: 269; 2002e: 180). It offers an image of consistency or orientation to which we can return with the assurance that it will not have changed; it draws the tripartite narrative gaze (comprising that of Ferber, the narrator and the reader) together in the contemplation of another image and so distracts from the differences in these three perspectives.[8] Moreover, it directs us to a peripheral object, specifically and paradoxically, to an instrument of vision which is not meant for seeing, or might be overlooked. Instead, the elusive magnifying glass from Rembrandt's painting emerges elsewhere when it is used by Ferber to look at a reproduction of another Old Master, Tiepolo (2001a: 276; 2002e: 185).[9] Ferber studies the reproduction after recalling his childhood viewing of the real fresco at the Würzburger Residenz, and both experiences induce dizziness. This episode brings spatial and temporal disorientation and marks the return in another place of the object which is lost from sight. The use of optical instruments wants to aid recollection in the narrative, but in fact exposes the failure of a visual mode of recall. As Derrida notes, such prostheses want to supplement sight, but are always already secondary to the eye, showing in displaced mode the gap which emerges in perception between subject and object, past and present: 'It immediately *stands out*, is immediately *detachable* from the body proper' (Derrida 1993: 70).

EFFACEMENT IN EXHIBITION

Sebald's use of shades, screens or adjunct objects in *Die Ausgewanderten* exemplifies the effacement in exhibition operative across the text. This follows the effects described by Derrida where the fetish objects of portraiture such as glasses and bandanas (or Sebald's green shades and magnifying glass) both distract and draw our attention to the face (as primary site of identity): 'This is what is called showing oneself naked, showing nakedness – a nakedness which is nothing without modesty' (Derrida 1993: 72). A particularly striking example of this gesture is found on the double-page spread, where Paul Bereyter is shown once clothed and with eyes visible through spectacles and again with naked torso, but with eyes shaded by sunglasses (2008b: 82–3; 2002e: 55–6 (the images have been divided by a page turn in the English)). Above all, these images are about the nakedness of exhibition and about the desire at once to look at and to look away from that which is exposed. To look at Paul Bereyter in either photograph is to view a restricted, or censored, image; where we see his eyes, his body is clothed and where we see his body, his eyes are masked. In order to find what is obscured in one, we look to the other. This restriction becomes visible itself only through the juxtaposition of the two images, and in turn gestures towards the way Sebald challenges normative processes of viewing and reading. Access is given to the emigrants' pasts only in the act of its limitation, and it is the narrator who self-consciously performs the inscription of these limits which reflect his own restricted knowledge. The sort of shading and showing between the two images of Paul is symptomatic for the way the narrator constantly exposes his position as he retreats into the shadows of the narrative. Furthermore, it signals a shift in the position that Sebald comes to adopt in his texts, where this pair of images marks an extended stage of the division produced on the author's passport photograph in *Schwindel. Gefühle* (1990). In this earlier text, Sebald performs a very deliberate act of self-effacement, where a black line obliterates his own image in the document. Moreover, the restriction of image is reciprocated by the partial nature of text: Sebald writes how the personal data entered by the Milan official are typed 'in punktierten Buchstaben' ('in dotted letters') (2001l: 134–5; 2000b: 114), reminiscent of Bereyter's punctuated 'Mückensehen'. The restricted view of Bereyter is marked in a double sense by the complete withdrawal of the author/narrator.

In *Die Ausgewanderten*, visual modes of representation are accompanied by textual ones. Thus, when moments of (self-)inscription are accompanied by (self-) erasure, they function as another form of effacement in exhibition. This effect becomes most apparent in 'Max Ferber', via an implied tension between the respective positions and functions of author and artist. Here, Sebald is particularly concerned with the protagonist as artist, with his work, his technique, and his influences. Since Ferber used to assist his art-dealer father, the studio and gallery figure key scenes of viewing and exhibition in the narrative. Sebald writes about and includes examples of different types of image, some unidentified or unidentifiable, some anonymous, others created by great artists, such as Tiepolo, Rembrandt, Courbet and Grünewald. The status of these images is often ambiguous: some are conspicuous in their absence from a text which is characteristic in its integration of non-textual material, while others are screened and distorted by other, anti-materials, such as dust and ash, which are layered compulsively in Sebald's work. Evoked in post-1945 narrative and after the ashen poetry of Paul Celan, such residual materials connote the violence of the Holocaust (the threat of which caused Ferber to emigrate). They are the veil which now obscures the beauty of the images which were produced before Auschwitz.

Ferber's technique is described by the narrator as 'die Vermehrung des Staubs' ('the increase of dust' (2008b: 238; 2002e: 161, translation modified)) and his medium is a residue of destruction.[10] Following the sacrificial mode in which the *trait* functions for Derrida, Ferber's portraits trace, again, the loss to which they bear witness. The acts of portraiture in *Die Ausgewanderten* do not work to attribute a fixed identity through physiognomic likeness, rather, the face is made invisible, erased, shaded or overwhelmed. With his portrait of the artist Ferber, Sebald uses textual description of visual technique (perhaps an extended form of ekphrasis) to inscribe and overwrite identities in a double sense.[11] Ferber's mode of production is described in terms of a ceaseless process of destruction and salvage (2001a: 238–9;

2002e: 161–2), yielding a faceless portrait (2008b: 260; 2002e: 174), a 'Zerstörungsstudie' ('exercise in destruction' (2008b: 269; 2002e: 180)) and variations on these things. The narrative mediates Ferber's production of images through destruction in textual form, and it also describes Ferber himself in the same terms, thus blurring any distinction between the artist and the images he creates. Thus, in the narrator's memory, Ferber's face becomes a shadow (2008b: 264; 2002e: 177) which doubles the faceless portrait. The artist seems to belong to the same genealogy as his images, albeit one which marks the end of the line, emerging, like his portraits: 'aus einer langen Ahnenreihe grauer, eingeäscherter, in dem zerschundenen Papier nach wie vor herumgeisternder Gesichter' ('from a long lineage of grey, ancestral faces, rendered unto ash but still there, as ghostly presences, on the harried paper' (2008b: 239–40; 2002e: 162)). The mutual implication of text and image, author and artist in this destructive practice is shown again where the Aurach/Auerbach sketch breaks up the word 'zerschundenen' ('harried'), thereby performing as well as illustrating the breakdown described in narrative.

Despite the change in title from 'Max Aurach' to 'Max Ferber', the last story of *Die Ausgewanderten* retains the echo of the author's preferred name, 'Max', which he adopted as an emigrant, because he sensed that Winfried Georg was too Germanic a formulation.[12] The suggested *Familienähnlichkeit* or *Brüderlichkeit* gestures towards the kind of fraternal rivalry outlined by Derrida in *Memoirs of the Blind*: the respective work of artist and author functions as a series of drawings and inscriptions of the *trait* whereby one always draws or writes over the other. The *trait* is the shared praxis of artist and author, but one mode of representation is replaced by the other: 'A substitution, then, a clandestine exchange: one *trait* for the other' (Derrida 1993: 37). As writer, Sebald seems to withdraw the images he uses as he inscribes the text that supplements his emigrant portrait. Particularly in the case of Ferber, the artist is displaced, that is, overwritten by the writer. In addition to the sketch, Sebald includes an image (one with qualities reminiscent of Tripp's hyperrealist drawing) of Ferber's eye, which, we are told, is subject to repeated scrutiny by the narrator (2008b: 265) (image not included in the English version).[13] Described as staring out of the photograph accompanying a newspaper article, we can assume that this image is an extract of a larger whole, presumably a photographic portrait, and that this section has been included to the exclusion of the rest. Reducing the portrait to the single eye represents the blinding, potentially castrating, violence inflicted on the artist by the narrator/author.

The effacement in exhibition which is effected in *Die Ausgewanderten* has to do with identificatory relationships between emigrants and, via the text–image relationship characteristic for Sebald's work, with the similarities and differences in artistic and authorial practice. Through his claim to a sort of *Brüderlichkeit* with Ferber, the narrator identifies as artist, but he also identifies as a writer through the iconography of the feather or quill. In his search for the origins of others, the narrator goes to the Jewish cemetery at Bad Kissingen. A photograph accompanying the description of his visit shows the quill depicted on the headstone of a female author, Friederike Halbleib. The narrator is moved to a particularly problematic gesture of identification, one which effectively withdraws Halbleib (and the fact of both gender and ethnic difference) in order to re-inscribe himself into the narrative: 'Ich dachte sie mir als Schriftstellerin, allein und atemlos über ihre Arbeit gebeugt, und jetzt, wo ich dies schreibe, kommt mir vor, als hätte *ich* sie verloren' ('I imagined her pen in hand, all by herself, bent with bated breath over her work; and now, as I write these lines, it feels as if *I* had lost her' (2008b: 336–7; 2002e: 224, emphasis in original)). Through the emblem of the quill, which functions as a shared tool of inscription, the narrator as author identifies with the writer Halbleib, although he never knew her. In his quest for knowledge of the other, the feather becomes a different sort of identificatory figure for the narrator as writer: the quest becomes one for his own origins.

RESTORATION OF VISION

The tools of inscription, emblematized in the quill, are at work throughout *Die Ausgewanderten* and used in different acts of a sort of surgery of the blind. As such, the narrative attempts the restoration of sight. Following the hypothesis of vision proposed by Derrida, this act of restitution responds to the failure of sight by revealing vision; which is to say, in encountering the blindness inscribed at the beginning of every act of representation, we witness how the blind are privileged with a kind of vision. Sebald's narrator adopts an interesting position in relation to such visionary moments, both performing a kind of eye surgery on his emigrant companions and becoming, momentarily, a kind of visionary, or blind witness himself.[14] Neither of these restorative roles is unproblematic, however, as the former requires an act of violence in the very surgical cut and the latter emerges despite having never witnessed the original experiences of the emigrants. The narrator oscillates between moments of vision and obscurity, and this movement can be understood as symptomatic for the gap between the narrative he produces and the memories proper to the emigrants. That this is vision (as opposed to sight) is indicated by the narrator's claims to alternative states of perception; fantasies, dreams and hallucinations are seen with clarity, but subject to disintegration and dissolution. Thus, paradoxically, the vision produced in blindness also works to obscure the portraits of the emigrants. The paradoxical effects of the vision that comes with blindness manifest themselves following the literal eye surgery performed on Bereyter. Paul's visual dysfunction develops from the childhood punctuations to cataracts and he undergoes an operation to remove them. With his eyes bound, he has lucid visions of the past: 'er [lag] im Sommer 1975 nach einer

Operation am grauen Star mit verbundenen Augen in einem Berner Spital und [sah], wie er sagte, mit reinster Traumklarheit Dinge, von denen er nicht geglaubt hatte, daß sie noch da waren in ihm' ('he was in hospital in Berne in 1975, his eyes bandaged after an operation for cataracts [and] he said that he could see things then with the greatest clarity, as one sees them in dreams, things he had not thought he still had within him' (2008b: 76; 2002e: 51)). Whilst seeming to illuminate his past, these dream visions (as fantasies) might render that past doubly inaccessible.

Vision and surgery are configured more symbolically in the first story, which traces the link between the surgeon protagonist Selwyn and his father, a lens-grinder, who bought into an optician's business (2008b: 32; 2002e: 20).[15] After leaving Prior's Gate, the narrator finds the surgeon's lancet still outside his window in botanical form, obscuring the view with greenish, grey leaves: 'Wir vermißten in der ersten Zeit die weite Aussicht, dafür aber bewegten sich jetzt vor unseren Fenstern die grünen und grauen Lanzetten zweier Weiden selbst an windstillen Tagen fast ohne Unterlaß' ('At first we missed the view, but instead we had the green and grey lancets of two willows at our windows, and even on days where there was no breeze at all they were almost never at rest' (2008b: 29–30; 2002e:18)). In more evident symbolism, the foliage which hangs in front of the windows comes to obscure the fact of a missing view. Since the etymology of glaucoma refers to a greenish, grayish color, the leaves also symbolize a configuration of visual dysfunction and the tool which would want to treat it. It is in this setting that the narrator and protagonist talk about Selwyn's past, a past which becomes available with increasing clarity in the process of this exchange. The doctor believed his memories lost, but finds in recent times that they return in particularly visual form (2008b: 31; 2002e:19); the visionary formulation 'ich sehe' is used repeatedly. In their colouring, the green and grey leaves suggest the visual dysfunctions, glaucoma and cataract, in German, *grüner* and *grauer Star* respectively. They anticipate Bereyter's cataracts and their surgical treatment, for which, the verb *stechen* (*gestochen*) is used and so provides a link to the punctuation of vision which obscures his childhood. The cut of surgery works, then, at once as the opening and marking of vision. The text produces a relay between the portraits which have, in the act of exhibition, been blinded. The double portrait of Paul Bereyter (2008b: 82–3; 2002e: 55–6), whose eyes are shaded where his torso is exposed and vice versa, looks across Sebald's text to encounter the single, black eye of Aurach/Ferber, which is marked by a fleck of white light. The eye which is shown (perhaps as an emblem of vision) is always in some sense scotomized or traumatized.[16]

In 'Ambros Adelwarth', Sebald includes a photographic portrait which in the Eichborn 1993 'Erfolgsausgabe' of *Die Ausgewanderten* is given emblematic status as its frontispiece. The narrator's great uncle had the picture taken at a photographer's studio on his last journey with Cosmo and it shows him wearing Arab dress. As the dust jacket image, it shows how Sebald produces his emigrant portraits on a photographic model or paradigm. The photographic portrait offers a model for Sebald both because it makes a claim to realism and because it is a haunted medium; it shows the lost object, whilst foregrounding its status as absent. In Sebald's work, it is the narrative (as attempted act of restitution) which works to fill in the gap left by the Barthesian *punctum*. As such, the photographic paradigm is supplemented or mediated through the repeated gesture of inscription and re-inscription made by the author/narrator, the traces of which are made visible on the image through the paradigm of drawing. The Adelwarth photograph is clearly composed as a portrait for the way its visual order has been organized. It also distracts our gaze from the unusually direct gaze of the sitter with the other, adjunct objects of the photographer's studio. In the story, it comes in place of the (oral) narrative Adelwarth failed to pass on to Tante Fini, functioning as a sort of screen image to cover the truth of his (sexual) identity: 'Es gibt jedoch ein Fotoporträt in arabischer Kostümierung von ihm aus der Jerusalemer Zeit' ('But there is a photographic portrait of him in Arab costume, taken when they were in Jerusalem' (2008b: 137; 2002e: 94–5, translation modified)). The image shows everything and nothing, as Fini's failure to comment further on the image suggests. Crucially, what Sebald adds to his portrait of Adelwarth with the insertion of this image is simultaneously what is withdrawn: his putative homosexuality. Costume and masquerade make visible what society insists on keeping invisible, something which was immediately clear to Sebald upon encountering this image: 'Now, as soon as I saw that picture, I knew the whole story. ... In a Catholic family that all gets repressed. It isn't even ignored – it's not seen, it doesn't exist. It doesn't fit in anywhere at all' (Angier 2007: 71). This picture marks the beginning of the narrative and the blindness always already inscribed in it. Sebald's narrator performs a kind of surgical act in making visible through his narrative description (as inscription or incision) what his family sought to disavow. In this sense, the striped costume comes to inscribe in metonymic fashion the traumatic cuts of the *trait*, marking the image with the same repeated gestures of inscription and obliteration made compulsively throughout *Die Ausgewanderten*.[17]

But perhaps with this mark made on Ambros Adelwarth's story, another aspect of his fate is made visible: Ambros is the only emigrant who is not Jewish in any part (although his companion, of course, is), but his homosexuality would have made him equally vulnerable to annihilation under National Socialism. Withdrawn in the service of Cosmo's eccentric father, Ambros spent the war years holed up in a grand house in the USA, and perhaps it was a kind of visionary clarity with which, following the decline of Cosmo, he saw the need to remain outside of the Fascist order prevailing in Europe. And for the other emigrants, it is a kind of visionary foresight, the brutality and ostracization they see experienced by others, that forces them elsewhere and thus makes them emigrants; which is to say, it is a kind of vision which allows them to survive, but at the cost of giving up their homeland. If, through its blindness, the narrative has a visionary power, what it makes visible is, ultimately, of a dark, obscure nature, since it is an image overshadowed by the violence to come, that of the Second World War and the Holocaust. For instance, the meaning of Paul's obsession with the railway and the uncle's foreboding reference to death on the railway has been read in an extended sense as a reference to the death of many deported by rail to death camps.[18] In the immediate context of the story, it refers to Bereyter's suicide, but in either case, Mme Landau fails to realize its implications at the time and only belatedly understands its full import: 'Die von meinem momentanen Fehlverständnis ausgelöste Beunruhigung – heute ist mir manchmal, als hätte ich damals wirklich ein Todesbild gesehen – war aber nun von der kürzesten Dauer und ging über mich hinweg wie der Schatten eines Vogels im Flug' ('The disquiet I experienced because of that momentary failure to see what was meant – I now sometimes feel that at that very moment I beheld an image of death – lasted only a very short time, and passed over me like the shadow of a bird in flight' (2008b: 93; 2002e: 63)). The protagonists emigrate (just) before the war years, but they foresee, via a system of more oblique references to (mass) violence, industrialization and modernization, its terrible effects.

If Sebald's narrative does in fact restore vision to his emigrants, it is particularly dark, overshadowed as it is by the truth of National Socialism. Moreover, even if the narrative produces moments of illumination, Sebald's own view is ultimately always marked by the blind spots of belatedness and failed witness. However, these marks, particularly the repeated gestures of the drawing, redrawing and withdrawing of the *trait*, on Derrida's model, are signs, at least, of the attempt at restitution which Sebald assigns to literature. We gain a deeper understanding of how this attempt links to the visual elements so key to Sebald's project when we read the restitutive gestures of the text in parallel with the gestures performed by Sebald as artist in the attempted restoration of sight to the blind.

NOTES

1 As well as Duttlinger, see for instance Jonathan Long (2003), Silke Horstkotte (2005), Lise Patt and Christel Dillbohner (2007).

2 For examples of Sebald scholarship which considers visual elements other than photography see Anne Fuchs (2006), Mattias Frey (2007), Laura Mulvey (2006) and Robert Buch (2010).

3 Critics have shown how these likenesses, read via Wittgenstein as *Familienähnlichkeiten*, extend to Sebald and his narrator, situating them in an uneasy relation to the emigrant protagonists, either overshadowing them, or emerging in composite form as fifth and sixth emigrants (see Christopher Gregory-Guider, 2005b and Susanne Finke, 1997). Jan Ceuppens suggests that Sebald is found in his text as a sort of Galtonian composite photograph (2006: 256).

4 I am grateful to Christina Howells, Andrew Webber and Stephen Joy for their discussions which helped to develop this argument.

5 Derrida has featured relatively infrequently in Sebald scholarship and Sebald himself seems to have shown little interest in poststructuralism or deconstruction, never mentioning them in interviews. Nevertheless, Derrida's deconstructive project has a distinct resonance for post-war, memory and trauma studies, all of which have a strong interest in Sebald's work. Paul Celan, in particular, offers an intermediary figure between Sebald and Derrida (see Ceuppens 2007), as might Walter Benjamin.

6 As Michael Wetzel notes in the afterword to his German translation, Derrida's title is a teasingly multivalent one, playing on the ideas of blinding, blind memories, memories of blindness, but, not least, also on the fact that the exhibition forces him to make a selection from a literally blinding abundance of images (Derrida 1997: 130). Derrida notes how he was also suffering from a sort of visual dysfunction at the time, a facial paralysis which affected his reflex ability to open and close his eye and which even afterwards left his face 'still haunted by a ghost of disfiguration' (Derrida 1993: 32). Through his selection of drawings which often show an obscured or shaded gaze, he puts his own blindness on display, but always in the act of distracting our gaze through these other images.

7 This book, a collection of Sebald's micropoems accompanied by a series of Tripp's hyperreal etchings of eyes, might offer a kind of allegory for the text–image relationship which informs Sebald's oeuvre. *Unerzählt* represents a later stage of Sebald's otherwise often unresolved engagement with different representational modes, where the status of images can be modified by textual inscription and narrative statements can be overshadowed by the insertion of visual elements.

8 The magnifying glass is found already in the hand of the narrator in the story preceding 'Max Ferber'. In 'Ambros Adelwarth', he recalls using the instrument to help him look for the source of the Hudson River, but he becomes lost in the other geographical features schematized on the map (2008b: 155; 2002e: 106).

9 Brad Prager describes how this painting produces disorientation in the reader as well as the protagonist, since Sebald's use of the fresco involves a viewing not intended by the artist (Prager 2005: 97).

10 Sebald speaks of the symbolic function he gives to dust, in particular, in order to circumscribe the violence of the Holocaust (Wachtel 2007: 53–4).

11 For a discussion of how Sebald's text–image relationship functions as the rhetorical device ekphrasis, see Horstkotte (2006).

12 The artist's choice of Max is also derivative, his full name being Friedrich Maximilian (2008b: 265; 2002e: 178).

13 According to Wohlleben, the high resolution and white flecks cause the reader to doubt whether this is a photograph or a photo-realist painting (Wohlleben 2007: 9).

14 Katja Garloff (2004) investigates the possibility of the emigrant as witness, although not using the paradigm of vision, as does Jan Cueppens (2007).

15 Together with the narrator's partner, Clara, the combined work of father and son with surgical and optical instruments evokes Hoffmann's fascination with traumatized and uncanny vision in *Der Sandmann*.

16 Sándor Ferenczi uses the term scotomization to describe how the traumatic moment is burnt onto the retina like photographic imaging, producing a point which comes to

mark the vision of the traumatized victim as a blind spot, persistently present in the visual field, but never visible in a meaningful sense (Ferenczi 1998: 113).

17 Striations figuring traumatized and traumatizing vision in metonymic mode offer a further example of the vision given by cutting the eye in the surgery of the blind. Both tropes are used in that primal scene of cinema's traumatic cut, Louis Bunuel's *Un Chien andalou*. Here, a striped tie and a striped box repeat and multiply its opening scene which slices an eye.

18 See for example, Stefan Gunther (2006).

6

'LIKE REFUGEES WHO HAVE COME THROUGH DREADFUL ORDEALS': THE THEME OF THE ANGLO-IRISH IN *DIE RINGE DES SATURN. EINE ENGLISCHE WALLFAHRT*

Helen Finch

INTRODUCTION

Jorge Luis Borges's short story 'The Theme of the Traitor and the Hero' (1944) sets its action 'in an oppressed yet stubborn country – Poland, Ireland, the republic of Venice, some South American or Balkan state [. . .] for convenience's sake; in Ireland, let us also say.'[1] The short story deals with a fictional nineteenth-century Irish conspirator, Fergus Kilpatrick, and his great-grandson, Ryan, who is writing the narrative of Kilpatrick's life. As he researches, he discovers that Kilpatrick's biography seems entirely copied from existing works of literature: 'The idea that history might have copied history is mind-boggling enough; that history should copy *literature* is inconceivable' (Borges 1998: 144). Given the story's arch introduction, scholars are divided as to whether the Irish theme is an essential part of the Borges story, or whether it invokes Ireland entirely 'for convenience's sake', as 'a red herring or a foil' (Finian 2010: 759). Given that the brief story refers to Yeats, Browning, Shakespeare, Leibniz, Chesterton and others within barely four pages, it is debatable whether the Irish location and tragic heroics of the Borges story are merely a pretext for writing about 'some South American state' – Borges's native Argentina – or whether they serve rather to suggest a supranational labyrinth of literary intertextuality.

Similar questions about the relevance and pretextual nature of Irish history also arise when discussing the presence of the Anglo-Irish themes in W. G. Sebald's *Die Ringe des Saturn (The Rings of Saturn)*. 'The Theme of the Traitor and the Hero' shares several concerns with *The Rings of Saturn*, besides a densely intertextual prosodics and an inquiry into the nature of history. Rebecca Sheehan, for instance, suggests that Borges's reference to Yeats's *The Tower* (1928) at the beginning of the story 'locates the disturbing conflation of subject and object beside a disruption to

111

diachronic history where the present, rather than being newer than the past, exists in limbo with it' (Sheehan 2009: 25). This suggestion of the simultaneity of history and present is also key to the textual strategies of Sebald's *The Rings of Saturn*, a text which owes an explicit debt to Borges, through a direct reference to his story 'Tlön. Uqbar. Orbis Tertius' (1944). This story provides the Sebaldian narrator with an allegory for the negative dialectics of Enlightenment that inform his entire text.[2] Gazing upon swallows at sunset, he tells us that he has read in 'Tlön, Uqbar, Orbis Tertius' 'von der Rettung eines ganzen Amphitheaters durch ein paar Vögel' ('of how a few birds saved an entire amphitheatre' (Sebald 1997b: 87; 1999a: 67)). Borges states that in Tlön, things 'tend to grow vague or "sketchy" and to lose detail when they begin to be forgotten' (Borges 1998: 78). However, memory can save objects from destruction, even the memory of beasts such as horses or birds. Sebald uses Borges's short story to hint at the redemptive potential of memory in the face of the terrible disintegration of the material world by radically idealist labyrinths. In 'Tlön. Uqbar. Orbis Tertius', this labyrinth is represented by the unreal world of Tlön. Sebald explains it thus: 'Die labyrinthische Konstruktions Tlöns, so merkt ein Nachtrag aus dem Jahr 1947 an, steht im Begriff, die bekannte Welt auszulöschen' ('The labyrinthine construction of Tlön, reads a note added to the text in 1947, is on the point of blotting out the known world' (Sebald 1997b: 91; 1999a: 70)). In Borges's story, which was in fact published in 1944, the historico-political import of Tlön's colonization of the material world is made explicit: 'Ten years ago, any symmetry, any system with an appearance of order – dialectical materialism, anti-Semitism, Nazism – could spellbind and hypnotize mankind. How could the world not fall under the sway of Tlön, how could it not yield to the vast and minutely detailed evidence of an ordered planet?' (Borges 198: 81). Borges here describes the destructive effect of Enlightenment in the twentieth century. Just as, in Tlön, the memory of birds and beasts can save the material world from destruction through forgetting, in *The Rings of Saturn*, a baroque prosodics of commemoration, materialism and mourning provides a source of resistance to such idealist and technocratic systemization. This literary resistance takes the form of a commitment to forgotten histories and figures stranded at the margins of history, exemplified by the Irish freedom fighter Roger Casement. Literary resistance to totalizing domination is thus, for Sebald, intimately bound up with the literary project of restitution.

Barbara Hui further argues that Sebald's literature of restitution is even more precisely invested in the local, and indeed shows an excessive commitment to the local material landscape of East Anglia at the expense of accurately representing further-flung marginal histories. While Sebald names the place where Borges wrote 'Tlön, Uqar, Orbis Tertius' as 'Argentina' (Sebald 1997b: 87; 1999a: 67), Hui notes that 'Salto Oriental' is in fact in Uruguay. Hui concludes that this inaccuracy demonstrates that 'Sebald is more interested in composing a cogent work of art and gathering compelling examples of the historical cycle of rise and decline than he is in exhaustively researching the basis of his descriptions for strict factual accuracy' (Hui 2010: 284). If, then, Borges provides for Sebald a compelling set of allegories for his wider prosodics of the negative effects of Enlightenment, and of memory and resistance, material evidence for which he gathers only in the East Anglian landscape, are the Irish and Anglo-Irish moments in *The Rings of Saturn* equally pretextual? Are they merely glancing references to what Hui terms 'far-off lands' that are irrelevant to the primacy of local East Anglian stories? In this essay, I suggest that the Anglo-Irish figures and moments in *The Rings of Saturn* are emblematic of certain key concerns of Sebald's, namely exile, the long history and after-effects of colonialism, the possibility of a literature of resistance, and the link between political oppression and the destruction of nature. Anglo-Irish figures appear at three main points in the text: first, the Irish freedom fighter Roger Casement appears in the context of a discussion of Joseph Conrad; second, Sebald links the poet Edward FitzGerald's poetic production to his Anglo-Irish ancestry; and third, the text's narrator himself wanders into a semi-ruined Anglo-Irish Big House near the Slieve Bloom mountains, and spends a night in it as the guest of the Ashbury family. This essay considers the extent to which these figures are linked in their poetic significance, and to what extent they are, as in the debate surrounding 'The Theme of the Traitor', merely a pretext for discussing concerns at the heart of Sebald's prosodics. Do the liminal Anglo-Irish characters stand in for the fate of humanity in general at the end of the twentieth century? Can Sebald be said to have an 'Irish' theme at all? If so, by eliding the specific complexities of Anglo-Irish history, does the pretextual nature of these references undermine Sebald's commitment to a literature of restitution?

Certainly, the themes of Irish history are close to Sebald's overarching concerns in *The Rings of Saturn*. In *Heathcliff and the Great Hunger* (1995), Terry Eagleton puts forward some provocative Benjaminian analyses of Irish history and literature, which suggest in turn why Irish themes might have attracted Sebald. Eagleton suggests that the Irish Famine is a catastrophe at the heart of Irish natural history that parallels Auschwitz, as it demonstrates how nature wreaks vengeance on history. 'Ireland's disaster was a kind of inverted image of European turmoil, one which you suffer rather than create, which strips culture to the poor forked Beckettian creature and which, in threatening to slip below the level of meaning itself, offers to deny you even the meagre consolation of tragedy' (Eagleton 1995: 12). Eagleton argues that, in the wake of the brutal depopulation of the Famine, Irish landscapes are 'decipherable texts rather than aesthetic objects, places made precious or melancholic by the resonance of the human' (1995: 6). Such a reading of the Irish landscape is in keeping with the melancholy prosodics of *The Rings of Saturn*, and would allow it metonymically to stand, as does the East Anglian landscape, at once for the twin European catastrophes of Enlightenment and Shoah, and for the longer natural history of destruction. However, Sebald does not address himself directly to the catastrophe of the Irish Famine, nor, unlike Borges's Irish traitor-hero, are his Irish figures 'native', Catholic or 'mere' representations of the literary trope of the 'imaginary Irish peasant' (as Edward Hirsch has termed him, Hirsch 1991). Instead, the Irish themes in *The Rings of Saturn* are more properly Protestant or Anglo-Irish themes. The term Anglo-Irish describes a disparate group of Protestant English settlers who sought their fortune and set up in grand style as the landlord class of Ireland in the wake of the religious wars and English conquests of Ireland in the seventeenth century. The Anglo-Irish never became 'more Irish than the Irish themselves', but instead occupied a space of shifting loyalties. In the nineteenth century, in the wake of the Act of Union in 1801, they oriented themselves towards English elites; in the twentieth century, in the wake of the Irish revolution, they were left stranded. Since they were not a diaspora with a distinct culture, but rather hybridized colonizers, they could not survive the destruction of their economic base by a series of land Acts that forcibly sold their estates back to the Irish peasantry.[3]

Casement, FitzGerald and the Ashburys exist in varying relationships to this post colonial narrative of conquest and loss. The common thread binding the three sets of figures, however, is their exile status. This distinguishes Sebald's Irish themes from those of, say, Heinrich Böll, who finds in Irish rural tradition and landscape an idealized counterpart to historically burdened German modernity.[4] The exile is, in Sebald's literature, the paradigmatic figure of modernity and of postmodernity. The exile is at once the victim of the destructive processes of history and, by virtue of being already an outsider, its privileged witness. Nonetheless, Sebald recognizes the double-edged status of the Anglo-Irish in the negative dialectic of Enlightenment. The Anglo-Irish are simultaneously both victims of the destructive progress of history (as illustrated by the Ashburys, living in a crumbling ruin at the bottom of the Slieve Bloom mountains) and among its first agents (as illustrated by the wealthy and powerful Anglo-Norman FitzGerald family). They thus provide a link between feudal premodernity, capitalist modernity and our own apocalyptic postmodern era. Again, in contradistinction to Böll's Irish peasants, who live close to the land and whose society is presented as the authentic expression of *Heimat*, Sebald's Anglo-Irish characters are always already irrevocably dislocated in time and space, uneasy 'hybrids', as Declan Kiberd terms the descendants of Anglo-Norman settlers (Kiberd 1995: 9). In this sense, they are both exiles in time and place, and members of a deterritorialized community in the sense of Deleuze and Guattari's theses in *Kafka: Towards a Minor Literature*.[5] Thus, the hybridity and deterritorial-ized status of the Anglo-Irish affords them access to liminal spaces and experiences, spaces in the interstices of the otherwise unremittingly calamitous world of the oppressive Enlightenment described in *The Rings of Saturn*.[6] The three sections of this essay examine the different ways in which the Anglo-Irish figures of *The Rings of Saturn* address these Sebaldian complexes.

ROGER CASEMENT

The Irish human rights defender, republican rebel and homosexual martyr Roger Casement appears in *The Rings of Saturn* as a figure from Joseph Conrad's Congo diaries. The narrative sequence is striking for Sebald's glowing representation of the complex and shadowy figure of Casement, and reveals most of the key moments that Sebald associates with the Anglo-Irish. Conrad becomes marked with guilt for entering the Congo – 'die Mühen, unter denen er zu leiden hat, [befreien] ihn nicht von der Schuld, die er durch seine bloße Anwesenheit im Kongo auf sich lädt' ('his own travails did not absolve him from the guilt which he had incurred by his mere presence in the Congo' (1997b: 147; 1999a: 120)), and he subsequently attempts redemption by producing his literature of restitution, *Heart of Darkness* (1902). By contrast, Casement's redemption from imperial complicity is achieved by heroic martyrdom. Thus, Anne Fuchs refers to the Casement section as a 'hagiography', portraying a 'tragischen Helden, der als Einzelkämpfer den heroischen Versuch unternimmt, in den schlechten Geschichtsverlauf verändernd einzugreifen' ('tragic hero, a solitary fighter who undertakes an heroic attempt to intervene to change the bad course of history' (Fuchs 2004: 200; my translation)). She correctly argues 'wie sehr es Sebald um eine Stilisierung Casements zum isolierten Fürsprecher der unterdrückten Kolonialvölker zu tun ist' ('how crucial it is to Sebald to portray Casement as an isolated advocate of the suppressed colonial peoples' (Fuchs 2004: 202; my translation)). Again, Casement is unusual in Sebald's work for the positive representation of his engagement in politically motivated violence. Heroic figures who engage in military adventures are, in Sebald's work, frequently exemplars of the dialectic of Enlightenment, rash adventurers whose grandiose plans come to grief and bring historical catastrophe in their wake, such as the 'Corsican comet' Napoleon. Moreover, elsewhere in *The Rings of Saturn*, minor nationalisms such as the Irish struggle are exemplified by the destructive Balkan turmoil prior to the First World War, and minor nationalist heroes by the luckless Gavrilo Princip. Princip's assassination of Franz Ferdinand sets in motion a European 'Unglückschronik' ('chronicle of disaster' (Sebald 1997b: 118; 1999a: 95)), and the Shoah is foreshadowed in his subsequent imprisonment in Theresienstadt, 'wo er im April 1918 der ihn seit seiner Jugend langsam zerfressenden Knochentuberkulose erlag' ('where in April 1918, he died of the bone tuberculosis that had been consuming him since his early youth' (Sebald 1997b: 119; 1999a: 96)). Princip's actions are thus bound into the longer history of the European catastrophe in the twentieth century. Casement's actions, too, foreshadow the historical tragedy to come in the Irish Civil war of 1922. His heroic revolt against Belgian and British colonialism, described in the fifth part of *The Rings of Saturn*, will indirectly lead to the independence of Ireland and the consequent isolation of the Ashburys, described in the eighth part. However, this is an indirect and subtextual link, rather than an explicit causal link such as that which Sebald makes between the assassination of Franz Ferdinand and the genocide both of the Jewish people in Theresienstadt and of the Serbian people in the Balkans. By way of contrast to the misguided Princip, Casement is presented as a moral man of clear judgement and right action; for Conrad, he is the 'einzige[r] geradsinnige[r] Mensch' ('only man of integrity' (Sebald 1997b: 126; 1999a: 104)) in a corrupt Congo.

Sebald directly links Casement's moral rectitude to his engagement in the cause of Irish freedom. 'Es lag in der Linie der Konsequenz' ('It was only to be expected'), Sebald tells us, 'daß er dabei schließlich auf die irische, das heißt auf seine eigene Frage stieß' ('that in due course he should hit upon the Irish question – that is to say, his own' (Sebald 1997b: 156; 1999a: 129)). However, the 'Irish question' is not quite Casement's own. Both Conrad and Casement are portrayed by Sebald as deterritorialized, men in self-chosen exile from their colonized homelands. (Indeed Conrad is further displaced out of his native Polish language into French and then English, while Sebald himself writes in German, despite living in England; linguistic displacement and hybrid linguistic affiliations also seem to form an essential part of a literature of resistance.) Whereas Conrad is an adventurer, journeying out from one empire into the heart of darkness of another in the spirit of exploration, Sebald depicts Casement as a man journeying away from imperial complicity to national reintegration. However, due to his hybridity, Casement's exilic status is still maintained, despite his *ritorno in patria*: he is, as Sebald points out, the son of a Catholic mother and an Ulster Protestant father. Casement's hybrid nature is emphasized throughout Sebald's account: for instance, the one image of Casement that is retained by the Sebaldian narrator from the BBC television documentary about Casement and the Congo is Conrad's description of seeing Casement 'nur mit einem Stecken bewaffnet und nur in Begleitung eines Loanda-Jungen und seiner englischen Bulldoggen Biddy und Paddy in die gewaltige Wildnis aufbrechen' ('swinging a crookhandled stick, with two bulldogs: Paddy (white) and Biddy (brindle) at his heels and a Loanda boy carrying a bundle' (Sebald 1997b: 126; 1999a: 104)).

The hybridity and liminality inherent in the Anglo-Irish position is clear here: Casement is accompanied by English bulldogs with Irish names, is perceived in a state between waking and dream and is radically deterritorialized, given that he is in the Congolese wilderness, yet appears 'als kehrte er gerade von einem Nachmittagsspaziergang im Hyde Park zurück' ('as though he had been for a stroll in the park' (Sebald 1997b: 126; 1999a: 104)). Indeed, Michael Hulse, when translating this section, noted that Sebald had made several changes to Conrad's original description in his German version that emphasize this aura of hybridity and exterritorialization: 'He added the comment that, in the Congo, the wilderness surrounds every settlement; he added the adjective "englisch" to the bulldogs, but removed their colours, [. . .] the park had become not just any park but one iconically recognizable to every German reader, Hyde Park' (Hulse 2011: 197). The hybrid Casement can bear witness to the horrors of the Congo, whereas the Congolese victims of Belgian atrocity, excluded from the bounds of the regulated public sphere as *homo sacer*, cannot.[7] Equally, Casement's privileged position as an Anglo-Irishman gives him precisely the critical perspective and connections that he needs to engage in the Irish cause. Casement, by education and upbringing 'gehörte seiner ganzen Erziehung nach zu denjenigen, deren Lebensaufgabe darin bestand, die englische Vorherrschaft über Irland aufrechtzuerhalten' (was predestined to be one of those whose mission in life was the upholding of English rule in Ireland' (Sebald 1997b: 157; 1999a: 129)), but he identifies with the cause of the indigenous 'weißen Indianer von Irland'. Casement's commitment to the Irish cause is shown as grounded in a transnational understanding of empire, connected to the enslavement of Irish people in the West Indies and their forcible expatriation via emigration; by contrast to Casement, Sebald portrays the Irish-Irish rebels of the Easter Rising as culpably romantic in their nationalism. 'Daß die Idealisten, die Dichter, Gewerkschafter und Lehrer, die in Dublin die Verantwortung trugen, sich selbst und diejenigen, die auf sie hörten, dennoch in einem siebentägigen Straßenkampf aufopferten, war eine andere Sache' ('If the idealists, poets, trade unionists and teachers who bore the responsibility in Dublin nonetheless sacrificed themselves and those who obeyed them in seven days of street fighting, that was none of his doing' (Sebald 1997b: 159; 1999a: 131)).

Casement's hybrid or liminal status is also shown in his queer sexuality, which once again is part of the truth of Casement's life that the Sebaldian narrator wishes to rescue from the decades of oblivion in which it has been shrouded. Sebald writes:

> Der einzige Schluß, der daraus gezogen werden kann, ist der, daß es möglicherweise gerade die Homosexualität Casements war, die ihn befähigte, über die Grenzen der gesellschaftlichen Klassen und der Rassen hinweg die andauernde Unterdrückung, Ausbeutung, Versklavung und Verschrottung derjenigen zu erkennen, die am weitesten entfernt waren von den Zentren der Macht. (Sebald 1997b: 134)

> (We may draw from this the conclusion that it was precisely Casement's homosexuality that sensitized him to the continuing oppression, exploitation, enslavement and destruction, across the borders of social class and race, of those who were furthest from the centres of power. (Sebald 1999a: 162))

Sebald asserts that homosexuality, which doomed Roger Casement to execution, enabled a politically transgressive vision. Here, an essay by Colm Tóibín on Casement in the *New York Review of Books*, whose starting point is this very moment in *The Rings of Saturn*, is particularly relevant: 'Afterward, when Sebald, intrigued by his own vague and twilit memories of the program, sets about finding out what he can about Casement, his imagination is fired by the relationship between Casement and Joseph Conrad' (Tóibín 2004). Later, Tóibín writes:

we all bring our own concerns to Casement's story: Sebald is interested in the literary connections; Dudgeon is interested in the gay Casement; McCormack entertains the idea of the text as shifting and unstable. (Tóibín 2004)

Sebald describes the history of Conrad and Casement as 'die von mir damals in Southwold (unverantwortlicherweise, wie ich meine) verschlafene Geschichte' ('the story I slept through that night in Southwold' (Sebald 1997b: 127; 1999a: 104)). In the original German version, crucially, the act of sleeping through the story is described in parentheses as 'irresponsible'. In keeping with the Sebaldian narrator's commitment to a literature of restitution, he devotes a chapter of the text to reconstructing their story and making good his sin of irresponsible sleep. As Peter Arnds has shown, *lethe* (sleep and forgetting) forms a key binary pair with *aletheia* (memory or truth) in *The Rings of Saturn* (Arnds 2010). Conrad cites Casement's commitment to *aletheia* as a contrast with his own culpable *lethe*, writing of how Casement 'Dinge berichten könnte, die er, Korzeniowski seit langem zu vergessen versuche' ('could tell things that he, Korzeniowski, had long been trying to forget' (Sebald 1997b: 154; 1999a: 127).

In bearing witness to suppressed injustice, both to the genocidal crimes of the Congo and to Casement's own martyrdom, Sebald's poetic mission mirrors Casement's political mission to speak truth to King Leopold of Belgium. Whereas the veterans of the Irish freedom movement found it unthinkable that one of their martyrs should be victim to the 'englischer Laster' ('English vice' (Sebald 1997b: 162; 1999a: 131)), and adjusted their official history of Ireland accordingly, Sebald attempts to restore Casement to his rightful heroic status. Yet, as Tóibín shows, the discovery of the 'truth' of Casement's diaries in 1994 has led to yet more projection and fantasy being invested both in the historical and in the textual Casement. Far from establishing the 'truth' of a queer martyr, they make Casement a nexus for widespread Irish public discourses surrounding queer rights, homophobia, the validity of the Irish revolution of 1916 and many more. Sebald's hagiography of Casement provides one possible reading of these complex discourses, but cannot establish a historical truth.

EDWARD FITZGERALD

If Casement is a deterritorialized Anglo-Irish freedom fighter, Edward FitzGerald, composer-translator of *The Rubá'iyát of Omar Khayyam*, is one of Sebald's melancholy bachelor-poets, akin to the hapless Algernon Swinburne. Nonetheless, the Anglo-Irish elements of his narrative echo those that we have already seen in Sebald's depiction of Casement. Like Casement, FitzGerald shares the privilege of the Anglo-Irish classes; like Casement, he too reacts with horror against such privilege. As Hutchinson says, 'Sebald lässt keinen Zweifel daran, dass er FitzGeralds "ekzentrische Gewohnheiten" als Widerstand gegen seine eigene Klasse versteht' ('Sebald leaves us in no doubt that he understands FitzGerald's "excentricities" as an act of resistance against his own class' (Hutchinson 2009b: 128; my translation)). In Sebald's *Arbeitsbibliothek* in the German Literary Archive in Marbach, Peter de Polnay's *Into an Old Room – The Paradox of Edward FitzGerald* (1950), the source text for much of Sebald's biographical material on FitzGerald, makes the Anglo-Irish nature of this class explicit. De Polnay writes:

> then and yesterday the Irish were all over the place, and are certainly everywhere to-day. To let his eye roam as far as the little tree near to the hedge beyond the garden and at the same time to see the minarets of Khorassan, had been granted to FitzGerald thanks to his origin and background. But the background often triumphed over the origin, which was one of the reasons why he stayed with the little tree and cared not to know the minarets. (de Polnay 1950: 10)

Just as Sebald attributes Roger Casement's imaginative solidarity with the oppressed to his Anglo-Irish perspective, so de Polnay ascribes FitzGerald's deterritorialized imagination to his Anglo-Irish origins. Indeed, he shares with Casement a hybridity between Protestant and Catholic origins, since, despite his Protestant parents, he numbered among his ancestors Irish Catholic rebels against British occupation: 'his background and early surroundings [...] were completely contradictory', argues de Polnay, 'and this must have contributed a great deal in forming his character' (de Polnay 1950: 10). Sebald describes the Anglo-Irish culture of FitzGerald's ancestors solely in terms of repression and greed:

> Der Klan der FitzGeralds war anglo-normannischen Ursprungs und über sechshundert Jahre ansässig gewesen [...] [Das] Familienvermögen [...] bestand, abgesehen von den Besitzungen in England, in erster Linie aus den schier unübersehbaren irischen Ländereien, aus der gesamten, auf diesen Ländereien sich befindenden beweglichen und unbeweglichen Habe sowie aus einer sich nach Tausenden zählenden, zumindest in der Praxis noch so gut wie leibeigenen Bauernschaft. (Sebald 1997b: 234)

> (The FitzGeralds were an old Anglo-Norman family and had lived in Ireland for more than six hundred years [...] The family fortune [...] consisted principally, apart from properties in England, of their vast land holdings in Ireland, together with the goods and chattels, and hosts of peasants who were effectively no more than their serfs. (Sebald 1999a: 197))

The reference to the FitzGeralds' 'enserfed' tenants draws a link to the other colonial practices exposed and condemned throughout Sebald's text, and confirms the Anglo-Irish complicity in the longer history of European colonialism prior to Enlightened modernity. They thus occupy a position in Sebald's natural history of destruction prior even to what Jonathan Long refers to as the two-hundred-year 'époque de longue durée' of modernity in Sebald's work (Long 2007: 170).

119

As de Polnay's account shows, unlike Sebald's Casement, FitzGerald does not wander the globe seeking to expiate his inherited feudal guilt. Rather, due to the 'Abneigung, die FitzGerald bereits in der Kindheit gegen seine eigene Klasse gefaßt hatte' ('aversion that FitzGerald had had since childhood to his own class' (Sebald 1997b: 241; 1999a: 202)), he eschews the dungeon-like family manor in favour of a 'winziges zweizimmriges Cottage am Rande des Parks' ('tiny two-roomed cottage on the perimeter of the estate' (Sebald 1997b: 237; 1999a: 199)). FitzGerald prefers elective affinities with distant and long-dead writers, such as Khayyam and Mme de Sévigné, to participating in the material customs of his class, such as 'das Ritual des gemeinsamen Tafelns' ('the ritual of communal dining' (Sebald 1997b: 240; 1999a: 202)). Moreover, like Casement, Sebald's FitzGerald is homosexual, thereby refusing to perpetuate the oppressive dynastic politics of his clan; but, unlike Casement, he does not engage in any actual sexual encounters, and instead is unrequitedly in love with 'eine Art Idealbild' ('the personification of an ideal' (1997b: 240; 1999a: 201)), his close friend William Browne. Sebald tells us, 'Die Liebeserklärung, die FitzGerald wahrscheinlich nie zu machen wagte, findet sich erst in dem Beileidsbrief an die Witwe' ('The love which FitzGerald probably never dared to declare was not expressed until he wrote his letter of condolence to Browne's widow' (1997b: 240; 1999a: 202)). In fact, de Polnay's biography of FitzGerald cites Havelock Ellis here, who records merely that FitzGerald wrote to Mrs Browne that he 'used to wander about the shore at night longing for some fellow to accost me who might give some promise of filling up a very vacant place in my heart' – while certainly queer, this is not quite an explicit romantic declaration of love for Browne (de Polnay 1950: 236). Thus Sebald's account embellishes and romanticizes the nexus of Anglo-Irishness and queerness found in his account of Casement, thereby underlining FitzGerald's outsider status and linking both figures in an exile from the reproductive and acquisitive patterns of their Anglo-Irish class. If Sebald ascribes Casement's passion for human rights to his homosexuality, de Polnay suggests that FitzGerald's poetry of reconciliation comes precisely from the denial of his homosexuality: 'It is feasible that if he had led an actual and active sex life the Rubá'iyát might never have been translated' (de Polnay 1950: 96). Sebald makes of FitzGerald's homosexuality a romantic literary inspiration, whereas both de Polnay and his source, Havelock Ellis, suggest that he was more or less unaware of his true sexual feelings.

Thus, Sebald makes of FitzGerald a somewhat queerer bachelor and exile than his source material would suggest. The Rubá'iyát becomes the medium in which FitzGerald uses his exile status in order to make good the depredations perpetrated by the property-owning classes; as Hutchinson says, 'der Widerstand FitzGeralds schlägt sich in seinen literarischen Tätigkeiten nieder' ('Fitzgerald's resistance finds expression in his literary activities' (Hutchinson 2009b: 128; my translation)). Although he embarks on countless failed literary projects, the Rubá'iyát is his sole success. His English verse is in itself a literature of restitution. Sebald tells us,

120

Die von ihm zu diesem Zweck ausgesonnenen englischen Verse fingieren in ihrer scheinbar absichtslosen Schönheit eine jeden Anspruch von Autorschaft weit hinter sich zurücklassende Anonymität und verweisen, Wort für Wort, auf einen unsichtbaren Punkt, an dem das mittelalterliche Morgenland und das erlöschende Abendland einander anders als im unseligen Verlauf der Geschichte begegnen dürfen. (Sebald 1997b: 200)

(The English verses he devised for the purpose, which radiate with a pure, seemingly unselfconscious beauty, feign an anonymity that disdains even the least claim to authorship, and draw us, word by word, to an invisible point where the mediaeval orient and the fading occident can come together in a way never allowed them by the calamitous course of history. (Sebald 1999a: 238))

Like Casement, FitzGerald too heals the wounds of history, though in an imaginary, poetic space rather than in the heroic world of human rights activism. What Casement achieves by intervening in the course of history, FitzGerald achieves in poetry, although both eventually suffer the depredations of domination on their own bodies.

THE ASHBURYS OF SLIEVE BLOOM

As with Roger Casement, Sebald first encounters FitzGerald in the liminal space of a dream. He describes playing dominoes with FitzGerald in his garden: 'Jenseits des Blumengartens erstreckte sich bis an den Weltrand, wo die Minarette von Khoranan aufragten, ein gleichmäßig grüner und vollkommen leerer Park' ('Beyond the flower garden an even green park, utterly deserted, extended to the very edge of the world, where the minarets of Khorasan soared' (Sebald 1997b: 247; 1999a: 208)). The reference to the minaret marking the edge of FitzGerald's park comes, as we have seen, from de Polnay's biography. However, Sebald's dream links FitzGerald to a third set of Anglo-Irish figures, the Ashburys of Slieve Bloom: 'Es war jedoch nicht der Park der FitzGeralds in Boulge, sondern der eines am Fuß der Slieve Bloom Mountains in Irland gelegenen Landsitzes' ('It was not, however, the park of the FitzGerald estate at Boulge, but that of a country house at the foot of the Slieve Bloom Mountains in Ireland where I had been a guest for a short time some years ago' (Sebald 1997b: 247; 1999a: 208)). This dream brings the narrative of *The Rings of Saturn* to the territory of Ireland itself. However, this is not a reterritorialization of the narrative, any more than Casement's return home is a happy reconciliation with his Irish *Heimat*. Mrs Ashbury, the head of the family, tells the narrator that when she moved to Ireland in 1946, 'sie habe damals [...] von den irischen Verhältnissen, die ihr bis heute fremd geblieben seien, nicht die geringste Ahnung gehabt' ('she had not had the slightest notions of Ireland's Troubles, and to this day they remained alien to her' (Sebald 1997b: 255; 1999a: 214)). The Ashburys remain exiles within their crumbling mansion, radically trapped within their minor culture. If FitzGerald withdraws from the world of feudal privilege into the world of the poetic imagination, the tide of history ebbs away from the Ashburys of Slieve Bloom, leaving them stranded in Gothic penury; the depredations of history are worked out not on their bodies, as with Casement and FitzGerald, but on the fabric of their Big House and gardens, which slowly fall into disrepair. This slow decay, the Sebaldian narrator suggests, is the way in which the Ashburys do penance and are absolved of their role in the colonization of Ireland and the negative history of human oppression: Mrs Ashbury challenges the narrator with an unspoken demand: 'ich möge bei ihnen bleiben und ihr Tag für Tag unschuldiger werdendes Leben teilen' ('to stay there with them and share in a life that was becoming more innocent with every day that passed' (Sebald 1997b: 262; 1999a: 220)). Equally (and like Roger Casement and Edward FitzGerald), the Ashburys are now no longer able to participate in the marital rituals of their class. The three adult daughters are 'wie von einem bösen Bannspruch getroffene Riesenkinder' ('like giant children under an evil spell' (Sebald 1997b: 252; 1999a: 212)), left unmarried because 'die Gesellschaft, zu der wir [the Ashburys] gehörten, längst schon zusammengebrochen war' ('the society we [the Ashburys] were part of had long since collapsed' (Sebald 1997b: 261; 1999a: 219)). The enforced chastity of the Ashburys, like the homosexuality of Casement and FitzGerald, prevents them from reproducing their class and, hence, the history of domination of the Anglo-Irish. To return to Borges, Sebald appraises the aphorism from 'Tlön, Uqbar, Orbis Tertius' that 'das Grauenerregende an den Spiegeln, und im übrigen auch an dem Akt der Paarung, bestünde darin, daß sie die Zahl der Menschen vervielfachen' ('the disturbing thing about mirrors, and also the act of copulation, is that they multiply the number of human beings') as 'denkwürdig scheinende [...] Sentenz' ('a memorable remark' (Sebald 1997b: 90; 1999a: 70)). In keeping with this aphorism, rather than merely refusing to reproduce their own class, Sebald's Anglo-Irish characters refuse to reproduce humankind and, hence, to extend human domination over the natural world. Their condition of exile and profound exterritorialization further becomes emblematic of humankind in general at the end of the history of destruction: 'It seems to me sometimes that we never got used to being on this earth', Mrs Ashbury tells the Sebaldian narrator (Sebald 1997b: 262; 1999a: 220).

Far more than the tales of FitzGerald and Casement, the tale of the Ashburys fits very closely the classic mystique of the Anglo-Irish Big House narrative, a stock trope of Anglo-Irish literature. The Ashburys are clinging on to existence in the ruins of their once grand house, living apparently off air while desultorily planning to take in guests. Matters were not always thus; the narrator is shown a film of the glory days of the house, when servants kept the house immaculate and the estate was run to keep the farm. But now, the lands are sold, the Ashburys had to give up farming since they could not pay the labourers' wages, they have sold the family silver and remain tied to the wreck of their once grand house. Mrs Ashbury tells the Sebaldian narrator that their fate is typical of the Anglo-Irish gentry in the twentieth century, except that they shared in the general decline rather later in the day. Moreover, she says, they are in a sense lucky, for unlike so many others, their house was not burned. The Ashburys are quintessential exiles, like the Sebaldian narrator himself: 'die Ashburys [lebten] unter ihrem eigenen Dach wie Flüchtlinge, die Furchtbares mitgemacht haben und die es nicht wagen, an dem Platz, an dem sie gestrandet sind, sich niederzulassen' ('the Ashburys lived under their roof like refugees who have come through dreadful ordeals and do not now dare to settle in the place where they have ended up' (Sebald 1997b: 250; 1999a: 210)). Thus, although Sebald makes play with the clichés of the Anglo-Irish 'Big House' novel such as Elizabeth Bowen's *The Last September*, the characterization of the Ashburys as strangers under their own roof, yet strangers who are complicit in the natural history of destruction, means that they serve to prefigure the diasporic fate of humanity in general in the post-industrial era.

In Sebald's work, though, the depiction of history is never a direct record, and what seems to be literary realism is anything but. Sebald aims to achieve the Barthesian *effet de réel* (Angier 1997: 48) – a simulacrum that appears flawless but that reveals itself, on careful inspection, to be merely a backdrop that is flung over the abyss that lies beneath all human endeavour. To claim to be able to reproduce perfectly a historical moment or actor would be to exercise the same kind of tyranny of the gaze over a suffering history as the panorama at Waterloo that Sebald condemns in the middle of his narrative about Conrad and Casement. Sebald's seemingly realistic account of the fate of the Ashbury family is shot through with intertextual devices that make it clear that this is no realistic depiction of a historical diaspora but, rather, an elaborate allegory. Thus, the three unmarried Ashbury daughters sit every day in one of the north-facing rooms, stitching scraps of silk together that they then unpick and resew the next day. Not only does this serve as an allegory for the futility of human endeavour, including the poetic endeavour to create a coherent text, but it is also clearly an allusion to the three Fates who, in Greek mythology, sit spinning and cutting the threads of life.[8] Similarly, although Catherine Ashbury might appear to be an eyewitness to a diasporic history, at the end of her story Sebald makes it clear that she, too, is but another poetic allegory: 'Jahre nach diesen wenigen zuletzt mit Catherine Ashbury gewechselten Worten habe ich sie noch einmal gesehen oder zu sehen geglaubt, in Berlin im März 1993' ('Years after that last exchange with Catherine Ashbury, I saw her again, or thought I did, in Berlin in March 1993' (Sebald 1997b: 263; 1999a: 221)). The narrator sees her appear on the stage of a small, scruffy theatre which he has entered by mistake:

[sie] erschien bereits auf der Bühne, unglaublicherweise in demselben roten Kleid, dem gleichen hellen Haar, dem gleichen Pilgerhut, sie, oder doch ihr Ebenbild, Catharina von Siena, in einem leeren Zimmer, und dann weitab von ihres Vaters Haus. (Sebald 1997b: 264)

(there she stood on the stage, incredibly wearing the same red dress, with the same light-coloured hair and holding in her hand the same pilgrim's hat, she or her very image, Catherine of Siena, in an empty room, and then far from her father's house. (Sebald 1999a: 221))

The intertextual reference is to a fragmentary play by the playwright Jakob Michael Reinhold Lenz, in which Saint Catherina of Siena flees her father's house and seeks refuge near a cave. Only fragments of the play exist, and the plots of these differ, but in more than one fragment it is made clear that the cave is no safe hiding place, but instead is a bottomless abyss: 'Ich warf einen Stein hinab und hörte ihn nicht niederfallen' ('I threw a stone down and did not hear it fall' (Lenz 1987: 440; my translation)). Catharina and her companions, whose names and identities change from fragment to fragment, must wander on as eternal pilgrims, without any textual resolution.

As in 'The Theme of the Traitor and the Hero', then, the Sebaldian narrator's rediscovery of Catherine as an actress and then as a literary character suggests the labyrinthine possibility 'that history should copy literature'. Catharina of Siena's cave metonymically refers to the 'dark grotto' or abyss underlying all of human history in Sebald's melancholy understanding (Sebald 1997b: 217; 1999a: 182). While specific, historical diasporas like the Anglo-Irish make us more aware of the closeness of the abyss, the Lenzian intertext suggests that exile is in fact the universal condition of humanity, and that the Anglo-Irish players Catherine, Casement and FitzGerald are merely pretextual, possibly interchangeable figures used to personify the universal deterritorialized nature of human existence. Such a reading of the Anglo-Irish themes would suggest that Hui is right, and that these three stories are ultimately interchangeable material gathered to create *l'effet de réel*, while developing the true Sebaldian themes of exile, the depredations of history and the evils of colonialism.

However, it must also be noted that Sebald's Anglo-Irish themes skim over the complexity of Anglo-Irish relations and border on the hagiographic. The Ashburys' narrative of genteel decline avoids both the reality that many Anglo-Irish families were brutally burned out and forced to flee the Free State of Ireland in fear of their lives in 1922, and the very real part that many such families had played in the impoverishment of their peasant tenants. More particularly, the Roger Casement narrative radically simplifies the complexities of the Easter Rising of 1916, to suggest that it was a righteous uprising of the downtrodden, if naïve, Irish Catholic idealists, poets and teachers against the 'fanatischen Widerstand der nordirischen

Protestanten' ('fanatical resistance of Ulster Protestants' (Sebald 1997b: 157; 1999a: 129)). Such unabashedly partisan accounts of Irish history have been out of favour in Irish historiography for at least two generations.[9] Moreover, the suggestion that Casement's homosexuality led him to an empathy with the oppressed and colonized again elides the more questionable aspects of his sexual adventures. Casement, after all, appears to Sebald in the dream accompanied by a Loanda boy, who does not speak, but who might well, if Casement's Black Diaries are to be believed (as Sebald suggests they should be), be paid by Casement in return for sexual favours. Such dubious paedophile tourism sits ill with Sebald's heroic portrayal of Casement, as it does with the forced link to FitzGerald's poetically unrequited homosexual yearnings for which, as we have seen, Sebald forces the evidence. It would seem, then, that in his attempt to champion the queer, deterritorialized and local, Sebald at times falls prey to a wilfully blinkered exoticism that deals in large and simplified clichés of Irish history, and elides ethically ambivalent elements. The literature of restitution has its blind spots, too.

NOTES

1 Borges (1998: 143). I am indebted to Barry McCrea of Yale University for this link to Borges.

2 See Ben Hutchinson (2009b) for an extended treatment of the workings of negative dialectics in Sebald's work.

3 See, for instance, de Vere White (1972) for an overview of the history and self-perception of the Anglo-Irish, or Dooley (2001).

4 See Böll (1957).

5 Judith Ryan suggests that just as Deleuze and Guattari state that in minor literature 'language is affected with a high coefficient of deterritorialization', so is Sebald's language of exile exemplary of a 'literature of deterritorialization' (Ryan 2007: 53).

6 The concept of liminality was first discussed by Arnold Van Gennep (1909) and then elaborated very usefully for literary and other critics by Victor Turner (1974; 1987: 3–19).

7 The Congolese *homo sacer* appears in an intertextual reference to Conrad in *The Rings of Saturn* (Sebald 1997b: 120; 1990a: 146).

8 As such, it cross-refers to the photograph of the three weavers in the Litzmannstadt ghetto included in *Die Ausgewanderten*. For a discussion of this latter photograph, see Graley Herren's essay in the present volume.

9 See, for instance, Boyce and O'Day (1996).

7

THE 'ARCA PROJECT': W. G. SEBALD'S CORSICA

Graeme Gilloch

To great writers, finished works weigh lighter than those fragments on which they work throughout their lives. (Walter Benjamin, 1996: 446)

Je mehr ich daran herumbastelte, desto minder kam es mir vor. [The more I tinkered with it, the less it seemed to me to become.] (W. G. Sebald 2008d: 211)

INTRODUCTION

Most writers are destined to leave something 'unfinished'. Indeed, as Benjamin memorably observes in *Einbahnstrasse*, it may even be the case that such incomplete labours are the most important and precious. Inevitably, they are the most intriguing and tantalizing. Benjamin's own now famous, fragmentary *Arcades Project* (1999a) is evidence of this. And this may prove to be true also of W. G. Sebald. His various writings on Corsica, an island he visited in the mid 1990s,[1] comprise not just the four brief essays brought together and published in the 2003 collection *Campo Santo*,[2] but also numerous texts and other materials now held in the German National Literature Archive (Deutsches Literaturarchiv [DLA]) in Marbach am Neckar.[3] These various materials were intended as elements of a much larger work, one that was to be set aside for the sake of other texts and studies and ultimately left incomplete – or unwritten – at the time of the author's untimely death in December 2001. While comparisons between Benjamin's writings and those of Sebald are nothing new,[4] and without wishing to overstate the parallels, I want to suggest that there may be some intriguing correspondences between the ill-fated *Passagenarbeit* and the Corsican *corpus*.

What form might such correspondences take? In the first instance, it might be fruitful to consider what one might see as an apparent 'structural' or compositional affinity. Sebald's tinkering and fiddling with his Corsican convolutes may have been far less extensive and of much shorter duration than Benjamin's fourteen-year brooding with the proliferating 'Arcades' materials, and, as von Bülow observes, Sebald's increasing frustration may have led to a final renunciation of the planned project altogether, but to conceive of these papers simply as some kind of textual 'missing link' (Sebald 2008d: 212) between the 1995 *Rings of Saturn* and the 2001

Austerlitz is to construct a rather teleological, developmental sequence of his writings and ideas which seems very much at odds with his own labyrinthine, highly Benjaminian mode of thought, with its endlessly repeated forays into the same subjects and preoccupations, his tireless iterations and reiterations of motifs and figures. A 'missing link'? Or, rather, something more akin to a fascinating, infuriating, expanding and enduring 'charmed circle[s] of fragments' (Benjamin 1996: 446) that stubbornly refuses to take final form, a veritable constellation[5] of writings in which themes and tropes are subject to both centripetal and centrifugal forces, drawn in from neighbouring texts here, expelled into other writings there, in one moment a locus of stylistic, technical and narrative experimentations and inventions,[6] in the next a site of incubation for concepts and characters that will finally be deployed under new names and in altered guises elsewhere.[7] No, surely not a 'missing link' in a linear evolutionary scheme; rather, the Corsica pieces remain unfinished business, teasing texts for Sebald then, for us now.

And then, of course, there are the actual thematic correspondences themselves. Both of these undertakings take as their focus distinctive features of French society of the recent past as read through the double optic of contemporary commentary and present-day interest. Both are panoramic historical-archaeological projects preoccupied with the ruinous residues of the nineteenth century and, in particular, the 'dreamworld' of empire (the First for Sebald, the Second for Benjamin).[8] Both are critical and redemptive explorations fascinated with the archaic and anachronistic remnants, with the fetishisms and phantasms of yesteryear persisting into and within the twentieth century. Decaying objects, fractured images, scarred spaces, arcane texts, eccentric imaginings – all these are identified and illuminated amid the debris and detritus of the contemporary cityscape / landscape. And both undertakings take obscure, lingering architectural features of this bygone age as points of departure and decisive motifs: in each case, enclosed structures serving as passages and thresholds, edifices lit only from above, and filled with dead and decaying things – for Benjamin, the collective 'dreamhouses' (*Traumhäuser*) of the Parisian arcades, museums, railways stations and World Exhibitions; less obviously but no less significantly, in the case of Sebald, the melancholy funerary monuments of the island. Of these, the simplest, yet perhaps most remarkable, were the *arca*, unassuming rustic stone constructions which once served as communal burial chambers: windowless, doorless buildings into which the bagged corpses of the landless and poorest were stuffed from an opening in the roof, the bodies left inside 'wie Kraut und Rüben durcheinanderlagen' ('all jumbled up like cabbages and turnips' (2003b: 27; 2005b: 25)).[9] Preoccupied with death, destruction, ghosts and haunting, imbued with melancholy, Sebald's Corsican studies constitute fragments of what might be termed 'The Arca Project', in which the edifices of death and mourning littering the island, its *Trauerhäuser* perhaps, constitute sites of intense scrutiny and brooding speculation.

In what follows, I do not propose any systematic reconstruction or exhaustive comparison of Benjamin's Parisian *Traumwelt* with Sebald's Corsican *Alptraum-*, or *Traumawelt*. More modestly, I offer a reading of Sebald which is deeply inflected by and imbued with Benjaminian figures and traces and which is, at the same time, mindful of the *leitmotif* of this current collection: the idea of 'restitution'. This notion, and both its historical necessity and (im)possibility, is understood here in two senses: on the one hand, as a return to or restoration of, an original state; and, on the other, as the very act of reconstruction itself (from *restituare*: Latin – 'to rebuild'). And if my focus is very much on Sebald's published essays in the *Campo Santo* collection, this is not to side-line the more recently available archive materials from which they emerged but, rather, to concentrate on their most polished but still provisional form. They are fragments, fragments born of fragments indeed, and anything but finished business.[10]

THE *TRAUERWELT* OF THE RECENT PAST: THE UNCANNY ISLAND

Let us begin our island excursions with the eponymous 'Campo Santo' piece itself. This characteristically enigmatic essay recounts Sebald's dreamlike discovery on an afternoon walk of the local cemetery at Piana. Perhaps death had a particular poignancy for him at this precise moment, having narrowly avoided being swept out to sea while swimming in the Bay of Ficajola earlier in the day. In any case, whatever his motives, Sebald ventures into the cemetery even though the site promises little of interest. It was, he recalls:

> ein ziemlich verwahrloster Platz von der in Frankreich nicht seltenen Art, wo man eher den Eindruck hat eines von der Kommune verwalteten, für den profanen Abraum der menschlichen Gesellschaft bestimmten Areals als den eines Vorhofs des ewigen Lebens. (2003b: 21)

> (a rather desolate graveyard of the kind not uncommon in France, where you have the impression not so much of an antechamber to eternal life as of a place administered by the local authority and designed for the secular removal of waste matter from human society. (2005b: 18))

Closer inspection proves rather rewarding, however. Overgrown and neglected, the gravestones shelter myriad wild plants whose simple charm and untamed beauty far exceed the artificial prettiness of those well-tended gardens of rest to which we northern Europeans are accustomed:

> Erst wie ich genauer mich umsah, fiel mir das Unkraut auf, die Saatwicken, der Quendel, der kriechende Klee, die Schafgarben und Kamillen, der Goldhafer und der Wachtelweizen und viele andere mir unbekannte Gräser, die um die Steine herum zusammengewachsen waren zu richtigen Herbarien und Miniaturlandschaften, halb grün noch und halb schon vertrocknet und gleich schöner, so dachte ich mir, als der

von deutschen Friedhofsgärtnern verkaufte, meist aus vollkommen gleichförmigen Erikastauden, Zwergkonifern und Stiefmütterchen bestehende, in strikt geometrischer Anordnung in makellose, rußschwarze Erde gesetzte sogenannte Grabschmuck. (2003b: 22)

(Not until I looked more carefully around me did I notice the weeds – the vetch, wild thyme, white clover, yarrow and camomile, cow wheat, yellow oat grass, and many other grasses with names unknown to me – that had grown around the stones to form actual herbariums and miniature landscapes, still showing some green but already half dead, far lovelier, I thought to myself, than the ornamental funerary plants sold by German cemetery florists, usually consisting of heathers, dwarf conifers and pansies of absolutely standard shape, planted in spotless, soot-black soil in geometric rows. (2005b: 19–20))[11]

The disorderliness of the Piana cemetery is slightly deceptive, though. Sebald comes to recognize the distinctive patterning of the older graves – not individual plots but great extended families all buried together, emphasizing the solidarity of Corsica's great feuding clans even in death. The narrator notes that:

Die Ceccaldi zu den Ceccaldi und die Quilichini zu den Quilichini zu liegen kamen, daß aber diese alte, auf nicht viel mehr als ein Dutzend Namen gegründete Ordnung seit längerem bereits zurückweichen mußte vor der des modernen Zivillebens, in dem jeder für sich allein steht und zuletzt auch nur für sich und seine nächsten Anverwandten einen Platz zugewiesen bekommt, der so akkurat wie möglich dem Maß seines Vermögens oder dem Grad seiner Armut entspricht. (2003b: 24)

(the Ceccaldi lay beside the Ceccaldi and the Quilichini beside the Quilichini, but this old order, founded on not more than a dozen names, had been forced some time ago to give way to the order of modern civil life, in which everyone is alone and in the end allotted a place only for himself and his closest relations, one which corresponds as accurately as possible to the size of his property or the depths of his poverty. (2005b: 21))[12]

Wandering amid the graves prompts a whole host of observations on the 'überaus elaborat' and 'hochdramatischen' ('extremely elaborate' and 'highly dramatic' (2003b: 28; 2005b: 25)) funereal practices and the deep-seated folk superstitions of the Corsicans, a people for whom the threshold between the living and the dead is so readily traversable in both directions.[13]

The dead are omnipresent, their 'kleine Leichenhäuser' ('little dwellings' (2003b: 26; 2005b: 24)) scattered everywhere on the island. The dates on the stones in the Piana graveyard testify to the fact that until the mid-nineteenth century the dead were not buried in specially demarcated and consecrated cemeteries but, rather, were laid to rest on the family land, often in particularly picturesque locations, sometimes favoured by panoramic views such that they could silently 'wachen über die Grenzen ihres Gebiets' ('continue to watch over the boundaries of their property' (2003b: 27; 2005b: 24)) and keep a careful eye on their current heirs. There they lie, the *antichi* or *antinati* (2003b: 28; 2005b: 26), close by, conveniently situated for regular visits and consultations by widow(er)s and orphans who are drawn to them for advice 'über die Nutzung des Landes und sonstige die rechte Lebensführung betreffende Fragen' ('on the cultivation of the land and other matters to do with the correct conduct of life' (2003b: 27; 2005b: 24–5)).

On Corsica, the dead make themselves very much 'at home' (2005b: 24) among the living. And this homeliness is, of course, unhomely, the very ambiguity of *heimlich–unheimlich* that Freud famously explored in his 1919 essay 'The Uncanny' (1955: 234–6). The uncanny, for him, is to be understood as that intense sense of disquiet occasioned by the sudden, unexpected return of that which has been repressed (ontogenetically, in and from our own childhood) or 'surmounted' (phylogenetically, in the course of humankind's ever more complex, more 'civilized' existence). Forgotten 'infantile complexes' and/or obsolete 'primitive beliefs' reappear as the strangely familiar which one recognizes with a shudder (Freud 1955: 249). And this experience of the uncanny seems to be the very hallmark of Corsica for Sebald: it is precisely the island of this double return, of haunting by troubling memories and troublesome spirits.

And Sebald himself offers a suggestive image or allegory of this in 'Campo Santo'. Back in the Piana graveyard, he observes that the grandest and largest monoliths are those placed over the graves of the rich. While this is surely in keeping with prevailing socio-economic hierarchies, Sebald suspects another, deeper reason: the wealthy are those with most reason to begrudge their fortunate heirs and determine to return and reclaim what was once theirs. The great stone marker is there, or so it seems to Sebald, to hinder, as best the living can, such unwelcome reappearances, to ensure the dead stay buried in the ground. The slab in the graveyard provides an *image* of the work of repression in this sense. But at the same time, the mere idea that such weighty masonry is required at all gives credence to our 'primitive' fear of the return of the dead. We are reminded of such threats and terrors, beliefs we thought that we, as civilized, rational, modern beings, had outgrown long ago. The *image* of repression reminds us precisely of the *need* for repression, and hence, paradoxically, that which is repressed assuredly returns as the psychoanalytical uncanny. Indeed, the very size and weight of the great stone slabs of the Piana cemetery attest to the power and persistence of the envious, vengeful dead, and their perpetual proximity unnerves us. For Sebald, Corsica is, above all, the island of the uncanny in that it is 'alive' with the dead.[14]

While the massive monoliths may prevent the rich from realizing their posthumous claims, their more impoverished brethren are, according to folklore, very much engaged in persecuting the living. Singly, Sebald tells us, these 'wandering shades' are thought to prey upon unwary travellers who venture too far from the safety of the main tracks, and/or restlessly, repeatedly seek admission to their former homes and those of their enemies. But the dead are also said to roam the island's *maquis* in great hordes, veritable 'Heerscharen der Toten [. . .] gekleidet in die weiten, wehenden Umhänge der Leichenbruderschaft oder die buntfarbenen Uniformen der Füsiliere, die gefallen waren auf den Schlachtfeldern von Wagram und Waterloo' ('armies of the dead . . . clad in the full billowing cloaks of the brotherhood of corpses, or the colourful uniforms of fusiliers who had fallen on the battlefields of Wagram and Waterloo' (2003b; 32–3; 2005b: 30)) – referred to locally as the *cumpagnia*, the *mumma*, or the *squadra d'Arozza* – ghostly regiments bent on desecrating churches with blasphemous masses of the dead and seizing hold of fresh recruits from among the feuding clans of the island.

The dead of the island make themselves at home in another sense, too: as Sebald points out, the parlour of the Corsican house is no living room, but, rather, seems to become a veritable shrine honouring the dead of the family, specifically reserved for use as a temporary mortuary for the recently deceased. It is here that the dead are 'laid out' prior to burial. It is here that the wake takes place. And it is here, too, that one finds the images of the dead, for the walls of the parlour are lined with portraits and photographs of ancestors and relations, a whole gallery of ghosts gazing down upon the living.

Sebald interests himself in the highly ritualized and dramatic performances of grieving which accompany funeral rites and in the conventional proprieties and dress codes of bereavement,[15] traditions which ensure that the islanders seem to be in a perpetual state of mourning. Indeed, Sebald observes: 'daß das hochgeschlossene schwarze Kleid mit dem schwarzen Kopftuch und der schwarze Manchesteranzug bis weit in das zwanzigste Jahrhundert hinein die korsische Nationaltracht zu sein schien' ('the high-necked black dress and black headscarf, or the black corduroy suit, seemed to be the Corsican national costume until well into the twentieth century' (2003b: 31; 2005b: 28)).

And these sombre, sorrowful figures themselves have something uncanny about them:

> Nach Berichten früherer Reisender ging von den schwarzen, überall in den Gassen oder Ortschaften und Städte und draußen am Land gegenwärtigen Gestalten eine Aura der Schwermut aus, die sich, sogar an den strahlendsten Tagen, wie ein Schatten über die grüne Blattwelt der Insel legte. (2003b: 31)

> (According to the accounts of travellers, there was an aura of melancholy about those black figures seen everywhere on the streets of villages and towns and out in the country, an aura that even on the brightest sunlit days lay like a shadow over the green and leafy world of the island. (2005b: 28–9))

THE MEXICAN AMBASSADOR AND A BAVARIAN LOCK-KEEPER

On Corsica one thing is certain: the dead are not to be forgotten, do not allow themselves to be forgotten – indeed, for the islanders 'Das Andenken an die Toten nahm eigentlich niemals am Ende' ('remembrance of the dead never really came to an end' (2003b: 31; 2005b: 29)). Corsica is a reminder of death in two ways for Sebald: he recalls how easy it is for death to be forgotten by us, how unremarkably its traces are (seemingly) erased in the hygienic orderliness and routines of modern life; and it serves as a prompt for memories of, and reflections on, his own uncanny encounters with sinister, ghostly figures elsewhere:

> Und seit einiger Zeit weiß ich auch: Je mehr einer, aus was für einem Grund immer, zu tragen hat an der der menschlichen Art wahrscheinlich nicht umsonst aufgebürdeten Trauerlast, desto öfter begegnen ihm Gespenster. Auf dem Graben in Wien, in der Londoner U-Bahn, auf einem Empfang, zu dem der Botschafter von Mexiko geladen hat, bei einem Schleusenhäuschen am Ludwigskanal in Bamberg, einmal da und einmal dort trifft man, ohne daß man es versieht, auf eines dieser irgendwie undeutlichen und unpassenden Wesen, an denen mir immer auffällt, daß sie ein wenig zu klein geraten und kurzsichtig sind, etwas eigenartig Abwartendes und Lauerndes an sich haben und auf ihren Gesichtern den Ausdruck tragen eines uns gramen Geschlechts. (2003b: 35–6)

> (And for some time, too, I have known that the more one has to bear, for whatever reason, of the burden of grief which is probably not imposed on the human species for nothing, the more often do we meet ghosts. On the Graben in Vienna, in the London Underground, at a reception given by the Mexican ambassador, at a lock-keeper's cottage on the Ludwigskanal in Bamberg, now here and now there, without expecting it, you may meet one of those beings who are somehow blurred and out of place and who, as I always feel, are a little too small and short-sighted; they have something curiously watchful about them, as if they were lying in wait, and their faces bear the expression of a race that wishes us ill. (2005b: 33))

This list of sites for possible encounters with these malevolent ghosts is, of course, highly suggestive: the Viennese street Graben (ditch, moat) most obviously invokes the grave (*Grab*); the London underground is also suggestive of the realm of the dead, as in *Austerlitz*, where Sebald describes the lower concourse of Liverpool Street Station as 'a kind of entrance to the underworld' (2002d: 180). But the reference to the Mexican ambassador's reception is a little obscure and that to the Bavarian lock-keeper on the Ludwigskanal obscurer still.

The name 'Ludwig' is certainly associated with death elsewhere in Sebald's writings: in the essay '*All' estero*' in *Vertigo* (1999b: 130–2) he mentions the infamous 'Ludwig' murders, ten horrific killings perpetrated in Italy beginning in 1977 and ending with the conviction of Mario Furla and Wolfgang Abel by a Veronese court in 1987. But a Bamberg lock-keeper? Perhaps a lock-keeper, as one who attends to the relationship between that which is above and that which is below, and therefore a figure of watery thresholds, is reminiscent of the ferryman of Greek mythology, Charon, who transports the dead across the River Styx. Perhaps. But the Ludwigskanal, built 1836–46 to connect the Main and the Danube, might be suggestive in other ways. At Bamberg, lock 100, the first or last of the locks, is one of the few still in working order, the canal itself having long been superseded by rail and road links and by another waterway (the Main–Donau Kanal). The Bamberg–Nuremberg section, for instance, has been partially transformed into the autobahn A73. So our lock-keeper keeps patient watch over a defunct water course, a ruin, a remnant of an obsolete mode of transportation. And one final point: the Main is connected to the canal by the Regnitz at Bamberg flowing through a channel with the evocative name 'Nonnengraben' (nuns' graves/ditches).

The Mexican reference[16] might be explained as a reminder of that very society which is famed for its preoccupation with death and the Day of the Dead, rituals and superstitions depicted so memorably in the paintings and murals of Diego Rivera. But for readers of Benjamin, the reference cannot but call to mind the enigmatic section in *One-Way Street* entitled 'Mexican Embassy' (Benjamin 1996: 448–9), a passage in which Benjamin relates the following curious dream:[17] in Mexico, at some kind of mission established among remote mountain caves, a Mass is being conducted. At the ceremonial climax, a fetish figure is brought before an image of the Christian God, whose head turns from side to side three times by way of denial, an act reminiscent of Peter's disavowal of Jesus.

But perhaps it is not Benjamin's dream but the epigram from Charles Baudelaire, which opens the fragment, that is most significant for us here: 'I never pass by a wooden fetish, a gilded Buddha, a Mexican idol without reflecting: perhaps it is the true God' (Benjamin 1996: 448). Baudelaire's radical uncertainty is instructive: he acknowledges that the face of the 'true God' may possibly be in any image, anywhere; that he has perchance already gazed upon it countless times unknowingly; that if humankind is in God's image, then S/He is in ours, too, such that one of us mere mortals may resemble Her/Him, so much so perhaps that one may blithely and unsuspectingly encounter God's double strolling in a Vienna street, slumped on a London commuter train, socializing at a consular reception, peering out from behind the curtains of a provincial canal-side cottage. And so it might be, Sebald muses, with the faces of the dead.

The Mexican embassy, the Mexican ambassador – the German term here is, of course, *Botschaft/Botschafter* ['message'/'messenger']. And what exactly is this message brought from the homeland of the Day of the Dead? It is perhaps this: remember the dead are all around you; remember that as you gaze upon the living, you see those who will certainly die, who may perhaps be ghosts already. And never forget that you must assuredly die too. Corsica, for Sebald, is a site of the uncanny in that it constitutes an insistent reminder of death, a *memento mori*.

THE DREAM HUNTERS

Of all the suspicious, sinister and malevolent figures stalking the island,[18] perhaps the most disturbing are not the dead themselves, but their unwitting accomplices among the living, the *culpa morti, acciatori* or *mazzeri*. Sebald explains: '[Es] war auf Korsika bis in die Jahrzehnte nach dem letzten Krieg noch die Vorstellung weit verbreitet von besonderen, gewissermaßen im Dienst des Todes stehenden Personen' ('there was still a widespread belief in Corsica, until well into the decades after the last war that some special people were in a way in the service of death' (2003b: 34; 2005b: 32)). These individuals were subject to somnambulism, leaving their beds to go on nocturnal forays into the depths of the island. In the darkness they would move stealthily, crouching down by a brook or pool to wait and watch for their prey – some unsuspecting wild animal come to drink. Having pounced on the poor creature, they would kill it with their bare hands, and as they did so, they were thought to recognize 'das Doppelbild eines Bewohners ihres Dorfes, unter Umständen sogar das eines engen Verwandten [...], der von diesem furchtbaren Augenblick an gezeichnet war auf den Tod' ('the image of some inhabitant of their village, sometimes even a close relation, who from that terrible moment on was doomed to die' (2003b: 34; 2005b: 32)). Sebald notes:

> Was diesem [...] äußerst bizarren Aberglauben zugrundeliegt, ist das in der Leidensgenossenschaft der Familie aus einer nicht abreißen wollenden Reihe schmerzhaftester Erfahrungen entstandene Wissen von einem bis in den hellichten Tag hinein sich erstreckenden Schattenreich, in dem, vermittels eines Akts perverser Gewalt, das Geschick vorbestimmt wird, das uns schließlich ereilt. (2003b: 35)
>
> (What lies behind this extremely bizarre superstition ... is the awareness, arising from the family's shared suffering of an endless series of the most painful experiences, of a shadow realm extending into the light of day, a place where in an act of perverse violence, the fate we shall finally meet is predetermined. (2005b: 32))

The idea of the *acciatori*, of these *'dream-hunters'* as they are evocatively termed by an earlier visitor (Dorothy Carrington), is highly suggestive.[19] For Sebald, it is another aspect of the insatiable violence that bedevils Corsica and the terrible destruction that its inhabitants wreak upon each other and upon their environment. In 'The Alps in the Sea', Sebald laments the disappearance of the ancient forests which once covered the island before succumbing to the axe in the nineteenth century and/or to devastating forest fires which continue today and some of which are deliberate acts of arson (see 2008d: 154). The Forest of Bavella, for example, once expansive home to immense native trees that were a source of awe and wonder to earlier visitors,[20] has now been reduced to 'schmächtiges Nadelholz, von dem man nicht denken kann, daß es ein Menschenleben überdauert, geschweige denn Dutzende von Generationen' ('slender conifers which cannot be imagined lasting a single human lifetime, let alone for dozens of generations' (2003b: 42; 2005b: 39)), all planted by the forestry department, and reminiscent of those dwarf conifers ornamenting the German cemetery.[21] And most of the animals that once flourished in these vast, dense sylvan habitats – unique indigenous island species of diminutive stature – have now been eradicated without trace. But even this has seemingly done little to assuage the bloodlust of the Corsicans for whom the autumn hunting season is a time of the most intense (and for Sebald 'pointless') killing 'fever' (2003b: 42–3; 2005b: 40–1).

HAUNTED FORESTS

Catastrophic destruction and senseless slaughter – these are, arguably, the central preoccupations of the 'First' and 'Second Versions' (and especially the latter), where Sebald is led to reflect upon two forms of primordial human violence brought to mind by the ecological impoverishment of Corsica: burning and hunting. Firstly, the terrible devastation wrought by forest fires is explicitly linked by Sebald to another act of incineration, the wartime fire-bombing of German cities, the fundamental theme, of course, of his subsequent essays found in *On the Natural History of Destruction* (2003). In the 'First Version' he observes that, however much one may calmly quantify and measure the extent of the damage done, what cannot be known but only imagined is the terror of the victims. He writes:

aber die Panik der Zeisige, deren Nester, noch bevor sie die Flammen erreichen, zu Asche verfallen, die Angst der unter den Blättern verborgenen Nachtfalter, der Nattern, Mäuse und Eidechsen, denen selbst, wenn sie sich ausruhen, das Blut in der Kehle klopft, diese Angst können wir mit keiner Statistik erfassen; sie ist uns so unbegreiflich wie nur unsere eigene es ist, wenn wir in unseren Städten verbrennen

(but the panic of the siskins, whose nests turn to ash even before the flames reach them, the fear of the moths hidden under leaves, of the adders, mice and lizards, whose blood throbs even as they rest – we cannot capture this kind of fear in a statistic; it is as incomprehensible to us as our own fear when we burn in our cities. (2008d: 154))

In the 'Second Version' this connection between the incinerated forests of Corsica and the burnt-out cities of Germany is evident from the very beginning.[22] But it is in the closing passages of the text that Sebald develops his theme most evocatively and provocatively. Here, reflecting upon the apparent forgetfulness and impassivity of Corsicans (and indeed of himself) before the spectacle of their own ashen landscape, he writes:

Nicht einmal der Schock der einen beim ersten Anblick einer vom Feuer vernichteten Gegend durchfährt, ... nicht einmal dieser Schock hält, wie ich verschiedentlich an mir selber feststellen konnte, lange vor. Irgendwie bringen wir es fertig, nicht zu erstarren vor dem Totengebirge, das oft von einem Tag auf den andern vor die schönsten Prospekte sich schiebt, reagieren kaum mehr auf die Verwandlung eines eben noch grün gewesenen Geländes in einen trostlosen Landstrich, in dem allenfalls ein paar verkohlte krumme Stecken übriggeblieben sind von der seit ungezählten Generationen sich fortpflanzenden Vegetation. Das Auge lernt abzusehen von dem, was es schmerzt

(Not even the shock felt at first seeing an area ravaged by fire, ... not even this shock lasts long, as I have observed in myself on various occasions. Somehow we manage not to be transfixed by the mountain of death that often overnight obscures even the fairest prospect; our reaction is scarcely greater to the transformation of a landscape that just a moment ago was green into a desolate tract, where at best a few charred and crooked sticks are all that remain of vegetation that has flourished for generations. The eye learns to look away from whatever pains it. (2008d: 208))

For readers of Benjamin, this image of a 'Totengebirge [mountain of death]' relentlessly, inexorably arising or amassing before one's eyes cannot but call to mind the 'Angel of History' from the 1940 theses 'On the Concept of History', Benjamin's famous invocation of the curious figure depicted in Paul Klee's *Angelus Novus*.[23] With the wind caught in his wings, the Angel is blown backwards into the future by the storm of progress, while at his feet the ruins and calamities of human history pile up unremittingly. But there is a fundamental and utterly unnerving difference between the Angel, wide-eyed in anguish at the mounting horrors before him, and Sebald's observer. What is truly shocking is how little we, Sebald and his contemporaries, are shocked. So inured are we to death and destruction (of unknown others and places elsewhere, of course) that we are unmoved by catastrophe. It is this indifference, and our facile faith in the beneficence of progress and the new, that *is* the catastrophe.

Haben wir nicht sogar ganze Völker verbrannt, unsere Städte abbrennen gesehen in meilenhohen Feuerstürmen, und haben wir nicht alles wieder aufgebaut, besser und schöner als zuvor, und keinen Schaden genommen an unserer Seele?

(Have we not burnt entire peoples, seen our cities burn in mile-high firestorms, and have we not rebuilt everything better and more beautiful than before, and left our soul unscathed? (2008d: 209))

Sebald presents us here with a double disaster: as if the violence and destruction of the recent past, indeed their continuation and intensification in the present, were not horror enough, we, the cheerfully complacent generations that look on today, are so easily reassured as to the possibility of an adequate reparation, of an appropriate restoration, of a full and final restitution – replanting a few conifers here and there,[24] rebuilding houses, streets and squares from the post-war rubble in the image of the new interspersed with sentimental replicas of the past. Our hands are clean, our conscience clear. We live in obscene oblivion.

136

Clean hands – this leads to the second aspect of human violence which preoccupies Sebald: the hunt. Hunting is a repeated motif in his writings, occurring in several other contexts in relation to various literary and mythological figures.[25] On Corsica, he recalls Gustave Flaubert's narration of the legend of St Julian: 'von der mit jeder Zeile tiefer in das Grauen eindringenden, von Grund auf perversen Erzählung über die Verruchtheit der Menschengewalt' ('an utterly perverse tale of the despicable nature of human violence, a story that probes horror further with every line' (2003b: 48; 2005b: 46)). Here hunting is no 'dream' but a series of nightmares: Julian is the hunter who one day, after causing the most terrible carnage, is moved to renounce hunting altogether, only to find himself the quarry pursued relentlessly by the avenging ghosts of the animals he has killed. In his desperation, he is driven to the ends of the earth searching for absolution for his sanguineous atrocities, and finds it eventually in the infectious embrace of a leper whose pitiful bed he is forced to share.

We northern European metropolitans are no St Julians. Our killing causes us no torments or suffering. We sleep soundly in our own beds. Just as we are keen to consign our own human dead to the municipal ornamental plots located out of sight and out of mind, so we are only too happy to ensure that the acts of industrialized animal slaughter which feed us are hidden away 'behind the scenes' of civilized everyday life, as the sociologist Norbert Elias (1994) describes it. And though the Corsican hunters, like Julian, may take pleasure in their brutal and bloody business, there is no denying at least a certain visceral energy and integrity in such acts, a great physical expenditure in contrast to the meagreness of the catch. How different all this is from our own prissy hypocrisy, our unearned profligacy, and our all too easily assuaged conscience. Here in Britain, recalls Sebald,

habe ich später kleine, kaum einen Zoll hohe Reihen grüner Plastikbäumchen gesehen, mit denen die in den Schaufenstern der sogenannten *family butchers* ausgestellten Fleischteile und Innereien umrandet waren. Die unabweisbare Einsicht, daß dieser immergrüne Plastikzierat irgendwo fabrikmäßig hergestellt werden mußte zu dem einzigen Zweck, unsere Schuldgefühle zu lindern angesichts des vergossenen Bluts, war mir, gerade in ihrer völligen Absurdität, ein Zeichen dafür, wie stark der Wunsch nach Versöhnung in uns ist und wie billig wir uns sie von jeher erkauften. (2003b: 46)

(I saw rows of little green plastic trees hardly an inch high surrounding cuts of meat and offal displayed in the shop windows of 'Family Butchers'. The obvious fact that these evergreen plastic ornaments must be mass-produced somewhere for the sole purpose of alleviating our sense of guilt about the bloodshed seemed to me, in its very absurdity, to show how strongly we desire absolution and how cheap we have always bought it. (2005b: 43–4))

Such Lilliputian plastic trees, like the geometrically arranged miniature conifers –

and the very antithesis of the great forests in which the game of Corsica once roamed – are now sufficient for us calmly to forget slaughter on a scale and regularity that dwarfs Julian's most violent excesses. Little wonder, then, that all this should remind Sebald of a traumatic incident from his childhood:

> So entsinne ich mich jetzt, wie ich auf meinem Schulweg einmal am Hof des Metzgers Wohlfahrt vorbeigekommen bin an einem frostigen Herbstmorgen, als gerade ein Dutzend Hirschkühe von einem Karren abgeladen und auf das Pflaster geworfen wurde. Ich vermochte mich lang nicht von der Stelle zu rühren, derart gebannt war ich vom Anblick der getöteten Tiere. (2003b: 45)

> (I remember, for instance, how on my way to school I once passed Wohlfahrt the butcher's yard on a frosty autumn morning, just as a dozen deer were being unloaded and tipped out on the paving stones. I could not move from the spot for a long time, so spellbound was I by the sight of the dead animals. (2005b: 43))

And here again is that return of the repressed, of nature in all its inescapable corporeality and incessant cruelty, confronting poor Sebald the schoolboy. And perhaps it is not just the sight of these animals which haunts him, but the terrible suspicion that they are looking back at him with their large, motionless, staring eyes. This fear of mutual recognition between humans and animals is the theme of 'Gloves' (Benjamin 1996: 448), the text immediately preceding the Mexican embassy fragment in *Einbahnstrasse*. Such a primordial terror is occasioned, Benjamin claims, above all by the sense of touch.[26] Physical contact may bring with it a deep-seated disgust prompted by our continually denied kinship with the animal world. Benjamin advocates not gloves, a tactic of tactile avoidance, but, optimistically, forlornly perhaps, the mastery of our relationship with animals. Until then, though, our relations with our fellow creatures will always be imbued with violence and the uncanny.

A final thought on Sebald's catastrophic 'natural history' of Corsica: in the stark and repeated contrasts made between the lush landscapes of the recent past, and the present ruinous condition of the island, a process of degradation whose modern intensification he dates to around the 1870s, around the end of the Second Empire, Sebald makes clear that we today are left with the residues and remnants of once-majestic panoramas and abundant wildlife. Visiting in 1852, the traveller Ferdinand Gregoriovius marvelled at the giant trees and plentiful fauna, especially those unique, miniature species of animals so characteristic of island habitat. For him, then, Sebald reflects, the island must have seemed 'wie ein Paradiesgarten oder eine Arche [like a garden of Paradise or an Ark]' (2008d: 200), an Eden that has irretrievably vanished. And here perhaps we have an alternative rubric for the Corsican writings: not so much the 'arca project' preoccupied with the funereal practices and death cults of the islanders, as the 'ark project' concerned with the ruination of once wondrous landscapes and the extermination of dainty species.

'Arca Project'? 'Arche Project'? Sebald's Corsican writings are both, of course, for these are inextricably interwoven: indeed this is precisely what Sebald intends under his proposal for a 'Natur- und Menschenkunde' [natural and human history]' (2008d: 211) of the island.

DREAMWORLD OF THE FIRST EMPIRE

Of all the dead of Corsica, there is one long-deceased son of the island who remains at a distance, exiled from his birthplace. While the fallen fusiliers of Wagram and Waterloo may feature among the unholy *squadra d'Arozza* wandering the *maquis* – and to their numbers we could add the *chasseurs* of Marengo and Austerlitz – their general, the Emperor himself, is not among them, buried still on remote St Helena. Whether Sebald's preoccupation with Corsica stems originally and/or entirely from his enduring fascination with Napoleon Bonaparte and his various campaigns and adventures is a moot point, but there is no denying the Napoleonic theme which links his *magnum opus*, *Austerlitz* (2001/2002), the Corsican writings and the first part of *Vertigo* (1999) – 'Beyle, or Love is a Madness Most Discreet' tells of Stendhal on the Italian campaign and at the Battle of Marengo.[27]

Yet, curiously, Sebald's 'little excursion to Ajaccio', during which he visits the Casa Bonaparte, seems a capricious and nonchalant affair, a matter of idling and accident rather than urgent interest. Sebald strays firstly into the Musée Fesch, Joseph Fesch being Napoleon's step-uncle, whose family connections and opportunism enabled him to become:

> einem der unersättlichsten Kunstsammler seiner Zeit, einer Zeit, in der der Markt im wahrsten Sinne des Wortes überflutet war mit Gemälden und Artefakten, die während der Revolution aus Kirchen, Klöstern und Schlössern geholt, den *Emigrés* abgenommen und bei der Plünderung der holländischen und italienischen Städte erbeutet wurden. (2003b: 8)

> (one of the most insatiable art collectors of his day, a time when the market was positively flooded with paintings and artefacts taken from churches, monasteries, and palaces during the French Revolution, bought from émigrés, and looted in the plundering of Dutch and Italian cities. (2005b: 4))

Comprising some thirty thousand pieces, Fesch's private collection ambitiously sought 'to document the entire course of European art history' (2005b: 4). And of course it does, though not in the way Fesch intended, for it provides the clearest proof of Benjamin's memorable contention in the seventh of his theses 'On the Concept of History' that:

> There is no document of culture that is not at the same time a document of barbarism. And just as such a document is never free of barbarism, barbarism taints the manner in which it was transmitted from one hand to another. (Benjamin 2003b: 392)

At the same time, and here the ambiguity of Benjamin's vision of the collector, of collecting and of the collection is brought sharply into focus, one might justly say of Fesch's artworks that they are artefacts rudely removed from their original and ritualistic context (religious sites and other galleries) and now reassembled in a new context upon this insular backwater, far from the great metropolitan centres of European art and culture. And that the artworks have been brought together through acts of war, vandalism and theft is of not such great consequence perhaps – as Benjamin suggests in 'Unpacking My Library' (1999c: 486–93), the most precious collectibles tend to be those one has 'borrowed' and forgotten to return – stolen, in other words.[28]

For Sebald, and this would certainly be true for Benjamin as well, the really fascinating collection in the Musée Fesch is not that formed by the works of art upstairs, all neatly classified by period, location and artist but, rather, the materials found in the museum's basement, a motley assemblage of Napoleonic memorabilia and imperial kitsch. Here Sebald discovers 'Memorabilien und Devotionalien' ('mementoes and devotional items' (2003b: 9; 2005b: 6)), fetishistic objects of all kinds dedicated to Bonapartist mythology and the cult of the Emperor. Such bric-a-brac includes: 'mit Napoleonköpfen und Initialien verzierte Brieföffner, Petschafte, Federmesser, Tabaks- und Schnupftabakdosen' ('objects adorned with the head and initials of Napoleon – letter openers, seals, penknives, tobacco and snuff boxes' (2003b: 9; 2005b: 6)) as well as painted cups and plates, an old, moth-eaten uniform of the Chasseurs de la Garde once worn by the great man, and such curios as 'ein mit einer ägyptischen Szene bemaltes Straußenei' ('an ostrich egg painted with an Egyptian scene' (2003b: 9–10; 2005b: 6)). Sebald adds:

> Außerdem sind zu sehen zahlreiche aus Speckstein und Elfenbein geschnittene Skulpturen des Kaisers, die ihn zeigen in den bekannten Posen und die, von zirka zehn Zentimeter angefangen, immer winziger werden, bis fast nichts mehr zu sehen ist als ein blindes Fleckchen Weiß, der erlöschende Fluchtpunkt vielleicht der Menschheitsgeschichte. (2003b: 10)

> (There are also many statuettes of the Emperor carved from soapstone and ivory showing him in familiar poses, the tallest about 10cm high and each of the others smaller than the last, until the smallest seems almost nothing but a white speck, perhaps representing the vanishing point of human history. (2005b: 6))

Such an array of incongruous and useless objects would surely delight any surrealist and would happily reside in any of the ruinous arcades of Paris they frequented in the 1920s and 1930s. In the basement of the Musée Fesch, Sebald stumbles upon what can only be described as the dreamworld of the First Empire, an assortment of decaying artefacts which were once the focus of nationalist fervour, imperial fantasies, the cult of personality and *la gloire* of military invincibility, illusions which were so quickly to be dispelled by failure and bloody defeat.[29]

The reference to the uniform of the chasseur is particularly significant. The dreamworld of empire, the preoccupation with hunting and the return of uncanny childhood memories all converge here. In the essay *'Il ritorno in patria'* from *Vertigo* (1994d: 187–287; 1999b: 169–263), Sebald recalls the strange figure of the so-called Grey Chasseur, the supposed ghostly occupant of a neighbour's attic, a place he was forbidden to go as a child. Venturing into this attic many years later, he became aware of:

> einer Erscheinung, die sich einmal deutlicher, einmal schwächer hinter dem schräg durch das Dachbodenfenster eindringend Licht zu erkennen gab, eine alte Schneiderpuppe, die mit hechtgrauen Beinkleidern und einem hechtgrauen Rock angetan war, dessen Kragen, Aufschläge und Vorstöße einmal von grasgrüner, die Knöpfe aber von goldgelber Farbe gewesen sein mußten. Auf dem Kopfholz trug die Puppe einen gleichfalls hechtgrauen Hut mit einem grünen Hahnenfederbusch. Vielleicht, weil sie verborgen gewesen war hinter dem durch das Lukenfenster in das Dachbodendunkel einfallenden Lichtschleier, in welchem unablässig die Glanzpartikel einer ins Schwerelose sich auflösenden Materie durcheinanderwirbelten, machte die Graue Gestalt sogleich einen äußerst geheminisvollen Eindruck auf mich. (1994d: 247–8)

> (something like a uniformed figure, which could now be seen more clearly, now more faintly behind the blade of light that slanted through the attic window. On closer inspection it revealed itself as an old tailor's dummy, dressed in pike-grey breeches and a pike-grey jacket, the collar, cuffs and edgings of which must have been grass green, and the buttons a golden yellow. On its wooden headpiece the dummy was wearing a hat, also pike-grey, with a bunch of cockerel's tail feathers in it. Perhaps because it had been concealed behind the shaft of light that cut through the darkness of the attic and in which swirled the glinting particles of matter dissolving into weightlessness, the grey figure instantly made a most uncanny impression on me. (1999b: 227))

The disintegrating uniform must have belonged, Sebald thinks, to one of the doomed Austrian irregulars who fought and perished at the Battle of Marengo. The only survivors of the catastrophe of war, the uniform of the vanquished in the attic and the uniform of the victorious in the basement of the museum, now both share the same miserable, moth-eaten fate.

From the museum, Sebald makes his way to the Casa Bonaparte, but only after a sojourn in the sun of the Place Letizia – and, given what transpires, one is entitled to wonder whether the visit itself is only a dream. Curiously, Sebald proceeds to say precious little about the building's history, its interiors, its furnishings and artworks; rather, his attention is almost completely taken up by the two women who work there. On meeting the first of these seemingly ordinary employees, the cashier, Sebald undergoes 'einer jener seltsam zerdehnten Augenblicke, an die man sich Jahre später noch manchmal erinnert' ('one of those moments strangely experienced in slow motion that are sometimes remembered years later' (2003b: 12; 2005b: 8)). He explains this strange sensation thus:

141

Weit eigenartiger aber als das Divamäßige ihrer Erscheinung war ihre erst auf den zweiten Blick deutlich werdende, dann freilich umso verblüffendere Ähnlichkeit mit dem Franzosenkaiser, in dessen Geburtshaus sie als Türhüterin amtierte. (2003b: 12–13)

(Far more striking than her diva-like figure, and something that became clear only at second glance but was all the more startling for that, was her resemblance to the French emperor in whose birthplace she acted as doorkeeper. (2005b: 9))

And the tour guide he meets moments later is equally remarkable:

Ich stieg die schwarze Marmortreppe hinauf und war nicht wenig verwundert, als mich an ihrem oberen Absatz eine weitere Dame empfing, die anscheinend gleichfalls der napoleonischen Linie entstammte beziehungsweise irgendwie mich erinnerte an Masséna oder Mack oder sonst einen jener legendären französischen Feldherren, wahrscheinlich weil ich mir diese von jeher als ein Geschlecht von zwergenhaften Heroen vorgestellt hatte. (2003b: 13)

(I climbed the black marble staircase, and was not a little surprised to be met on the top landing by another lady who also seemed to be of Napoleonic descent, or rather who somehow reminded me of Masséna or Mack or another of the legendary marshals of France, probably because I had always imagined them as a race of dwarfish heroes. (2005b: 10))

These 'beiden diskreten Botschafterinnen aus der Vergangenheit' ('two discreet messengers from the past' (2003b: 14; 2005b: 10)), as Sebald terms them – and we might think of them as ghosts or as 'imperial ambassadors' – so disconcert Sebald that he has little thought and few words for the interiors in which he finds himself circling 'planlos' ('aimlessly' (2003b: 14; 2005b: 10)). Only one thing catches his eye – a strange picture of the genealogy of the Bonaparte clan painted as a tree with the names of relatives and descendants cut on little pieces of white paper and hanging from the branches and twigs (2005b: 11–12):

Alle waren sie hier versammelt, der König von Neapel, der König von Rom und der König von Westphalen, Marianne Elisa, Maria Annunciata and Marie Pauline ... der arme Herzog von Reichstadt ... Charles Lucien, Plon-Plon, der Sohn von Jérôme und Mathilde Letizia, seine Tochter, der dritte Napoleon ... die Bonapartes von Baltimore und viele andere mehr. (2003b: 15)

(They were all assembled here: the King of Naples, the King of Rome and the King of Westphalia, Marianne Elisa, Maria Annunciata and Marie Pauline ... the unfortunate Duke of Reichstadt ... Charles Lucien, Plon-Plon, son of Jérôme, and Mathilde Letizia, his daughter, Napoleon III ... the Bonapartes of Baltimore and many more ... (2005b: 12))

Sebald smiles to himself: so many great and royal personages-to-be once sat daily as children around the dinner table in the Bonaparte household (2005b: 14)! And from this his thoughts come to dwell on the many contingencies of history and the inscrutability of fate:

> Aber was wissen wir schon im voraus vom Verlauf der Geschichte, der sich entwick-elt nach irgendeinem, von keiner Logik zu entschlüsselnden Gesetz, bewegt und in seiner Richtung verändert oft im entscheidenden Moment von unwägbaren Winzigkeiten, durch einen kaum spürbaren Luftzug, durch ein zur Erde sinkendes Blatt oder durch einen von einem Auge zum anderen quer durch eine Menschenversammlung gehenden Blick. Nicht einmal in der Rückschau können wir erkennen, wie es wirklich vordem gewesen und zu diesem oder jenem Weltereignis gekommen ist. (2003b: 17)

> (But what can we know in advance of the course of history, which unfolds according to some logically indecipherable law, impelled forward, often changing direction at the crucial moment, by tiny, imponderable events, by a barely perceptible current of air, a leaf falling to the ground, a glance exchanged across a great crowd of people? Even in retrospect we cannot see what things were really like before that moment, and how this or that world-shaking event came about. (2005b: 14))

The strange family tree in the Casa Bonaparte, with its names, titles, dates and destinies, looks down on the living in the same way as those pictures of ancestors in the parlours of other, more humble Corsican homes. The whole imperial dynasty itself keeps watch over their distant descendants – the uncanny employees perhaps, the women who make time pass slowly and who usher idling tourists through the rooms which once were theirs.

THE CORSICAN AMBASSADOR . . . UNFINISHED BUSINESS

In the Casa Bonaparte, Sebald muses upon the unknowable futures of those in the past. Most importantly, his Corsican writings, the Arca Project as I have termed them, are concerned with the *future of the past*. At the end of 'Campo Santo' he shares his deepest fears for what will come to pass. The ever-growing populations of our great global cities mean that there is decreasing space for the dead and ever less time for their proper remembrance. Today, we have become so many that our own passing will be of all too little consequence:

> In den Stadtschaften des ausgehenden zwanzigsten Jahrhunderts [hingegen], in denen jeder, von einer Stunde zur andern, ersetzbar und eigentlich bereits von Geburt an überzählig ist, kommt es darauf an, dauernd Ballast über Bord zu werfen, alles, woran man sich erinnern könnte, die Jugend, die Kindheit, die Herkunft, die Vorväter und Ahnen restlos zu vergessen. (2003b: 37)

143

(In the urban societies of the late twentieth century ... where everyone is instantly replaceable and is really superfluous from birth, we have to keep throwing ballast overboard, forgetting everything that we might otherwise remember: youth, childhood, our origins, our forebears and ancestors. (2005b: 35))

Sebald finally envisages the nightmare of a world without memory, where the dead have no place, and to which they are unwilling to return. It is a world in which the dead have, so to speak, given up the ghost. Sebald writes: '[wir werden] am Ende selber das Leben lassen ohne das Bedürfnis, eine Weile wenigstens noch bleiben oder gelegentlich zurückkehren zu dürfen' ('in the end we shall relinquish life without feeling any need to linger for a while, nor shall we be impelled to pay return visits from time to time' (2003b: 38; 2005b: 35)).

All memories involve a return of that which has been repressed. This is why Corsica is uncanny: haunted by ghosts, it is where no one is forgotten, where no one is permitted to forget. If it is the Mexican ambassador who insists: remember the dead, then the urgent message borne by Sebald, the Corsican ambassador, is something even more fundamental: remember to remember.

The notion of the incomplete work is of particular significance here. The unfinished/'unwritten' text has a special poignancy, no less so than ruins. Ruins suggest the vanity of humankind, the collapse of once-mighty temples and palaces and their slow but inexorable reclamation by nature. And ruins are evocative of the ghosts of those who once laboured and lived amid what is now so much debris and decay. Simon Ward eloquently and persuasively contends that 'the ruin is central to both the content and the form of Sebald's literary production' (Ward 2004: 58). But, for me, ruins, especially literary remains as ruins, seem to invite reparation, restoration and renewal, to promise the possibility of restitution, the very restitution indeed that Sebald himself seems to deny. Yet neither Benjamin's Parisian 'prehistory' nor Sebald's Corsican constellation are ruins in need of reconstruction; rather, they are incomplete, imperfect, perpetual works in progress. As such, these writings are suggestive not so much of the dead, of redemption and resurrection, as of the fragility and contingency of life itself. The unfinished is something interrupted, left for further work, suspended, postponed for another time. It is something the author intends to pick up once more, to return to, but death intervenes. The unfinished always involves a sense of an anterior futurity in that it begs the question: how might it have been completed? Or, more precisely: how might it have been completed *if only*? If only the writer had survived that fateful moment of crisis, that fatal accident. 'If only ...': this is the gesture of the unfinished work. It is a future gesture, perhaps a utopian one, perhaps a wish. 'If only...': this is what Sebald's unwritten 'Arca' or 'Arche Project', like Benjamin's unwritten *Arcades Project* before it, reminds us to remember.

NOTES

1 According to von Bülow (Sebald 2008d: 129), Sebald spent two weeks on the island, 3–17 September 1995, and returned for a second visit in 1996. Written in diary form, the entries constituting the *Erste Fassung* ['First Version'] are dated 3–15 September 1995.

2 Published in English translation in 2005. The essays are: the eponymous 'Campo Santo' (first published 2003); 'A Little Excursion to Ajaccio' (1996); 'The Alps in the Sea' (2001) and '*La coeur de l'ancienne école*' (1997).

3 Of these, the most significant are, doubtless, the prose pieces designated as the *Erste Fassung* ['First Version'] and *Zweite Fassung* ['Second Version'] published in *Wandernde Schatten*, the 2008 Marbachkatalog on the occasion of a Sebald exhibition at the neighbouring Literaturmuseum der Moderne. There is also much more, as von Bülow helpfully points out: two box files marked 'Korsika' containing: 'umfangreichen Materialien, Zeitungsauschnitten, Kopien, Bildern, Karten, Exzerpten, und Notizen [extensive materials, newspaper cuttings, copies, images, cards, excerpts and notes]' (2008d: 211). Some of this material is further organized into seven small folders or convolutes (see 2008d: 216) under provisional chapter titles, a nomenclature that is sometimes recognizable in relation to the published essays ('Campo Santo', 'Ajaccio'), sometimes intelligible in connection with the two published 'versions' ('Anflugs,' 'Politik'), and sometimes rather obscure ('L'interieur', 'Motten', 'Seraphine and Danielle').

4 Indeed, the recognition and exploration of diverse themes and motifs shared by these two writers is a reasonably familiar feature of the critical secondary literature on Sebald. This is no surprise. Comparing Benjamin's urban flâneries in his 'A Berlin Childhood around 1900' with Sebald's rural wanderings in *The Rings of Saturn*, David Darby (2006: 266) rightly notes: 'The affinities between Benjamin and Sebald ... are manifold. References to Benjamin, explicit and oblique, occur throughout Sebald's writings'. In a discussion of *Austerlitz*, Mark Ilsemann (2006: 304) observes that: 'Sebald's anthropology is so indebted to Walter Benjamin's reading of Kafka as to warrant more than just one footnote to Benjamin's famous essay on that author from 1934'.

5 This Benjaminian term has a particular relevance for Sebald in the context of the Corsican writings. In the 'Second Version', Sebald's narrative of the fictional nocturnal flight to the island with Douglas X at the controls of his plane contains a series of reflections on the spectacle of the night sky and the images produced by the Hubble telescope. In what one might read as a metaphor for the creative process of textual production, Sebald writes of the distant Eagle nebula ['Adlernebel']: 'Wie riesige drei Finger treten auf einem der Bilder die Ausläufer dieser Nebel hervor, die angeblich die Geburtsstätten oder Krippen neuer Sterne sind, wo das interstellare Gas unter seiner eigenen Schwerkraft sich zu Klumpen zusammenzieht und so den Prozess der Sterngeburt einleitet [In one of the images the fringes of this nebula stretch forth like three gigantic fingers and are apparently the birth places or nurseries of new stars, where the interstellar gas-cloud condenses under the influence of its own gravity into globules, inducing the birth of a star]' (2008d: 169).

6 Some of Benjamin's best-known texts from the 1930s such as 'Berlin Chronicle', the 'Berlin Childhood' fragments and even the famous 'Work of Art' essay were seen by

Benjamin himself as textual, historiographical and methodological experiments for the wider 'Arcades Project'. Sebald's experimentation with the diary form in the 'First Version' is very much in keeping with this sense of testing out the possibilities and potentialities of different narrative techniques.

7 Von Bülow's essentially philological commentary on the 'First 'and 'Second' versions focuses in particular on tracing the source of figures for *Austerlitz*. See Sebald (2008d: 220–2). The marked links with, for example, *On the Natural History of Destruction* (2003) remain unexplored.

8 Sebald's fascination with the literature of the Second Empire should also not be overlooked. In the 'First Version', a diary entry dated 11.IX notes his preoccupation with Gustave Flaubert's novel *Sentimental Education*: 'weil ich mich immer wieder verirrte in dem kaleidoskopischen Wortschatz, der in diesem Roman zur Beschreibung der Kostüme und Interieurs und überhaupt der gesamten Pariser Warenwelt aufgeboten wird [because time and again I would lose myself in the kaleidoscopic vocabulary mustered in this novel to describe the costumes, interiors and indeed the entire commodity-world of Paris]' (2008d: 145).

9 It is not only the dead that end up in such totally enclosed structures: Sebald notes the case of a priest in Sartène who, in the year 1834, walled himself into his home rather than undertake a feud revenge killing demanded of him (2008d: 142–3).

10 It should be made clear that the four essays contain within them in reworked form numerous passages and episodes from the 'First' and 'Second Versions'. For example, Sebald's visit to the Piana graveyard detailed in 'Campo Santo' is similarly described in the 'First Version' in a diary entry dated 7.IX.1995 (2008d: 137–40). Five days later, a visit to the Casa Bonaparte and the Musée Fesch is recorded (2008d: 148–51), material that will be developed in 'A Little Excursion to Ajaccio' essay. In the 'Second Version' much is made of the destruction of the once-imposing forests and plentiful fauna of the island, with reflections in particular upon the fate of the Bavella Forest (2008d: 198–9) and the legend of St Julian (2008d: 203–4), both of which feature in 'The Alps in the Sea'. The essays are, one might say, culled from the materials of the 'First' and 'Second Version'.

11 This rather romantic account of the wild flowers growing in the neglected Corsican graveyard is certainly at odds with the account in the 'First Version'. Here one reads: 'Und die bunten Schiessbudenblumen aus Kunstseide und Plastik, die auf dem Friedhof von Piana wie überall sonst in Frankreich zu Bouquets gebündelt und als Sträusse in Steckvasen die Graeber schmücken, sind sie wirklich ein Zeichen der fortwährenden Zuneigung oder nicht vielmehr eine Art Eingeständnis, dass man den Toten nichts bieten muss als einen billigen Ersatz [And the motley fairground flowers of synthetic silk or plastic, bunched together into bouquets jammed into flower-holders to adorn the graves in the cemetery at Piana as they do all across France – are they really a sign of lasting affection or aren't they more likely to be an acknowledgement of sorts that we need offer the dead nothing but a cheap imitation]' (2008d: 137–8). It is not easy to reconcile this apparent contempt for the dead with Sebald's stress upon the Corsicans' reverence for, and fear of, the deceased.

12 Benjamin observes that the city, through its street names and signage, becomes a 'linguistic cosmos' (1999a: 522). One might extend this to the naming and inscriptions of the

Corsican graveyard, a necropolis where naming itself becomes a new ordering principle.

13 As Jo Catling notes, in an interview published in the *New York Times* (11 December 2001), Sebald is reported as saying: 'These borders between the dead and the living are not hermetically sealed ... There is some form of travel or gray zone. If there is a feeling, especially among unhappy people, that there is such a thing as a living death, then it is possible that the revers [sic] is also true' (quoted in Görner 2003: 47).

14 For a discussion of Sebald's other travels in terms of the uncanny, see Zilcosky (2004: 102–20).

15 Sebald notes that the proper mourning period was five years (2008d: 139). The prevalence of black on the island finds a kind of mimetic expression in Sebald's writings by means of repetition. See, for example, the remarkable recurrence in the text of the adjective *schwarz* [black] during a brief stop at the Café des Sports in Eviza (2008d: 152–3).

16 There is another Mexican reference in the Corsican writings: in the 'First Version' Sebald attends and marvels at a performance given by a small touring circus, during the course of which a fire-eater makes his entrance dressed in a 'schwarz-silbern mexikanischen Anzug [black and silver Mexican outfit]' (2008d: 136).

17 Benjamin is not the only one to have such nightmares: while searching for traces of his family in Prague, Jacques Austerlitz has a Kafkaesque dream in which he climbs 'up and down flights of steps, ringing hundreds of doorbells in vain' until he finally comes upon a caretaker. Austerlitz hands him a note but the man declares he is unable to help, 'saying that unfortunately the tribe of Aztecs had died out years ago, and that at best an ancient perroquet which still remembered a few words of their language might survive here and there' (2002d: 210). Is Austerlitz, as Aztec messenger, the 'Mexican ambassador'? Are the 'Aztecs' here, then, a stand-in for that other destroyed people, Central European Jewry?

18 And there are many of these, not least among them the (albeit benign) 'hunchback' figures Sebald describes at the opening of the 'First Version': a fellow passenger on the flight from Gatwick who strangely manages to precede the author to the hotel in Piana, and the hunchback woman whom he remembers as a consequence: again a curious passenger on a flight years earlier to Vienna who also inexplicably moved more swiftly between connections – onto the Circle Line at Liverpool Street Station for instance (see 2008d: 129–33). This sense of being shadowed by a hunchback, and Sebald's own invocation of an old German folk rhyme (2008d: 131), cannot but call to mind, as von Bülow (2008d: 213) rightly points out, Benjamin's figure of the 'little hunchback' found in his 'Berlin Childhood' reflections (2002: 384–5) and, in another guise, in the first of his 1940 theses in 'On the Concept of History' (2003b: 389). It should be recalled that this latter text was conceived by Benjamin as a sketch of the historical epistemological-methodological principles of the 'Arcades Project'.

19 For me, the figure of the unwitting murderous sleepwalker cannot but call to mind Cesar in Robert Wiene's celebrated expressionist film *The Cabinet of Dr Caligari*, a drama with its own island nomenclature and origins which fascinated Siegfried Kracauer (1947), among others, and which presents us with the very image of a ghostly apparition stalking the Holstenwall Fair, the phantasm in a public place or 'phantasmagoria'. The *acciatori* are *phantasmaquis*.

20 Sebald mentions the French historian Etienne de la Tour, the English writer Edward Lear, and the Dutch traveller Melchior van der Velde (2008d: 198–9).

21 The mass destruction of forests by natural forces (by the 'Great Storm' of 1987 and by Dutch elm disease) is related in *The Rings of Saturn* as part of what Greg Bond describes as 'Sebald's apocalyptic English landscape' (2004: 31).

22 The suggestively named Gerald Ashman (later, Douglas X), the pilot who flies Sebald to Corsica, traces his fascination with aviation to watching as a child the American Liberator bombers flying out of the local East Anglian airstrip in the last years of the war, and to the death of his uncle Hamish, an aircraft gunner, whose plane failed to return from a raid (see 2008d: 165–6).

23 See thesis IX in Benjamin 2003b: 392.

24 Or even 7,000 oaks. See Christa-Maria Lerm Hayes's consideration of Sebald in relation to the work of the artist Joseph Beuys and, in particular, his 7,000 Eichern project presented at the Dokumenta 7 in Kassel and 1982 (Lerm-Hayes 2007: 413–14).

25 See, for example, his curious invocation of the story of Gracchus the hunter in *Vertigo*. In a 1997 interview with Eleanor Wachtel, Sebald mentions the Corsican cult of the dead and approvingly embraces the epithet 'ghost hunter' for his own literary practice (Wachtel 2007: 40 and 42).

26 Interestingly, according to local superstitions in Mexico, the curse of the 'evil eye' can be undone only by touching the person who has cast the spell.

27 For a discussion of Sebald's fixation with Napoleon Bonaparte see Fuchs (2004: 183–91).

28 For a discussion of Sebald's fascination with collections and collecting see Long (2007: 27–45).

29 Fuchs (2004: 189) makes a similar point regarding this ruinous collection and its 'ironische Entheroisierung des Gedächtnisorts Napoleon [ironic de-heroization of the memorial site of Napoleon]'.

8

TWISTED THREADS: THE ENTWINED NARRATIVES OF
W. G. SEBALD AND H. G. ADLER

Peter Filkins

Towards the end of W. G. Sebald's *Austerlitz*, the title character spends his evenings and weekends reading H. G. Adler's 1955 monograph, *Theresienstadt 1941–1945: Das Antlitz einer Zwangsgemeinschaft*. Deeply moved by the 'gewissermaßen futuristische [. . .] Verformung des gesellschaftlichen Lebens' ('almost futuristic deformation of social life' (2001b: 335; 2001e: 236)) captured by the intensive study of Theresienstadt undertaken during Adler's two-and-a-half year internment there, Austerlitz finds that '[d]ie Lektüre, die mir Zeile für Zeile Einblicke eröffnete in das, was ich mir bei meinem Besuch in der Festungsstadt aus meiner so gut wie vollkommenen Unwissenheit heraus nicht hatte vorstellen können' ('Reading this book [. . .] line by line gave me insight into matters I could never have imagined when I visited the fortified town' (2001b: 334; 2001e: 233)). He then goes on to summarize Adler's encyclopaedic description of Theresienstadt's 'allumfassende [. . .] Internierungs- und Zwangarbeitssystem' ('comprehensive system of intern-ment and forced labor' (2001b: 341; 2001e: 241)) over the next twelve pages of the novel, which also include a map of the ghetto and a breakdown of the work done by the labourers reprinted from the first edition of Adler's seminal study. 'Deshalb scheint es mir heute unverzeihlich, daß ich die Erforschung meiner Vorvergangenheit so viele Jahre hindurch zwar nicht vorsätzlich, aber doch selber verhindert habe und daß es darüber nun zu spät geworden ist, Adler, der bis zu seinem Tod im Sommer 1988 in London gelebt hat, aufzusuchen' ('It seems unpar-donable to me today that I had blocked off the investigation of my most distant past for so many years,' Austerlitz laments once he realizes that 'now it is too late for me to seek out Adler, who had lived in London until his death in the summer of 1988' (2001b: 335; 2001e: 236).

 Coming as it does after Austerlitz's complete breakdown in late 1993 after returning from Prague, where he finally learns the story of his mother's imprison-ment in Theresienstadt, the encounter with Adler's text both helps to heal Austerlitz's mental distress and reveals deeper levels of his mother's experience.[1] After his release from St Clements Hospital in April 1994, Austerlitz spends the next two years immersed in the business of deciphering 'die von der in Theresienstadt alles beherrschenden Fach- und Verwaltungssprache der Deutschen' ('the pseudo-technical jargon governing everything in Theresienstadt' (2001b: 334; 2001e: 233)) as documented by Adler. However, despite Adler's meticulous account, Austerlitz finds himself unable 'mich in das Ghetto zurückzuversetzen und mir vorzustellen, daß Agáta, meine Mutter, damals gewesen sein soll an diesem Ort' ('to cast my mind back to the ghetto and picture my mother Agáta there at the time' (2001b: 346; 2001e: 244)). This then spurs him on to track down the infamous film made for the Red Cross visit to Theresienstadt in 1944, in which the town is shown off as a 'model' community dubbed as 'Hitler's Gift to the Jews'. Thinking that 'wenn nur der Film wieder auftauchte, so würde ich vielleicht sehen oder erahnen können, wie es in Wirklichkeit war' ('if only the film could be found I might perhaps be able to see or gain some inkling of what it was really like' (2001b: 346; 2001e: 245)), Austerlitz finally finds a copy from the Federal Archives in Berlin.

Austerlitz then describes the content of the film and his desperate search for a glimpse of Agáta within it. Although he thinks he sees her at one point, doubt still lingers, thus causing him to make a second and final trip to Prague 'Zu Beginn dieses Jahres' '[a]t the beginning of this year' (2001b: 355; 2001e: 252)), which would be roughly January 1997, or, in other words, between the time that the narrator first re-encounters Austerlitz after visiting a Czech ophthalmologist[2] in London in December 1996, and their subsequent meeting at the house on Alderney Street soon after Austerlitz sends the narrator a postcard from there on 19 March 1997. Once deciphered, the linear narrative can be seen to move from Austerlitz's breakdown in 1993/94 after his first visit to Prague, followed by his two years of reading Adler, followed by his finding the Theresienstadt film, which likely happens in the summer or fall of 1996, followed by his meeting the narrator again for the first time in twenty years in December 1996, which then is followed by his second trip to Prague and discovery of his mother before returning by March of 1997 to tell the narrator of it.

The period 1996–97, then, is Austerlitz's 'anno mirabilis', and Adler's book is the impetus for it, just as, so often in the novel, books or bookstores mark a critical crossroads in Austerlitz's evolving awareness of the past and his own identity. This alone would make Adler's book an important text to consider in its role in the making of *Austerlitz*. However, as we all know, there is frequently more than meets the eye in Sebald, and Adler himself is no exception. For if Vladmir Nabokov is the presiding spirit over *The Emigrants*, and Kafka is the muse of *Vertigo*, and Freud and Sir Thomas Browne are the inspiration for *The Rings of Saturn*, Marcel Atze has also pointed out that not only is Adler's *Theresienstadt 1941–1945* a key text for *Austerlitz*, but so too are Adler's *Eine Reise* (1962) and *Die unsichtbare Wand* (1989) (Adler 2004: 17–30). Atze also contends that the 'hybrid form of paraphrase and quotation' (Atze 2005: 92) used by Adler in his Theresienstadt study is similar to the combination of historical and fictional renderings that are foundational to Sebald's working method in all four of his narratives.

But who was Adler and what was the nature of what Jürgen Serke describes as the 'Gesamtkunstwerk' (Serke 1987: 327) of the history, sociology, philosophy, fiction and poetry he wrote? More specifically, how frequent and convincing are the ties between *Austerlitz* and Adler's novels, and if they do exist, what then are the consequences for Sebald if such ties remain completely unacknowledged? Lastly, if indeed Austerlitz gains his identity as much through Adler's book as through his visits to Prague, as Atze contends, how then does Sebald's use of Adler's fiction inform his role and identity as a writer attempting to render aspects of the Holocaust?[3]

To get at some of these questions, it would help first to know more about Adler himself, for Sebald provides little background on him, and without it there is the risk that the uninformed reader could even think that he is one of Sebald's fabled inventions.[4] Born in Prague in 1910, H. G. Adler grew up in a secularized Jewish family and later studied musicology at the Karl Universität in Prague, where, in 1935, he wrote a thesis on 'Klopstock and Music'. Like so many of his generation, however, his dream of becoming a professor and writer was soon postponed. Though he made attempts to emigrate before the Germans marched into Czechoslovakia, visas were difficult to come by, circumstances ever changing and confusing, the needs of family and friends too pressing to ignore. Adler was still in Prague when the Nazis arrived in 1939, and, after marrying Gertrud Klepetar, he was transported with her and her parents to Theresienstadt on 8 February 1942, where he immediately began taking notes for what would become *Theresienstadt 1941–1945*. There his wife's father died, while later, in Auschwitz, Gertrud would join her mother on 'the bad side' of the ramp as they came off the trains, in order that the mother not die alone in the gas chambers. Adler's own mother and father would also meet their death in other camps, a total of eighteen family members eventually disappearing into the horror.

As was the case for so many survivors, a combination of good health, sharp wits and pure luck saved Adler himself. After spending two weeks in Auschwitz he was transported to Niederorschel, a neighboring camp of Buchenwald, and eventually to Langenstein, where he worked in a factory that made sheet metal for airplanes. It was there that he was liberated by American troops on 13 April 1945, returning to Prague on 22 June, barely alive. Eventually he regained his health and, after the rise of the Communists in Czechoslovakia, emigrated to London in 1947, where he reunited with the Czech sculptor and painter Bettina Gross, married, and had a son, Jeremy, who would become a writer, scholar and critic in his own right. However, he also remained an exile for the rest of his life, dying in 1988 after having published twenty-six books of poetry, fiction, philosophy and history, as well as over two hundred articles and essays on the Holocaust, Jewish history, literature and philosophy. Never resting, never settling in any one field or genre, Adler described himself simply as a 'freelance writer and scholar', preferring to approach his subject matter through both literature and social science in order to carefully detail what he'd experienced, as well as render it in art so that it could be imagined by others.

In a television interview in 1986, Adler remembered feeling upon his arrival at Theresienstadt that: 'When I was deported I said to myself: I won't survive this. But if I survive, then I will describe it, and I will do so in two key ways. I want to do it by setting down the facts of my individual experience, as well as to somehow describe it artistically. I have indeed done both, and the fact that I have done so is not that important, but is at least some justification for my having survived those years' (1998: 45).[5] Hence, key to Adler's work is the dovetailing of fact and fiction in trying to both scientifically and imaginatively encompass his experience. Obviously, this approach echoes Sebald's own use of the 'documentary' and 'factional' renderings in his prose works, he himself refusing the terms 'novel' and 'fiction' to describe them. However, if Adler's combination of 'the talents of a historian with the sensibility of a writer' (Atze 2004: 17) in his Theresienstadt book provides a window onto Sebald's work,[6] what then of his fiction? Certainly Sebald was well enough read to know of Adler's novels,[7] but if this is so, it immediately raises the question of what kind of latent residue from them might exist in *Austerlitz*. Furthermore, if such a residue is more blatant than at first appears, and yet remains unacknowledged, what are the consequences for the ethics of Sebald's own effort to reconstitute a past that, like Austerlitz, he can only begin to glimpse through Adler?

Atze is again key to forwarding this discussion, for he has pointed out a number of parallels not only between *Theresienstadt 1941–1945* and *Austerlitz*, but also with *Eine Reise* and *Die unsichtbare Wand*, the final instalment in the trilogy that centres on Adler's Theresienstadt experience. I would argue that *Panorama*, the first instalment in that trilogy, also contains uncanny ties to both *Austerlitz* and Sebald's work, for the very idea of the panorama, a machine that displays pictures of far-off places as sites of wonder before the viewer's eyes, would seem to anticipate Sebald's unique use of photographs to highlight and complicate his prose narratives.[8] More specifically, Austerlitz himself remembers as a child devouring 'Geographie und Geschichtsbücher, Reisebeschreibungen, Romane und Lebensschilderungen ... Nach und nach enstand so in meinem Kopf eine Art idealer Landscaft [...] in einem einzigen Panorama' ('works on geography and history, travel writings, novels, biographies' until his 'mind gradually created a kind of ideal landscape... [and] formed a single panorama' (2001b: 89; 2001e: 61)). Add to this the 'Noctorama' in Antwerp and the way Austerlitz finds that the animals' eyes mimic those of philosophers, or the way that Věra's memory of staring at the Prague landscape from Petřín Hill makes it seem 'als schaute ich wieder [...] in ein Diorama' ('as if I were gazing at a diorama' (2001b: 227; 2001e: 158)), and we see that the aspect of looking at the past through a sort of viewfinder or staged setting is very akin to the panorama that Josef Kramer, the protagonist of Adler's novel, visits as a boy in the book's opening 'Vorbild', and which serves as the novel's recurrent metaphor.[9] This is then followed by ten separate 'scenes' or instalments running from his childhood and education in Prague to his internment in and eventual liberation from a concentration camp, further emphasizing Adler's use of the 'hybrid' as an aesthetic that constructs a narrative whole out of parts or fragments.

Arguably, then, elements from all three of Adler's Theresienstadt novels are entwined with the narrative of *Austerlitz*. And just as the thread of the time line is deeply embedded in the book's purposeful convolution, Austerlitz's view of time as 'verschiedene, nach einer höheren Stereometrie ineinander verschachtelte Räume' ('various spaces interlocking according to the rules of a higher form of stereometry' (2001b: 265; 2001e: 185)) can also serve as a metaphor for the interlocking of Adler's fiction with Sebald's. Indeed, just as Adler's *Eine Reise* concerns itself with the journey of the Lustig family to Theresienstadt with only the son Paul returning, *Austerlitz* encompasses an eventual journey to the same place, with Adler's book serving as both inspiration and guide. However, the links with *Eine Reise* (or *The Journey*, as I've chosen to title it in my translation, *Die Reise* being the title Adler preferred before it was changed by his publisher) are more subtle and elaborate. Beyond the motifs of rubbish, the journey and the museum pointed out by Atze (2004: 26) there are a number of other shared motifs, scenes and narrative structures that, when added up together, make for uncanny echoes between the two.

As Atze points out, the dustbins and rubbish details carried out on funeral wagons in Theresienstadt show up in both texts. In addition, Austerlitz curiously decides after retiring from teaching to dispose of all of his research when:

> Eines Abends [...] habe ich meine sämtlichen gebündelten und losen Papiere, die Notizbücher und Notizhefte, die Aktenordner und Vorlesungsfaszikel, alles, was bedeckt war mit meiner Schrift, aus dem Haus getragen, am unteren Ende des Gartens auf den Komposthaufen geworfen und schichtweise mit verrottetem Laub und ein paar Schaufeln Erde bedeckt' (2001b: 180)

> (One evening [...] I gathered up all my papers, bundled or loose, my notepads and exercise books, my files and lectures, anything with my writing on it, and carried the collection out of the house to the far end of the garden, where I threw it on the compost heap and buried it under layers of rotted leaves and spadefuls of earth. (2001e: 124))

This, indeed, mimics the work done by the aged Dr Leopold Lustig on the rubbish detail in *Eine Reise*. Atze also argues that Austerlitz's visit to the museum in Theresienstadt invokes Arthur Landau's deep ambivalence in directing a museum of Jewish artefacts after the war in *Die unsichtbare Wand* (Atze 2004: 28). In *Eine*

Reise, Leopold Lustig's wife, Caroline, also finds herself imprisoned in the 'Technology Museum' before being transported, and later has a long, phantasmal nightmare about trying to retrieve her sister Ida's belongings from a Holocaust museum, only to find that they now belong to the state.

In addition, both Austerlitz and Paul experience moments of revelation inside of theatres. For Austerlitz this occurs when Věra gives him the two photographs from his mother's volume of Balzac, one of which shows a theatre set with a forest background (the other being the 'staged' picture of himself as the attendant to the Rose Queen), as well as when he visits the Estates Theatre in Prague, where 'das Proszenium, auf dem Agáta einmal gestanden hatte, war wie ein erloschenes Auge' ('the stage on which Agáta had once stood seemed like a blind eye' (2001b: 231; 2001e: 160)). Meanwhile, Paul's revelation in *Eine Reise* occurs upon his arrival in Unkenburg, where he sits within a bombed-out theatre, contemplating the empty stage as he thinks, 'I'm standing on the stage, like a dead man fleeing a specter' (Adler 2008: 236). Half-dead, desperate for shelter and sleep, Paul is led by a native of Unkenburg to an abandoned barracks, where he falls into a deep dream of being buried alive, only to rise from the grave upon awakening, much as Austerlitz quotes from memory Colonel Chabert's account of being buried alive in a 'mass grave' in the Balzac volume, realizing like Paul Lustig that 'the border between life and death is less impermeable than we commonly think' (Adler 2008: 283).

Beyond these shared motifs and scenes, however, there is also a central narrative strategy that would seem to tie *Austerlitz* even more pointedly to *Eine Reise*. Věra Ršanová, whose first name means 'truth', holds possession of not only Agáta's apartment, but also her memory, not to mention Austerlitz's non-existent memory of himself. In *Eine Reise*, the houselady, Frau Lischka, whose name means 'vixen' in Czech, takes over the Lustigs' possessions and watches over their apartment, albeit for personal gain, once they are deported. In both novels, then, a neighbour occupies and possesses the locale and memorabilia left behind. Whereas Adler's protagonist, Paul, ends the novel in setting out on the journey back to his home, we never see its completion, and so Frau Lischka still holds sway over the past at the end of the novel. Similarly, neither Austerlitz's return to Prague nor his journey to Theresienstadt brings him any sense of completion beyond the melancholy knowledge of his mother's demise and his own lost childhood. Indeed, at the novel's end he is in Paris, for him a nether region inhabited by the ghosts of his own research and his failed love for Marie de Verneuil, herself perhaps another Adler stand-in, as her gift of a medical book is what restores Austerlitz's lost sense of himself and his memory (2001e: 271) during an early breakdown in 1959, just as Gertrud Klepetar helped save her husband, H. G. Adler, and many others as a medical doctor in Theresienstadt, before her eventual murder in Auschwitz.

The real figure in charge of maintaining Austerlitz's memory, however, is Sebald himself. That he does so through the open quotation of Adler's scholarly monograph illustrates the key role that Adler plays in this process, such borrowings from Adler's scholarly work also granting a kind of imprimatur of genuineness to Austerlitz's reconstructed memory and identity. If this then begins to raise the problem of appropriation inherent to any non-survivor trying to construct the survivor's experience, such problems become even more vexed if we consider the possible appropriation of Adler's fictional themes and motifs *without* any direct acknowledgement by either Austerlitz or Sebald himself.

In considering this troubling issue, the 'Paris Epilogue' begins to loom larger in relation to Sebald's invocation and attempted reconstitution of the past. As Austerlitz learns when visiting the new Bibliothèque National in Paris, 'Auf dem Ödland ... auf dem heute diese Bibliothek sich erhebt, war beispielsweise bis zum Kriegsende ein großes Lager, in dem die Deutschen das gesamte von ihnen aus den Wohnungen der Pariser Juden geholte Beutegut zusammenbrachten', as part of a 'bis ins letzte durchorganisierten Enteignungs- und Weiterverwertungsprogramm' ('where this Babylonian library now rises, there stood until the end of the war an extensive warehousing complex to which the Germans brought all the loot they had taken from the homes of the Jews in Paris' as part of a 'highly organized program of expropriation and reutilization' (2001b: 403; 2001e: 288)). Given that Austerlitz himself describes Adler's Theresienstadt book as a 'Babylonian text' (2001e: 233), the question we have to ask of ourselves is whether or not Sebald's method,[10] however brilliant, sensitive and ultimately aimed at evoking both the burden and inability to remember, is in any way parallel to the 'expropriation and reutilization' that Austerlitz realizes is buried beneath this 'Babylonian library'.[11] Put another way, if Adler's fiction is buried beneath Sebald's, what are the consequences for Sebald's unacknowledged use of it?

The short answer is that, for all of his ground-breaking technique, Sebald remains caught in the same dilemma inherent to issues of representation and appropriation that have always haunted Holocaust fiction, particularly that written by non-survivors.[12] However, though Atze says of Sebald's open use of *Theresienstadt 1941–1945*, 'Sebald does not fabricate a palimpsest: the information found in the hypo-text is not written over, but rather reproduced, its semantic potential having crossed over into the new text itself'(Atze 2004: 27), any unattributed fictional borrowings are a trickier problem. Yes, such reproduction is of course found throughout Sebald's works, be it the use of Kafka's 'Gracchus' fragment in *Vertigo*, the biography of Sir Thomas Browne in *The Rings of Saturn*, the use of Ambros Adelwarth's (supposed) diaries in *The Emigrants*, or the numerous allusions to, or unattributed quotes from, Proust, Celan, Levi, Améry and others. Nor is the technique of unattributed literary or classical allusions unique to Sebald. Yet many such figures are not direct survivors of the Holocaust, nor do most of their writings immediately involve the accumulation and interpretation of evidence and experience gathered in the face of the very peril they seek to depict. The fact that Adler spent forty years trying to chronicle his experience of Theresienstadt in both fiction and scholarly studies underscores the bipartite nature of his accomplishment, for Adler felt there was no other way to go about it. If Sebald's mixing of fictional and non-fictional techniques is directly descended from Adler's, it is important to recognize that it springs from a different necessity, one less related to what Adler and many others endured, but instead driven more by what Sebald seems constitutionally unable to ignore or to square with his own lived experience.

For in *Austerlitz*, Sebald is caught in a bind from which he cannot extricate himself, namely that of having to remain a witness to a witness. As Emmanuel Levinas writes in *Ethics and Infinity*:

> The witness testifies to what was said by himself. For he has said "Here I am!" before the Other; and from the fact that before the Other he recognizes the responsibility which is incumbent on himself, he has manifested what the face of the Other signified for him. The glory of the Infinite reveals itself through what it is capable of doing in the witness. (Levinas 1985: 109)

For Sebald, however, no such glory can be immediately or conditionally available, nor does he pretend that it is in real terms. Adler, on the other hand, as a first-hand witness to others and to his own lived experience, can aspire to lay claim to such ethical revelation. Yet Sebald also cannot seem to let go of his pursuit of meaning. Sara Friedrichsmeyer observes that his obsession with 'oddly fated encounters' (2006: 77) reveals that he is 'struggling for an antidote to what experience tells him: that the world and everything in it is random, without meaning, and thus an inescapable source of profound suffering' (Friedrichsmeyer 2006: 87). In regard to this, Richard Sheppard concludes: 'It is as though Sebald's growing consciousness of meaningless suffering continually threatens, like "the horror" in Conrad's *Heart of Darkness* or the corrosive echo of the Marabar caves in E. M. Forster's *A Passage to India*, to overwhelm him. So having precluded the possibility of religious antidotes, and lest he be overwhelmed, he distracts both himself and the "knowing reader" in highly sophisticated, but ultimately inconsequential narrative play' (Sheppard 2009: 112).

To Sebald's credit, the clues left behind that help us to see Adler's influence are as evident as the time line that he buries throughout *Austerlitz*. Indeed, the reproduction of Adler's map and a page from *Theresienstadt 1941–1945* mark the only time Sebald incorporates full pages from another writer's text into his four narratives. Thomas Browne's quincunx illustration and a snippet of Grimmelhausen's Baldanders narrative in *The Rings of Saturn* could also qualify as such, but each is fragmentary and illustrative, in contrast to the self-contained documents formulated by Adler. Hence a different game would seem to be afoot. To arrive at this from another direction, one only need to ask why, then, if Sebald were interested only in blatant appropriation, would he leave so many clues linking the texts? Still, that Sebald points to Adler both directly and indirectly, and on several fronts, only complicates our reading of his true intent.

Consider, for instance, Sebald's inclusion of the map of Theresienstadt that appears on the inside cover of Adler's book (Figures 8.1 and 8.2). Interestingly, Sebald places it right at the start of Austerlitz's account of reading Adler, thereby lending an air of authenticity, be it unspoken, to our 'reading' of Austerlitz reading. On the other hand, because in typical manner Sebald provides no reference or context to the image, Austerlitz's passing comment 'bei meinem Besuch in der Festungsstadt' ('I myself [having] visited the fortified town' (2001b: 334; 2001e: 233)) might also make us think that the map is a vestige document from Austerlitz's own journey there, rather than from the book he is now reading to try to better understand where he has already been. Indeed, the way these two possibilities seem simultaneously present makes evident Martin Swales's claim for the twin strands of the 'literary' and the 'documentary' running throughout Sebald (Swales 2004: 23).

Closer inspection of the map, however, gives rise to even more intriguing problems. Any copy of Adler's original text, for instance, shows that the map is *very* clearly printed, and that there are none of the shadings or seeming deterioration in the map itself as are implied by the reproduction in *Austerlitz*. In fact, there is no reason why Sebald could not have copied the map so that it would appear as crisp and detailed as that which appears in Adler's book under the title 'Theresienstadt – Sommer 1944', which, interestingly enough, Sebald excludes, along with Adler's key to the various locations on it. The effect of such poor copying, however, is what gives the map a 'patina' of age or decay,[13] thus transforming a 'documentary' artefact into a 'literary' one. As such, Adler's 'map' becomes Sebald's 'text,' which in turn posits a subtle but important demarcation between Adler's 'factual,' first-hand mapping of Theresienstadt through experience, memory and the shaping of them, and the gulf of Sebald's remove as a writer writing about a character who confesses to how little practice he had in using his memory (2001e: 139).

If the discrepancy in the appearance of these two maps is not enough to remind us of the difference between reading the account of a survivor and a novel about a survivor who, along with its author, has no account he can lay claim to, there is one more element embedded in Sebald's reproduction of Adler's map which should give us pause – namely the library bar code that appears in the upper right-hand corner. Given Sebald's manipulation of the copying of the map, as well as his having removed Adler's title from it, he could have also easily removed or blocked out the library bar code. However, he did not. Instead, the bar code is what confirms the map as a 'literary' artefact, for one can assume that even if Austerlitz brought back a map from his travels, it would not contain such a symbol. This points to Adler's book as the likely source for the map, while the motif of a 'library' bar code introduces Sebald's role in gathering the materials that the novel maintains are gathered by Austerlitz.[14] In such manner, Sebald risks participating in the 'highly

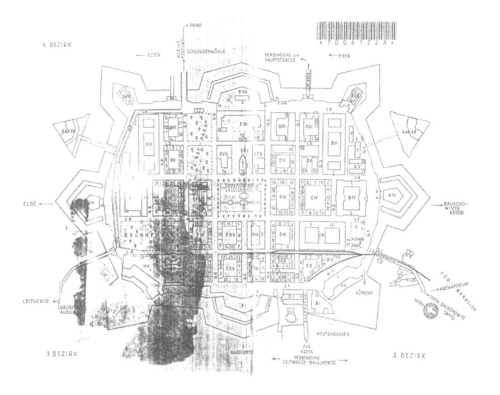

Figure 8.1 W. G. Sebald's reproduction of H. G. Adler's map as it appears on pages 234–5 of *Austerlitz*, published in 2001

organized program of expropriation and reutilization' inherent to the 'Babylonian library' that also represents the archive of the past scattered across the many libraries and government offices that both he and Austerlitz visit. True, if we are careful enough readers willing to do comparative research, Sebald's hand is revealed, but one also has to wonder just how many readers are willing or capable of doing just that, or whether, when such a game of cat-and-mouse between fact and fiction extends too far, the moral consequences of the novel are blurred, if not drowned in its own fictive play.

This method, however, is not just restricted to Sebald's use of Adler's book, but also points to an important evolution in Sebald's method in *Austerlitz*, whereby the residue of his role as a collector becomes an important if subtle part of the images he collects.[15] Again, Adler seems to be the key catalyst to this change, for the next illustration in *Austerlitz* is a copy of a list of designated work assignments produced by the administration at Theresienstadt to account for the economic worth of the work done at the camp, 'no matter how insignificant and totally ridiculous such operations really were' (Adler 1960: 437) as Adler reports. Hence, even Adler's

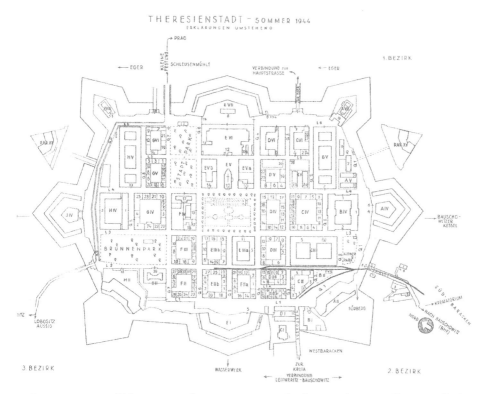

Figure 8.2 Map of Theresienstadt as it appears on the front endpapers of H. G. Adler's
Theresienstadt 1941–1945: Das Antlitz einer Zwangsgemeinschaft, published in 1955

'factual' document is a document about a fraud purporting Theresienstadt's
economic worth, despite the inefficiency of its actual economy. As if to underscore
this silent hoax, Sebald's next illustration is of a postage stamp bearing the bucolic
likeness of Theresienstadt and the surrounding countryside. This image is not from
Theresienstadt 1941–1945, but instead can be found in Adler's 1958 collection, *Die
verheimlichte Wahrheit: Theresienstädter Dokumente*, further confirming Sebald's use
of other Adler texts. Meanwhile, the vestige of a post office cancellation on the
stamp reminds us of the German government's role in perpetrating such outra-
geous and fraudulent views, a practice that culminates in the making of the
Theresienstadt film.

In fact, the next two illustrations in *Austerlitz* are not from Adler but, rather, from
the infamous film that Austerlitz gets a copy of in the hopes of finding an image of
Agàta. And yet, though the ten-pages-long sentence awash with observations from
Adler's book has at last come to an end, the techniques used to render that book in
the novel have not. The first still image from the Theresienstadt film is spread over
two pages and, like the earlier map, is of very poor quality, part of the frame that

shows two male internees looking as if it has eroded away or been burned by the projector. Austerlitz is frustrated by the quality of the fourteen-minute fragment and '[d]ie Unmöglichkeit, genauer in die gewissermaßen im Aufscheinen schon vergehenden Bilder hineinblicken zu können' ('the impossibility of seeing anything more closely in those pictures, which seemed to dissolve even as they appeared' (2001b: 348; 2001e: 246)). This then leads to his ordering 'a slow-motion copy' that lasts an hour, a still from which provides Sebald's next illustration and convinces Austerlitz that the woman who appears in it is '[g]erade so wie ich nach meinen schwachen Erinnerungen und den wenigen übrigen Anhaltspunkten, die ich heute habe, die Schauspielerin Agàta mir vorstellte' ('just as I imagined the singer Agàta from my faint memories and the few other clues to her appearance that I now have' (2001b: 354–5; 2001e: 251)).[16]

As we know, Věra soon dismisses this conjecture as wrong, saying that the woman looks nothing like Agàta did. However, even before this there is a problem for us as readers. For though Austerlitz refers to 'der Zeitanzeiger in der oberen linken Ecke des Bildschirms' ('the time indicator in the top left-hand corner of the screen') as well as 'die Zahlen, die einen Teil ihrer Stirn verdecken, die Minuten und die Sekunden, von 10:53 bis 10:57' ('the figures covering part of her forehead [which] show the minutes and seconds, from 10:53 to 10:57' (2001b: 355; 2001e: 251–2)), no mention is made of the date, 09-05-89, that also appears in the same corner. Whether this refers to 9 May 1989 or 5 September 1989 (given the film's European origin, it is likely the former), neither of these dates corresponds to the time when Austerlitz views the film, which is the summer or fall of 1996. Thus, like the library bar code on the map of Theresienstadt, the time indicator on the video still reminds us that what we or Austerlitz, or even Sebald, are looking at is not something looked at in 'real time', or even in 'narrative time'. Instead, the record of time is a false one belonging to the organizational demands of the archive itself, ironically in this case the Federal Archives in Berlin facilitated by the Imperial War Museum in London. Furthermore, the film is not a film at all but, rather, a copy of one, and on videotape rather than celluloid. Hence, Austerlitz is not watching a film of Theresienstadt, and what he thinks is the image of his mother but, rather, a copy of a film formulated in a time outside of the time in which it was filmed, but which Sebald has further telescoped by emphasizing its irrelevance to the narrative time that he has constructed.

At the end of these temporal and narrative dead ends, we arrive at the last illustration in what I would posit as the 'Adler sequence', namely the photograph from the theatrical archives that Věra claims is Agàta. By now, however, nothing can be trusted, Austerlitz's own constructed fiction for the woman in the photograph seeming as poignant as it is necessary. From here Sebald quickly moves on to the Paris episode and Austerlitz's search 'nach dem Verbleib des Vaters ('[for] traces of his father's last movements' (2001b: 357; 2001e: 253)). As part of this, Austerlitz remembers his first breakdown in Paris in the 1950s and later watching the Alain Resnais film *Toute la mémoire du monde*, which causes him to think that 'entlang der Nervenbahnen sozusagen, und wie die in ihrer Gesamtheit mit dem Bibliotheksapparat verbundenen Forscher ein höchst kompliziertes, ständig sich fortentwickelndes Wesen bilden, das als Futter Myriaden von Wörtern braucht, um seinerseits Myriaden von Wörtern hervorbringen zo können' ('[amid the] library's nervous system, . . . scholars, together with the whole apparatus of the library, formed an immensely complex and constantly evolving creature which had to be fed with myriads of words, in order to bring forth myriads of words in its own turn' (2001b: 367; 2001e: 261)). Such ambivalence towards the function of the library and the research that goes on within it lies at the heart of the novel's denouement. The question, however, is whether such ambivalence applies to Sebald and his own method and, if so, on what kind of plane of regard he ultimately stands in relation to it.

Sebald, like Adler, employs both fact and fiction to reconstitute the past. In *Austerlitz*, however, his open use of Adler's factual study only shows the limitations he faces as a non-survivor. But if, indeed, Sebald consciously or unconsciously employs fiction without acknowledgement, he also risks ending up a non-survivor, in a quite different sense, of his own fictional project. '*A quoi bon la literature?*' Sebald poignantly asks in his speech opening the Stuttgart Literaturhaus, 'Ein Versuch der Restitution' ('An Attempt at Restitution'). The answer he supplies is: 'Einzig vielleicht dazu, daß wir uns erinnern und daß wir begreifen lernen, daß es sonderbare, von keiner Kausallogik zu ergründende Zusammenhänge gibt' ('Perhaps only to remember, and teach us to understand that some strange connections cannot be explained by causal logic' (2003b: 247; 2005b: 213–14)). At the end of the same speech, he goes on to conclude that 'Der synoptische Blick . . . ist verschattet und illuminiert doch zugleich das Andenken derer, denen das größte Unrecht widerfuhr' ('The synoptic view . . . is both overshadowed by and illuminates the memory of those to whom the greatest injustice was done'),[17] and that 'einzig aber in der literarischen [Form des Schreibens] geht es . . . um einen Versuch der Restitution' ('only in literature . . . can there be an attempt at restitution over and above the mere recital of facts and over and above scholarship' (2003b: 248; 2005b: 215)). But if we ask ourselves who is 'remembering' and whose 'memory' is being restored in *Austerlitz*, particularly in relation to the actual memory constituted in the figure of Adler, and yet which is passed by glancingly, the ground beneath our feet begins to fall away. Anne Fuchs, through Dori Laub, points to the possibility of Austerlitz's interior 'thou' or 'du' being restored through the narrator's help (Fuchs 2004: 42). Yet, for a fictional character, there is no actual interiority that can be restored or witnessed in the sense outlined by Levinas above. Hence, the 'synoptic view' cannot help but remain 'overshadowed' *rather than* 'illuminated . . . by the memory of those to whom the greatest injustice was done'. As such, Sebald's fictional project in *Austerlitz* must remain an 'attempt at restitution', but one that cannot help but fail, no matter how compelling such failure may be for the reader.[18]

Paradoxically, Sebald's failed hopes for the ability of fiction to attain restitution in *Austerlitz* align him all the more poignantly with Austerlitz's failure to convincingly reconstitute his past. There is something quite moving in this, and, despite Sebald's shared inability to access or restore the past, his empathy for anyone caught in such a dilemma is clear and deep. Ultimately, however, Sebald's non-survival of his own project pales in comparison to the necessity for Adler to have survived his actual experience, and then struggled for the next forty years to render it. For though Sebald acknowledges the import of Adler's Theresienstadt book for *Austerlitz*, and while clear ties exist to Adler's fiction as well, Sebald did not mention Adler in the numerous interviews he gave about *Austerlitz* before his tragic death. One wonders, however, if Sebald had lived, how long it would have been before an interviewer or scholar pressed this question, perhaps revealing a keener and deeper knowledge of Adler than has thus far been apparent. Meanwhile, Sebald's use of Adler does call into question his own enterprise, but not in simplistic terms of appropriation or misappropriation, nor the failure to reconstitute the past, but to point to the importance and inevitability of such failure. For Sebald's experience is not the same as Adler's, nor can it be, and yet Sebald is the one who points us to Adler through *Austerlitz*, if not constructing a densely layered homage to him. That he does so overtly is what sets us on the trail; that he does so in such circumspect manner only underscores the challenge that he expects us to take up. In the end, though the parallels between Sebald and Adler exist right before our eyes, they require our own efforts to see them, much like the moral scope demanded of us in confronting 'eine großformatige graue Photographie' ('large-format photograph') that Austerlitz at the novel's end finds in a journal which shows 'die den bis an die Decke hinauf mit offenen Fächern versehenen Raum [...], in welchem heute die Akten der Gefangenen aufbewahrt werden in der sogenannten kleinen Festung von Terezín' ('the room filled with open shelves up to the ceiling where the files on the prisoners in the little fortress of Terezín, as it is called, are kept today' (2001b: 397; 2001e: 283)).

NOTES

1 Marcel Atze in fact argues that Austerlitz gains access to his mother more through Adler's documentation in *Theresienstadt 1941–1945* than from his actual visit because of the numerous direct borrowings from Adler's book used in describing Agáta's deportation and internment. See Atze (2005).

2 Though the ophthalmologist is named Zdenêk Gregor, it's tempting to think of the Prague-born Adler, or at least his book, serving as the doctor who restores Austerlitz's vision of his own past. As so often happens in Sebald, however, fact feeds fiction, for a

quick online search reveals that a Zdeněk Gregor does indeed work as an ophthalmologist at The Moorfields Hospital in London.

3 Hans-Christoph Graf v. Nayhauss also raises similar questions in relation to Sebald's use of Adler's Theresienstadt book, but does so only to compare Sebald's use of Adler with Günter Grass's use of Erwin Lichtenstein in *Aus dem Tagebuch einer Schnecke*, which Sebald criticizes in 'Constructs of Mourning: Günter Grass and Wolfgang Hildesheimer', in *Campo Santo*, 2005. See Nayhauss (2009): 447–57.

4 Richard Sheppard catalogues a number of invented persons and documents uncovered by scholars in his report on Sebald scholarship from 2005 to 2008, Sheppard (2009: 111).

5 Throughout this chapter all translations from Adler are my own.

6 Atze points out that Sebald wrote a critical appreciation of Heinrich Böll's 'Frankfurt Lectures', in which the latter praises *Eine Reise*. See Atze (2005: 95).

7 In a 29 April 2011 email to me, Jeremy Adler confirms that Sebald and H. G. Adler never met, but that in the late 1980s or early 1990s Sebald invited Jeremy Adler to Norwich to speak on *Panorama*. Though Jeremy Adler did not take him up on the invitation, his colleague John White did speak on *Panorama* at East Anglia. Sebald also sent a copy of *Austerlitz* with a warm note to Jeremy Adler upon its publication, to which the latter responded with equally warm wishes. In addition, Jo Catling reports that a copy of *Eine Reise*, as well as a copy of *Ortlose Botschaft*, the catalogue for the 1998 Marbach exhibition on Adler, Franz Baermann Steiner and Elias Canetti, were in Sebald's personal library in Norwich. See Catling (2011: 381).

8 Mattias Frey, in arguing for a broader interpretation of the language and forms of cinema at work in Sebald, quotes Lev Manovich's *The Language of New Media* (Cambridge: MIT Press, 2001), p. 71: '"Cinema" thus includes the mobile camera, representations of space, editing techniques, narrative conventions, spectator activity – in short, different elements of cinematic perception, language, and reception. Their presence is not limited to the twentieth-century institution of fiction films; they can be found already in panoramas, magic lantern slides, theater, and other nineteenth-century cultural forms; similarly, since the middle of the twentieth century, they have been present not only in films but also in television and video programs.' See Frey (2007: 231).

9 In a 1997 interview with Christian Scholz, Sebald talks about the attraction of photographs for him, saying: 'For me it has an effect that is familiar from my childhood: there were these "Viewmasters" into which you could look. You had the feeling that with the body you are still in your normal bourgeois reality. With the eyes, however, you are already in an entirely different place.' See Scholz (2007: 105). Interestingly, Josef Kramer's experience of the panorama as a little boy is much the same, as Adler writes: 'If he doesn't turn his gaze away from the peepholes and presses his face hard against the shield, he feels completely alone with the pictures. The daily world disappears and is gone. The viewer and the picture become one on the inside, no one can get in. Josef himself, however, cannot wander off into the pictures, for he remains sitting on his stool, his upper body bent forward slightly … The otherwise familiar world has disappeared. Here is another world which one can only gaze at, there being no other way to enter but to gaze. Only these little holes are there for the eyes. Josef can see so for himself, simply by touching the glass, that there is no other way in. All the people and the distant lands

that one encounters in these pictures remain untouchable behind the glass walls that are only large enough for the eyes.' See Adler (2011: 4–5).

10 Atze invokes Renate Lachmann's notion of 'Einlagerung' (burial or emplacement) of one text within another in discussing Sebald's use of Adler. See Atze 2005: 89. Another interesting model to consider is the idea of 'superimposition' set forth by Bettina Mosbach, who argues: 'The evocation of "superimposed" images governing the framework narrative and the design of the autobiographical narrative of the protagonist are read as a constellation of contradictory narrative programs.' See Mosbach (2007: 390).

11 It is interesting to note that in his essay on Jean Améry published in *A Natural History of Destruction*, Sebald cites Améry and Primo Levi's description of Auschwitz as a 'Babylonian conglomeration'. See Sebald (2004a: 165).

12 The literature on the ethics of appropriation is of course vast, and I make no claims here to being able to resolve such large issues in regard to Sebald's entire oeuvre, but, rather, to look at what seem to me the specific and obvious problems inherent to his use of Adler in *Austerlitz*. In his critical overview that opens *W. G. Sebald and the Writing of History* (Fuchs and Long 2007), J. J. Long provides an excellent discussion of various positions on appropriation, history and intertextuality in Sebald taken by Stuart Taberner, Anne Fuchs, Peter Fritzsche, Angela Reineke and Jan Ceuppens, while himself arguing that '[t]he ethics of quotation … are irreducibly ambiguous', having explored as well the problems inherent to memory and its retrieval in 'Disziplin und Geständnis: Ansätze zu einer Foucaultschen Sebald-Lektüre' (2006) and his book *W. G. Sebald – Image, Archive, Modernity* (2007). Meanwhile, Fuchs (2004) draws upon the work of Edith Wyschogrod and Dori Laub in arguing for Sebald's ethical engagement with the victims he writes about. Fritzsche (2006: 298–9) takes the position that, in Sebald, it is as if 'History has come to an end', and as a result, 'Sebald threatens to undo the historical work of recovery that he has laboriously accomplished. He ties the years of his prewar lives off in what can only be taken as the finality of a natural disaster'. John Sears (2007: 209) argues that Sebald's texts forward a 'problematic, uncertain fictional status'. Ruth Vogel-Klein (2005a: 115) argues that Sebald aspires to return the dead to life through what she terms the 'Gegen-zeitigkeit' of his texts. Lastly, Jan Ceuppens (2004: 191–2) sees 'repetition or representation, even if it is a "hopeless" endeavor, as a way of remaining faithful to an irrecuperable past and of opening a space for a promise', while in Ceuppens (2006: 263) he points out that Sebald's use of texts by others 'will every so often – and even by necessity – miss the singularity of a specific fate'.

13 In a casual dinner conversation during the conference at East Anglia, a former graduate student at the university reported that he once brought up Sebald's name at the copying centre. The response he received went along the lines of 'Oh, that guy! He was always in here, saying "make it look old, make it look old"!'

14 Amir Eshel astutely reminds us that Austerlitz gives his collection of black-and-white photographs to the narrator, which means that they 'were configured with the text *after* the narrator received the keys to Austerlitz's interior, both literally and metaphorically'. However, what this does not answer is whether the two pages from Adler's text are part of that collection, since they are not, per se, photographs, a conundrum that also applies to Sebald's later use of film stills. See Eshel (2003: 79).

164

15 In writing about Sebald's relationship to the 'ruins' he often describes, Simon Ward contends that 'in Sebald's work, [the ruin] is a site of broken narration, a realm where the imagination actively engages with, indeed transforms, the material environment, and where the mediating writer inhabits an interstitial space, both past and present, pointing to the mediated nature of writing (someone else's) memories'. If we think of Adler's map as a kind of 'virtual ruin', Sebald's habitation of an interstitial space through the incorporation of the bar code and his role in controlling the quality of the reproduction echoes this same mediation. See Ward (2006: 190).

16 It is interesting that Bell translates 'Schauspielerin' as 'singer' instead of 'actress' or 'performer'.

17 The verb 'illuminiert' is clearly in the active tense in the German, but for some reason Bell renders it as passive. Thus the correction made here.

18 I say 'compelling', for indeed a counter response to the ethical dilemma in *Austerlitz* is argued by Ben Hutchinson when he says: 'The representation of history depends upon a willed suspension of chronology, and this is where art, and in particular a self-consciously narrative art such as that of Sebald, serves both to distort and to design these fragments shored against his ruin' (2006: 182).

9

STATIONS, DARK ROOMS AND FALSE WORLDS IN
W. G. SEBALD'S *AUSTERLITZ*

David Darby

Austerlitz begins with the description of an arrival and a darkening. But it is an arrival at no destination, an aimless arrival, or at least an arrival with no known aim. The Centraal Station in Antwerp may be central to the city, but its integration into the surrounding topography is in *Austerlitz* idiosyncratic. It serves not simply as a point of deliberate arrival and departure but, rather, as a place of chance meeting between more or less fictional characters, between worlds and lives present and past, true and false. While departures in *Austerlitz* – at least for the figure of Austerlitz, if not for Sebald's narrator – tend toward finality, arrivals, as elsewhere in Sebald's writing, rarely signal conclusive ends to journeys, real or metaphoric. The arrival with which *Austerlitz* begins is not even quite described: we see the approach to the station in radiant early-summer sunshine, but, as the train crosses the viaduct and enters the station, the world turns dark, as it does again and again in this book, countless times from the first page to the closing sentence of the last. The narrator is next seen wandering back and forth through the centre of Antwerp in a state of physical and mental unease. The arrival itself is elided, a mysterious crossing into an inner zone suggestive of the possibility, or at least the memory of the possibility, of some kind of unrealized redemption. Its narrated topography is bounded between Jeruzalemstraat, Paradijsstraat and Immerseelstraat, the last of which is, incidentally, in reality nowhere near the city centre but, rather, several kilometres distant from the station in the opposite direction, toward the outer suburbs. From the station the narrator saves himself – he remembers 'wie ich mich schließlich, von Kopfschmerzen und unguten Gedanken geplagt, in den am Astridplein, unmittelbar neben dem Zentralbahnhof gelegenen Tiergarten gerettet habe' ('plagued by a headache and my uneasy thoughts, I took refuge [literally: saved myself] in the zoo by the Astridplein, next to the Centraal Station' (2001b: 5–6; 2001g: 3)) – first into the adjacent zoo and then into the day-for-night false world of its Nocturama. Its most compelling and memorable inhabitant is the racoon, who 'immer wieder denselben Apfelschnitz wusch, als hoffe er, durch dieses, weit über jede vernünftige Gründlichkeit hinaus-

gehende Waschen entkommen zu können aus der falschen Welt, in die er gewissermaßen ohne sein eigenes Zutun geraten war' ('washing the same piece of apple
over and over again, as if it hoped that all this washing, which went far beyond any
reasonable thoroughness, would help it to escape the unreal [literally: false/wrong]
world in which it had arrived, so to speak, through no fault of its own' (2001b: 6–7;
2001g: 4)). As if the last hope for the reversal of the Fall were in the hands of this
single raccoon. As if the vanity of its obsessive compulsion were the last remnant in
this world of the notion of messianic deliverance.

The status of the four mainline stations in *Austerlitz* is remarkable. The degree of
elaboration in the descriptions of the Centraal Station, Liverpool Street Station,
Prague's Wilson Station and the Gare d'Austerlitz – Martin Swales refers to them as
'great set pieces' (Swales 2003: 83) – corresponds to their importance in the
network of the text's three main narratives. They are crucial locations: first, in the
forgotten prehistory of Austerlitz and his family; second, in Austerlitz's story of
how he remembers his own childhood; and third, in Sebald's narrator's account of
his acquaintance with Austerlitz and of hearing the first two stories. This essay
explores the significance of the stations, and in particular the key role they play in
the recollection and construction of memories. On the one hand, the set-piece
descriptions in *Austerlitz* suggest resemblances between these locations with regard
both to the organization of key interior spaces and to the way in which the stations
enable the operation of specific memory processes and determine the kinds of
memories that can be generated within them. On the other hand, while these
stations function in *Austerlitz* as complex threshold zones between worlds that are
usually considered to be discrete, they are also complicit in a historical process that
has resulted in a systematic and irredeemable falsification of the world and of the
lives lived in it.

STATIONS, PHOTOGRAPHY, MEMORY

Sebald's stations are characteristically dark spaces, in which seeing is described in
terms of photographic processes. In the thickening artificial gloom of the Centraal
Station, for instance, the narrator fixes and saves images, not just of the architecture
but also of human presences. These images subsequently become confused with
those that appeared as his eyes adjusted to the darkness in the Nocturama.[1] The
frame subsequently narrows to select the first image of Jacques Austerlitz, explicitly
a film-like image, his hair resembling that of Siegfried in Fritz Lang's 1924
Nibelungen film. But the image then reverses. In a *mise-en-abyme* echoed in the
narrative embeddings that operate throughout the text of *Austerlitz*, the perceived
and fixed object becomes the viewer and recorder of other, less penetrable images:
from Austerlitz's rucksack, itself the subject of a subsequent photograph, appears
the camera, with which its owner then takes photographs of the enormous, dark

mirrors of the *salle des pas perdus*. The photographs that Austerlitz takes are to become part of the collection that almost three decades later will devolve into the narrator's safekeeping. The moment at which Austerlitz takes these pictures is virtually simultaneous with that of the final extinction of the day's light. There is no suggestion at all in the narrative of the passing of any time between the narrator's first sight of the mirrors, a page earlier, and his vision of Austerlitz's photographing them. When the narrator first sees the mirrors, their capacity to reflect any image is already severely impaired; Sebald's German text speaks of the day's fading light, of which, in their partial blindness, they catch the last glimmer: 'Noch war der Gold- und Silberglanz auf den riesigen halbblinden Wandspiegeln gegenüber der Fensterfront nicht vollends erloschen' ('The gleam of gold and silver on the huge, half-obscured [literally: half-blind] mirrors on the wall facing the windows was not yet entirely extinguished' (2001b: 9: 2001g: 6)). When Austerlitz photographs them, seemingly no time later, they are 'ganz verdunkelt[]' ('now quite dark' (2001b: 11; 2001g: 7)). It is as though Austerlitz is attempting to capture images just at the moment of the disappearance of their last traces from old-fashioned photographic plates. Whatever the mirrors have seen before their blindness, whatever images they have reflected in the past, all that is lost and forgotten, just beyond the reach of Austerlitz's capacity to see or save it. The world we are introduced to here is a world coloured by 'the post-Baudelairean poetic consciousness that all that is present is already past, already lost' (Eshel 2003: 84). And besides, even if any trace of the memories that are presumed to haunt the *salle des pas perdus* and the blind photographic surfaces within were still present, what possibility could there be that, in the complete darkness, it could be captured in any recognizable form in the hand-held snapshots taken with Austerlitz's Ensign?

The opening passages of *Austerlitz*, then, place considerable emphasis on ways of seeing. The first four images reproduced in the text show pairs of eyes – of night animals, and of certain painters and philosophers – all committed to penetrating the darkness of the world in which they find themselves. But, despite the emphasis on seeing, the only visual representation of Delacenserie's station that the reader of Sebald's text is allowed actually to see is the fifth image in the text: a rather amateur-ish daylight snapshot showing the interior of its dome (2001b: 15; 2001g: 11). What Austerlitz and Sebald's narrator see, or try to see, as – raccoon-like – they attempt to penetrate the darkness of their respective worlds cannot be shown in these pages. It is as though seeing is subject to an entropic process at the end of which lies darkness, the impenetrable blackness of the mirrors, the disappearance or absence of images from memory. The Centraal Station and the Nocturama are places where, we are told, painstaking attempts to fix images in memory prove to be in vain, as the images fade to black in the very moment of their appearance.

When we speak of images in *Austerlitz*, we must distinguish between at least three primary categories of image. First, there are the images of various kinds that are reproduced at irregular intervals and in variously complex relationships to the verbal text throughout Sebald's fictional oeuvre. These have of course been the subject of intense scholarly attention. Second, the narrator describes and eventually takes possession of a potentially immense photographic archive assembled by Austerlitz over decades. There is some overlap between this archive and the images depicted in *Austerlitz*, though of course the overwhelming majority remains unseen and unrecounted. Within the archive, one sub-category alone, consisting of the so-called 'Banlieu-Ansichten' [sic] (*'banlieu*-photographs' [sic] (2001b: 372); 2001g: 265), taken on the outskirts of Paris, contains images that number in the hundreds and are notable only for their emptiness. Silke Horstkotte distinguishes here between 'visible photographs' and 'narrated photographs' (Horstkotte 2005: 270). I propose a third category, consisting of images (commentators describe them variously as hallucinations, memories, dreams and products of the imagination) that are seen and recounted only by Austerlitz (or occasionally only by the narrator) and whose appearance – and often disappearance – is described in metaphors based explicitly on photographic processes and technologies. Just as Sebald is interested in 'the non-static, ontological moments of photography' (Patt 2007: 72), so too he focuses on the experience of moments at which memories both become and recede.[2] Most prominent among the places where these momentary images are revealed are the book's four major railway stations. It is in Sebald's metaphoric darkrooms, dark zones of transition between the visible and invisible, the remembered and the forgotten, that these images, perhaps constituting a memory of some authentic world and life, can sometimes be glimpsed 'an der Grenze der Sichtbarkeit' ('on the edge of visibility' (2001b: 237; 2001g: 165)).

The most important of these described, pseudo-photographic images in Sebald's book, at least in terms of its function as a crucial turning point in Austerlitz's adult life, is that which confronts Austerlitz during his return as an adult to the Ladies' Waiting Room at Liverpool Street Station. There, as in Antwerp, the crucial image is described but can, of course, never be seen by the reader. This image exists on neither film nor photographic paper, but it is nevertheless explicitly photographic in nature. The images of the animals in the Nocturama and of the people in the *salle des pas perdus* present themselves to Sebald's narrator by emerging mysteriously from the darkness. The process by which the crucial lost images of childhood develop before Austerlitz's eyes has its analogue in Austerlitz's own earlier account of his darkroom work as a schoolboy: there he speaks of 'der Augenblick, in dem man auf dem belichteten Papier die Schatten der Wirklichkeit sozusagen aus dem Nichts hervorkommen sieht, genau wie Erinnerungen . . . die ja auch inmitten der Nacht in uns auftauchen und die sich dem, der sie festhalten will, so schnell wieder verdunkeln, nicht anders als ein photographischer Abzug, den man zu lang im Entwicklungsbad liegenläßt' ('the moment when the shadows of reality, so to speak, emerge out of nothing on the exposed paper, as memories do in the middle of the night, darkening again if you try to cling to them, just like a photographic print left in the developing bath too long' (2001b: 113; 2001g: 77)). Anthea Bell's English translation effects a subtle but illuminating change of emphasis from the German original here. In Sebald's text it is not exactly the emergence of the image that is the focal point of the analogy but, rather, the subjective experience of *seeing* it emerge. While in Bell's text photographic images are described as emerging 'as memories do', in the German text they are *seen* to do so 'genau wie', precisely as, one *sees* memories. Thus, what the German text emphasizes is not an approximate analogy between how photography and memory function but, rather, a very exact analogy between the ways two different visual phenomena – one real, the other hallucinatory – are experienced. The importance of this is revealed later in Sebald's text: as Rolf G. Renner notes, Austerlitz, by the time he visits Věra in Prague, makes no distinction at all between 'psychische und technisch erzeugte Bilder' (Renner 2009: 335) ('mental and mechanically produced images').[3]

Austerlitz, though, is not alone in having such experiences. Between the depictions of the railway stations in Antwerp and London, the text's German narrator relates the first of his own darkroom experiences, which occurs on the day following the second of his conversations with Austerlitz. In its photographic dimension, and in view of the unstated trauma informing the memories that his vision provokes, this episode clearly anticipates Austerlitz's experience at Liverpool Street. It occurs in Breendonk, when he penetrates to the deepest, darkest part of the fortress, the casemate where prisoners were tortured and killed just two or three decades earlier. Staring into this space, images of his own childhood – the laundry room, a butcher's shop – emerge from the darkness. 'Genau kann niemand erklären, was in uns geschieht, wenn die Türe aufgerissen wird, hinter der die Schrecken der Kindheit verborgen sind', he comments ('No one can explain exactly what happens within us when the doors behind which our childhood terrors lurk are flung open' (2001b: 37; 2001g: 25)). As Claudia Öhlschläger comments (2006: 119), the way into the casemate opens the interior spaces of the psyche and dissolves the boundaries between exterior and interior space, between history and individual memory. The analogy to Austerlitz's later experience is obvious (Öhlschläger 2006: 127). Further memories follow, hinting at childhood memories of domestic violence. In the near-panic of the moment, fragments of personal memory fuse with what the narrator knows of the history of torture and murder in which this room played its part around the time of his own birth.

The second episode takes place in a waiting room, this time that of the narrator's opthalmologist in London, immediately following his arrival at Liverpool Street Station, which is described for the first time in terms of its darkness and subterranean quality (2001b: 53; 2001g: 36). The memory is of the onset of winter, of the childhood wish for everything to be snowed over and silenced completely, and of imagining the redemption brought by the spring: 'wie es wäre, wenn wir im Frühjahr wieder auftauten und hervorkämen aus dem Eis' ('what it would be like when we thawed out again and emerged from the ice in spring' (2001b: 54; 2001g: 37)). As with Austerlitz's childhood memory, none of this is recorded on the photographs that punctuate or are mentioned in the verbal text. Andrea Gnam's observation with regard to Austerlitz's vision in the Ladies' Waiting Room – that the memory of individual scenes of his early childhood occurs independently of the rediscovered photographs (2007: 36) – applies equally well to the narrator's involuntary memories.

The memory sites of the four mainline stations in *Austerlitz* are all reminiscent of photographic darkrooms: Antwerp's *salle des pas perdus* is 'ein zweites Nocturama', 'another Nocturama', filled with 'ein unterweltliches Dämmer', 'a subterranean [literally: underworldly] twilight' (2001b: 9; 2001g: 6); and the waiting room at Liverpool Street is entered through both a door and, like a darkroom or a nine-teenth-century studio camera, a kind of heavy blackout curtain.[4] The entrance functions as 'eine Art Eingang zur Unterwelt' ('a kind of entrance to the under-world' (2001b: 184; 2001g: 127–8)); or a portal to 'ein [].. . falsche[s] Universum' ('a deranged [literally: false] universe' (2001b: 195; 2001g: 135)). Into neither does light penetrate normally from outside. For the adult Austerlitz in Prague, Wilson Station appears illuminated, darkroom-like, by 'ein rotlilafarbenes, wahrhaft infernalisches Licht' ('[a] sickening red-hued light . . . a positively infernal glare' (2001b: 310; 2001g: 218)); and later still the Gare d'Austerlitz, an only slighter less infernal subterranean labyrinth, is, despite the time of day, 'nur von einem spärlichen Licht erhellt[]' ('filled with a feeble light' (2001b: 408; 2001g: 292)), giving Austerlitz the impression of being 'am Ort eines ungesühnten Verbrechens' ('on the scene of some unexpiated crime' (2001b: 409; 2001g: 292)). The relatively few recurrent elements in Sebald's description of key memory places are as striking as the architectural family resem-blances that Austerlitz traces obsessively between the buildings he studies.[5]

The notion that photographic processes provide an analogue to the processes of memory, that (as Austerlitz puts it) photographic images emerge 'out of nothing' on photosensitive surfaces more or less *exactly* like memories, is scarcely original. Prominent among its explorers is of course Walter Benjamin, and for Sebald, a writer concerned to a large degree with tracing connections between architecture, photography, memory and the history of modernity, reference to Benjamin is, as is suggested by the frequency with which the comparison is made in the critical liter-ature on Sebald, all but inevitable. But, however much his writing plays on Benjamin, Sebald's photographic imagination of memory relies on an analogy that is fundamentally different from that informing Benjamin's. Benjamin focuses again and again on the suddenness of an image's appearance on the photosensitive recording surface of memory. In the 'Berliner Chronik', for instance, he writes:

Es ist also durchaus nicht immer Schuld einer allzukurzen Belichtungsdauer, wenn auf der Platte des Erinnerns kein Bild erscheint. Häufiger sind vielleicht die Fälle, wo

171

die Dämmerung der Gewohnheit der Platte jahrelang das nötige Licht versagt, bis
dieses eines Tages aus fremden Quellen wie aus entzündetem Magnesiumpulver
aufschießt und nun im Bilde einer Momentaufnahme den Raum auf die Platte bannt.
(1985: 516)

(It is not [always], therefore, due to insufficient exposure time if no image appears on
the plate of remembrance. More frequent, perhaps, are the cases when the half-light
of habit denies the plate the necessary light for years, until one day from an alien
source it flashes as if from burning magnesium powder, and now a snapshot transfixes
the room's image on the plate. (1999b: 632–3))

While it clearly shares much with Benjamin's metaphor, Sebald's analogy between
photography and memory concentrates rather on the darkroom process, the effect
of which is a metaphor that accommodates an infinitely extendable interval
between, on the one hand, the initial, remembered and forgotten experience and,
on the other, the formation or recall of its secondary image on paper in the developing bath.[6] In completely separating not just the time but also the medium,
process and even agent of the initial capture of an image from those of its later
rediscovery, Sebald's darkrooms suggest themselves as a more exact and evocative
metaphor for the secondary process of what has come to be known by Marianne
Hirsch's term 'postmemory'.[7] While images occasionally do flash up – the
Benjaminian term 'Aufblitzen' is used in *Austerlitz* (2001b: 135) – in Sebald's
darkroom the appearance of the image, while equally mysterious, is more often
gradual.[8] Like much in *Austerlitz* – including, as Nathalie Binczek notes (2008: 19),
Austerlitz himself in the station in Antwerp – these pseudo-photographic images
constitute themselves 'sozusagen aus dem Nichts' ('out of thin air [literally: out of
nothingness], so to speak' (2001b: 385; 2001g: 274)). Various commentators have
suggested that what Austerlitz experiences at Liverpool Street Station is a variety of
mémoire involontaire; nevertheless, the emergence of his childhood memory cannot
be compressed into a single, Proustian *madeleine* experience. Of particular interest
here is Franz Loquai's study, which, working in part from Sebald's own annotations
in his copy of the various volumes of the German translation of Proust's *magnum
opus*, traces in detail the degree to which that text informs this episode in particular
(Loquai 2005: 213).[9] The images that present themselves to Austerlitz in the dark
spaces of the Ladies' Waiting Room stand, however, only at the beginning of his
thought and memory work. Beyond them lie other journeys and other images, lost,
found, and decipherable in many cases only with painful uncertainty.[10]

There are, however, differences in the way that memory functions in the pseudo-
darkrooms of the second half of Sebald's text. Following Austerlitz's Liverpool
Street experience and the beginning of his own active *recherche du temps perdu*, he
visits such locations in the hope that images of his parents will emerge out of the
nothingness. In the newly renovated theatre in Prague, for instance, there is consid-

erable mental exertion involved in his production of memory images as he stares into the darkness of the proscenium arch, which is compared to 'ein erloschenes Auge' ('a blind [literally: extinguished] eye' (2001b: 231; 2001g: 160)). The authenticity of the key image of one of the blue, sequined shoes worn by Agáta on stage is subsequently subject to Věra's confirmation, in a way that Austerlitz's earlier pseudo-photographic images – the Liverpool Street image, and his momentary nocturnal memory as a child in Bala of his parents in Prague (2001b: 66; 2001g: 45) – simply are not. Austerlitz's attempt to envision his childhood departure from the Wilson Station is no less an exercise in *mémoire volontaire*. He describes how for half an hour at the station he has tried 'zurückzudenken durch die Jahrzehnte' ('to think my way back through the decades' (2001b: 311–12; 2001g: 218)). He sees nothing, except that sometimes, for a fraction of a second, he believes, he does recollect sense impressions, which, however, disappear when he attempts to capture them or, invoking another photographic metaphor, to bring them into focus (2001b: 312; 2001g: 219).

The attempt to visualize his mother's presence in Theresienstadt, years after his visit to Terezín, involves a remarkable mix of dream state 'an der Schwelle des Erwachens' ('on the verge [literally: threshold] of waking from sleep' (2001b: 276; 2001g: 194)) and deliberate postmemory: 'Ich weiß noch, wie ich im Halbschlaf versuchte, das pulvergraue, manchmal in einem leisen Luftzug erschauernde Traumbild festzuhalten und zu erkennen, was in ihm verborgen war, aber es löste sich immer mehr auf' ('I still remember how, in my half-conscious state, I tried to hold fast to my powdery gray dream image, which sometimes quivered in a slight breath of air, and to discover what it concealed, but it only dissolved all the more' (2001b: 276–7; 2001g: 194)). The images that come to him in the night immediately following his visit to Terezín, be he sleeping or waking, are those of what he himself has seen of the fortress and the ghetto museum and of what he has gleaned from Věra's account of Agáta's leaving Prague (2001b: 287–8; 2001g: 201–2). Postmemory fails him: the past – the utterly false world of Theresienstadt – is beyond Austerlitz's capacity to see. The Gare d'Austerlitz, the last of the pseudo-darkrooms in *Austerlitz*, reveals no suggestion that it has images to conceal or reveal. Austerlitz can do nothing but imagine – that is, generate fantastic mental images of – his father's experience there: 'Ich bildete mir ein, sagte Austerlitz, ihn zu sehen, wie er sich bei der Abfahrt aus dem Abteilfenster lehnt, und sah auch die weißen Dampfwolken aufsteigen aus der schwerfällig sich in Bewegung setzenden Lokomotive' ('I imagined, said Austerlitz, that I saw him leaning out of the window of his compartment as the train left, and I saw the white clouds of smoke rising from the locomotive as it began to move ponderously away' (2001b: 407–8; 2001g: 291)). The wide-format photograph included in the text at this point gives a sense only of the station's massive emptiness of human life or movement of any kind at the moment of its taking: it reveals absolutely nothing of Maximilian Aychenwald's imagined departure (2001b: 406–7; 2001g: 290–1). It really cannot be otherwise: by this time Austerlitz's image making, be it with a camera or with words, has ceased to have anything to do with processes of memory.

There is of course much of Benjamin in Austerlitz's fascination with 'die ganze Bau- und Zivilisationsgeschichte des bürgerlichen Zeitalters' ('the whole history of the architecture and civilization of the bourgeois age'), not least the notion of that history's pointing 'in die Richtung der damals bereits sich abzeichnenden Katastrophe' ('in the direction of the catastrophic events already casting their shadows before them at the time' (2001b: 201; 2001g: 140)). Particularly incisive and critical among the numerous studies that comment on the importance of Benjamin in Sebald's writing is that by Irving Wohlfarth, who begins by describing Benjamin's writings as perhaps the most central resource for the '*poeta doctus* Sebald' (Wohlfarth 2008: 186); he then states that Benjamin's traces are to be found nowhere more clearly than in *Austerlitz*, and he points in this respect especially to Benjamin's theses on the concept of history and his studies of Paris (Wohlfarth 2008: 196, 207).[11] Just as for Benjamin, the narration of Austerlitz's knowledge becomes 'die schrittweise Annäherung an eine Art Metaphysik der Geschichte' ('a gradual approach to a kind of historical metaphysic [literally: metaphysics of history]' (2001b: 18–19; 2001g: 13)). Various commentaries, beginning with Iris Radisch's characterization of Sebald as 'kein Erzähler, sondern ein materialistischer Geschichtsmetaphysiker [no storyteller, but a materialist metaphysician of history]' (Radisch 2001: 55), have noted such affinities. Eshel, for instance, sees here and elsewhere in Sebald's writing 'culture-critical laments echoing the rhetoric of Marx, Adorno, and Foucault,' which 'unquestionably result in a dark allegorical philosophy of history in the vein of the Frankfurt School', and comments further on Sebald's specific 'affinity with Benjaminian "*kulturkritische*" metaphysics' (2003: 87).

There is an equally clear resonance of Benjamin's work in the ambition and formal organization of Austerlitz's research, which, despite its author's ideas with regard to its eventual systematic articulation, scarcely progresses beyond provisional notations that extend over thousands of pages. It is organized in Sebald's German text into 'Konvolute' (2001b: 47, 175), an unusual word in German, variously translated by Bell as 'stacks' (2001g: 32) and 'bundles' of paper (2001g: 121), both English terms blurring the clarity of the analogy with the sections of Benjamin's sprawling and unfinished *Passagen-Werk*; translators have simply adapted the German to generate the English term 'convolute'. It is, Wohlfarth states, as though Austerlitz had quietly decided to continue to work on Benjamin's arcades project (Wohlfarth 2008: 222).

For Benjamin, railway stations in particular constitute or contain thresholds – *Schwellen* – between realms of experience: magical places, not boundaries, but relatively extensive zones of transformation and passage. The verb *schwellen*, to swell, also connotes, according to Benjamin in the *Passagen-Werk*, 'Wandel, Übergang, Fluten' ('[t]ranformation, passage, wave action' (1982: 618; 1999a: 494)).[12] It entails, in Samuel Weber's understanding, both 'the breakdown of the clear-cut opposition between inside and outside' and 'a crisis in the function of containment' (2003: 23), 'a zone of indefinite expansion and inflation' (2003: 26). A threshold experience is, for Benjamin, 'not a linear transition *from* one state to another ... but rather an *experience* that *traverses* a zone no longer bounded by the familiar oppositions' (Weber 2003: 28). Benjamin suggests the zone between sleeping and waking as perhaps the only threshold experience left to us (1982: 617; 1999a: 494).[13] The concept is explicated by Winfried Menninghaus in terms of such locations' being connected to caesurae in the continuum of space and time (1986: 8). Benjamin's assertion that 'Die Moderne hat die Antike wie einen Alb, der im Schlaf über sie gekommen ist' ('Modernity has its antiquity, like a nightmare that has come to it in its sleep' (1982: 470; 1999a: 372)) conflates both these dimensions of the concept; it also clearly anticipates the tendency of time levels and true and false worlds in Sebald's narrative, and in the processes of memory that it describes, to fold and intersect with one another. Equally pertinent is Benjamin's sketching of the myriad thresholds where he hovered 'auf der Schwelle ins Nichts' ('on the edge of the void' (1985: 472; 1999b: 600)) on his walks through the Berlin of his childhood. In the *Berliner Chronik* he recounts: 'So wurden mir auf diesen Irrgängen ganz besonders die Bahnhöfe vertraut ... der Schlesische, der Stettiner, der Görlitzer, Bahnhof Friedrichstraße' ('So on these erring paths the stations became my special habitat ... the Silesian, Stettin, Görlitz stations, and Friedrichstrasse' (1985: 472; 1999b: 600)). The echo of this in Austerlitz's 'sogenannte Bahnhofsmanie' (Sebald 2001b: 49), his 'obsession with railway stations' (2001g: 34), is unmistakable.

It is in the railway stations and their immediate surroundings in *Austerlitz* that such threshold zones are found most prominently. The narrator's arrival at Antwerp's Centraal Station, not to mention its neighbouring Nocturama, is described, as noted earlier, as a passage into an underworld, a day-for-night world. The zoo and station mark a general turn into a wrong world, an unredeemable fall into the heart of a wider, inescapable darkness that engulfs Sebald's history of modernity in *Austerlitz* and elsewhere. The railway network, present throughout the false worlds of Sebald's books, is closely linked with this fall into history, into chronology. At one end of that history we read of the world's submission to the domination of time, its syncronization that began with the introduction of railway time, the beginning of an eventually global 'Gleichschaltung' (2001b: 18). Far from the neutrality of the notion of time's being 'standardized' (2001g: 12), Sebald's word is loaded in German with the darkest connotations as a metaphor for the process of aligning the organs of the totalitarian Nazi state. At the other end stands the perfection of a network, still in place today, that links Breendonk, Theresienstadt, the Galéries d'Austerlitz in Paris, the internment camp at Gurs in the Pyrenean foothills and the death camps of Eastern Europe.

The station in Antwerp is, however, an anomaly among the mainline stations in *Austerlitz*. Its function is primarily allegorical (Fuchs 2004: 47) or programmatic (Öhlschläger 2006: 111): within the information that Austerlitz dispenses on it, following the narrator's initial description, there unfold the fundamental assumptions and organization of Austerlitz's metaphysics of history. Liverpool Street's place within that history is more complex. While the architecture of the station is not read in anything like the same detail as that of the station in Antwerp, the prehistory of its actual site locates it in relation to a centuries-long history of suffering and death. It is a haunted place, where the dead return, and it is from its underworld that the child Austerlitz returns from oblivion. In these senses, and as a pseudo-photographic darkroom, it represents a threshold zone between present and past, between historical memory and personal memory, between memory and forgetting, a zone of passage between the living and the dead. It is a place of return and of impossible encounters, where Austerlitz's relationship to his own and his century's history undergoes a far-reaching transformation. And it is at this location that Austerlitz's claim, 'daß sämtliche Zeitmomente gleichzeitig nebeneinander existierten' ('that all moments of time have co-existed simultaneously' (2001b: 148; 2001g: 101)), is realized to the fullest degree.[14]

Liverpool Street Station's threshold function is repeatedly emphasized by a leit-motivic resonance in the German text between different kinds of *Schwellen*, Sebald's repeated use of Benjamin's term leaving little doubt about the nature of Austerlitz's experiences. *Schwellen* confront Austerlitz at intervals throughout his research and explorations: in the fabric of the network of railways that fascinates him, in memory and in his writing. The railway itself is in part constructed of 'Schwellen' (2001b: 184–5), the German term for sleepers (2001g: 128); in his account of the crisis that leads to Austerlitz's night wanderings in London (which in turn lead him to Liverpool Street) we read in the German text of the panic he feels 'vor der Schwelle eines jeden zu schreibenden Satzes' ('on facing the start [literally: threshold] of any sentence that must be written' (2001b: 178; 2001g: 123)); and among the memories that come to Austerlitz in the Ladies' Waiting Room is one of mist crossing 'die Schwelle' of the church in Salle in Norfolk (2001b: 196).[15] Beyond Liverpool Street, his first 'Schwelle' experience in Prague brings Austerlitz face to face with nobody other than a Kafkaesque 'Türhüter' (2001b: 209), whose literary ancestry is somewhat lost in Bell's translation 'porter' (2001g: 145).[16] We later read of Marie de Verneuil's having told Austerlitz in Marienbad that it was as if he were standing before a 'Schwelle' (2001b: 308), 'a threshold' (2001g: 216), and dared not step over it.

These locations function in *Austerlitz* very clearly as thresholds between, on the one hand, false, wrong, perverse or deranged worlds, and, on the other hand, something that must be presumed to have been, or that at least might have had some connection to, their opposite. Echoing the raccoon's displacement into its false world is Austerlitz's experience of living a false life, 'sein[] falsch[es] englisch[es] Leben' ('the false pretenses of his English life' (2001b: 357; 2001g: 254)), and of being 'in einem falschen Leben' in a 'falsch[es] Universum' ('living the wrong life' in a 'deranged universe' (2001b: 302, 195; 2001g: 212, 135)). As J. J. Long notes, the falsity or derangement of this life echoes Theodor W. Adorno's notion of the 'beschädigtes Leben', the 'damaged life', of the subtitle of his *Minima Moralia*, and in particular the final sentence of section 18, which reads: 'Es gibt kein richtiges Leben im falschen' ('Wrong life cannot be lived rightly' (Adorno 1980: 43; 1964: 39)).[17] The conclusion of that book talks of a philosophy that confronts and defies despair. Its final page is punctuated by repeated reference to the intertwined categories of 'Erkenntnis', 'Licht', and Erlösung' ('knowledge', 'light', 'redemption' (1980: 281; 1964: 247)), the release from a displaced or estranged world. This is where the analogy with Sebald's thought begins to break down. Although Long argues that 'the way in which the terms ... are used in *Austerlitz* ... ostensibly assumes that ... one can find one's way back to a life and a world that are not "falsch", that inauthenticity is produced by a specific historical or personal caesura which, once identified, can be overcome in a return to the *status quo ante*' (Long 2007: 158), I see in *Austerlitz* absolutely no assumption of the possibility of a return, a reversal of the fall into the darkness of modernity. Another kind of life and world must have existed prior to some wrong turn, but it is impossible to assume that such things still exist or will exist again in the future. Swales writes of Austerlitz's 'epiphany' at Liverpool Street Station: 'if it is a rebirth, it is one that neither restores nor liberates, nor in any significant sense quickens. Rather, it seems to compound the deprivation that is at the heart of the life. Revelation there is; but it is somehow un-negotiable, beyond analysis or comprehension' (Swales 2003: 85). The fall that has taken place admits no possibility of restitution for losses incurred. In Austerlitz's wrong world something bad, some 'Unglück', some misfortune has happened, and it is 'als höre es nie mehr auf und als sei es durch nichts und von niemandem mehr gutzumachen' ('as if the little accident ... were always happening over and over again, and nothing and no one could ever remedy it' (2001b: 20; 2001g: 14).

It is in this pessimism that various critics see an unbridgeable difference between Austerlitz's (along with Sebald's) and Benjamin's understandings of history. Wohlfarth, for example, illustrates this difference with reference to the lasting preoccupations that Sebald's and Benjamin's thought share: the question of the disenchantment of the world that an understanding of time as linear and mechanical has wrought (Wohlfarth 2008: 202) and an understanding of undying suffering, of pain as the deepest stratum, the substructure, of history (Wohlfarth 2008: 217). The difference, argues Wohlfarth, lies in the absence in Sebald of the messianic, the profanely illuminated, dimension of Benjamin's philosophy of history (2008: 210). He argues further that there is almost no echo in Sebald's writings of the Benjaminian constellation of melancholy and revolution (2008: 234) and that, in the absence of the capacity to use the failings of our false world to imagine a more authentic one, all that remains for Sebald is 'das traurige Benennen' (2008: 190), the sad naming, of the catastrophe of history.[18]

Sebald's commentators have noted that the description of Liverpool Street Station in *Austerlitz* depicts an interior clearly reminiscent of the architectural fantasies in Giovanni Battista Piranesi's *Carceri d'inventione*.[19] What preoccupies the tiny figures that move about Sebald's labyrinth is very simple: they are understood by Austerlitz to be seeking 'einen Ausweg ... aus diesem Verlies' ('some way of escape from [literally: way out of] their dungeon' (2001b: 194; 2001g: 135)). *Ein Ausweg*, a way out: this is exactly the word that Kafka's Rotpeter in the story 'Ein Bericht für eine Akademie' ('A Report to an Academy') – finding himself, so to speak, through no fault of his own, in yet another false world – carefully chooses to name his highest realizable aspiration, in explicit contradistinction to any possible idea of restoration or redemption. Austerlitz himself sees in Stower Grange his 'einziger Ausweg' (2001b: 88), his 'only escape route' (2001g: 60), from the false life into which he has fallen, through no fault of his own, with his Welsh foster-parents. There is no question of a simple, physical return to home and hearth. The repeated, failed attempts of Austerlitz's splendidly named schoolmate Robinson to escape and return to Andromeda Lodge prove that. As a child in Bala, Austerlitz may have dreamed of opening a locked door and stepping over 'die Schwelle ... in eine freundlichere, weniger fremde Welt' ('[the threshold] into a friendlier, more familiar world' (2001b: 65; 2001g: 44)). But the only time Sebald's book speaks of 'Erlösung' (release, redemption), the redemption in question offers anything but a sound analogy with Adorno's defiantly illuminated restoration of an undamaged life. The novel's narrator recounts, rather, a 'Vision der Erlösung', through the extinction of the faculty of sight, 'von dem ewigen Schreiben- und Lesenmüssen' ('a vision of release ... [from] the constant compulsion to read and write' (2001b: 52; 2001g: 35–6)): an involuntary retreat to a wicker chair in a garden that is no longer visible.

In false worlds false lives are lived. The practicalities of the German occupation of Prague induce in Věra the thought that from now on we must live 'in einer falschen Welt' ('in a world turned upside down' (2001b: 247; 2001g: 171)). In such a world systems of rules become suddenly inverted. There is no disorder. There is no question of the world's deregulation, its decoupling from the network of the rules of its *Gleichschaltung*. Another, comprehensive system of more far-reaching rules now applies, determining 'das Modell einer von der Vernunft erschlossenen, bis ins geringste geregelten Welt' ('the model of a world made by reason and regulated in all conceivable respects' (2001b: 284; 2001g: 199)), a world that in *Austerlitz* finds its most perfect, most inescapable and most rational of materializations in Theresienstadt.

Crucial to this false world is the perfectibility of its network, the capacity of its constitutive system for closure and completeness. Such networks – for example 'd[as] gesamte[] System der Eisenbahnen' ('the entire railway system' (2001b: 49; 2001g: 33)) – are in essence threshold-free. Once one has entered such a world, there is no way out: one is committed to riding the metaphoric train to its inevitable destination.[20] In the work of Benjamin and of Adorno, as in *Austerlitz*, that destination, a consequence of modernity's perverse confusion of enlightened reason with instrumental rationality (Taberner 2004: 191; Öhlschläger 2006: 117), is the catastrophe of our history, whether or not the catastrophe may admit the possibility of a later messianic return to an undamaged life, to a more authentic world. Of the messianic potential in both Benjamin's and Adorno's thought there is, as discussed above, little left in *Austerlitz* beyond the vain attempt of the raccoon to restore its piece of apple to its original state.

Austerlitz, nevertheless, does contain the suggestion of another way of living in the world at hand. Like Benjamin's *Arcades Project*, *Austerlitz*'s scholarship resists systematization and regulation: it may have begun as a dissertation project but, after 'endlose Vorarbeiten', 'endless preliminary sketches', decades later it has resulted in the 'Denkversuche' (2001b: 48), the 'tentative ideas' (2001g: 33) that Austerlitz begins to relate to the narrator in Antwerp. While it was motivated initially by intentions entirely coincident with the 'Ordnungszwang' and the 'Zug ins Monumentale' ('the compulsive sense of order and the tendency toward monumentalism' (2001b: 48; 2001g: 33)), and even the 'Tendenz zu paranoider Elaboration' (2001b: 23–4), the 'tendency towards paranoid elaboration' (2001g: 16) that characterize the architectural structures that it purported to study, its realization is indefinitely deferred.[21] It simply never becomes a history. When Austerlitz describes his intention of resuming the work in the 1990s in Paris, he speaks this time of his 'Plan eines mehrbändigen systematisch-deskriptiven Werks', or alternatively 'ein[e] Reihe von Versuchen' ('a systematically descriptive work in several volumes ... a series of essays' (2001b: 174; 2001g: 120–1)).[22] Both possibilities echo and exceed the study or studies that Benjamin might have written. What remains, at least until Austerlitz destroys them, is the collecton of *Konvolute*, his papers that contain only 'Entwürfe ... die mir jetzt unbrauchbar, falsch und verzeichnet erschienen' ('sketches which now seemed misguided, distorted, and of little use' (2001b: 175; 2001g: 121)). What is salvageable can be reshuffled, 'um vor meinen eigenen Augen noch einmal, ähnlich wie in einem Album, das Bild der von dem Wanderer durchquerten, beinahe schon in der Vegessenheit versunkenen Landschaft entstehen zu lassen' ('in order to re-create before my own eyes, as if in the pages of an album, the picture of the landscape, now almost immersed in oblivion, through which my journey had taken me' (2001b: 175; 2001g: 121)). The *Konvolute* thus become a further memory place, another archive of images whose order can be shuffled to produce subjective, contingent meanings and which are useless for the construction of a systematic, monumental historical project of the kind for which they were originally begun.

The organization and usefulness of the *Konvolute* represent the antipode of the systems of military architecture described in *Austerlitz* that were completed – 'vervollkommnet' (2001b: 23) – in the eighteenth century, of which some found a use later as places of torture and murder (Breendonk, Vauban, Terezín and so on).[23] The life contained in the *Konvolute* exists not in the perversely rigid organization of the new Mitterand library, of which we read 'daß ... die allumfassende, absolute Perfektion des Konzepts in der Praxis durchaus zusammenfallen kann, ja letztlich zusammenfallen muß mit einer chronischen Dysfunktion und mit konstitutioneller Labilität' ('that the all-embracing and absolute perfection of the concept can in practice coincide, indeed ultimately must coincide, with its chronic dysfunction and constitutional instability' (2001b: 394–5; 2001g: 281)).[24] It exists, rather, in a world characterized by the lost wide embrace (2001b: 386–7; 2001g: 276–7), congeniality and half-light of the old Bibliothèque Nationale – the haunt of both Benjamin and Austerlitz – whose means of communication, bookstacks and scholars formed 'ein höchst kompliziertes, ständig sich fortentwickelndes Wesen ... das als Futter Myriaden von Wörtern braucht, um seinerseits Myriaden von Wörtern hervorbringen zu können' ('an immensely complex and constantly evolving creature which had to be fed with myriads of words, in order to bring forth myriads of words in its own turn' (2001b: 367; 2001g: 261)). It exists not in the room at Terezín where the orderly files on the prisoners are stored, but in Austerlitz's own study in Bloomsbury, its floor, shelves and desks filled in no obvious systematic order with books, magazines, folders, colour slides, stacks of papers and whatever else.[25] Such a defiance of closed systems, such a way of thinking about the world, is likewise made explicit in two earlier Sebald texts: in *Schwindel. Gefühle* (*Vertigo*) we read of Henri Beyle's 'vollendetes oder doch der Vollendung zustrebendes System' ('perfect system, or at least one that was aspiring to perfection' (Sebald 2001l: 18; 2000b: 14)), and in *Die Ringe des Saturn* (*The Rings of Saturn*), the apparent chaos of Janine Dakyns's office at the University of East Anglia represents 'so etwas wie eine vollendete oder doch der Vollendung zustrebende Ordnung' ('a perfect kind of order, or an order which at least tended towards perfection' (Sebald, 2001k: 17; 1998b: 9)), where in both cases the 'oder doch', 'or at least', has the clear sense of a corrective 'or rather'.

It is to such worlds, the crucial principle of whose order and systems is their logical and practical imperfectability, that the stations, darkrooms and thresholds of *Austerlitz* belong. The stations are of course especially ambiguous. On the one hand, as nodes in the railway system and as buildings whose architecture offers an allegorical representation of the capitalist ideologies and economies that have driven the history of modernity, they are utterly complicit in the catastrophe that so preoccupies both Benjamin and Austerlitz. On the other hand, they offer zones of transit between a life lived inescapably in the false world of that history and momentary memories of another world, before its falsification and fall into darkness.[26] That is to suggest neither that these thresholds permit a return nor that the memories themselves, or at least the sudden experience of such moments, are in many cases anything but painful or traumatic. These darkrooms' characterization as 'Glücks- und Unglücksorte zugleich' ('places marked by both blissful happiness and profound misfortune' (2001b: 49; 2001g: 34)) emphasizes their resistance to alignment within a single system. They are zones of tension between the presumed authentic and the false, and the access they give to an unsuspected underworld in which both coexist is in defiance of the asserted wholeness of the network of whose architecture, history and catastrophe they are essential elements.

NOTES

1 As Bettina Mosbach suggests, both the photographic technique of double exposure and the technique of a dissolve (Sebald here uses the term 'Überblendung' (2001b: 9)) between film frames or projected transparencies function as analogies through which the confusion of these images can be understood (Mosbach 2008: 225). In another essay Mosbach examines the photographic technique of 'Überblendung' as a narrative strategy in *Austerlitz* (2007: esp. 390–3).

2 Patt defines such moments, in contrast to the 'frozen, "decisive moments" fixed on photographic paper', as 'the few, powerful, non-static moments of the photograph's becoming and receding: the moment of its clicked inception, when light is captured on a piece of film; those blind moments of faith when film is developed into a negative; and those magical moments of the photograph's public coming-out, when under cover of arterial colored light, the negative is coaxed to give up some (but never all) of its secrets' (2007: 72).

3 Renner later discusses how photographic processes both imitate and influence the processes of memory in *Austerlitz* (2009: 341).

4 Patt discusses how 'Jacques Austerlitz gravitates to sites, either rooms that are mirrored and transparent (like the camera), or spaces that are dark and duplicitous (like the darkroom), so that he can give voice to the secrets he holds in reserve (often even from himself) ... With an eerie consistency, Austerlitz describes his world as if it were a black and white photograph' (2007: 73).

5 Urszula Terentowicz-Fotyga argues that 'while the spaces and their histories are indeed meticulously placed and represented, they are not quite described. Austerlitz and the narrator rarely represent places, buildings, and objects in an extensive way. Spatial semiotics does not progress through straightforward description. We do not get to know places through a progression and accumulation of detail, rather through a careful

selection of representative or synecdochical elements, a reduction of multiplicity to a few meticulously selected, named, and defined objects or images' (2009: 321).

6 Alexandra Tischel, for instance, writes of the 'innere Dunkelkammer' (inner darkroom) in which Austerlitz's memories reveal themselves (2006: 32–9).

7 Developed most fully in Hirsch's *Family Frames*, where it is described as characterizing 'the experience of those who grew up dominated by narratives that preceded their birth' (1997: 22), the concept finds a particularly precise definition in a more recent essay: 'Postmemory describes the relationship of the second generation to powerful, often traumatic, experiences that preceded their births but that were nevertheless transmitted to them so deeply as to seem to constitute memories in their own right' (2008: 103). For a consideration of the theory, practice and ethics of postmemory in relation to *Austerlitz*, see Crownshaw (2004).

8 In his theses 'Über den Begriff der Geschichte' ('On the Concept of History') Benjamin writes: 'Nur als Bild, das auf Nimmerwiedersehen im Augenblick seiner Erkennbarkeit eben aufblitzt, ist die Vergangenheit festzuhalten' ('The past can be seized only as an image that flashes up at the moment of its recognizability, and is never seen again' (1974: 695; 2003a: 390)). He continues: 'Vergangenes historisch artikulieren heißt nicht, es erkennen "wie es denn eigentlich gewesen ist". Es heißt, sich einer Erinnerung bemächtigen, wie sie es im Augenblick einer Gefahr aufblitzt' ('Articulating the past historically does not mean recognizing it "the way it really was". It means appropriating a memory as it flashes up in a moment of danger' (1974: 695; 2003a: 391)). See also Taberner (2004: esp. 192–3).

9 Loquai goes on to trace the white turban of the railway employee (a figure who has provoked various critical interpretations), whom Austerlitz follows toward the waiting room, to Proust's invocation of the Sultan who rules over life and death in the *1001 Nights* (Loquai 2005: 219). This figure in *Austerlitz* is prefigured by the man, also wearing a white turban, who photographs the narrator's eyes during his appointment with his Harley Street opthalmologist (Sebald 2001b: 56; 2001g: 38–9).

10 Russell J. A. Kilbourn (2004) challenges the general assumption that Austerlitz's Liverpool Street experience constitutes his 'Proustian moment, where his "involuntary memory" is engaged through a series of serendipitous events'; for Kilbourn, 'the differences are telling: rather than a catalyst for involuntary memory, the station and waiting room operate in a more complex manner as the externalised concrete representation of the structure (*topos*) of Austerlitz's hitherto suppressed and/or displaced long-term memory, laid bare to him for the first time, in a description that signifies at both individual and socio-historical levels' (2004: 145–6).

11 Wohlfarth later discusses Benjamin's life and thought as having been the 'Pate' (godfather) of Austerlitz's fictional biography (2008: 219); then, after listing resemblances, Wohlfarth proceeds to discuss how motifs from Benjamin's workshop are 'verarbeitet' ('processed') by Sebald (Wohlfarth 2008: 221).

12 Samuel Weber translates this as 'Change, passage, flooding' (2003: 23).

13 Binczek understands Sebald's thresholds in relation to the cultural-historical and aesthetic paradigms that mark the image of the threshold in the nineteenth and twentieth centuries: the technique of *mémoire involontaire*, depth-psychological theory of

dream, trauma, and association, Stifter, Kafka, Benjamin (Binczek 2008: 21).

14 Regarding the Benjaminian dimension of this claim, see Brockmeier (2008: 359, 361). See also Horstkotte (2005: 274–5).

15 In the English translation there is no mention of a threshold: the mist simply 'crept slowly into the church porch' (2001g: 136).

16 The echo is of the figure of the 'Türhüter', the 'doorkeeper' in the parable 'Vor dem Gesetz' ('Before the Law'), which is related in the ninth chapter of Kafka's novel *Der Prozeß* (*The Trial*). Both Taberner (2004: 191) and Hutchinson (2009: 46) point toward further echoes of *Der Prozeß* in *Austerlitz*.

17 See also Hutchinson (2009: 95, 111).

18 Connected with this argument, and important to an understanding of the crucial differ- ence between Austerlitz's and Benjamin's scholarship, is the correction of the notion that Benjamin's *Passagen-Werk* might have been unfinishable: Wohlfarth argues that Benjamin left convincing evidence to the contrary in his papers and in the completed parts of the Baudelaire study (2008: 225).

19 For example, Tischel (2006: 34–5); Arnold-de Simine (2006: 159–60); and Martin (2007: 88–90). Arnold-de Simine uses the etching 'La torre circolare' (the round tower) to illus- trate the comparison, while Martin identifies 'Il ponte levatoio' (the drawbridge) as the etching in question in *Austerlitz* (Wilton-Ely 1994: 53, 60). Martin argues that there is an implicit, indirect reference to Giambattista Vico, whose understanding of the recurrence of earlier stages of history in the present was of interest to Piranesi, and he sees a further connection between the architectural imaginings of Sebald and Piranesi in the difficulty of determining whether the etchings depict ruins or buildings under construction (2007: 90). Renner compares Sebald's description of the architectural order not just of the railway stations but also of the new Bibliothèque Nationale to the architectural fantasies of both Piranesi and M. C. Escher (2009: 343).

20 Taberner describes Austerlitz's 'conception of the deformations of modernity' in similar terms (2004: 190); Eshel, on the other hand, is sceptical of 'Sebald's *kulturkritische* notions', which 'amount at times to a questionable teleology in which modernity is all too clearly configured as necessarily leading to Theresienstadt' (2003: 88).

21 Long describes Austerlitz's knowledge as 'motivated by a desire for totality and complete systematisation' (2007: 153).

22 Wohlfarth sees in these intended projects echoes of the work of Maxime Du Camp and Dolf Sternberger (2008: 222).

23 Bell renders *vervollkommnet* as 'improved' (2001g: 16).

24 Eshel describes Sebald's critique of the new Bibliothèque Nationale as 'pedantic' (2003: 88).

25 Gnam (2007: 41) makes a connection between the image of Austerlitz's 'Arbeitsplatz' (Sebald 2001b: 47), 'where he worked' (2001g: 32), in Bloomsbury and that of what is later described as his 'wahrer Arbeitsplatz' (2001b: 397), his 'true place of work' (2001g: 283), in the archive at Terezín; the echo is lost in Bell's translation.

26 Wohlfarth comments on the mixture of mistrust and fascination that informs Austerlitz's attitude to the railway network (2008: 215). Binczek too points to this contra- diction in discussing Austerlitz's own use of the synchronized rail network not just to

trace his own past but also to reach a conception of time as asynchronous or even atemporal (2008: 18): 'doch ist es mir immer mehr, als gäbe es keine Zeit, sondern nur verschiedene, nach einer höheren Stereometrie ineinander verschachtelte Räume' ('I feel more and more as if time did not exist at all, only various spaces interlocking according to the rules of a higher form of stereometry' (Sebald 2001b: 265; 2001g: 185)).

Part III

'PROSE' AND PHOTOGRAPHY

10

FIELDS OF ASSOCIATION: W. G. SEBALD AND CONTEMPORARY PERFORMANCE PRACTICES

Simon Murray

I am not seeking an answer. I just want to say this is very odd indeed. (Sebald in Schwartz 2007: 165)

This process means dismembering logical plot structures, building up scenes, not by textual reference, but by reference to associations triggered by them, juggling with CHANCE or junk, ridiculously trivial matters which are embarrassingly shameful, devoid of any meaning or consequence . . . (Kantor 1993: 60)

This chapter traces modes of association between W. G. Sebald's writing and particular tropes of contemporary performance making. Sebald's engagement with visual art, especially photography, has been well explored over the decade since 2003,[1] but little has been articulated around possible synergies between his writing and selected practices within the territory of contemporary theatre. Whilst Sebald edited a collection of papers entitled *A Radical Stage: Theatre in Germany in the 1970s and 1980s* (1988), theatre, in any explicit sense, hardly features in his fictions – there is little apparent interest in theatre as an art form from Sebald's characters and narrators.[2] Nonetheless, in *A Radical Stage*, Sebald hints at where his theatrical sympathies lie when he affirms post-war documentary drama in West Berlin as having 'very positive implications for theatre as an art form, at least inasmuch as it went against all preconceived notions of what a play ought to look like' (Sebald 1988a: 2). Similarly, in his essay on the theatre of Herbert Achternbusch, Sebald seems to applaud the fact that Achternbusch's output 'clearly defies any notion of an orderly body of work. One text grows out of another, or alternatively into another . . . disorder is turned into a system' (Sebald 1988a: 174). From the evidence of this collection (1988a), Sebald felt strongly that the conventions governing Brechtian theatre – let alone those of naturalism and realism – were now unable 'to deal with our traumatised consciousness' (1988a: 175). Such statements suggest that the theoretical frameworks of theatre and performance studies might constitute an important, if under-researched, perspective on Sebald's work.

Drawing confidence from Sebald's affirmation of working against 'preconceived notions of what a play ought to look like', this essay identifies and reflects upon shared formal dispositions between Sebald's strategy for fictional writing and the dramaturgical and compositional practices of contemporary devised theatre. Here, I particularly elaborate upon what appear to be some striking associations between Sebald and these makers of performance in terms of approaches to narrative structure: the construction of reader-spectators as witnesses inevitably complicit in events that unfold on page or stage; a playful disregard for the immutability of boundaries between fact and fiction/the real and the imaginary; a quality of attention tethered loosely in lightness and circling; and the necessity of speaking through multiple voices, not as some ironic postmodern game, but as an ethical and ideological imperative for restitution which might begin to address the fractures of the twentieth and twenty-first centuries.

FINDING SEBALD WITHIN DEVISED PERFORMANCE: VOLCANO, GOAT ISLAND AND CUPOLA BOBBER

As a preface to what follows I must indicate the opaque and diverse landscapes of contemporary theatre and performance towards which I am gesturing.[3] Of course, *contemporary* theatre will include modern playwriting, but in this account I am referring largely to performance practices where work is collaboratively *devised*, that is to say, a process whereby all members of the company or group are (self-consciously) co-authors/co-creators – although not necessarily equal ones – of the material to be performed. Above all, despite the manifold compositional strategies embraced by devised theatre makers, the project implicitly or transparently is positioned against 'preconceived notions of what a play ought to look like' (Sebald 1988a: 2). Such processes do not preclude the role of director, composer, choreographer and scenographer or, indeed, writer, but do presuppose that any of these (specialist) functions are carried out in collaboration with the actor/performers. Increasingly within devised practices we are likely to find work being performed in spaces not formally designated as theatres, and indeed such work may be experienced as being far removed from what is conventionally understood as 'theatre'. Following Hans Thies-Lehmann, we might offer a shorthand for these practices as 'postdramatic theatre' (Lehmann 2006), where 'narrative fragmentation, heterogeneity of style, hypernaturalist, grotesque and neo-expressionist elements' (Lehmann 2006: 24) are typical, but not exhaustive features.

In contemporary devised performance we are less likely to find 'characterisation' than we are performers working with task and action and playing with the boundaries between their own presence and more conventional forms of representational acting. Here, there is a disposition to talk of 'performance' rather than 'theatre', largely so as to distance the work and its intention from the more habitual practices of play-based theatre making with a linear narrative structure and a disposition 'to tell stories'. Here, too, performance makers are as likely to be in dialogue with the theories and conventions of contemporary visual arts, film and digital technologies, cultural theory, philosophy, dance and experimental writing as they are with the traditions and structures of theatre. This is not a rejection of theatre and its histories, but an insistence that theatre is a mongrel art form which delights in drawing upon a multiplicity of artistic and critical practices.

I have offered this foregrounding of the account which follows because I am proposing that Sebald's fictions bear a similar formal relationship to the dominant conventions of novel writing as devised theatre does to the hegemonic (Western) protocols of play-driven theatre production. Of course, to claim such an association raises awkward questions about modalities of authorship and I return to these issues later in the chapter.

Amongst the most resonant of contemporary Western theatre makers whose work falls into the patterns identified above we should include: Tim Etchells and Forced Entertainment; Chicago-based company Goat Island;[4] Lone Twin; Volcano; Cupola Bobber; Gob Squad; Reckless Sleepers; Wooster Group; Elevator Repair Service; Wrights and Sites; Mike Pearson; and the dance theatre of the late Pina Bausch or Jerome Bel. Of these companies and artists, Volcano, Goat Island and Cupola Bobber have explicitly engaged with Sebald, translating material from his fictions into their performance. Others like Tim Etchells, Mike Pearson, Carl Lavery and Phil Smith of Wrights and Sites relate to Sebald more obliquely, finding an affinity not only with his radical subversion of existing writing conventions, but also with the generative power of his associative and digressive poetics.

The most explicit harnessing of a Sebald text is to be found in *i-witness* (2008), from Volcano, a company based in south Wales whose work is regularly signed as 'physical or visual theatre'. Not unused to bringing unlikely texts to the stage (e.g. *The Communist Manifesto* and Shakespeare's *Sonnets*), Volcano became obsessed and haunted by Sebald's *The Rings of Saturn*. Claudine Conway writes:

> *i-witness* grew out of a problem. We had found this fascinating book that spoke so profoundly to us and seemed to demand some kind of response, but it was unstageable. . . . But what really makes the book so extraordinary is the vastness of the moral and political world opened up by Sebald's digressions. 'Hopscotching' is the word we use in the show to describe what his mind and the book does [sic]. (Volcano website)

The structural conceit for the performance is that each of the four actors traces his/her own response to the book, and uses this response as a discursive strategy to construct and compose the piece. They place the book centre stage and make their own differences, disagreements and struggles with the text the driving impulse. The four performers each play versions of themselves – competing voices that articulate dissent and irritation; political and moral high seriousness; an experience of walking the narrator's own route; and an increasing obsession with coincidences. Originally Volcano had advertised that there were going to be five performers, but in the event only four were in the piece. The absence of the fifth performer became 'in a gratifyingly Sebaldian way' (Volcano website) a mysterious absence leaving traces of her presence in the show. Reflecting on her own walking of the Suffolk route, one performer represents her findings as a slide show and diary:

> You start to become the narrator, you become the 'I' that is Sebald. He gets into your body, into your senses. His musings and meditations become yours, and you begin to congratulate yourself – at your eloquence, your sensitivity and your astute observations as well as your breadth of knowledge. (Volcano website)

Goat Island's eighth piece, *When will the September roses bloom? Last night was only a comedy* (2002–5) was driven and shaped by the question: 'how do you make a repair?' Source material for the work ranged from 1950s repair manuals to the voices and imagery of Paul Celan, Jean Améry, Simone Weil, Thomas Bernhard, Tommy Cooper, James Taylor, Lillian Gish, dogs and Sebald himself. They interpreted Celan's writing as a project of 'repair' for the German language in Europe following the end of the Second World War and drew upon Sebald's project of 'restitution' (without using the term explicitly) in *Austerlitz*, *Vertigo* and *On the Natural History of Destruction*. These voices' melancholic recollections 'constitute an attempt, if not at repair, at least of repetition. These texts ... enact a compulsive, compulsory return to historical experience. They hover at the edge of memory' (Ridout 2005).

Goat Island's work resonates with a sense of loss, a light and distracted melancholy articulated through juxtapositions of imagery, text (found and created), movement and stillness. Never directly *about* something, the work is a process of discovering meaning through making and enacting performance material: 'we discovered a performance by making it', says Matthew Goulish (Goat Island website). The material performed is precise, delicate, often remorseless, technically skilful but never self-consciously virtuosic, forever implicating the audience though never didactic, always unresolved and open. An example of unsettling but associative juxtaposition in *September roses* occurs when Goulish performs some text from *Austerlitz*, intercutting in a disturbing way memories of a torture survivor with Tommy Cooper jokes:

> Joke telling and torture turn out to be strangely connected; both crafted to elicit involuntary responses from the victim. ... in laughing at the jokes, and at the same time feeling acute discomfort at doing so, in this context the viewer of *September roses* might experience this connection viscerally. (Bottoms and Goulish 2007: 63)

In another scene Goulish performs a passage from *Austerlitz* where the speaker visits the prison cell in which Jean Améry was tortured. Here the calmness of Améry's own account contrasts with the frantic anxiety generated by the character who visits the cell, but who never actually experienced torture. Goulish explains thus: 'it's this kind of witnessing from the edges of a really traumatic experience . . . trying to approach the trauma through its echoes' (Goulish 2004).

Cupola Bobber, founded in 2000, works out of a Chicago West side studio. Like Goat Island and Volcano, Cupola Bobber's method is to research and assemble materials for performance without preconceived narrative, working slowly to use a 'simple aesthetic to explore the world for an hour or two, look at it from arms' length, creating a new system for an audience to discover meaning. Intimacy, delicacy and confusion are important' (Cupola Bobber website). In *In Way Out West, the Sea Whispered Me* (2009), the company used *The Rings of Saturn* as a primary text, drawing particularly on the section around Lowestoft and Dunwich and its material on fishermen and the dust storm. As significantly, Sebald's Suffolk walk inspired a mode of composition and research actions which in turn generated material for the piece. Stephen Fiehn and Tyler Myers – who are Cupola Bobber – undertook various walks along the Lancashire coast, consciously using the lens of Sebald's walk to see the world of an Edwardian factory town and a seaside resort and their interrelations, real and imagined. A piece of text from the work indicates a direct connection with Sebald's Dunwich and its parish churches:

> (The sea) has my left shoe, my toothbrush, my father's encyclopaedias, my coffee cup, my favorite fork, my bath towel folded just so, the parish churches of St James, St Leonard, St Martin, St Bartholomew, St Michael, St Patrick, St Mary, St John, St Peter, St Nicholas and St Felix, one after the other, sliding down the steadily receding cliff-face and sank in the depths, along with the earth and stone of which the town had been built. The town, for its part, has decided to look forward. It looks forward to its new future, reinventing itself westward as the water reinvents the shore each day. It makes its progress west, followed by the water, looking forward to its future while reflecting on its past. (Text from *In Way Out West, the Sea Whispered Me*, 2009)

That three contemporary theatre companies might draw material for their work from a twentieth-century European writer of fiction is hardly remarkable in itself. What is significant here is that the relationship in these pieces to Sebald is well beyond a curiosity with his subject matter. For the purpose of this account, however, it is a conscious association and affinity with Sebald's writing as a register of form, dramaturgy and mode of composition that seems an equally vital part of the relationship.

WRITING AGAINST – AND AROUND – THE GRAIN

The danger in trying to establish commonalities and connections between the compositional strategies of a most particular writer and the practices of contemporary performance makers is that one presses too hard, searching for bonds in order to establish a neat pattern or matrix that 'proves' a hypothesis or theory.

Consequently, what follows is an attempt not to construct a theoretical edifice but, rather, to assemble and observe a range of resemblances between the way that Sebald composes his 'fiction' and the dramaturgical strategies of some significant makers of contemporary performance. To paraphrase Sebald himself: this chapter is not seeking answers but, rather, noting the *oddness* of things and their interrelations.

In so far as Sebald offered explanations for the way he wrote, he positioned himself against the weight of the conventions of novel writing, finding in the play of fictional characters charting their journey through a narrative structure that offers closure or resolution a mode of representation which can do little justice to the monstrous enormities of lived experience in the twentieth century. Sebald acknowledges a 'debt of gratitude' to the Austrian writer Thomas Bernhard (1931–89), who, he says, moved

> away from the standard pattern of the standard novel. He only tells you in his books what he heard from others. So, he invented, as it were, a kind of periscopic form of narrative. You're always sure what he tells you is related at one remove, at two removes, at two or three. That appealed to me very much, because this notion of an omniscient narrator who pushes around the flats on the stage of the novel … one can't do very easily any more. (Sebald in Schwartz 2007: 83)

We can locate a similar reaction in many contemporary performance makers who refuse to find in the single-authored and 'well-made' play any beneficial strategy to engage with the exigencies of contemporary life. The pleasure of found materials and a gleeful raiding of existing and overheard texts implicitly, but productively, problematize simplistic notions of authorship and creativity. Here, too, heroic and – sometimes – hopeless attempts at collective authorship, an engagement with the visual and visceral dimensions of theatre and a resistance to the seamlessness of naturalistic dramatic construction offer an alternative model for live performance which possesses the potential to be in sharp dialogue with the pressing issues of twenty-first-century life. In searching for different modes of narrative structure for page and stage, Sebald shares with companies like Goat Island, Volcano or Cupola Bobber an insistence that to represent and remember the atrocities of the twentieth century with integrity and adequacy we need to discover new relationships between forms of fictional and non-fictional writing (documentary and autobiographical) and – together – their dramaturgical association with the visual image. In a Volcano or Goat Island piece the spectator is presented with dense textual material within or alongside physically draining dance theatre. The text may, for example, be poetic and composed, or 'found' and technical. These elements form a complex information system inviting spectators to 'complete the circuit' (Bottoms and Goulish 2007: 15). Of Goat Island's work Sara-Jane Bailes argues that we will experience:

shards of [the] scenic and choreographed … working from any sources, such as personal narrative, documentary footage, found images or observed and copied gestures … work that resists the usual hierarchy of formal features … or the development of meaning through linear narrative, instead the performance unfolds as a network of associations. (Bailes 2001)

In the same way, the reader of *Austerlitz* must negotiate a map, a frozen video image and the photo of a railway station within a complex verbal discourse in order to construct meaning, to 'complete the circuit'. Quite early in the account, Jacques Austerlitz recalls a journey back from South Wales (Sebald 2001b: 74–83; 2001c: 70–8) with his preacher foster-father, Elias. Over eight pages hellish stories of bombed-out smouldering ruins, drowned valleys, moonlit all-night football matches and a biblical illustration of an encampment for the Children of Israel jostle with each other to help construct the narrative hinterland of the lives of both Austerlitz and Elias. These passages refer to photographs shown to Austerlitz by Elias at the same time as three associative images, apparently referring to the realities described, present the reader with the challenge of making sense of (dubious) photographic evidence in relation to their apparent signalling in the text itself.

Sebald's first three works of fiction to be published in English (*The Rings of Saturn*, *The Emigrants* and *Vertigo*) as well as, to a lesser extent, *Austerlitz*, all exhibit a marked strategy towards composition, which entails a very particular approach to dealing with subject and content. Sebald speaks of the productive delights in *circling* a subject or theme rather than approaching it directly, and admits that even his own doctoral research was undertaken in a 'random haphazard manner' (Sebald in Schwartz 2007: 94). Such unsystematic searching is not without an endpoint, and yet is a strategy which yields a range of unexpected but salient findings around the discourse in question. And this haphazard mapping for Sebald was not some callow response to the difficulties of writing:

> And the more I got on the more I felt that, really, one can find something only in that way, i.e., in the same way in which, say, a dog runs through a field. If you look at a dog following the advice of his nose, he traverses a patch of land in a completely unplottable manner. And he invariably finds what he is looking for. (Sebald in Schwartz 2007: 94)

Amongst a range of propositions put forward to explain and position Sebald's swirling lines of thought, his use of non-linear coincidence and delight in the porosity of borders and boundaries, two particular kinds of compositional strategy resonate with the tactics and approaches of contemporary performance makers.

LIGHTNESS OF ATTENTION

The first of these resides in what is perhaps the emblematic question for all artistic endeavour from the mid-twentieth century: how to represent and engage with that which is unspeakable. The multiple voices (and forms) assembled and curated through Sebald's writing are a response to the question of how art deals with matters of human behaviour beyond understanding, beyond representation and beyond imagination. Sebald shares with many contemporary performance makers a sense that the conventional languages of representation, narrative and dramatic structure can no longer convey – if they ever could – the materiality of twentieth- and twenty-first-century atrocity and destruction. Approaching such matters from a tangent does not remove the *weight* of responsibility from the artist but, rather, *lightens* the task by redirecting it, by offering multiple angles of incidence into – or rather around – the subject matter. Here, arriving from the oblique is a writing and compositional strategy in response to excessive exposure, to a surfeit of information and to that sensory overload which dulls and desensitizes our ethical and political antennae.

Habitually, Sebald would find no obligation to explain or justify this strategy, but occasionally he articulated his position without ambiguity:

> To write about the concentration camps is practically impossible. So you need to convince the reader that this is something on your mind but that you do not necessarily roll out ... on every other page. I think it is sufficient to remind people, because we've all seen images, but these images militate against our capacity for discursive thinking, for reflecting upon these things. And also paralyze as it were, our moral capacity. So the only way in which one can approach these things, in my view, is obliquely, tangentially, by reference rather than by direct confrontation. (Sebald in Schwartz 2007: 80)

Here is an echo of Italo Calvino, who, in his essay on 'Lightness', in *Six Memos for the Next Millennium* (2009), found the Medusa-like weight of the world and its events turning his imagination to stone. Calvino notes that, to cut off Medusa's head without being turned to stone, Perseus was carried by 'the very lightest of things, the winds and the clouds, and fixes his gaze upon what can be revealed only by indirect vision' (2009: 4). For Calvino, and by implication for Sebald, this myth must be an allegory for the artist's relationship to the world, 'a lesson to follow when writing' (2009: 4).

Of course, no one acquainted with Sebald's work would ever consider him 'light' in the sense of being superficial or inconsequential, and, given the writer and his narrators' propensity for a profound and often melancholy seriousness, *lightness* seems a perverse phrase with which to signal the tenor and register of his writing. But here I am indicating that lightness is a quality sought in the form of attention given to the subject – a quality of touch and texture, a profoundly embodied event as well as a metaphysical one. And this quality is in a symbiotic relationship to circling, to the rhythms of the drift and a disposition to be around rather than *in* or *on* the subject matter. Significantly, given the texture of melancholy often attributed to Sebald's writing, Calvino's memo on 'Lightness' suggests that the quality has a special connection with melancholy, arguing that the latter 'is sadness that has taken on lightness, so humor is comedy that has lost its bodily weight' (2009: 19).[5] Moreover, it is a lightness not to be confused with either frivolity or a lack of care or attention. It is a tactic for dealing with the weight of things, intended 'to prevent the weight of matter from crushing us' (Calvino 2009: 8). Calvino extols 'lightness of thoughtfulness' (2009: 10) as a disposition for the new millennium, and clearly, by implication, a quality sought by any art work.

In the context of contemporary performance it is this very lightness that is sought both as a *texture* of acting and in the manner of how subject matter is touched dramaturgically by the theatre makers. For Australian performance maker Barry Laing, and iconic French teacher of theatre Philippe Gaulier, lightness is a disposition which finds generative qualities in a refusal to look directly at the object/subject – not a refusal of the world, but an attempt to escape from its weight, inertia, noise and opacity. For Gaulier, lightness has a radical quality, allowing the performer/theatre maker to ease the weight of the text by circling it, through an indirect glance, playfully and with generous disrespect. A disposition to relax the sinews attaching performer to character, to find an engaged distance, to avoid knowing too much and trying too hard. Explicitly for Gaulier, 'lightness' has an ideological dimension as well as a performative one, and he often gives meaning and potency to the term by contrasting this elusive quality with the *weight* and *darkness* of stamping – Fascist – boots. Returning to Sebald, we note how he approaches the problem of memory as the predicament of weight. He speaks and often writes of the frailty of memory: 'vast tracks of your life … vanish in oblivion' whilst 'what survives in your mind acquires a considerable degree of density, a very high degree of specific weight … once you are weighed down with these kinds of weight, it's not unlikely that they will sink you' (Sebald in Schwartz 2007: 54).[6]

Lightness is in both the grain and texture of Sebald's writing as well as its formal structures. In *The Emigrants*, for example, whilst the subject matter of the four accounts is incontestably tragic, the unfolding narrative as each life reaches its conclusion through suicide has an almost casual and dispassionate quality. The text is peppered with comments – 'Wie ich mich erinnere oder wie ich mir vielleicht jetzt nur einbilde' ('as I recall, or perhaps merely imagine' (Sebald 1994a: 36; 2002e: 23)) or 'Es war Anfang des Frühjahrs, wenn ich mich recht entsinne' ('It was early the following year, if I remember correctly' (1994a: 234; 2002e: 158)) – which offer a light and contingent distance to the narrator's engagement with his subject, para-doxically heightening its poignancy and melancholy. Formally, the propulsion of the narrative by chance encounters rather than through a clear teleological unfolding lightens the relationship to the subjects whilst never abdicating an ethical commitment to their plight. Notwithstanding this lightness, the narrator remains 'witness', rather than detached onlooker. Lightness is given form through what J. J. Long calls the 'poetics of digression' and 'ambulatory narratives' (Long 2009: 61). It is these deceptively casual tactics of meandering digression which prevent the 'kind of leaden heaviness (that) weighs the reader down in a way that makes him blind' (Sebald in Siedenberg 1997: 147).

DESTABILIZING THE READER-SPECTATOR

The second 'tactic' employed by Sebald which offers parallels with the processes of contemporary performance making leads us to the nature of the engagement sought with readers or audiences. Here, in both cases, a refusal to offer reader-audiences the solace of either a tidy unity of form (in writing or performance) or the seductive conventions of a story told with unfolding linear development destabilizes the reception of the work, making demands which exercise and strain the imagination in order to forge connections between things and events. Conceptually, what links Sebald with these performance makers is a commitment to change the habitual 'contract' with the reader-spectator: a celebration of the performative nature of 'reading', whether it be of a written fiction or a piece of devised theatre, an understanding that not only the text but also reading may be considered performative, since reading brings into existence an interpretative engagement which did not exist prior to the act itself. John Hall proposes that:

> the performance writer writes the space between the writing and
> the performing,
> where the writing is always about to leave to become
> something else;
> where the I is about to become at least another I,
> whoever's I that is, however many eyes there are. (Hall 2007: 11)

Sebald suggests that to make discoveries which might not otherwise be formulated through a more predictable compositional strategy, 'you have to take heterogeneous materials in order to get your mind to do something it has not done before' (Sebald in Schwartz 2007: 95). Inviting the body-minds of readers and audiences to 'do something they have not done before' lies at the heart of what both Sebald and a significant number of contemporary performance practices are searching for. For Sebald, destabilizing reception and straining the reader's imagination takes a number of forms which include: the juxtaposition of text and image; the ambiguous function of images as unreliable 'evidence'; the elision of different modalities of writing (fiction, historical documentation, biography, travelogue, for example); a pleasure in celebrating the porosity of the borders between these modes; and a refusal to indulge the reader with the comfort of the narrative scaffolding of linearity.

In *Certain Fragments* (1999), for example, Tim Etchells, writer and director with Forced Entertainment, articulates the trajectory and aspiration of the company's work:

> It had to forgo the suspect certainties of what other people called political theatre [. . .] we worked with a growing confidence that a reliance on intuition, chance, dream, accident and impulse would not banish politics from the work, but ensure its veracity – a certainty that old rules did not apply. (1999: 19)

Forced Entertainment remains an emblematic company within the landscape of contemporary European devised performance. For this group – and many others – the urgency of the times demands a shifting of the boundaries of looking, hearing, sensing and constructing meaning, and with this movement a refreshed and alert form of witnessing is demanded: 'the sense that the watching is at the edges of its contract, on the edge of something new' (Etchells 1999: 21).

The loss of one's bearings as one moves through a Sebald novel or experiences a piece of *Tanztheater* from the late Pina Bausch, the repetitive but playful re-enactments of Chicago's Goat Island, or Sheffield's Forced Entertainment, unsettles our reception as it is obliged to move into a fundamentally different frame and register. In the same way as Deane Blackler (2007) proposes that Sebald creates the 'disobedient' reader, spectators at a piece by Goat Island or Forced Entertainment have little choice but to engage actively in the performance of the text. This straining and exercising of the imagination places the reader-audience in a quasi-Brechtian relationship with the work, but this is Brecht without didacticism. An invitation to *witness* rather than merely spectate and listen, to be quietly engaged with the ethical tenor of the writing, or, in the case of contemporary theatre, with the textual and visual languages of performance. For Tim Etchells, this is an 'on stage' condition of *investment*, when things seem to matter, to touch, to threaten or to please the performers. A condition which, when present, becomes part of the transaction with an audience, part of the deal. 'Investment' says Etchells, 'is slippery and evasive and isn't often found where we'd expect it . . . I ask: "are you at risk in this"? That's all I want to know' (1999: 48). To engage with, for example, *The Emigrants*, the Sebald reader is quietly drawn in to construct the relationship between the four protagonists – Selwyn, Bereyter, Adelwarth and Ferber – to (dis)place them in relation to histories of exile, loss and destruction. Distracted by Sebald's meditative register, the reader becomes – performs – an inconsolable witness to unspeakable events and histories. Similarly, Sebald's fictional narrator in *Austerlitz* constructs readers into witnesses bearing a present ('now') ethical engagement with the catastrophes which have marked our collective past.

One of the qualities that I believe Sebald shares with these performance makers is that the work opens up a space of invention, an opportunity to provide what is not obviously there. An occasion to welcome the disobedient reader-spectator, for, as Blackler notes: 'Sebald's example is better understood using Lévi-Strauss's notion of *bricolage*, which is less determined and more random in its appropriativeness than the more authoritarian, modernist idea of montage . . . His is a bolder, emancipatory poetics' (Blackler 2007: 26). Mike Pearson, echoing Sebald's affirmation of bricolage as a strategy for writing (Sebald in Schwartz 2007: 159), constitutes performance as 'a "field" of activity . . . as a discontinuous and interrupted practice of different modes of expression, of varying types and intensities, in which different orders of narrative can run simultaneously . . .' (Pearson 1998: 40). And this notion of 'field' rather than 'discipline', 'subject' or even 'art form' is crucial to our understanding of how contemporary theatre positions itself in relation not only to other arts practices, but beyond these towards worlds of non-fiction and the sciences. Sebald might speak for Mike Pearson and many other contemporary performance makers when he says:

> if you grow up not with toys bought in the shop but things that are found around the farmyard, you do a sort of bricolage . . . Bits of string and bits of wood. Making all sorts of things, like webs across the legs of a chair. And then you sit here like a spider.
> (Sebald in Schwartz 2007: 159)

It is perhaps Sebald's disposition to open up spaces of readerly invention in his fictions (and other writings) which allows or indeed encourages such divergent treatment from diverse types of performance practitioners. The complex and looping heterogeneity of Sebald's prose construction offers theatre makers multiple routes through the journey from page to stage in a way that more conventional narrative structures would inhibit. Certainly, Sebald's fiction does not prescribe or encourage an uncomplicated embrace of either dramatic linearity or the apparent certainties of naturalism. In this sense, the evident affinity between contemporary performance makers and Sebald's writing is not hard to unravel.

DRAMATURGIES IN SEBALD'S FICTION AND CONTEMPORARY PERFORMANCE

In this section I focus on notions and practices of dramaturgy. In a curious way, there are similarities between a dramaturg working within devised theatre and the writer assembling or curating materials which will find their way onto the 'page', or its (im)material equivalent. Although Sebald's writing, as cultural production, is self-evidently distinct from the collective and collaborative dynamics of devising, his mode of assembling and constructing material shares many of the same qualities and dispositions. Sebald's assemblage of materials is a startling act of imagination, and links us both historically to Duchamp and Beuys in their collection and re-presentation of *objets trouvés*, and synchronically to the compositional practices of companies and artists already considered in this account.

Most significantly, Sebald and contemporary performance makers meet in their shared debt to a paradigm, rooted in Dada and Surrealism, which blurs and breaks down distinctions between the fictional and the 'real' and between art as heroic inspiration and as 'work', organization and collection. Through approaches to assembling and making material, through shameless and gleeful raiding of sources outside theatre, and through a willing engagement with cultural and critical theory, contemporary performance makers have consistently challenged the boundaries of theatre and offered transgressive propositions about what it means to be creative and an artist.

What devising particularly proposes and demands, however, is a rethinking of the practice of expertise or expert knowledge. It does not refuse to acknowledge or deny such qualities; rather, it insists that expert knowledge is *practised* differently in the devising relationship than in the normative rehearsal conventions of play-based drama. Here, paradoxically, expert knowledge is (playfully) respected at the same time as it is acknowledged to be context bound, mutable and contingent. The conditions and processes of invention within devised theatre practices have a tangible and dialectical relationship with the work itself. In *Devising Performance: A Critical History*, Deirdre Heddon and Jane Milling explain:

> Devising ... potentially enables the production of a different kind of performance structure that in some senses reflects its collaborative creative process – typically compartmented or fragmented with multiple layers and narratives ... This repetition of fragmented dramaturgy has undoubtedly altered our comprehension of 'narrative', and of the possible shapes or trajectories by which narratives can or should be represented. (2006: 221)

Clearly, it would be erroneous to argue that *only* devising can generate these dramaturgical forms: the work of Samuel Beckett, Heiner Müller and Peter Handke exemplify complex and layered narrative structures, and demand modalities of acting far removed from the conventions of naturalism and realism. However, it is in the presentation of 'found' material within a range of performance languages, and alongside more obviously imaginary sources of writing, that contemporary devised performance becomes harmonious with Sebald's composition. The 'found' material of many of Sebald's images and their careful placing within the text of *The Rings of Saturn* (for example, Rembrandt's *The Anatomy Lesson* (Sebald 1997b: 24–5; 1999a: 14–16) and a grainy photograph of the Bergen Belsen concentration camp at liberation (Sebald 1997b: 78–9; 1999a: 60–1)) work dramaturgically – playing elastically with the 'real' and the fictional – in a similar way to the cardboard signs in Forced Entertainment's *Emanuelle Enchanted* (1992) or the Wooster Group's projected images of film footage from Paul Morrissey and Andy Warhol in *Vieux Carré* (2010).

By offering radically different dramaturgical structures and choices to the hegemonic configurations and conventions of drama, companies such as Goat Island, The Wooster Group and Forced Entertainment are presenting a powerful, but often ambiguously playful, challenge to theatre and its own terms of reference. Notwithstanding differences of style, aesthetic and political focus, these artists and companies lead us far away from dramatic theatre. Hans-Thies Lehmann, reflecting on Polish artist and performance maker Tadeusz Kantor, notes that his theatre was: 'a rich cosmos of art forms between theatre, happening, performance, painting, sculpture, object art ... and ongoing reflection on theoretical texts, poetic writings and manifestoes' (Lehmann 2006: 71).

My contention here is that these figures of contemporary performance stand in a similar challenging relationship to the dominant conventions of theatre and drama as Sebald does to the prevailing and weighty customs of fiction and other quotidian modes of 'creative writing'. And this, as I have argued, is manifested as a delight in interdisciplinarity, a playful approach to the fictional and the real, an invitation to read openly and 'disobediently', a (deep and sustained) suspicion towards the dominant protocols of character and narrative structure, and a witnessing commitment to matters both ethical and political, but with an exquisite attention and touch that is both light and indirect.

As a final aside, it is worth noting that these compositional practices problematize and render complex singular notions of authorship, no less for Sebald than amongst contemporary performance makers. The shared 'magpie-like' approach to found materials and the destabilizing of authorial voice do not, within the finished texts of page or stage, remove or weaken an unmistakable sense of signature. Arguably, the texts of Sebald's fictions, or Forced Entertainment and Goat Island's performances, possess a distinctive and resonant identity, paradoxically both imitable and 'unique'. If the grain of Sebald's voice is unmistakable it is because of how it speaks through, within and alongside the relational assembly of 'found' materials – maps, photographs, newspaper cuttings and paintings such as Rembrandt's *The Anatomy Lesson* – presented in his fictions and other writings. The distinctiveness of Sebald's signature resides in the relationship between printed word and visual image: an embrace of multiple 'languages' and registers rather than heroic authorial singularity. And it is this disposition to compose and 'perform' work constructed associatively and relationally from various forms and materials which is shadowed by the collaborative process of authorship in contemporary devised performance. The register of the voice remains distinct, regardless of the multiple and digressive dramaturgical strategies which make up its construction, shape and texture.

DIGRESSIONS, BYWAYS AND INEFFICIENCY: CONCLUDING NOTES

Our categories should always be treated as questions – temporary groupings in which every element is nomadic – rather than as answers: as comforters, but not as fetishes. (Phillips 1997: 91)

In this account I have argued that there are unambiguous formal connections as well as serendipitous associations to be identified between Sebald's fiction and the dramaturgical tropes embraced by a number of the most significant contemporary Western performance companies and artists. A dimension of such a shared landscape not engaged with in this account concerns the generative dramaturgies of walking both in Sebald's fictions and as a (performative) arts practice. Although this is rich territory already well explored within Sebaldian scholarship, the dramaturgical function of walking in his fictions has yet to be examined through the lens of performance studies. In these concluding comments it is appropriate to note that a distracted (and distractable) walking serves as a salient metaphor whilst also providing form and structure both in Sebald's writing *and* in the work of particular performance makers. Emblematically, J. J. Long's observation about walking in *The Rings of Saturn* offers an acute perspective on the writing and performance considered in this account:

> [Walking is] ... deliberately inefficient and one might say, anti-disciplinary. This tendency to explore byways rather than make beelines goes hand in hand with a narrative technique that is multiply digressive: it repeatedly shifts focus, as each digression is soon abandoned in favour of another digression. (Long 2009: 67)

A poetics of digression which challenges existing literary and dramatic cartographies seems an adequate enough frame within which to connect Sebald's fiction with the dramaturgical strategies of contemporary performance. I have proposed that some of the most significant contemporary performance practitioners share with Sebald an approach to form, composition and dramaturgy of the material that they use to assemble their work. The lens of production dramaturgy functions as a generative angle of incidence into understanding how Sebald writes, as well as suggesting the curious parallels this process has with the practices of devised performance. David Williams, dramaturg to Lone Twin, proposes that dramaturgy:

> Is about the rhythmed assemblage of settings, people, texts and things ... the composing of events for and in particular contexts, tracking the logic of materials, their implications and connective relations, and shaping them to find effective forms. [...] The dramaturg's role is ambivalent, multiple, protean and always contextually determined, to be invented. (Williams 2010: 197–8)

To identify these associations is not to force an artificial yoking of Sebald's writing practice to the compositional strategies of contemporary performance makers, but to propose that the innovative conventions constructed by Sebald and these theatre practitioners possess curious but mutual qualities which speak urgently, although often softly, of the temper of the times. I have proposed that between Sebald and these players of contemporary performance there are shared dispositions which reject the 'suspect certainties' (Etchells 1999: 19) of a clamorous political 'theatre' and offer instead an attempt to stage – and blur – the shifting landscape between the real and the imaginary. A commitment to restitution through the acts both of witnessing and of producing the reader-spectator as 'witness'. Through the toil of making theatre or writing fiction there is an ethical commitment, as Peggy Phelan suggests, 'to continue a conversation that without your intervention would cease ... (allowing) the dead, the disappeared, the lost, to continue to live as we rediscover their force in our ongoing present' (Phelan in Etchells 1999: 13).

NOTES

1 Almost all accounts of Sebald's work engage, unsurprisingly, with his use of images within the text. For example, see Long and Whitehead (2004), Blackler (2007a) and Patt and Dillbohner (2007).

2 Austerlitz's mother, Agáta, who worked as an actress in Prague before the war, is perhaps the exception that proves the rule.

3 My thanks go to Matthew Goulish, Mike Pearson, Carl Lavery, Phil Smith, Kay Denyer (Volcano), Tyler Myers and Stephen Fiehn (Cupola Bobber) and David Williams for email and other conversations around their practice and the work of W. G. Sebald.

4 Founded in 1987, Goat Island's final performance was in 2009. The spirit of the company's work continues through the performance practices of Lin Hixson, Matthew Goulish and other original members of the ensemble.

5 Hutchinson (2009b: 147–50) shows that Sebald actually annotated Calvino's 'Six Memos', often in a manner which supports these arguments.

6 For a discussion of Sebald's attempts to escape the 'burden' of memory, see Hutchinson (2009a).

11

STILL LIFE, PORTRAIT, PHOTOGRAPH, NARRATIVE IN THE WORK OF W. G. SEBALD[1]

Clive Scott

Early on in *Austerlitz*, we are given a good idea of Sebald's photographic orientations in Jacques Austerlitz's own account of his photographic practices at school, Stower Grange (Figure 11.1):

> In der Hauptsache hat mich von Anfang an die Form und Verschlossenheit der Dinge beschäftigt, der Schwung eines Stiegengeländers, die Kehlung an einem steinernen Torbogen, die unbegreiflich genaue Verwirrung der Halme in einem verdorrten Büschel Gras. Hunderte solcher Aufnahmen habe ich in Stower Grange meist in quadratischen Formaten abgezogen, wohingegen es mir immer unstatthaft schien, den Sucher der Kamera auf einzelne Personen zu richten. (2001b: 112–13)

> (From the outset my main concern was with the shape and the self-contained nature of discrete things, the curve of banisters on a staircase, the moulding of a stone arch over a gateway, the tangled precision of the blades in a tussock of dried grass. I took hundreds of such photographs at Stower Grange, most of them in square format, but it never seemed to me right to turn the viewfinder of my camera on people. (2001c: 108–9))

The 'self-contained nature [of discrete things]' is a translation of the German 'Verschlossenheit', which suggests, rather, the aggressively withheld and the sealed-off, and reminds one of those closed doors on the top floor of Emyr Elias's manse, doors that Austerlitz dreams will open onto a more familiar world: 'Noch heute träumt es mir manchmal, daß eine der verschlossenen Türen sich auftut und ich über die Schwelle trete in eine freundlichere, weniger fremde Welt ('Even today I sometimes dream that one of the locked doors opens and I step over the threshold into a friendlier, less alien world' (2001b: 65; 2001c: 61)). Sebald's photographs are like so many closed doors in the text, which, like the doors in Terezín/ Theresienstadt, 'den Zugang versperrten zu einem nie noch durchdrungenen Dunkel' ('obstruct[ed] access to a darkness never yet penetrated' (2001b: 276; 2001c: 268)) (Figure 11.2). But about this general perception of photography, two things should be said. First, if photographs block us off from the darkness, if they are chemistry lab had not been used for years, but the wall cupboards and drawers still held several boxes with rolls of film, a large supply of photographic paper and a miscellaneous collection of cameras, including an Ensign such as I myself owned later. From the outset my main concern was with the shape and the self-contained nature of discrete things, the curve of banisters on a staircase, the moulding of a stone arch over a gateway, the tangled precision of the blades in a tussock of dried grass. I took hundreds of such photographs at Stower Grange, most of them in square format,

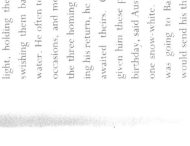

but it never seemed to me right to turn the viewfinder of my camera on people. In my photographic work I was always especially entranced, said Austerlitz, by the moment when the shadows of reality, so to speak, emerge out of nothing on the exposed paper, as memories do in the middle of the night, darkening again if you try to cling to them, just like a photographic print left in the developing bath too long. Gerald enjoyed helping me, and I can still see him, a head shorter than I was, standing beside me in the dark-room, which was dimly illuminated only by the little reddish light, holding the photographs in tweezers and swishing them back and forth in a sink full of water. He often told me about his family on these occasions, and most of all he liked talking about the three homing pigeons who would be expecting his return, he thought, as eagerly as he usually awaited theirs. Gerald's Uncle Alphonso had given him these pigeons a year ago for his tenth birthday, said Austerlitz, two of them a slaty blue, one snow-white. Whenever possible, if someone was going to Bala or Aberystwyth by car, he would send his three pigeons to be freed at a distance, and they always infallibly found their way

Figure 11.1

closed doors, they are also what *emerge* from the darkness, to which, however, they threaten to return:

> Besonders in den Bann gezogen hat mich bei der photographischen Arbeit stets der Augenblick, in dem man auf dem belichteten Papier die Schatten der Wirklichkeit sozusagen aus dem Nichts hervorkommen sieht, genau wie Errinerungen, sagte Austerlitz, die ja auch inmitten der Nacht in uns auftauchen und die sich dem, der sie festhalten will, so schnell wieder verdunkeln, nicht anders als ein photographischer Druck, den man zu lang im Entwicklungsbad liegenläßt. (2001b: 113)

> (In my photographic work I was always especially entranced, said Austerlitz, by the moment when the shadows of reality, so to speak, emerge out of nothing on the exposed paper, as memories do in the middle of the night, darkening again if you try to cling to them, just like a photographic print left in the developing bath too long. (2001c: 109))

A photograph may, then, be either an obstruction or a fragile memory which we would be well advised not to try to hold on to. Secondly, even if all the doors are shut in Terezín, even if the 'Verschlossenheit' is a symptom of 'Verlassenheit' (abandonment), there are at least some breaches in the walls: namely, the windows of the antiques shop – Antikos Bazar – which are also photographs (Figure 11.3; Figure 11.4). What goods we see in the windows are only the tip of the iceberg of objects which stretches back into the inner recesses of the shop. These objects which fill the windows, these objects which are also photographs, promise, either in themselves, or in their relationships, to provide answers, if only we knew what questions to ask. More importantly still, Austerlitz refers to these windows as 'diese vier, offenbar vollkommen willkürlich zusammengesetzten Stilleben' ('these four still lifes obviously composed entirely at random' (2001b: 278; 2001c: 274)). The larger, related proposals that I would like to make are these:

1   that the landscapes, the architectural photos, the photographed texts and documents are subgenerical manifestations of the superordinate genre 'still life'; all photographs in Sebald's work live the life of a still life;[2]
2   that the particular drama of the portrait photograph lies in its attempt to re-inhabit, to acquire substance in, the world of the still life;
3   that, conversely, still life photographs have appropriated the power of portraits which the portraits themselves have surrendered.

Sebald sharpened his own reflections on still life through the perusal of the hyperreal portraits (derived from photographs) and the still lifes of his friend Jan Peter Tripp. He tells us that he 'rediscovered' Tripp in Stuttgart in May 1976, having previously been to school with him in Oberstdorf (2005a: 209–10). Tripp's portraits are all, more or less, in Sebald's words, 'pathographic': the very meticulousness, the

obstructing access to a darkness never yet
penetrated, a darkness in which I thought, said

Figure 11.2

rezin. Es nimmt die ganze Vorderfront eines der größten Häuser ein und geht, glaube ich, auch weit in die Tiefe. Sehen konnte ich freilich nur, was in den Auslagen zur Schau gestellt war und gewiß nicht mehr als einen geringen Teil des im Inneren des Bazars angehäuften Trödels ausmachte. Aber selbst diese vier, offenbar vollkommen willkürlich zusammengesetzten Stilleben, die auf eine, wie es den Anschein hatte, naturhafte Weise hineingewachsen waren in das schwarze, in den Scheiben sich spiegelnde Astwerk der rings um den Stadtplatz stehenden Linden, hatten für mich eine derartige Anziehungskraft, daß ich mich von ihnen lange nicht losreißen konnte und, die

Stirne gegen die kalte Scheibe gepreßt, die hundert verschiedenen Dinge studierte, als müßte aus irgendeinem von ihnen, oder aus ihrem Bezug zueinander, eine eindeutige Antwort sich ableiten lassen auf die vielen, nicht auszudenkenden Fragen, die mich bewegten. Was bedeutete das Festtagstischtuch aus weißer Spitze, das über der Rückenlehne der Ottomane hing, der Wohnzimmersessel mit seinem verblaßten Brokatbezug? Welches Geheimnis bargen die drei verschieden großen Messingmörser, die etwas von einem Orakelspruch hatten, die kristallenen Schalen, Keramikvasen und irdenen Krüge, das blecherne Reklameschild, das die Aufschrift *Theresienstädter Wasser* trug, das Seemuschelkästchen, die Miniaturdrehorgel, die kugelförmigen Briefbeschwerer, in deren Glassphären wunderbare Meeresblüten schwebten, das Schiffsmodell, eine Art Korvette unter geblähten Segeln, der Trachtenkittel aus einem leichten, hellleinenen Sommerstoff, die Hirschhornknöpfe, die überdimensionale russische Offiziersmütze und die dazugehörige olivgrüne Uniformjacke mit den goldnen Schulterstücken, die Angelrute, die Jagdtasche, der japanische Fächer, die rund um einen Lampenschirm mit feinen Pinselstrichen gemalte endlose Landschaft an einem sei es durch Böhmen, sei es durch Brasilien still dahinziehenden Strom? Und dann war da in einer schuhschachtelgroßen Vitrine

Figure 11.3

von der letzten Hoffnung verlassenes weibliches Wesen zu sich emporzuziehen und aus einem dem Beschauer nicht offenbarten, aber ohne Zweifel grauenvollen Unglück zu retten. So zeitlos wie dieser verewigte, immer gerade jetzt sich ereignende Augenblick der Errettung waren sie alle, die in dem Bazar von Terezin gestrandeten Zierstücke, Gerätschaften und Andenken, die aufgrund unerforschlicher Zusammenhänge ihre ehemaligen Besitzer überlebt und den Prozeß der Zerstörung überdauert hatten, so daß ich nun zwischen ihnen schwach und kaum kenntlich mein eigenes Schattenbild wahrnehmen konnte. Noch während ich vor dem Bazar wartete, hob Austerlitz nach einer Weile wieder an, hatte es leise zu regnen begonnen, und da sich weder der Inhaber des Ladenlokals, der als ein gewisser Augustýn Němeček ausgewiesen war, noch irgend jemand sonst zeigen wollte, bin ich schließlich weitergegangen, ein paar Straßen hinauf und hinunter, bis ich auf einmal, an der nordöstlichen Ecke des Stadtplatzes, vor dem sogenannten, von mir zuvor übersehenen Ghettomuseum stand. Ich stieg die Stufen hinauf und betrat den Vorraum, in dem hinter einer Art Kassentisch eine Dame unbestimmten Alters saß in einer lilafarbenen Bluse und mit einer altmodisch gewellten Frisur. Sie legte die Häkelarbeit, mit der sie beschäftigt war, beiseite und reichte mir, indem sie

auf einem Aststummel hockend dieses ausgestopfte, stellenweise schon vom Mottenfraß verunstaltete Eichhörnchen, das sein gläsernes Knopfauge unerbittlich auf mich gerichtet hielt und dessen tschechischen Namen – veverka – ich nun von weit her wieder erinnerte wie den eines vor langer Zeit in Vergessenheit geratenen Freunds. Was, so fragte ich mich, sagte Austerlitz, mochte es auf sich haben mit dem nirgends entspringenden, nirgends einmündenden, ständig in sich selbst zurückfließenden Strom, mit veverka, dem stets in der gleichen Pose ausharrenden Eichhörnchen, oder mit der elfenbeinfarbenen Porzellankomposition, die einen reitenden

Helden darstellte, der sich auf seinem soeben auf der Hinterhand sich erhebenden Roß nach rückwärts wendet, um mit dem linken Arm ein unschuldiges,

Figure 11.4

very insistence, of the painter's scrutiny pushes these figures into an existential loneliness (Figure 11.5).

> Die Kehrseite dieser Abschilderung einer im Verlauf des Zivilisationsprozesses immer ungeheurer werdenden Art sind die verlassenen Landschaften und insbesondere die Stilleben, in denen – weit jenseits der Ereignisse – nurmehr die bewegungslosen Gegenstände Zeugnis geben von der vormaligen Anwesenheit einer sonderbar rationalistischen Gattung. (Sebald 2000a: 172–3)

> (The reverse side of this depiction of a species becoming more and more monstrous in the course of a civilisation's progress is the abandoned landscapes and especially the still lifes in which – far beyond the events – now only the motionless objects bear witness to the former presence of a peculiarly rationalistic species. (Sebald and Tripp, 2004a: 79))

The validity of this remark as a guide to Sebald's own intentions and practice is borne out by a remark made much later,[3] in the essay 'Ein Versuch der Restitution' ('An Attempt at Restitution'), again in connection with Tripp's work:

> Tripp hat mir damals einen von ihm gefertigten Stich als Geschenk mitgegeben, und auf diesen Stich, auf dem der kopfkranke Senatspräsident Daniel Paul Schreber zu sehen ist mit einer Spinne in seinem Schädel [...] auf diesen Stich geht vieles von dem,

Figure 11.5

was ich später geschrieben habe, zurück, auch in der Art des Verfahrens, im Einhalten einer genauen historischen Perspektive, im geduldigen Gravieren und in der Vernetzung, in der Manier der *nature morte*, anscheinend weit auseinander liegender Dinge. (2003b: 243–4)

(At the time Tripp gave me a present of one of his engravings, showing the mentally-ill senatorial president Daniel Paul Schreber with a spider in his skull [. . .] and much of what I have written later derives from this engraving, even in my method of procedure: in adhering to an exact historical perspective, in patiently engraving and linking together apparently disparate things in the manner of a still life. (2005a: 210))

One may detect here an apparent contradiction: how do we reconcile adherence to an exact historical perspective and the linking together of apparently disparate things?

To explain this paradox, two perspectives for the photograph might be proposed: an archaeology of the photograph, and a teleology of the photograph. The archaeology of the photograph, the replacement of the photograph in its original context of taking, the fixing of a referent to a photograph's indexicality, is one possible work of the viewer, the reconstruction of a first kind of history, the chronometric, external kind. And in this archaeology, the narrator's *interlocutor* is an indispensable guide. This is the perspective of the photograph which supposes that the whole *can* be given and that, thus, a higher Whole (History Mark I) can also be elaborated. That the establishment of the truth of origins was vital for Sebald we cannot doubt, judging from what he has to say about the writing of Hans Erich Nossack: 'Das Ideal des Wahren, das in der Gestalt eines gänzlich unprätentiösen Berichts beschlossen ist, erweist sich als der unwiderrufliche Grund aller literarischen Bemühung. In ihr kristallisiert sich Resistenz gegen die menschliche Fähigkeit, all jene Erinnerungen zu verdrängen, die die Fortführung des Lebens irgend verhindern könnten' ('The ideal of truth contained in the form of an entirely unpretentious report proves to be the irreducible foundation of all literary effort. It crystallizes resistance to the human faculty of suppressing any memories that might in some way be an obstacle to the continuance of life' (2003b: 86; 2005a: 86)).

But whatever Sebald's own moral commitments to this view, he seems naturally to gravitate more towards the teleological perspective, as it is partly represented by the writing of Alexander Kluge: 'Kluge "does not allow the data to stand merely as an account of a past catastrophe", writes Andrew Bowie; "the most unmediated document . . . loses its unmediated character via the processes of reflection the text sets up. History is no longer the past but also the present in which the reader must act"' (2003b: 99–100; 2005a: 100). The teleological perspective is the perspective of the photograph itself, as a material object which has broken free from the context of its taking and has become an indexicality *without* a referent, an indexicality looking for a *new* referent, not the referent of its taking, but the referent of its being seen by a spectator, a referent which may include a Barthesian *punctum*,[4] an involuntary memory, a surfacing of the unconscious. The teleological perspective projects the photograph out across its future, towards its encounters with countless spectators for whom it is ostensibly unfamiliar, but who strike up with it relationships of mysterious familiarity. Photos may not be ours, but it may be as if we had taken them.[5] In their taking, photographs belong to History Mark I; as projections they belong to History Mark II, a Bergsonian history, not a history made up of consecutive events, which have only empirical relations with each other, but an invisible history, a history of *advents*, to use Merleau-Ponty's word, the 'promise of events', 'secret, modest, nondeliberated, involuntary and, in short, living historicity' (Johnson, 1993: 105–6, 99), cumulative, progressively multiple.

Still lifes, at least the still lifes of objects as opposed to flowers, fruit, meat, occupy an extremely slow time, a time of gradual, accumulative patience, in which the world and its fugitive inhabitants leave their traces on what persists. Still lifes are not subject to the principle expressed by Roland Barthes in these words: 'What the Photograph reproduces to infinity has occurred only once: the Photograph mechanically repeats what could never be repeated existentially' (1984: 4). Looking at still lifes, one does not think of their instantaneousness, but of their capacity to shrug off the photographic instant, to embrace existential repeatability. And photographs as material objects, like still-life objects, outlast the moments they trace as images. As Austerlitz puts it in his closing comment on the window of the antiques shop:

> So zeitlos wie dieser verewigte, immer gerade jetzt sich ereignende Augenblick der Errettung waren sie alle, die in dem Bazar von Terezín gestrandeten Zierstücke, Gerätschaften und Andenken, die aufgrund unerforschlicher Zusammenhänge ihre ehemaligen Besitzer überlebt und den Prozeß der Zerstörung überdauert hatten, so daß ich nun zwischen ihnen schwach und kaum kenntlich mein eigenes Schattenbild wahrnehmen konnte. (2001b: 281)

> (They were all as timeless as that moment of rescue, perpetuated but for ever just occurring, these ornaments, utensils and mementoes stranded in the Terezín bazaar, objects that for reasons one could never know had outlived their former owners and survived the process of destruction, so that I could now see my own faint shadow barely perceptible among them. (2001c: 276–7))[6]

Sebald's essay on Tripp equally underlines, of course, the ability of things to outlast us ('überleben', 'überdauern'), to have a greater knowledge of us than we ourselves (Figure 11.6):

> Da die Dinge uns (im Prinzip) überdauern, wissen sie mehr von uns als wir über sie; sie tragen die Erfahrungen, die sie mit uns gemacht haben, in sich und *sind* – tatsächlich – das vor uns aufgeschlagene Buch unserer Geschichte. [...] Die *nature morte* ist bei Tripp, weit deutlicher als je zuvor, das Paradigma unserer Hinterlassenschaft. An ihr geht uns auf, was Maurice Merleau-Ponty in *L'Œil et*

l'Esprit den 'regard préhumain' genannt hat, denn umgekehrt sind in solcher Malerei die Rollen des Betrachters und des betrachteten Gegenstands. (Sebald 2000a: 173–4)

(Because (in principle) things outlast us, they know more about us than we know about them: they carry the experiences they have had with us inside them and are – in fact – the book of our history opened before us. [. . .] The *nature morte*, for Tripp, much more conspicuously than ever before, is the paradigm of the estate we leave behind. In it we encounter what Maurice Merleau-Ponty, in his *L'Œil et l'esprit*, called the *regard pré-humain* [the pre-human gaze], for in such paintings the roles of the observer and the observed objects are reversed. (Sebald and Tripp, 2004a: 79–80))

Photographs have the same value as the Trippian object, the Trippian still life; for all the technology of their production, photographs constitute Merleau-Ponty's 'pre-human gaze', where we can no longer differentiate between who sees and who is seen.

Austerlitz's final comment on the window of the antiques shop, his sighting of his own faint shadow as a reflection among the objects (but see notes 5 and 6), spells for me not only the fadingness of the human but also the desire of the human to re-inhabit the world of the still life. From a psychoanalytical point of view, the space of the still life is characteristically the space of the feminine, of the mother, of the mother's body; for the male painter/spectator, it is therefore the place of the uncanny – hence the peculiarly photographic way of seeing it – both a place of taboo and, at the same time, the place of the heart's desire. As Norman Bryson puts it:

This sense of the space of still life as alien to the male painter, incapable of being occupied from the inside, and at the same time as a place of fascination and obsessive looking, points to an ambivalence which the discourse of psychoanalysis does much to clarify (1990: 173–4).

In Sebald's work, the desire is also somewhat different. The trajectory of objects, as we have seen, is a double and contradictory one: as the object travels through time it becomes a gravitational point for the gathering of memories, existential traces, affective associations, but at the same time its incoherence in relation to other objects, its sense of being marooned and the subject of puzzlement, increases. But, however much still life evicts the human and nullifies human agency, it presupposes the human, sketches out the potential presence of the human, invites us to think its objects back into a habitat. In order to reunite the human being with his objects, since these objects are what give the human its substance, its necessary anchorages, its channel of dialogue with the world and the self, the Sebaldian portrait seems to adopt several strategies: (i) the intensification of the pose, where the pose is a form of self-reification (there are relatively few unposed portraits in Sebald's work); (ii) the drift towards studio conditions, where the studio species, which is not to be found in any bestiary – their preference for crowding close together, their semi-gregarious, semi-aggressive demeanour, the way they put their throats back in emptying their glasses, the increasingly excitable babble of their voices, the sudden hasty departure of one or another of them – as I was watching all of this I suddenly noticed a solitary figure on the edge of the agitated crowd, a figure who could only be Austerlitz, whom I realized at that moment I had not seen for nearly twenty years. He had not changed at all in either his carriage or his clothing, and even had the rucksack still slung over his shoulder. Only his fair, wavy hair was paler, although it still stuck out oddly from his head as it used to. None the less, while I had always thought he was about ten years older than I, he now seemed ten years younger, whether because of my own poor state of health or because he was one of those bachelors who retain something boyish about them all their days. As far as I remember, I was overcome for a considerable time by my amazement at the unexpected return of Austerlitz. In any case, I recollect that before approaching him I had been thinking at some length about

his personal similarity to Ludwig Wittgenstein, and the horror-stricken expressions on both their faces. I believe it was mainly the rucksack, which Austerlitz told me later he had bought for ten shillings from Swedish stock in an army surplus store in the Charing Cross Road just before he began his studies, describing it as the only truly reliable thing in his life, which put into my head what on the surface was the rather outlandish idea

of a certain physical likeness between him and the philosopher who died of the disease of cancer in Cambridge in 1951. Wittgenstein always carried a

Figure 11.6

itself is a still life, a world of props, painted backdrops and fancy dress (Figure 11.7); (iii) the minimization of physical identity, of the legibility of the face, in favour of clothing (Figure 11.8), particularly in verbal descriptions: the initial description of Austerlitz, for example, runs like this:

> Eine der in der *Salle des pas perdus* wartenden Personen war Austerlitz, ein damals, im siebenundsechziger Jahr, beinahe jugendlich wirkender Mann mit blondem, seltsam gewelltem Haar, wie ich es sonst nur gesehen habe an dem deutschen Helden Siegfried in Langs Nibelungenfilm. Nicht anders als bei all unseren späteren Begegnungen trug Austerlitz damals in Antwerpen schwere Wanderstiefel, eine Art Arbeitshose aus verschossenem blauem Kattun, sowie ein maßgeschneidertes, aber längst aus der Mode gekommenes Anzugsjackett (2001b: 10)

> (One of the people waiting in the *Salle des pas perdus* was Austerlitz, a man who then, in 1967, appeared almost youthful, with fair, curiously wavy hair of a kind I had seen elsewhere only on the German hero Siegfried in Fritz Lang's *Nibelungen* film. That day in Antwerp, as on all our later meetings, Austerlitz wore heavy walking boots and workman's trousers made of faded blue calico, together with a tailor-made but long outdated suit jacket. (2001c: 6))

Against the *transferability* of physical features is set the *permanence*, the insistent repetitions, of the single set of clothes. Indeed, it might be suggested that Sebald no longer wishes to house identity in the physical body, but precisely in objects: the antiques shop will remind us of the Surrealist flea-market and of the indispensability of the alienated or displaced object to the experience of 'hasard objectif' [objective chance], that strange encounter we have with our own desires and psychic images.

And, of course, Austerlitz creates his own *linguistic* still life in response to the items seen in the windows of the antiques shop:

> Welches Geheimnis bargen die drei verschieden großen Messingsmörser, die etwas von einem Orakelspruch hatten, die kristallenen Schalen, Keramikvasen und irdenen Krüge, das blecherne Reklameschild, das die Aufschrift *Theresienstädter Wasser* trug, das Seemuschelkästchen, die Miniaturdrehorgel, die kugelförmigen Briefbeschwerer, in deren Glasssphären wunderbare Meeresblüten schwebten, das Schiffsmodell, eine Art Korvette unter geblähten Segeln, der Trachtenkittel aus einem leichten, hellleinenen Sommerstoff, die Hirschhornknöpfe, die überdimensionale russische Offiziersmütze und die dazugehörige olivgrüne Uniformjacke mit den goldnen Schulterstücken, die Angelrute, die Jagdtasche, der japanische Fächer, die rund um einen Lampenschirm mit feinen Pinselstrichen gemalte endlose Landschaft an einem sei es durch Böhmen, sei es durch Brasilien still dahinziehenden Strom? (2001b: 279)

> (What secret lay behind the three brass mortars of different sizes, which had about them the suggestion of an oracular utterance, or the cut-glass bowls, ceramic vases and earthenware jugs, the tin advertising sign bearing the words *Theresienstädter*

had to fetch more money, said Aunt Fini; and then on the third evening, when he broke the bank again, Cosmo won so much that Ambros was busy till dawn counting the money and packing it into a steamer trunk. After spending the summer in Deauville, Cosmo and Ambros travelled via Paris and Venice to Constantinople and Jerusalem. I cannot tell you anything of what happened on that journey, said Aunt Fini, because Uncle Adelwarth would never answer questions about it. But there is a photo of him in Arab

costume, taken when they were in Jerusalem, and, said Aunt Fini, I have a kind of diary too, in tiny writing, that Ambros kept. For a long time I had quite forgotten about it, but, strange to say, I tried only recently to decipher it. With my poor eyes, though, I could not make out much more of it than the odd word; perhaps you should give it a try.

With long pauses, during which she often seemed very far away and lost, Aunt Fini told me, on my last day at Cedar Glen West, of the end of Cosmo Solomon and the later years of my Great-Uncle Ambros Adelwarth. Shortly after the two globetrotters returned from the Holy Land, as Aunt Fini put it, the war broke out in Europe. The more it raged, and the more we learnt of the extent of the devastation, the less Cosmo was able to regain a footing in the unchanged daily life of America. He became a stranger to his former friends, he abandoned his apartment in New York City, and even out on Long Island he soon withdrew entirely to his own quarters and at length to a secluded garden house known as the summer villa. Aunt Fini said that one of the Solomons' old gardeners once told her that in those days Cosmo would often be steeped in melancholy all day, and then at night would pace to and fro in the unheated summer villa, groaning softly. Wildly agitated, he would string our words that bore some relation to the fighting, and as he uttered these words of war he would apparently beat his forehead with his hand, as if he were vexed at his own incomprehension or were trying to learn what he said by heart. Frequently he would be so beside himself that he could no longer even recognized Ambros. And yet he claimed that he could see clearly, in his own head, what was happening in Europe: the inferno, the dying, the rotting bodies lying in the sun in open fields. Once he even took to

Figure 11.7

myself descending the gangway of a large ferry, and hardly had I stepped ashore but I resolved to take the evening train to Venice, and before that to spend the day with Ernst Herbeck in Klosterneuburg.

Ernst Herbeck has been afflicted with mental disorders ever since his twentieth year. He was first committed to an institution in 1940. At that time he was employed as an unskilled worker in a munitions factory. Suddenly he could hardly eat or sleep any more. He lay awake at night, counting aloud, his body was racked with cramps. Life in the family, and especially his father's incisive thinking, were corroding his nerves, as he put it. In the end he lost control of himself, knocked his plate away at mealtimes or tipped his soup under the bed. Occasionally his condition would improve for a while. In October 1944 he was even called up, only to be discharged in March 1945. One year after the war was over he was committed for the fourth and final time. He had been wandering the streets of Vienna at night, attracting attention by his behaviour, and had made incoherent and confused statements to the police. In the autumn of 1980, after thirty-four years in an institution, tormented for most of that time by the smallness of his own thoughts and perceiving everything as though through a veil drawn over his eyes, Ernst Herbeck was, so to speak, discharged from his illness

and allowed to move into a pensioners' home in the town, among the inmates of which he was scarcely conspicuous. When I arrived at the home shortly before half past nine he was already standing waiting at the top of the steps that ran up to the entrance. I waved to him from the other side of the street, whereupon he raised his arm in welcome and, keeping it outstretched, came down the steps. He was wearing a glencheck suit with a hiking badge on the lapel. On his head he wore a narrow-brimmed hat, a kind of trilby, which he later took off when it grew too warm for him and carried beside him, just as my grandfather often used to do on summer walks. At my suggestion we took the train to

Figure 11.8

Wasser, the little box of seashells, the miniature barrel organ, the globe-shaped paper-weights with wonderful marine flowers swaying inside their glassy spheres, the model ship (some kind of corvette under full sail), the oak-leaf-embroidered jacket of light, pale, summery linen, the stag-horn buttons, the outsize Russian officer's cap and the olive-green uniform tunic with gilt epaulettes that went with it, the fishing rod, the hunter's bag, the Japanese fan, the endless landscape painted round a lampshade in fine brush-strokes, showing a river running quietly through perhaps Bohemia or perhaps Brazil? (2001c: 275))

What makes enumeration so strange in writing is its undoing of discourse, of syntax: it has no ostensible organizing principle, it does not predict its own ending – when are enough items enough? – and, consequently, it has no perspectival drive towards a vanishing point, the full stop, or, in this particular case, the question mark. It undermines the foundation of the sentence, the main clause, which becomes submerged in the process of pure nomination, a process which nullifies the distinction between main and subordinate; in this particular instance, the main clause – 'What secret lay' – is quickly lost sight of, and by the end of the sentence we relate the question mark much more to whether the river runs through Bohemia or Brazil than to the initial question. Like the still life, enumeration denies both human agency and event, and it belongs to the temporality of utterance only because the process of naming itself takes place in consecutive time: but this still life really belongs to the world of juxtaposition and simultaneity. If this still life has an uncanniness equivalent to its visual counterpart, it derives from (i) the 'mesmerising effect' of the signifier, here aided by the German language's powers of compounding, as if the objects had come into existence as a result of strange, impenetrable laws of etymology and morphology; (ii) the recalcitrance, the intractability, that *pure* naming enacts: Sebald resists those escapes from the object into an anthropomorphizing appropriation of them provided by metaphor and simile; here, the only real narratorial intervention occurs apropos of the three brass mortars, in the clause 'which had about them the suggestion of an oracular utterance'; but this remark is applicable to all the items mentioned; (iii) the fact that objects deprived of a specific function in relation to a particular individual or household suddenly become available to a whole range of new, and perhaps improbable, possibilities.

If the constituents of still lifes are significant by virtue of what they hold, of what they know of us, of the traces they have of us, by virtue, in short, of this cumulative autonomy, photo-portraits are significant not by virtue of their searching depiction of a particular human being, but by virtue of their relationship with the medium of photography itself, by virtue of what significance the medium itself bestows upon them. If the medium acts in documentary fashion for the still life, it acts in spiritualist fashion for the portrait. Here, the black and white photo-graph, as an in-between of two states, comes into its own:

217

I believe that the black-and-white photograph, or rather the gray zones in the black-and-white photograph, stand for this territory that is located between death and life. In the archaic imagination it was usually the case that there was not only life and then death, as we assume today, but rather that in between there was this vast no-man's-land where people were permanently wandering around and where one did not know exactly how long one had to stay there, whether this was a purgatory in the Christian sense or just a kind of desert that one had to traverse until one reached the other side. (Sebald in Schulz, 2007: 108)

This metaphysicalization of the photo-portrait may take many forms. For instance, Věra, Austerlitz's nurserymaid, believes that portrait photographs have a memory of their own, remembering the roles that both we, the survivors, and those already dead had played in former lives (2001b: 262; 2001c: 258). Elsewhere, in his review essay 'Kafka Goes to the Movies', Sebald expresses the view that photographic portraits act vampirically, and draw into themselves that reality of which they are in fact only a copy, usurping reality's authenticity and identity: 'And because the copy lasted long after what it had copied was gone, there was an uneasy suspicion that the original, whether it was human or a natural scene, was less authentic than the copy, that the copy was eroding the original, in the same way as a man meeting his doppelganger is said to feel his real self destroyed' (2005a: 164). Of the image of himself as the page to the Rose Queen (Figure 11.9), Austerlitz says: 'Soweit ich zurückblicken kann, [. . .] habe ich mich immer gefühlt, als hätte ich keinen Platz in der Wirklichkeit, als sei ich gar nicht vorhanden, und nie ist dieses Gefühl stärker in mir gewesen als an jenem Abend in der Šporkova, als mich der Blick des Pagen der Rosenkönigin durchdrang ('As far back as I can remember, [. . .] I have always felt as if I had no place in reality, as if I were not there at all, and I never had this impression more strongly than on that evening in the Šporkova when the eyes of the Rose Queen's page looked through me' (2001b: 265; 2001c: 261)). In ostensibly giving us back our memories, images of our earlier selves actually deprive us of our memory; as the narrator tells Lukas Seelos/Ambrose(r), in 'Il ritorno in patria' (*Vertigo*): 'Je mehr Bilder aus der Vergangenheit ich versammle, sagte ich, desto unwahrscheinlicher wird es mir, daß die Vergangenheit auf diese Weise sich abgespielt haben soll, denn nichts an ihr sei normal zu nennen' ('The more images I gathered from the past, I said, the more unlikely it seemed to me that the past had actually happened in this way or that way, because nothing about it could be called normal' (1994d: 231; 1999c: 212)).

The life of the Sebaldian still life object might be described as a journey from the domestic interior to the antiques shop, or indeed to the German warehousing complex, mentioned in *Austerlitz*, which occupied the site of the new Bibliothèque Nationale. It is not difficult to find a parallel in the journey of the photograph from the family album, or contact sheet, to the Sebaldian text. It is as if the Sebaldian text must itself go through this process of dispossession, dispersal, in order for its own

ner Abreise aus Prag. Du durftest Agata auf einen Maskenball begleiten im Haus eines ihrer einflußreichen Verehrer, und eigens zu diesem Anlaß wurde das schneeweiße Kostüm geschneidert für dich. Jacquot Austerlitz, paže růžové královny, steht auf der Rückseite geschrieben in der Hand deines Großvaters, der damals gerade zu Besuch gewesen ist. Das Bild lag vor mir, sagte Austerlitz, doch wagte ich nicht, es anzufassen. Andauernd kreisten die Worte paže růžové královny, paže růžové královny in meinem Kopf, bis mir aus der Ferne ihre Bedeutung entgegenkam und ich das lebende Tableau mit der Rosenkönigin und dem kleinen Schleppenträger zu ihrer Seite wieder sah. An mich selber in dieser Rolle aber erinnerte ich mich nicht, so sehr ich mich an jenem Abend und später auch mühte. Wohl erkannte ich den ungewöhnlichen, schräg über die Stirne verlaufenden Haaransatz, doch sonst war alles in mir ausgelöscht von einem überwältigenden Gefühl der Vergangenheit. Ich habe die Photographie seither noch vielmals studiert, das kahle, ebene Feld, auf dem ich stehe und von dem ich mir nicht denken kann, wo es war; die dunkel verschwommene Stelle über dem Horizont, das an seinem äußeren Rand gespensterhaft helle Kraushaar des Knaben, die Mantille über dem anscheinend angewinkelten oder, wie ich mir einmal gedacht habe, sagte Austerlitz, gebrochenen oder ge-

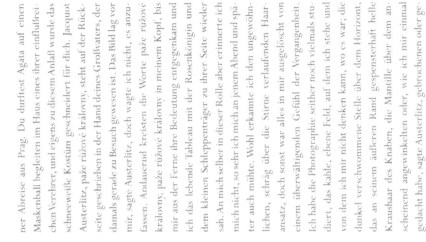

Schneewolke zu sehen glaubte und bis ich Věra weitersprechen hörte von dem Unergründlichen, das solchen aus der Vergessenheit aufgetauchten Photographien zu eigen sei. Man habe den Eindruck, sagte sie, es rühre sich etwas in ihnen, als vernehme man kleine Verzweiflungsseufzer, gémissements de désespoir, so sagte sie, sagte Austerlitz, als hätten die Bilder selbst ein Gedächtnis und erinnerten sich an uns, daran, wie wir, die Überlebenden, und diejenigen, die nicht mehr unter uns weilen, vordem gewesen sind. Ja, und das hier, auf der anderen Photographie, sagte Věra nach einer Weile, das bist du, Jacquot, im Monat Feber 1939, ein halbes Jahr ungefähr vor dei-

Figure 11.9

syntax to make sense, for the networking to find its efficacy. In his study of the still life, Bryson remarks that the construction of still life – and particularly the still life of the domestic table – is based on Renaissance perspective deprived of a vanishing point. The vanishing point is the guarantee of significance, the magnet of an inevitable orientation or organization. Objects disperse, photographs increasingly occupy their own particular space, withdraw into themselves; and as they do so, the vanishing point, the eye of God, and of coherence, disappears. But if the Sebaldian vision peculiarly gravitates towards the still life, it is wedded to a syntax of perambulation, in which the vanishing point constantly displaces itself. Sebald's abandonment of paragraphing in *Austerlitz* tells us something about the rejection of horizons. Why might Merleau-Ponty's account of Cézanne's vision[7] so appeal to Sebald? Because it has a similar teleological perspective at its heart, that teleology without a finality, in which everything is projected forward, 'transcendentally', but can always be begun again. Writing is walking, bodily being in language, where syntax is our movement, our constant self-relocation, where meaning is not being expressed, but is constantly coming into existence. Surely part of Sebald's gradual abandonment of paragraphing is the destruction of a textual outside. In Merleau-Ponty's thinking, Cartesian perspective is what puts the viewer outside space, immobilizes him in a viewing position without a point of view and confirms the separate operation of mind and body; Cartesian perspective is what locks objects into measurable spatial relations (see Johnson, 1993: 130–9; Merleau-Ponty, 2008: 37–43). But, I would argue, Sebald's work is about the human trying to re-inhabit the world of the still life, trying to dynamize and reconfigure connections between things. For Merleau-Ponty, body and mind must be fused as part of our re-entry into space, where our mobility constantly reconfigures our relationship with things, where space is no longer what confines and defines objects, but what comes into existence at their edges. The paragraph is an act of moving outside writing, of engineering a mental shift, of 'measuring' a distance elapsed in narrative or in argument, of generating a perspectival frame for the chapter or story. In order to be free to move, I must sacrifice paragraphing, lose my bearings, or, rather, I must lose my bearings in order that textual space starts from me, the reader, as the zero point; I do not see textual space according to its exterior envelope; I live it from the inside, I am immersed in it.

I look upon Sebald's description of the Waterloo Panorama in *The Rings of Saturn*[8] as a delineation of the three stages of his own construction of the historical memory. First, there is the general account that we have inherited from official history, clear but inanimate, without any direct, personal links: 'Wir, die Überlebenden, sehen alles von oben herunter, sehen alles zugleich und wissen dennoch nicht, wie es war' ('We, the survivors, see everything from above, see everything at once, and still we do not know how it was' (1997b: 152; 1998c: 125)); then, we try to get nearer specific events; this is perhaps when we look at photo-

graphs. Sebald's listening to the account of the battle in Flemish, only fragments of which he understands, is like looking at the fragments and splinters that photographs are: 'Verstanden habe ich von den verschiedenen Vorgängen höchstens die Hälfte' ('Of the various circumstances and vicissitudes described I understood no more than the odd phrase' (1997b: 152; 1998c: 125)). Finally, there is the retreat into the self, the recourse to personal vision and association, which draws one into fiction: 'Erst als ich die Augen schloß, sah ich, daran erinnere ich mich genau, eine Kanonenkugel, die auf schräger Bahn eine Reihe von Pappeln durchquerte, daß die grünen Zweige zerfetzt durch die Luft flogen. Und dann sah ich noch Fabrizio, den jungen Helden Stendhals [...] in der Schlacht herumirren' ('Only when I had shut my eyes, I well recall, did I see a cannonball smash through a row of poplars at an angle, sending the green branches flying in tatters. And then I saw Fabrizio, Stendhal's young hero, wandering about the battlefield, [...]' (1997b: 153; 1998c: 126)). This is that act of self-immersion of which I have just spoken, the move into a textual space of one's own, in which the promptings of one's intertexts can be freely responded to. Here, intertexts can become powerful spiritual witnesses.

I would like briefly to apply the Waterloo Panorama schema to the story of Paul Bereyter in *The Emigrants*, but, this time, to relate all three stages to photographic equivalents. First I want to observe that the story begins and ends with diagrams – of Bereyter's classroom and of one of the railway maps he was in the habit of drawing on the blackboard (Figure 11.10); we enter and exit the story with ground-plans and aerial views which are meant to provide us with complete pictures, but which reveal nothing of human circumstance, of those secondary, apparently insignificant details which are likely to be the key to discovery and involuntary memory. Between these two pillars of self-deluding comprehension which are, in fact, admissions of loss, we find group photographs and the portraits of Bereyter himself, alone or in the company of others – which are like the sightings of a rare species rather than attempts to capture, photographically, the depths of personality. At best these are the odd phrases of Flemish that we understand, the tantalizing glimpses, which activate imaginative projections and fabulations. But within the photographic range of the portrait should also be included those images which relate to still life, to the still life of letter racks, open books and other textual material, and, more particularly, Bereyter's notebooks, containing quotations from his voracious reading of writers, most of whom had taken their own lives, or been close to doing so (Figure 11.11). This is another point at which photographs cross over into fiction, the point at which writing itself becomes a still life. This is a handwriting in whose very graphological idiosyncrasies a voice is lurking, a handwriting which, the narrator tells us, resorts to Gabelsberg shorthand to accelerate the process by which Bereyter identifies himself as an exile in S rather than as one of its real inhabitants. Finally, at least in the Waterloo Panorama model, we have to leave photographs behind to engage our own imaginations. But this is not so in 'Paul Bereyter', where a photograph *is* able to enact the withdrawal into one's own

subjectivity. Because the first photograph is not, after all, the ground-plan of the classroom, but one of the few 'unconventional' photos to appear in Sebald's work, a worm's-eye view along the railway line on which Bereyter met his end (Figure 11.12). Is this presented to us as Bereyter's own view, as he lies across the rails, shortly before his death, a fearful anticipation? Or is this a view reconstructed by the narrator, a documentation now melancholic, eerily without imminence, a remembering? Or does this photograph have a point of view that belongs to no one and to everyone? The camera sees with another eye, with an angle of vision but without a point of view, or, rather, with a disembodied point of view, a dispersed or available subjectivity. Certainly the narrator takes up the photograph's implicit challenge: 'Er hatte, in meiner Vorstellung, die Brille abgenommen und zur Seite in den Schotter gelegt. Die glänzenden Stahlbänder, die Querbalken der Schwellen, das Fichtenwäldchen an der Altstädter Steige und der ihm so vertraute Gebirgsbogen waren vor seinen kurzsichtigen Augen verschwommen und ausgelöscht in der Dämmerung. Zuletzt, als das schlagende Geräusch sich näherte, sah er nurmehr ein dunkel Grau, mitten darin aber, gestochen scharf, das schneeweiße Nachbild des Kratzers, der Trettach und des Himmelsschrofens' ('As I pictured him, he had taken off his spectacles and put them on the ballast stones by his side. The gleaming bands of steel, the crossbars of the sleepers, the spruce trees on the hillside above the village of Altstädten, the arc of the mountains he knew so well, were a blur before his short-sighted eyes, smudged out in the gathering dusk. At last, as the thunderous sound approached, all he saw was a darkening greyness and, in the midst of it, needle sharp, the snow-white silhouettes of three mountains: the Kratzer, the Trettach and the Himmelsschrofen' (1994a: 44; 2002e: 29)). We no longer have a photograph *of* writing, but a photograph which accedes to writing, a writing which is the equivalent of the cannonball smashing through the row of poplars.

My final point relates to Sebald's preoccupation with eyes, which also stems from the portrait-work of Jan Peter Tripp. What matters for us, in this ocular preoccupation, is the inclusion of the eyes of animals, and particularly of dogs. Photographs look at us with eyes that are incomprehensible, though they may themselves seem to comprehend us. And the awareness of this paradox seems to increase as Sebald's work progresses. In this connection, and remembering Tripp's etching of the eyes of Sebald's dog Maurice/Moritz in *Unrecounted*, one might refer to Sebald's under-lining of lines in John Berger's essay 'Why Look at Animals?' which run: 'The animal scrutinises [man] across a narrow abyss of non-comprehension. [...] The man too is looking across a similar, but not identical, abyss of non-comprehension. And this is so wherever he looks. He is always looking across ignorance and fear' (Berger 1980: 3).[9] This may have been an important passage for Sebald, not least for that 'similar, but not identical', that possibility of a divergence of gazes between the spectator and the image. It may have been important, too, for a word, 'abyss', because this is the word that appears in Sebald's crucial assessment of the dog

herunter, als müßte eine tintige Flüssigkeit gleich herauslaufen aus ihm. Meine Schläfen schmerzten mich so unsäglich, daß ich mich niederlegen mußte, und ich erinnere mich genau, daß, als das Aspirin, das Paul mir gegeben hatte, langsam zu wirken begann, hinter meinen Lidern zwei seltsame, unheilvolle Flekken lauernd sich bewegten. Erwacht bin ich erst wieder in der Abenddämmerung, die an diesem Tag allerdings bereits um drei Uhr einsetzte. Paul hatte mich zugedeckt, war aber selber nirgends in der Wohnung zu sehen. Unschlüssig im Vorzimmer stehend, bemerkte ich, daß die Windjacke fehlte, von der Paul am Morgen beiläufig gesagt hatte, daß sie bald vierzig Jahre schon an der Garderobe hänge. In diesem Augenblick wußte ich, daß Paul in dieser Jacke fortgegangen war und daß ich ihn lebend nicht mehr sehen würde. Ich war also gewissermaßen vorbereitet, als es bald darauf an der Haustüre klingelte. Nur die Todesart, dieses mir unvorstellbare Ende, brachte mich zunächst völlig aus der Fassung, wenn sie auch, wie ich bald schon begriff, durchaus folgerichtig gewesen ist. Die Eisenbahn hatte für Paul eine tiefere Bedeutung. Wahrscheinlich schien es ihm immer, als führe sie in den Tod. Fahrpläne, Kursbücher, die Logistik des ganzen Eisenbahnwesens, das alles war für ihn, wie die Wohnung in S. sogleich erkennen ließ, zeit-

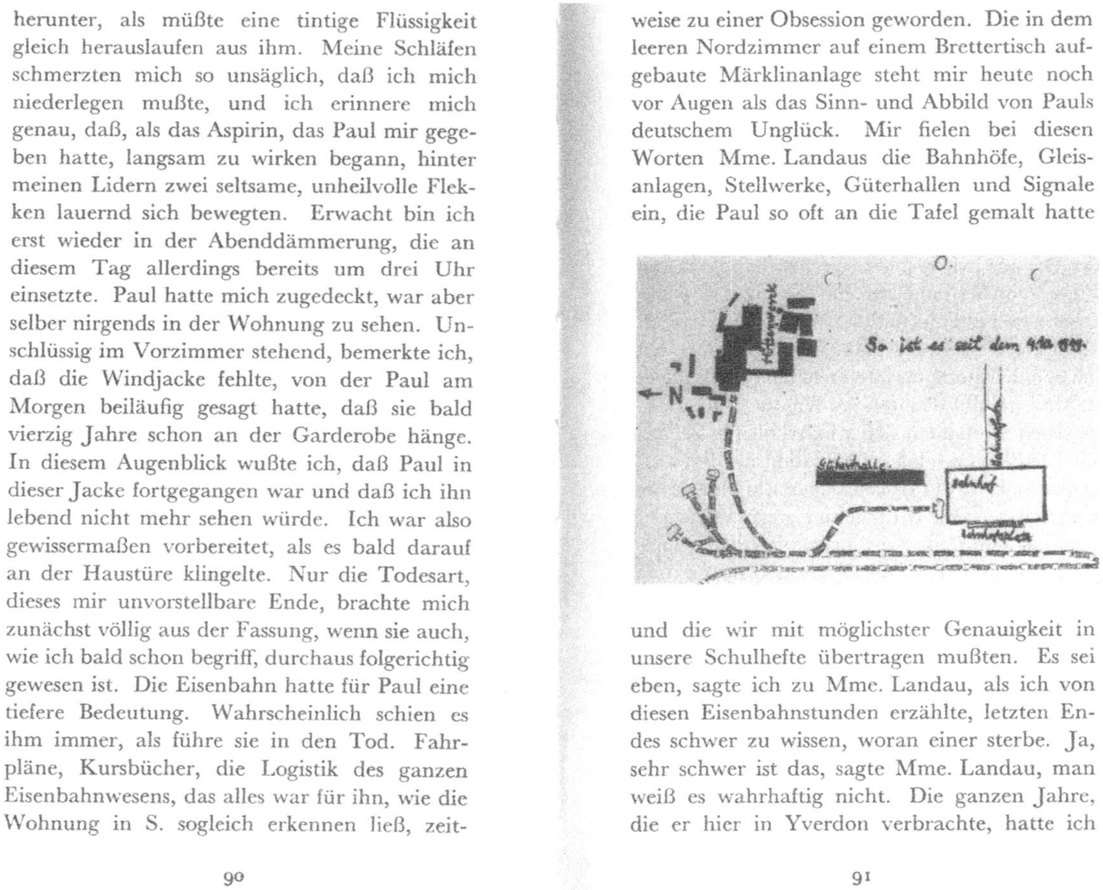

weise zu einer Obsession geworden. Die in dem leeren Nordzimmer auf einem Brettertisch aufgebaute Märklinanlage steht mir heute noch vor Augen als das Sinn- und Abbild von Pauls deutschem Unglück. Mir fielen bei diesen Worten Mme. Landaus die Bahnhöfe, Gleisanlagen, Stellwerke, Güterhallen und Signale ein, die Paul so oft an die Tafel gemalt hatte

und die wir mit möglichster Genauigkeit in unsere Schulhefte übertragen mußten. Es sei eben, sagte ich zu Mme. Landau, als ich von diesen Eisenbahnstunden erzählte, letzten Endes schwer zu wissen, woran einer sterbe. Ja, sehr schwer ist das, sagte Mme. Landau, man weiß es wahrhaftig nicht. Die ganzen Jahre, die er hier in Yverdon verbrachte, hatte ich

Figure 11.10

ten, sondern es habe immer bei ihm bis in die frühen Stunden die Lampe gebrannt. Er habe gelesen und gelesen — Altenberg, Trakl, Wittgenstein, Friedell, Hasenclever, Toller, Tucholsky, Klaus Mann, Ossietzky, Benjamin, Koestler und Zweig, in erster Linie also Schriftsteller, die sich das Leben genommen hatten oder nahe daran waren, es zu tun. Seine Exzerpthefte geben einen Begriff davon, wie ungeheuer ihn insbesondere das Leben dieser Autoren interessiert hat. Hunderte von Seiten hat er exzerpiert, großenteils in Gabelsberger Kurzschrift, weil es ihm sonst nicht geschwind genug gegangen wäre, und immer wieder stößt

man auf Selbstmordgeschichten. Es war mir, sagte Mme. Landau, indem sie mir die schwar-

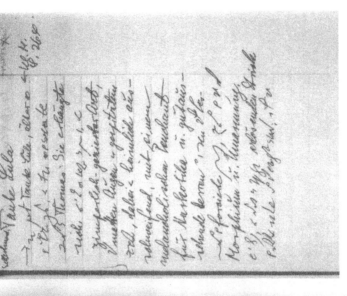

zen Wachstuchhefte aushändigte, als habe Paul hier eine Beweislast zusammengetragen, deren im Verlauf der Prozeßführung zunehmendes Gewicht ihn endgültig zu der Überzeugung

Figure 11.11

In January 1984, the news reached me from S that on the evening of the 30th of December, a week after his seventy-fourth birthday, Paul Bereyter, who had been my teacher at primary school, had put an end to his life. A short distance from S, where the railway track curves out of a willow copse into the open fields, he had lain himself down in front of a train. The obituary in the local paper was headed "Grief at the Loss of a Popular Teacher" and there was no mention of the fact that Paul Bereyter had died of his own free will, or through a self-destructive compulsion. It spoke merely of the dead man's services to education, his dedicated care for his pupils, far beyond the call of duty, his great love of music, his astonishing inventiveness, and of much else in the same vein. Almost by way of an aside, the obituary added, with no further explanation, that during the Third Reich Paul Bereyter had been prevented from practising his chosen profession. It was this curiously unconnected, inconsequential statement, as much as the violent manner of his death, which

Figure 11.12

which looks out of Tripp's picture entitled *Déjà vu or The Incident* of 1992 (Figure 11.13, detail):

> Der Hund, der Geheimnisträger, der mit Leichtigkeit über die Abgründe der Zeit läuft, weil es für ihn keinen Unterschied gibt zwischen dem 15. und dem 20. Jahrhundert, weiß manches genauer als wir. Aufmerksam ist sein linkes (domestiziertes) Auge auf uns gerichtet; das rechte (wilde) hat um eine Spur weniger Licht, wirkt abseitig und fremd. Und doch fühlen wir uns gerade von diesem überschatteten Auge durchschaut. (Sebald 2000a: 188)

> (The dog, bearer of the secret, who runs with ease over the abysses of time, because for him there is no difference between the fifteenth and the twentieth centuries, knows many things more accurately than we do. His left (domesticated) eye is attentively fixed on us; the right (wild) one has a little less light, strikes us as averted and alien. And yet we sense that it is the overshadowed eye that sees through us. (Sebald and Tripp, 2004a: 94))

The photograph's eye, which is the camera's eye, is at once domesticated and untamed, direct and peculiarly remote. And even though the photo may demand imperiously to be replaced in the moment when the shutter was released, even though it may claim its particular niche in a sequence from which it was untimely wrenched, so equally it goes out to confront all *subsequent* spectators across time-spans between which it makes no differentiation. All this could be said, too, of the still life. In its *dissemination*, the photograph, like the dog, like the still life, does not know the difference between the fifteenth and the twentieth centuries. In this sense, the photograph has the capacity constantly to rejoin history, to be part of all histories subsequent to it.

We should also notice the other feature of the dog's looking: its right eye 'wirkt abseitig und fremd' ('strikes us as averted and alien'). 'Abseitig' ('averted') will remind us of the dark eye of Max Aurach which 'ins Abseits blickte' ('looked sideways'). And 'abseitig' will remind us, too, of 'abgewandt' ('turned away, averted'), a word which occurs in the text of *Unrecounted* opposite the eyes of Rembrandt:

> Gleich einem Hund
> sagt Cézanne
> so soll der Maler
> schauen das Auge
> still & fast
> abgewandt (Sebald 2003: 45)
> (Like a dog
> Cézanne says
> that's how a painter
> must see, the eye
> fixed & almost averted (2004a: 51))

Figure 11.13

and in the text opposite the eyes of Sebald's daughter Anna:

> Unerzählt
> bleibt die Geschichte
> der abgewandten
> Gesichter (Sebald 2003: 69)
> (Unrecounted
> always it will remain
> the story of the averted
> faces (Sebald and Tripp; 2004a: 75))

Such a look may well be deflected by trauma, or by some other elsewhere which continues to haunt. But it also strikes me as a look that is directed into the wings, or, put photographically, into the blind field. This calls to mind Barthes's distinction between fixated pornographic looking which stays within the frame, and erotic looking which takes the spectator outside the frame, and 'it is there' as Barthes puts it, 'that I animate this photograph and that it animates me' (1984: 59). The averted eyes of the dog, and Max Aurach, and many others besides, invite us into the space which animates us and where we animate them.

227

NOTES

1 This chapter was written in conjunction with another paper, 'Sebald's Photographic Annotations' (2011). Both grew out of the same body of reading, which includes: for still life, not only Bryson's (1990) study referred to in the text of this article, but also Rosemary Lloyd's *Shimmering in a Transformed Light* (2005), and the volume on *trompe-l'œil* edited by Sybille Ebert-Schifferer (2002); on the photographic portrait, particularly Graham Clarke (ed.), *The Portrait in Photography* (1992) and Marianne Hirsch's *Family Frames* (1997), although Alexsander Rodchenko's 1928 'manifesto', 'Against the Synthetic Portrait, For the Snapshot' (1988), remains a crucial point of reference; for work on photography in Sebald, and particularly on how it relates to memory, trauma and narrative, one should consult: Stefanie Harris, 'The Return of the Dead: Memory and Photography in W. G. Sebald's *Die Ausgewanderten*' (2001), Elinor Shaffer, 'W. G. Sebald's Photographic Narrative' (2003), J. J. Long, 'History, Narrative, and Photography in W. G. Sebald's *Die Ausgewanderten*' (2003); Heiner Boehncke, 'Clair obscur: W. G. Sebalds Bilder' (2003); Markus R. Weber, 'Die fantastische befragt die pedantische Genauigkeit: Zu den Abbildungen in W. G. Sebalds Werken' (2003); the essays collected in Part V ('Haunting, Trauma, Memory') of *W. G. Sebald: A Critical Companion*, edited by J. J. Long and Anne Whitehead (2004) and Carolin Duttlinger's 'Traumatic Photographs: Remembrance and the Technical Media in W. G. Sebald's *Austerlitz*', in the same volume; Richard Crownshaw, 'Reconsidering Postmemory: Photography, the Archive, and Post-Holocaust Memory in W. G. Sebald's *Austerlitz*' (2004); George Kouvaros, 'Images That Remember Us: Photography and Memory in *Austerlitz*' (2005); Samuel Pane, 'Trauma Obscura: Photographic Media in W. G. Sebald's *Austerlitz*' (2005); Silke Horstkotte, 'Fantastic Gaps: Photography Inserted into Narrative in W. G. Sebald's *Austerlitz*' (2005); Elizabeth Chaplin, 'The Convention of Captioning: W. G. Sebald and the Release of the Captive Image' (2006); Section 3 ('History and Trauma') of *W. G. Sebald: History, Memory, Trauma*, edited by Scott Denham and Mark McCulloh (2006), and Maya Barzilai, 'On Exposure: Photography and Uncanny Memory in W. G. Sebald's *Die Ausgewanderten* and *Austerlitz*' and Lilian R. Furst, 'Realism, Photography, and Degrees of Uncertainty', in the same volume; and *Searching for Sebald: Photography after W. G. Sebald*, edited by Lise Patt with Christel Dillbohner (2007) is full of sharply relevant contributions. On the more general relationship between photography and trauma, Ulrich Baer's *Spectral Evidence: The Photography of Trauma* (2002) is indispensable. Finally, I might add that, beside the expected underpinnings of any photographic enquiry (Benjamin, Sontag, Berger, Barthes), I have, for this particular study, drawn with much profit on François Soulages's *Esthétique de la photographie* (1998), Emmanuel Garrigues's *L'Écriture photographique* (2000) and Clément Rosset's *Fantasmagories* (2006).

2 If we have any doubts about regarding all of Sebald's photographs as still-life objects that turn up in antique shops, then we should listen to his own words: 'For many years I have found images in a most unsystematic manner. One finds such things enclosed in old books that one buys. One finds them in antique shops or thrift shops. That's typical for photographs after all, that they lead such a nomadic existence and then are "rescued" by someone' (Sebald in Scholz, 2007, 104).

3 Sebald wrote his first essay on Tripp, 'Wie Tag und Nacht – über die Bilder Jan Peter

228

Tripps' [As Day and Night, Chalk and Cheese: On the Pictures of Jan Peter Tripp], for a book on Tripp's work published in 1993; the translation of that essay, which we have just quoted from, is to be found in the English translation of Sebald's collaborative work with Tripp, *Unrecounted* (2004).

4 Barthes's *punctum* is, initially, a visual detail in a photograph which penetrates or lacerates a particular spectator, because it is the irresistible activator of something deeply buried in the spectatorial psyche. It has nothing to do with the aesthetics of the photograph, nor with its general purport (*studium*). The experience of *punctum* cannot be predicted; and crucially, perhaps, it is produced by a photograph taken by someone else, rather than by a photograph of one's own. Crucially, too, *punctum* acts regardless of time: a photograph of 1910 may 'prick' a spectator in 2010. The *studium*, on the other hand, relates to the photograph's intended message, its 'average' significance and affect; *studium* is culturally determined, educative and available to all spectators indiscriminately (Barthes 1984, 23–8, and *passim*). Later in *Camera Lucida*, Barthes identifies another *punctum*, shared by all photographs, part of the photographic condition: the '*that-has-been*', an illusory resurrection at the expense of a death foretold (1984, 76–97). For a full re-appraisal of the significances of *punctum*, see the essays in Batchem (2009).

5 This claim may seem fanciful: *the reader feels as if he/she might have taken the photographs that appear in the Sebaldian text*. This is the sense that I derive from the dervish boy episode in 'Ambros Adelwarth'. The photograph of the boy in the text corresponds to the circumstances of the first encounter, described in Ambros's diary: shading their dazzled eyes against the sun's brightness, Cosmo and Ambros see the boy in his wide gown, jacket and high, brimless, camel-hair toque. Cosmo vows to come out again to take the photograph we have just seen: 'The sun had set, the water was a shadowy plain, but higher up a light still moved here and there. Cosmo, at the tiller, says he wants to come out shortly once again, with a photographer, to take a souvenir photograph of the boy dervish . . .' (2002e, 135). But the sun has gone down. How long is 'shortly'? How can one know that the dervish boy will still be in the alley? And why does this sentence end with suspension points, if not to suggest something that never happened, perhaps, or something the details of which we may not enquire into? As we were reading the passage, we took the photo, which Ambros and Cosmo were in no position to take. Alternatively, the photographer that Cosmo took back with him was in fact the reader who already knew what photograph to take, or knew, too, that to take photographs – as elsewhere the narrator does, as elsewhere Austerlitz does – is an integral part of the writing or reading experience.

6 That this reflected image in the window ('my own faint shadow') is the image of Sebald himself should not, I think, deflect us into a discussion of auto-fiction or of the whereabouts, in *Austerlitz*, of the Sebaldian identity, for two reasons: (i) Sebald's photographic sourcing of his work is extremely eclectic, and he resorts to his own photographs as and when necessary; (ii) Sebald projects the position of the photographer as an *available* position; as already suggested, it is important that every reader feels that he/she might easily have taken these photographs (or their equivalent); the power of the photograph lies in its ability to cast the spectator as the photographer, in the same way that the responsibility for narrative must also be felt to be freely transferable.

7 See particularly 'Cézanne's Doubt' and 'Eye and Mind' in Johnson (1993, 59–75 and 121–49).

8 The passage, in its entirety, runs: 'This then, I thought, as I looked round about me, is the representation of history. It requires a falsification of perspective. We, the survivors, see everything from above, see everything at once, and still we do not know how it was. The desolate field extends all around where once fifty thousand soldiers and ten thousand horses met their end within a few hours. The night after the battle, the air must have been filled with death rattles and groans. Now there is nothing but the silent brown soil. Whatever became of the corpses and mortal remains? Are they buried under the memorial? Are we standing on a mountain of death? Is that our ultimate vantage point? Does one really have the much-vaunted historical overview from such a position? Near Brighton, I was once told, not far from the coast, there are two copses that were planted after the Battle of Waterloo in remembrance of that memorable victory. One is in the shape of a Napoleonic three-cornered hat, the other in that of a Wellington boot. Naturally the outlines cannot be made out from the ground; they were intended as landmarks for latter-day balloonists. That afternoon in the rotunda I inserted a couple of coins in a slot machine to hear an account of the battle in Flemish. Of the various circumstances and vicissitudes described I understood no more than the odd phrase. De holle weg van Ohain, de Hertog van Wellington, de rook van de pruisische batterijen, tegenaanval van de nederlandse cavalerie – the fighting will have surged to and fro in waves for a long time, as is generally the case. No clear picture emerged. Neither then nor today. Only when I had shut my eyes, I well recall, did I see a cannonball smash through a row of poplars at an angle, sending the green branches flying in tatters. And then I saw Fabrizio, Stendhal's young hero, wandering about the battlefield, pale but with his eyes aglow, and an unsaddled colonel getting to his feet and telling his sergeant: I can feel nothing but the old injury in my right hand' (1998c, 125–6).

9 As intimated in note 1, I have elsewhere (2011) investigated Sebald's annotations of four photographic texts, namely Susan Sontag's *On Photography* (UK publication 1978), John Berger's *About Looking* (1980), Roland Barthes's *La Chambre Claire: Note sur la photographie* (1980) in its English translation by Richard Howard (*Camera Lucida: Reflections on Photography*, 1984) and my own *The Spoken Image: Photography and Language* (1999). In relation to this particular underlining, it is worth noting that the non-comprehending reciprocal scrutiny of animal and human, reappears in *Austerlitz*, in the observation of Marie de Verneuil: 'said Austerlitz, she said something which I have never forgotten, she said that captive animals and we ourselves, their human counterparts, view one another *à travers une brèche d'incompréhension*' (2002b, 368–9).

12

THE RETURN OF THE REPRESSED MOTHER IN W. G. SEBALD'S FICTION

Graley Herren

Anxieties about the Holocaust often assume the form of anxieties about lost mothers in Sebald's fiction. His narrator[1] is relentlessly drawn to victims who were separated from their mothers during the war, mothers who then disappeared with scarcely a trace into the camps. In Sebald's treatment of the Holocaust, Nazi 'crimes against humanity' are often translated as 'crimes against the family'. Mark M. Anderson identifies the central importance of the family drama in Sebald's work:

> In a very literal sense, his stories are 'familiar' – not just because of their casual presentation of his subjects' quotidian activities but because they explicitly focus on family relations. And although the narrator keeps himself quietly out of the spotlight, his own family narrative is subtly intertwined with that of his protagonists. Family photograph albums, memoirs, and diaries play a fundamental role in the telling of these stories, both formally and affectively. (2008: 141)

Sebald's literature of reparation is rooted in large part to a troubled paternal legacy as the son of a soldier in the *Wehrmacht*. However, with a few notable exceptions, the maternal dimension of these 'crimes against the family', particularly the severing of the mother–child bond, have not been fully appreciated.[2] Sebald addresses this subject most explicitly in the Luisa Lanzberg section of *The Emigrants* and in the search for Agáta Austerlitzová in *Austerlitz*. However, I am more interested in less direct manifestations of this crisis of maternity, visual and textual instances where the mother's identity is obscured or suppressed. In this chapter I will concentrate primarily upon two such instances from *Vertigo* and *The Emigrants*. Here Sebald's indictments extend well beyond the Nazi perpetrators of 'crimes against the family', and these indictments hit uncomfortably close to home.

My preference for the generic label 'fiction' to categorize Sebald's work is important to establish at the outset. The near-identity of the narrator with his author makes it tempting to equate the two and thus to think about Sebald's works categorically as memoir, travel narrative or essay. Indeed, Sebald at times encouraged such a reading, affirming for instance in his interview with Carole Angier: 'What matters is all true. The big events [. . .]. The invention comes in at the level of minor detail most of the time, to provide *l'effet du reel*' (Angier 2007: 72). It is interesting to note, however, that, far from being reassured by the author's affirmation, Angier was clearly disconcerted by his manipulation of source material. As Sebald 'confessed' to one creative intervention after another in *The Emigrants*, Angier could barely conceal her unease: 'This is the answer to my question, then: *The Emigrants* is fiction. And the photographs and documents are part of the fiction. It's a sophisticated undertaking, and perhaps a dangerous one, given its subject' (2007: 73). I share Angier's conclusion that Sebald's works are best understood as works of fiction, though I find little cause for distress in this fact. One of the more fascinating dynamics at play in the fiction is the *distortion* of autobiography – Sebald's wilful manipulation of raw material from his own experiences to produce a narrator whose perspective on those experiences is instructively incongruent with that of his author. To put it in terms of an instructive analogy, the narrator is to Sebald as Stephen Dedalus is to James Joyce. Critics customarily focus so much upon the narrator's explicit and implicit critiques of German history, ideology and behaviour that they often fail to recognize that the narrator himself is frequently held up for critique as well. Far from being immune from the faults that he diagnoses in the collective German psyche, the narrator is at times a walking case study of the very pathologies he decries. Nowhere is the narrator's proclivity for denial, distortion and repression more evident than in matters maternal.

Sebald's narrator laments the corruption of sacred maternal virtues as a deplorable casualty of the Second World War. I use the term 'sacred maternal virtues' advisedly, knowing from the outset that, rather than lending credence to such moral platitudes, Sebald invests his narrator with these values only to disappoint them. Sebald was raised in a Catholic family. His quasi-autobiographical narrator periodically invokes the same childhood background, though as an adult he has ostensibly become a religious sceptic, particularly when it comes to Christianity's complicity in violence. Nevertheless, the narrator still clings to strikingly traditional attitudes toward women, evidence of residual Catholic values at least in the arena of gender relations. Though he is apparently married to a woman named Clara (Sebald's own wife was named Ute), he is persistently revolted at the sight of sex,[3] and he shudders anytime a woman so much as touches him with less than virtuous intent.[4] Carnal knowledge – at least of the heterosexual variety – is consistently portrayed as dirty and disgusting. This is routinely offered as evidence of the narrator's closeted homosexuality,[5] but we might just as well chalk it up to a severe symptom of closeted Catholicism. In general, the narrator either idolizes women as divine Mothers (Madonna) or reviles them as carnal predators (Whore), with little acknowledgment of depth or nuance between these two extremes in matters of gender and sexuality. Again, it is worth emphasizing the crucial distinctions between Sebald and his narrator. In his provocative book *On Creaturely Life*, Eric L. Santner argues that the notion of 'creaturely life' – 'the peculiar proximity of the human to the animal at the very point of their radical difference' (2006: 12) – is an abiding concern in Sebald's work, and that sexuality is a key index for gauging this complex creaturely exchange. Yet when it comes to the depiction of mothers by Sebald's narrator, the fictional proxy reverts nostalgically to naive (and distinctly Catholic) maternal ideals at odds with the author's more complex and nuanced project outlined at length by Santner.

The narrator assumes a default position of the Mother as the family's virtuous source of affection, nurture, mercy and domestic tranquillity. He frequently invokes his ideal image of motherhood through reference to fine art. Anne Fuchs characterizes Sebald's approach to fine art as providing 'a therapeutic haven of contemplation [...] that enshrines moments of transcendence' (2006: 168). With striking frequency, the objects of contemplation and transcendence in these works of art are mother-figures enacting the traditional maternal virtues. His ideal mother tries steadfastly to protect her child, like the mother in the Paulino painting he admires in Corsica (Sebald 2005c: 5). When the inevitable trouble comes, she clings to her child like the Mary of Grünewald's Isenheim altarpiece (Sebald 1996: 160), and if he must flee she watches over him in exile like the Mary of Rembrandt's *The Flight into Egypt* (Sebald 2001f: 120). Finally, if the worst comes – torture, decrepitude, death, or even self-defilement – she is there to hear her children's lamentations and to heal their suffering, like Tiepolo's St Thecla (Sebald 1999d: 51). It should be noted that these religious images fit comfortably within the political context of the rise of German Fascism, which likewise promoted an elevated ideal of motherhood. The easy affinity between Catholic belief and Nazi ideology on this score helps to explain Sebald's characterization of his family background in the Angier interview: 'I come from a very conventional, Catholic, anti-Communist background. The kind of semi-working-class, petit bourgeois background typical of those who supported the fascist regime, who went into the war not just blindly, but with a degree of enthusiasm. They all fell up the ladder in no time at all, and until 1941 they all felt they were going to be lords of the world. Absolutely, there's no doubt about it, though nobody ever says it now' (Angier 2007: 66).[6]

As with all deeply held myths, the believer seems to find confirmation of his beliefs everywhere, in things both great and small. A less iconic, but no less revealing, instance of idealized maternal values can be found at the beginning of the final chapter in *The Emigrants*, when the narrator recalls his first arrival in Manchester. From the air he sees a city blanketed in fog as if it is suffocated in ash, and as the taxi drives him through the dilapidated and largely evacuated heart of the city, he feels as if he has wandered into a 'Totenhaus' ('necropolis' (Sebald 1994a: 220–1; 1996: 150–1)). Out of this darkness and death, the narrator finds sanctuary in the form of a hotel announcing its name in bright neon lights: the AROSA. There he is treated with graceful kindness by the proprietress, Mrs Gracie Irlam, who instantly makes him feel right at home. This should come as no surprise to students of Sebald, who can literally read the writing on the wall: AROSA. Max Sebald was born to Georg and Rosa Sebald on 18 May 1944. To emphasize Gracie's maternal identification even further, upon entering the hotel the narrator notices a photo of Gracie as a pretty young woman, dressed in Salvation Army uniform and carrying a distinctly German flugelhorn. The photo is dated 17 May 1944 – the day before Sebald was born – implicitly hearkening back to a prelapsarian ideal when he was literally at one with his mother. The narrator thus finds serendipitous sanctuary in a hotel which graphically bears the name of Sebald's mother. He is greeted at the door by a woman dressed in a pink candlewick robe, 'rosa' also being the German word for 'pink'. Gracie leads him to his cosy room where he discovers that the bedspread is made of the same material as her pink robe. The landlady also bestows a memorably quirky gift upon the narrator: the teas-maid. Most readers find this item comically bizarre, but the narrator invests this little gadget with surprisingly deep – and uncannily maternal – significance:

> [Die teas-maid] phosphoreszierte, wie sich in der hereinbrechenden Dämmerung bald schon zeigte, in einem mir auf der Kindheit vertrauten stillen Lindgrün, von dem ich mich in der Nacht immer auf unerklärliche Weise behütet fühlte. Darum vielleicht ist es mir, im Zurückdenken an die Zeit meiner Ankunft in Manchester, mehrfach so gewesen, als sei der von Mrs. Irlam [...] mir auf mein Zimmer gebrachte Teeapparat [...] es gewesen, das mich [...] am Leben festhalten ließ damals, als ich mich, umfangen, wie ich war, von einem mir unbegreiflichen Gefühl der Unverbundenheit, sehr leicht aus dem Leben hätte entfernen können. (Sebald 1994a: 227–8)

> ([The teas-maid] glowed a phosphorescent lime green that I was familiar with from childhood and which I had always felt afforded me an unaccountable protection at night. That may be why it has often seemed, when I have thought back to those early days in Manchester, as if the tea maker brought to my room by Mrs. Irlam [...] kept me holding on to life at a time when I felt a deep sense of isolation in which I might well have become completely submerged. (Sebald 1996: 154–5))

This surrogate mother Gracie, with her weirdly comforting, illuminating, protective gadget, blesses the exiled narrator with maternal virtues when he needs them most. Late in his essay 'The "Uncanny"' Freud equates uncanny places with 'the entrance to the former *Heim* [home] of all human beings, to the place where each one of us lived once upon a time and in the beginning. [...] [W]henever a man dreams of a place or a country and says to himself, while he is still dreaming: "this place is familiar to me, I've been here before", we may interpret the place as being his mother's genitals or her body' (Freud 1955: 245). Likewise in *The Emigrants*, though the narrator finds himself exiled in a foreign country, the uncannily familiar sanctuary provided by Gracie and her teas-maid in the Arosa hotel makes him feel as if he has returned home to the womb.

Despite the narrator's nostalgic attachment to maternal ideals, Sebald's depictions of motherhood ultimately emerge as far more ambivalent. Consider, for instance, the sequence involving the Gypsies in the final chapter of *Vertigo*. After years away from his home-town, the narrator crosses the Ach bridge leading into W. He recalls that an area at the foot of the bridge served as a summer campsite for a group of Gypsies after the war. These Gypsies were shunned by the community, and even by his own mother, who would pick him up and quickly carry him past the interlopers whenever she passed by the camp with her son.[7] These recollections lead him back to a seminal image from the family album:

> Ich [durchblättere] das Fotoalbum [...], das der Vater zur ersten sogenannten Kriegsweihnacht der Mutter als Geschenk mitgebracht hat. Es enthält Bilder von dem sogenannten Polenfeldzug, sämtliche säuberlich mit weißer Tinte beschriftet. Auf einigen der Bilder sind Zigeuner zu sehen, die man zusammengefangen hat. Freundlich schauen sie durch den Stacheldraht, irgendwo weit hinten in der Slowakei, wo der Vater mit seinem Werkstattzug Wochen vor dem sogenannten Ausbruch des Krieges schon gelegen war. (Sebald: 1994d: 201–2)

> ([...] I leaf through the photo album which my father bought as a present for my mother for the first so-called Kriegsweihnacht. In it are pictures of the Polish campaign, all neatly captioned in white ink. Some of these photographs show gypsies who had been rounded up and put in detention. They are looking out, smiling, from behind the barbed wire, somewhere in a far corner of Slovakia where my father and his vehicle repairs unit had been stationed for several weeks before the outbreak of war. (Sebald 1999d: 184–5))

This image (Figure 12.1) is surely one of the most unsettling in all of Sebald. It is unsettling to him as an adult, in a way that it never was as a child, because it provides incontrovertible proof that his father knew about the concentration camps from the very beginning of the war. His father's position among the perpetrators is visibly emphasized by his camera position on the free side of the prison's barbed wire fence, and his father's silent assent to the Nazi project is implicit in the very fact that he would take a tourist photo of such a scene and send it home to his wife.[8] Yet this practice, far from aberrational, was common up and down the ranks of the *Wehrmacht*. Janina Struk observes in *Photographing the Holocaust: Interpretations of the Evidence*: 'The practice of making photo albums was so popular among all military ranks that it seemed tantamount to a duty. [...] The photographs shift seamlessly from picture-postcard views, drinks parties and social occasions, to poverty-stricken indigenous peoples in destroyed towns and cities, deportations, hangings, murders and executions. It was as though the atrocities

Figure 12.1 Gypsy Mother. Image from *Vertigo*.

were just another sight along the way, all part of the foreign adventure' (2004: 66). What might have been intended as a tourist memento by the photographer, however, becomes a *memento mori* for the adult son who returns to it years later.

While the Gypsy photo does not capture any overt acts of atrocity, it does open a window into the ideology that would eventually justify such atrocities. As J. J. Long astutely observes:

> the ethnographic gaze that is inscribed in the gypsy photograph implicitly aligns the narrator's father with Nazi racial ideology and implicates him in the genocidal war in Eastern Europe. Furthermore, while the photograph itself was originally a gift, intended as a memento of war experience, it is also [. . .] the heavily coded bearer of ethnographic assumptions. As such, it contributes to the reinforcement of stereotypes designed to reproduce Nazi racial ideology within the family. (2006: 60)

Long's analysis is convincing. But I would also point out that, though he uses the collective term 'family', Long's immediate focus is on the complicity of the father and the ramifications for the son. Mark M. Anderson likewise places exclusive focus upon the father–son dimension: 'The inclusion of the family photo in this story documents what the father would not tell his son – a gap in narration that has a collective dimension, since it also exists for the millions of German children in his generation who had a father who served "somewhere in the East"' (2008: 145). Long and Anderson are both right as far as they go, but what get lost in the discussion are the specifically maternal implications for this image. The photo is, after all, a picture of mother and child, one made all the more disturbing by her inexplicable smile. Why would she be smiling? Because that is simply what one does when one's photo is being taken? Or because at least she still has her child? (Is that a child in her arms? Or is it just a bundle of cloth?) Perhaps she is smiling because that is what the vanquished always do when appealing for mercy from the vanquisher. Remember that the Gypsy woman is not staring at just any photographer, but at a group of uniform-clad German soldiers. For his part, Georg Sebald may have been moved to capture this image not simply as a souvenir from his adventures in Slovakia, but specifically because it presented such a benign image of the camps. Like Genewein's photos of the Litzmannstadt ghetto, perhaps the intended visual message here is, 'Look. See? Things aren't so bad here after all.'

So much for the paternal gaze; it is the maternal gaze that is most interesting in this case. Recall that it was an episode involving the narrator's mother, and a very different averted gaze, that prompted him to recall this photograph in the first place: '[wir] mußten [. . .] bei den Zigeunern vorbei, und jedesmal hat mich die Mutter an dieser Stelle auf den Arm genommen. Über ihre Schulter hinweg sah ich die Zigeuner von den verschiedenen Arbeiten, die sie stets verrichteten, kurz aufschauen und dann den Blick wieder senken, als grauste es ihnen' ('we would pass by the gypsies, and every time as we did so my mother picked me up and carried me in her arms. Across her shoulder I saw the gypsies look up briefly from what they were about, and then lower their eyes again as if in revulsion' (Sebald 1994d: 200–1; 1999d: 183)). Here the narrator's mother engaged in what could seem, out of context, an act of maternal virtue, sweeping her child into her arms and protecting him – in purely iconic terms a gesture which mirrors the one captured in the photo of the Gypsy mother. However, located within the context of racism exposed in this sequence, the German mother's actions become something to cringe over, inspiring retrospective shame rather than filial gratitude. Rosa did not wield the camera or wear the uniform like Georg did, but this anecdote suggests that she shared the same ethnographic assumptions.

Other evidence outside the photographic frame incriminates the narrator's mother as well. The album page with its caption of '*Zigeuner*' ['Gypsy'] is particularly revealing. Janina Struk comments upon the significance of presentation in the racially pure German family album:

Although making albums was a personal activity, it was part of a wider collective responsibility. It gave individuals an opportunity not only to order their own experiences and decide how the past should be remembered and preserved, but also to express commitment to National Socialist ideals. Organizing photographs and handwriting captions was a way of combining these aims and an opportunity to give a personal interpretation to a photograph and to direct the viewer in how to read it. (2004: 68)

Long directs us how to read the Gypsy photo with an incisive reading of its caption: 'the compiler of the album leaves gender unmarked by employing the generic masculine plural term *Zigeuner*. The women are thus reduced to an example of type' (2007: 57). Interestingly, Long himself leaves gender unmarked in his reference to the compiler of the album. Who did compile this album? Can we know? Thus far, critics have taken it for granted that the photographer and the compiler are one and the same. But we are told only that the father bought the album (obviously without the photos in it) and presented the album as a gift to his wife for 'the first so-called Kriegsweihnacht [War-Christmas]' (1996: 184). It seems at least as likely that Georg bought the album for Rosa, sent it to her for Christmas 1939, and subsequently sent her photographs that he shot and developed over a period of time during the Slovakia campaign. In other words, the circumstantial evidence points to Rosa as quite possibly the compiler of the album and the author of the captions. Already a wife and mother herself (though her only son was not born until 1944), she surely had the most personal vested interest in the family to elide the gender of the Gypsy mother – in effect suppressing the fact that not only enemy combatants but also civilian women and children were being rounded up and imprisoned in camps from the very beginning of this war. No other image in all of Sebald offers a more concentrated indictment of Nazi 'crimes against the family' as such than this image from *Vertigo*. Most damning of all is the implication that the narrator's mother was a co-conspirator against maternity, years before she even became his mother.

Of course, none of this is spelled out explicitly by the narrator. Sebald rarely does spell things out explicitly; the attraction of his prose depends upon subtlety, indirectness, obfuscation – and no one would wish it otherwise. He is a master prose stylist, not a preacher or pamphleteer, and his measured rhetorical approach is a welcome antidote to the vehement rhetorical excess we normally associate with Fascism. Nevertheless, sometimes critics are too quick to read Sebald's indirectness in exclusively stylistic terms. For instance, the narrator's reluctance to dwell upon any of the disturbing ramifications of the Gypsy mother photograph tells us at least as much – if not considerably more – about the narrator's repressive impulses as it does about Sebald's prose style. The narrator passes a spot by the road outside his home-town that reminds him of the Gypsy camp there after the war. This thought immediately makes him recall – *not* his father, who was deeply complicit in Nazi internment policies as a German soldier during the war – but his *mother*, who shamefully whisked him away rather than let her son get near such undesirables. When he then recalls his father's involvement, he does so through the mediation of his mother's (presumed) framing and labelling of the 'Zigeuner' photo. Yet the narrator conspicuously declines to damn the image, nor does he damn the photographer who captured that image or the compiler who attempted to sanitize it in the family album. Instead, the narrator recalls these disturbing facts and images only to change the subject quickly, continuing his narrative without any commentary – a gesture of evasion and elision every bit as significant as the 'Zigeuner' caption.

Here it becomes crucial once again to spell out the differences between Sebald and his narrator. The author has equipped the narrator with a past that mirrors his own, right down to reproducing an image from the Sebald family album as 'evidence'. However, the author's and narrator's respective approaches to that evidence are markedly different. In an interview with Christian Scholz, Sebald described the effect of returning to his family album as an adult and looking at the old photos through new eyes: 'Because in the meantime you have learned what history is. You know what happened. You have suspicions about the societal role of your own parents and relatives in this context, and now you suddenly and with complete clarity see it before yourself as visual evidence. And the shock then is typically inevitable' (Sebald in Scholz, 2007: 106). Elsewhere, he explained his obsession with uncovering the truth about his national and familial past with regard to the war and the Holocaust: 'If you know in the generation before you that your parents, your uncles and aunts were tacit accomplices, it's difficult to say you haven't anything to do with it. I've always felt I had to know what happened in detail, and to try to understand why it should have been so' (Jaggi 2001: 3). Where is the 'typically inevitable' shock in the *narrator*'s reaction to the Gypsy photo? Where is *his* compulsion 'to know what happened in detail', 'to try and understand'? Certainly, the narrator does frequently display such impulses throughout the fiction – but, tellingly, *not* here. Not when the subject hits so close to home. Not when his own mother is implicated. The narrator approaches the moral and psychic precipice, only to turn away and reverse course. Sebald equips the reader with sufficient detail to be shocked, but he does so through the vehicle of a narrator who, in his very reluctance to confront such unpleasant truths directly, proves himself a legitimate heir to a national and familial conspiracy of silence.

The final maternal image that I want to consider is the most famous withheld image in all of Sebald: the sempstresses of Litzmannstadt,[9] or, as the narrator reimagines them, the Sisters of Fate. Sebald ends *The Emigrants* with an unforgettable ekphrastic evocation of a photograph he once saw in a Frankfurt exhibition. The photos were taken by a Nazi accountant in the Litzmannstadt ghetto, Walter Genewein. The narrator was thunderstruck by one photo in particular, and its haunting after-effects are worth repeating at length:

> Hinter einem lotrechten Webrahmen sitzen drei junge, vielleicht zwanzigjährige Frauen. Der Teppich, an dem sie knüpfen, hat ein unregelmäßig geometrisches Muster, das mich auch in seinen Farben erinnert an das Muster unseres Wohnzimmersofas zu Hause. Wer die jungen Frauen sind, das weiß ich nicht. Wegen des Gegenlichts, das einfällt durch das Fenster im Hintergrund, kann ich ihre Augen genau nicht erkennen, aber ich spüre, das sie alle drei herschauen zu mir, denn ich stehe ja an der Stelle, an der Genewein, der Rechnungsführer, mit seinem Fotoapparat gestanden hat. Die mittlere der drei jungen Frauen hat hellblondes Haar und gleicht

irgendwie einer Braut. Die Weberin zu ihrer Linken hält den Kopf ein wenig seitwärts geneigt, während die auf der rechten Seite so unverwandt und unerbittlich mich ansieht, daß ich es nicht lange auszuhalten vermag. Ich überlege, wie die drei wohl geheißen haben – Roza, Lusia und Lea oder Nona, Decuma und Morta, die Töchter der Nacht, mit Spindel und Faden und Schere. (Sebald 1994a: 355)

(Behind the perpendicular frame of a loom sit three young women, perhaps aged twenty. The irregular geometrical patterns of the carpet they are knotting, and even its colours, remind me of the settee in our living room at home. Who the young women are I do not know. The light falls on them from the window in the background, so I cannot make out their eyes clearly, but I sense that all three of them are looking across at me, since I am standing on the very spot where Genewein the accountant stood with his camera. The young woman in the middle is blonde and has the air of a bride about her. The weaver to her left has inclined her head a little to one side, whilst the woman on the right is looking at me with so steady and relentless a gaze that I cannot meet it for long. I wonder what the three women's names were – Roza, Luisa and Lea, or Nona, Decuma and Morta, the daughters of night, with spindle, scissors and thread. (Sebald 1996: 237))

The narrator includes so very many photos, some of quite trivial objects, that it is fair to question why he neglects to include this vitally important image. Perhaps he is sparing us the accusatory gaze of the sisters, or sparing us the experience of standing in Genewein's shoes as spectators. But since he does not pull his punches in providing other disturbing images elsewhere, these explanations ring false. The narrator's reaction to this photo is highly personal, as if the woman on the right has a message addressed specifically to him. So his suppression of this photo hardly seems altruistic; if he is sparing anyone discomfort here, it is himself. Yet he remains unspared, for the return of the repressed image continues to haunt him. The real question, then, is why does this particular image haunt him, out of all the images he saw in the Frankfurt exhibition and out of all of the far more graphic Holocaust photos he might have chosen (or that might have chosen him)? Why can't he bear to face the gaze of the woman on the right (our left)?

In order to dissect this buried image properly, it would be useful first to exhume it. This photo (Figure 12.2) from the Frankfurt exhibition catalogue certainly seems to be the one the narrator has in mind.[10] In the middle sits the blonde woman, whom the narrator imagines as Luiza, an appellation that clearly connects her to the ill-fated Luisa Lanzberg. To her left is the woman with the tilted head, whom he imagines as Lea, probably an allusion to Israel's wife Leah, the mother of Judah, forefather of the Jews. Finally, chillingly, we see the woman on the right, our left, with the penetrating gaze, whom the narrator christens Roza, a clear proxy for Sebald's own mother. The narrator singles Roza out for her relentless gaze, but the accidental composition of the photo seems to single her out as well. The narrator reveals that the pattern they are working on reminds him of the settee in his childhood home, but pay particular attention to the pattern behind them. The white shape above and behind the woman on our left seems to be pointing straight down at her, like an aimed gun, or like the downward-turned thumb of the Roman emperor at the Coliseum, or like the Sword of Damocles, marking her for death. This image calls to mind the one explicit mention of the name 'Rosa' in connection with the narrator's mother. It comes from his Aunt Fini in *The Emigrants*, in reference to a school photo: 'Das Kind ganz rückwärts mit dem Kreuzchen über dem Kopf ist deine Mutter, die Rosa' ('The child right at the back, with a cross marked over her head, is your mother, Rosa' (Sebald 1994a: 110; 1996: 75–6)). In the case of the school photo, the picture has been marked to single Rosa out of the crowd for distinction, as if to say, 'This person is special: she is my sister, your mother.' Of course, the so-called Roza of the Litzmannstadt photo is effectively being singled out for a much harsher fate, where she will take her place among a crowd of over six million. Sebald makes reference to his mother's class photo in *After Nature* as well, though he does not mention her by name. In the final section ('Dark Night Sallies Forth') he locates the photo at the end of the First World War (1917 at Allarzried) and adds this foreboding detail: 'auf der rückwärtigen Seite/ des fleckigen grauen Kartons/ die Worte 'in der Zukunft/ liegt der Tod uns zu Füßen'/ einer jener Dunklen Orakelspruüche/ die man nie mehr vergißt' ('on the reverse of the/ spotted grey cardboard mount/ the words "in the future/ death lies

Figure 12.2 Three Weavers. 'Litzmannstadt-Getto Teppichweberei' (Lodz-311)

at our feet",/ one of those obscure oracular sayings/ one never again forgets'
(Sebald 2008c: 72; 2002a: 84–5)). The oracle's enigmatic prophecy finally yields its
bitter fruit in the sweatshop of Litzmannstadt.

Now return to Sebald's description of the photo, since that is all the reader is
actually given. The narrator notes with clear discomfort that: 'ich stehe ja an der
Stelle, an der Genewein, der Rechnungsführer, mit seinem Fotoapparat gestanden
hat ('I am standing on the very spot where Genewein the accountant stood with his
camera' (Sebald: 1994a: 335; 1996: 237)). This is certainly true, not only for this
photo but for all photos: we see what the camera saw, no more, no less. The empa-
thetic narrator does not share Genewein's heart, but he cannot help but share his
eye – an uneasy convergence which Simon Ward characterizes as 'the most high-
risk dialectic of the book' (2004: 69). In this context, think back a moment to the
Gypsy photo. The same dynamic is seemingly at play there, too. The narrator does
not share his father's ethnographical assumptions, but he does see through his
father's eyes, stands in his shoes – sort of. Actually that would strictly be true only
if the photo had been included by itself. Instead, what we actually receive is Rosa's
photo album page, meaning what the narrator is really doing – and what we are
doing too – is looking through Rosa's eyes looking through Georg's eyes at the
Gypsy woman. Contrast that dynamic with the ending of *The Emigrants*. The
narrator is no longer gazing through Rosa's eyes; instead, he imagines that he is
gazing at Rosa's eyes, having effectively shoved her through the looking-glass, cast
her behind the persecuted side of the fence, or in this case, the loom.

The narrator in effect tries to empathize his way into the world of the photo,
enacting an imaginative exercise in "What If": what if these three sisters had been
my sisters (Sebald did in fact have three sisters)? What if one of these women had
been my mother? What if I had to endure the experience of losing my family to the
Holocaust? This is, to be sure, a very slippery ethical move.[11] If Rosa was guilty of
'crimes against the family' in the first case, surely a son who vicariously condemns
his mother to hard labour in Litzmannstadt has violated the family ideal as well.
Furthermore, such a presumption of the subject position is highly dubious,
empathizing to the point of identification with suffering that neither Rosa nor the
narrator actually experienced. As historian Dominick LaCapra judiciously warns,

> If we who have not been severely traumatized by experiences involving massive losses
> go to the extreme of identifying (however spectrally or theoretically) with the victim
> and survivor, our horizon may unjustifiably become that of the survivor, if not the
> victim, at least as we imagine her or him to be. [...] We may even undergo surrogate
> victimage – something that may at times be unavoidable but, in terms of ethical,
> social, and civic responsibility, is open to question, particularly in its effects in the
> public sphere. (2001: 211)

On the other hand, the desire for identification is counterbalanced with certain gestures toward 'empathic unsettlement', to borrow LaCapra's term.[12] For instance, the narrator acknowledges that the weaver in question is not in reality his mother: he spells her name differently ('Roza' instead of 'Rosa'), and he prefaces his meditation by admitting, 'Wer die jungen Frauen sind, das weiß ich nicht' ('Who the young women are I do not know' (Sebald 1994: 335; 1996: 237)). Furthermore, he declines to replicate the ethnographic gaze of Genewein, seizing some measure of control over the image by reproducing it verbally rather than visually. Again, this deflective strategy is one of Sebald's signatures. Though one can sense the centripetal pull of the Holocaust throughout his work, the narrator rarely faces this vortex directly lest he lose himself in its darkness. As Sebald told Maya Jaggi shortly before his death, 'I don't think you can focus on the horror of the Holocaust. It's like the head of the Medusa: you carry it with you in a sack, but if you looked at it you'd be petrified' (Jaggi 2001: 5).[13] In the case of the Litzmannstadt photo, the narrator avoids the weaver's dreadful gaze by suppressing her image. But in this case removing the head of Medusa does not completely destroy her power, nor does it relieve her adversary from the burden of carrying her with him wherever he goes. Of course, the narrator's real battle is not against the forced labourers in Litzmannstadt; his battle is against truths that he does not want to be true but cannot wish away; his battle is with congenital culpability. He cannot bear to look in his sack because he suspects that the face staring back at him will bear a family resemblance.

Sebald's anxiety is historically and psychologically specific, yet his indirect approach displaces the source of that anxiety, cloaking its origins in a fog of metaphysical noir. The resulting narrative reads like *Oedipus Rex* refracted through Kafka and Beckett. Like Oedipus, Sebald's narrator wanders through a waste land, corrupted by some vast but shadowy crime from the past. Whoever is responsible for this crime must be rooted out and punished with exile, even if the investigation leads to the investigator's own hearth. For Sebald as for Kafka and Beckett, the protagonist's exile is an established fact from the start, so he is really working backwards from the punishment in an effort to discover the unnameable original crime. The narrator traverses Europe in search of clues, compiling evidence, searching for justice, atonement, and reparation. However, the more evidence he accumulates, the more the trail leads him back to where he started – his corrupt family home, the primal scene of the crime. His father's complicity was already understood, and indeed he paid some penance for his crimes with a stint in a prisoner of war camp. Yet the narrator's investigations increasingly point to another unindicted co-conspirator in the home. He resists this knowledge, he deflects it – he tries to keep her true identity *sub rosa*.

By the end of *The Emigrants*, the narrator effectively chooses to blind himself

243

rather than face the full implications of his family crisis head on. In wilfully choosing blindness, he proves himself not only a literary successor to Oedipus but, more importantly, an inheritor of what Sebald has diagnosed as German historical blindness. Speaking in his own voice without the mediation of a fictional narrator, Sebald berated his compatriots during his 1997 Zurich lectures for collective failure to confront the nation's recent history head on. In the preface to the published lectures (included in *On the Natural History of Destruction*), he boldly states that:

> wir Deutsche heute ein auffallend geschichtsblindes und traditionsloses Volk [seien]. Ein passioniertes Interesse an unseren früheren Lebensformen und den Spezifka der eigenen Zivilisation, wie es etwa in der Kultur Großbritanniens überall spürbar ist, kennen wir nicht. Und wenn wir unseren Blick zurückwenden, insbesondere auf die Jahre 1930 bis 1950, so ist es immer ein Hinsehen und Wegschauen zugleich. Die Hervorbringungen der deutschen Autoren nach dem Krieg sind darum vielfach bestimmt von einem halben oder falschen Bewußtsein, das ausgebildet wurde zur Festigung der äußerst prekären Position der Scheibenden in einer moralisch so gut wie restlos diskreditierten Gesellschaft. (Sebald 2002h: 6–7)

> ([W]e Germans today are a nation strikingly blind to history and lacking in tradition. We do not feel any passionate interest in our earlier way of life and the specific features of our own civilization, of the kind universally perceptible, for instance, in the culture of the British Isles. And when we turn to take a retrospective view, particularly of the years 1930 to 1950, we are always looking and looking away at the same time. As a result, the works produced by German authors after the war are often marked by a half-consciousness or false consciousness designed to consolidate the extremely precarious position of those writers in a society that was morally almost entirely discredited. (Sebald 2004b: viii–ix))

In the non-fictional formats of public lecture and published essay, Sebald's approach to the problem of German historical blindness is to compel confrontation. In his fiction, however, he often draws attention to the problem of blindness by *replicating* it through his narrator. At the end of *The Emigrants* the reader finds a perfectly representative re-enactment of 'looking and looking away at the same time', of 'half-consciousness or false consciousness'.

The narrator's mother instilled him with Catholic reverence for the maternal virtues, a reverence perfectly compatible with the ethos of German Fascism. His attitudes toward women remain deeply informed by these values. However, his various investigations occasionally lead him to evidence that his own mother betrayed those values – betrayed other mothers as well as other women who would never get a chance to become mothers. Were the narrator to confront this evidence directly, he would be forced both to reconsider the value system by which he adjudicates gender propriety and to denounce his mother as a tacit accomplice to the Holocaust's 'crimes against the family'. Rather than do either of those things, he half-sees and then looks away. Nevertheless, Sebald provides his readers with sufficient evidence to see beyond the narrator's averted gaze and thus to reach the very conclusions that his literary avatar avoids. This privileged insight not only permits us a fuller vision of the familial 'scene of the crime', but it also allows us to see that, in his blindness, the narrator is still very much his father's and mother's son.

NOTES

1 Given the network of cross-references and the consistency of voice, I work on the assumption that the first-person narrator is the same for *Vertigo*, *The Emigrants*, *The Rings of Saturn*, and *Austerlitz*. However, as will be clear from the present chapter, I do not equate this narrator as strictly autobiographical.

2 For two exceptional treatments of the maternal dimension in Sebald's work, see Barzilai (2004: 203–16) and Kempinski (2007: 456–71).

3 Consider the narrator's traumatic response as a child upon seeing Schlag and Romana having sex in *Vertigo* (Sebald 1999d: 238–3), or his revulsion as an adult when chancing upon a similar scene off the Covehithe cliffs in *The Rings of Saturn* (Sebald 1998b: 68–9).

4 See, for example, the narrator's unnerved response to Luciana touching his shoulder in *Vertigo* (Sebald 1999d: 97).

5 Maya Barzilai usefully applies Eve Kosofsky Sedgwick's concept of homosocial desire for an understanding of Sebald's male protagonists vis-à-vis other male characters and various secondary female characters in the fiction (Barzilai 2004: 208). Eric L. Santner explores the element of 'homosexual panic' in Sebald's work in chapter 4 ('On the Sexual Lives of Creatures and Other Matters') of *On Creaturely Life: Rilke/Benjamin/Sebald* (2006: 143–96).

6 For an iconic fusion of these two value systems, consider Hengge's mural of the reaper woman in *Vertigo*.

7 Though prejudice against the Gypsies had been prevalent in Europe for centuries, persecution in modern Germany seems to have been particularly pronounced in Sebald's home region of Bavaria. Time and again, in his extensive study *The Nazi Persecution of the Gypsies*, Guenter Lewy (2000) singles out Bavaria for leading the way in anti-Gypsy policies. In 1899 Bavaria established the *Zigeunerzentrale* (Central Office for Gypsy Affairs), specifically designed to police Gypsies. In 1926 'the Bavarian legislature approved the Law for the Combating of Gypsies, Travelers and the Work-Shy' (Lewy 2000: 7). In 1934, when the central government was looking for a more unified national policy toward Gypsies, Bavaria was held up as a model: 'As in the past, the *Zigeunerzentrale* (Central Office for Gypsy Affairs) in Munich was well ahead of everyone else in suggesting measure for attacking "the Gypsy problem" and in pressing for united action' (Lewy 2000: 18). Even after the war, Bavaria distinguished itself for its anti-Gypsy prejudice. In 1947, the 1926 law was overturned. But in 1953, 'the Bavarian legislature approved a new law that dealt with "travelers" (*Landfahrerordnung*). The word "Gypsy" did not appear in the legislation; travelers were defined sociologically as those who itinerate as a result of a deep-seated inclination or out of a strong aversion to leading a sedentary life. However, in terms of substance the new law for the most part repeated the prohibitions of the 1926 legislation' (Lewy 2000: 200). The *Zigeunerzentrale* was

replaced nominally by the *Landfahrerzentrale* (Central Office for Travelers), but the records and even some of the personnel simply carried over. This office was not closed until 1965, and the legislation remained on the statute books until 1970.

8 Though German photography complemented the aims of Nazi ideology, and though amateur photography by German soldiers attested to the widespread success of this aim, the Nazi leadership officially discouraged such photography among soldiers – apparently because they foresaw its potential as incriminating evidence against the regime. Hanno Loewy observes, 'the Wehrmacht supreme command and the SS leadership issued repeated circulars and decrees prohibiting photos being taken of executions and maltreatment, or of ghettos at all. [...] The point, it would seem, was not whether photographs were taken or not, but the awareness of the photographers that, in taking these pictures, they became conspirators, accomplices, perpetrators, and thereby fully subscribed to the regime and its aims' (1997: 106).

9 The native Polish name for this settlement is Łódź. When the Reich annexed and closed off the Jewish ghetto in early 1940, Łódź was renamed Litzmannstadt in honor of Karl Litzmann, a distinguished German general from the First World War. Since all of my references are to the Reich-controlled ghetto as such, I opt for the appellation 'Litzmannstadt'.

10 The photo is labelled no. 311 in the exhibition catalogue, with the caption 'Litzmannstadt-Getto Teppichweberei'. See Loewy and Schoenberner (1990: 119). Though he does not examine this particular photograph, I am nevertheless indebted to Ulrich Baer's (2002) probing analysis of Genewein's photographic project.

11 For several particularly provocative considerations of the ethical implications of suppressing the photo and the women depicted therein, see Ward (2004: 68–70); Franklin (2007: 140–2); and Horstkotte (2009: 178–83).

12 'I would argue that the response of even secondary witnesses (including historians) to traumatic events must involve empathic unsettlement [...]. But a difficulty arises when the virtual experience involved in empathy gives way to vicarious victimhood, and empathy with the victim seems to become an identity. And a post-traumatic response of unsettlement becomes questionable when it is routinized in a methodology or style that enacts compulsive repetition, including the compulsively repetitive turn to the aporia, paradox, or impasse. I would like to argue that the perhaps necessary acting-out of trauma in victims and the empathic unsettlement (at times even inducing more or less muted trauma) in secondary witnesses should not be seen as foreclosing attempts to work through the past and its losses, both in victims or other agents and in secondary witnesses' (LaCapra 2001: 47).

13 As Ben Hutchinson notes, Sebald's Medusa metaphor is appropriated from Primo Levi (Hutchinson 2009: 148). In *The Drowned and the Saved*, Levi insists, 'I must repeat: we, the survivors, are not the true witnesses. [...] We survivors are not only an exiguous but also an anomalous minority: we are those who by their prevarications or abilities or good luck did not touch bottom. Those who did so, those who saw the Gorgon, have not returned to tell about it or have returned mute, but they are the "Muslims", the submerged, the complete witnesses, the ones whose deposition would have a general significance. They are the rule, we are the exception' (Levi 1988: 83–4).

13

THE QUESTION OF GENRE IN W. G. SEBALD'S 'PROSE' (TOWARDS A POST-MEMORIAL LITERATURE OF RESTITUTION)

Russell J. A. Kilbourn

Artists create potentials for the future by exploiting the resources of the past. In literature, the most important carrier of past resources – the central organ of memory – is genre. (Bakhtin in Morson and Emerson 1990: 288)

INTRODUCTION

Writing in *The New Republic* in 1998, James Wood noted that the first appearance of *The Emigrants* caused him to recall 'Walter Benjamin's remark in his essay on Proust that all great works found a new genre or dissolve an old one. Here was the first contemporary writer since Beckett to have found a way to protest the good government of the conventional novel-form and to harass realism into a state of self-examination' (1998: 38).[1] In *Understanding Sebald* Mark McCulloh remarks that after the publication of *The Emigrants*, critics proclaimed

> that a 'new genre' had been created. Many commented that Sebald's work was like nothing they had ever read. Sebald's new type of fiction – part dream sequence, part travelogue, part photo album, part history, part memoir, part cultural-historical fantasy – confounded some and dazzled many ... But most who encountered the late-blooming writer in Germany and subsequently in the English-speaking world were in agreement regarding the uniqueness of Sebald's prose. The question remains, however, whether Sebald's accomplishments truly ascend to the level of an utterly new kind of literature. (2003: xix)[2]

Through a selective survey of the scholarship as well as key examples from Sebald's prose works, I hope to show that, insofar as Sebald produced or anticipated a 'new kind of literature' – which I call a 'literature of restitution' – he did so precisely through means which are anything but new. The majority of critics seem to agree that his first three idiosyncratic prose texts, *The Emigrants* (1992; 1996), *The Rings of Saturn* (1995; 1998b) and *Vertigo* (1990; 1999d), are not properly novelistic[3] – *Austerlitz* (2001g) presents unique challenges for classification, which I return to below – and this says as much about the difficulties posed by genre as it does about

247

the transgeneric character of Sebald's narratives. When the question of genre does arise it is generally determined by the two-part truism that (1) Sebald himself avoided calling his prose narratives 'novels',[4] and that (2) these texts display extraordinary generic and intertextual 'hybridity'. I follow the general practice of this volume in using the terms 'prose' and 'prose narrative', if only because these are the least loaded, most ideologically neutral terms: the books in general consist of prose and not poetic discourse, strictly speaking; and they do recount narratives of various kinds and qualities. Everything else – even their degree of fictionality – is open to question.

Historically, one of the things that continues to separate 'artistic' literary fiction from mass-market fiction, as Tsvetan Todorov reminds us, is that it is 'considered a sign of authentic modernity in a writer if he ceases to respect the separation of genres' (Duff 2000: 194).[5] M. M. Bakhtin is one of the more important thinkers to theorize a 'middle term between Saussure's *langue* and *parole*, a term which [E. D.] Hirsch calls the *"type* of utterance" as distinct from the individual utterance (*parole*) and the language-system itself (*langue*)' (Duff 2000: 15).[6] This 'quasi-linguistic concept of *type*' forms the basis of a definition of genre that unites Hirsch with Bakhtin in thinking of the 'non-unique' and 'non-arbitrary' character of much of what passes for everyday speech and literary or artistic discourse alike – especially in popular culture and in the kinds of historical 'primary genres' exploited so effectively by Sebald in his prose texts. However, this key recognition of the category of the 'type of utterance' also opens up a new set of problems about textual authority (not to speak of the author him- or herself), moving away from the Romantic cult of the author, whose hegemony we have yet to see come to an end,[7] throwing the burden of interpretation unequivocally onto the reader in the moment of reception – which is really just another way of describing the relatively conservative dependency of the production of meaning in all narrative fictions, literary or otherwise, upon pre-established codes and conventions.

Ideologically speaking, genre embodies a contradiction between revolution and reaction, reflecting 'historical and social tensions': on the one hand, '[g]enres come equipped ... with class connotations and social evaluations. In modern literature, the novel, rooted in the common-sense world of bourgeois facticity, challenges the romance, often linked to aristocratic notions of courtliness and chivalry' (Stam 2005: 6).[8] On the other hand, once established and canonized, genres work to stabilize and perpetuate the aesthetic and formal and therefore the ideological status quo. In this context I outline two postulates or focal points around or between which I will explore the question of genre in Sebald: (1) that genre – like literary self-reflexivity – stands counter to realism as a basis for analysis; i.e., as soon as genre is identified or invoked as the initial or primary category of analysis, 'realism' is put into context as an aesthetic effect produced out of the relation between the reader and the text.[9] And (2) that generic hybridity is the primary or salient characteristic of postmodern literature. While these postulates may very well be modified in what follows, I acknowledge here that they are complementary: the first, antirealism, entailing genre as an approach to categorization and analysis, operating on the level of reception and interpretation; the second, genre hybridity, operating on the level of a text's production.

Bakhtin's formulation (from 1941) serves as a baseline definition of the modern novel as 'the sole genre that continues to develop, that is as yet uncompleted. The forces that define it as a genre are at work before our very eyes: the birth and development of the novel as a genre takes place in the full light of the historical day. The generic skeleton of the novel is still far from having hardened, and we cannot foresee all of its plastic possibilities' (1981: 7). For Bakhtin, the novel is the Trismegistean genre, its centre everywhere and its circumference nowhere. However one categorizes Sebald's texts, Bakhtin's ideas remain significant for their relation to genre: '[N]ovel is the name Bakhtin gives to whatever force is at work within a given literary system to reveal the limits, the artificial constraints, of that system' (1981: xxxi). On a broader cultural level, Bakhtin's historical account of the novel is deeply relevant to Sebald in terms of the critique of modernity central to the latter's work.[10]

In the 1941 essay 'Epic and Novel', Bakhtin notes that, '[f]aced with the problem of the novel, genre theory must submit to a radical re-structuring' (1981: 8). The question of genre in Sebald's prose narratives does not signal a problem with these texts so much as with genre itself; that is, with the cultural impulse, beginning with the reception of Aristotle's *Poetics*, to classify works of literature according to pre-existing and predictable categories as a way of assigning meaning and formal closure.[11] If, as Alistair Fowler reminds us, 'the single most important factor separating modern from earlier genre theory' is 'the perception that literary genres ... change or "evolve" across time' (2000: 232), then Sebald's prose texts represent *both* the novel in its later twentieth-century completion *and* what might be called the twenty-first-century 'post-novel' as a form in a perpetual state of becoming.[12] To look at this another way: if we are going to continue to discuss Sebald's prose narratives in terms of their generic 'hybridity', we must do so in the full awareness of the texts' common characteristic as self-reflexive meta-critiques of genre; as, in effect, aestheticized works of genre theory. Only in acknowledging this can we understand the collective status of the prose works as a 'literature of restitution'.

SEBALD AND THE QUESTION OF GENRE

What follows is a selective discussion of the debate around the generic status of Sebald's prose works – a 'debate' that is mostly a rhetorical construct; in practice most readers of Sebald invoke the question of genre, if at all, as a point of departure, only rarely considering it in a sustained, critical manner. In order to provide a framework within which patterns, connections or some kind of coherent picture can emerge, I follow J. J. Long's 'Bibliographical Essay on Current Research' (Fuchs and Long 2007: 11–30), organizing this discussion under ten interconnected categories around each of which a set of themes, formal parameters and readerly habits of mind coalesce: Genre Hybridity; Memory; History/Historiography; Travel; Realism; Intertextuality/Intermediality; Adaptation/Remediation; Visual Culture; Gender; the Holocaust. Besides genre itself the governing category is 'Postmodernism', encompassing the prosthetic, second-order inflections of the categories of 'Memory' and 'the Holocaust', especially, when modified by 'Post-'. Specific examples or counter-examples from Sebald's books will be marshalled where relevant, but in general literary terms I invoke 'postmodern' to qualify the novel's development since the Second World War as late capitalist narrative mode, implying, among other stylistic features, an amplified self-reflexivity through the privileging of intertextual remediation over literary mimesis.[13] Substantively, this mode is characterized by the presentation of narrative subjects constituted in relation to technologies of cultural production and reproduction, prosthetic 'organs' of cultural memory, including genre.[14] This list of potential genre categories is necessarily elastic and incomplete, with considerable internal overlap and contradiction – much like the concept of genre itself. For, if there is one thing to be learned from the study of genre in Sebald, it is that only readers (and some writers) demand the comfort of generic fixity; the texts themselves conform to expectations only rarely, and in a selective manner.

At one end of the scale are those who attempt to pin the narratives down to a single category. Stanley Corngold attributes to Sebald's prose works the status of modern 'tragedy' in terms of a 'modern tragic sense' (2008: 4), corresponding more to Raymond Williams' 'structure of feeling'[15] than to a distinct literary genre. Patrick Madden (2008), writing in the journal *Fourth Genre*, by contrast, argues that in fact they belong to the 'fourth genre' of the essay.[16] On the other hand, as noted, the genre hybridity characteristic of Sebald's prose texts has itself become a way of categorizing a strain of contemporary postmodern writing.[17] Carsten Strathausen argues persuasively that Sebald's 'poetics' 'cannot adequately be described in traditional terms such as "interaction" or "intertextuality" or "intermediality" or "intergenre"', for, to assume that Sebald's books 'initiate a new genre' presupposes '*a stable frame of reference maintained by a distinct set of fixed coordinates or concepts . . .* between which we are able to establish and trace various lines of connection – be that a particular literary motif, a historical reference, or a stylistic pattern . . . [T]he distinctive feature of Sebald's prose is precisely that it obliterates this stable frame of reference' (Patt 2007: 478; my emphasis). As will be seen below, this highly productive negativity is central to the texts' constitution as a 'literature of restitution'.

Similarly, Long argues in a seminal essay that the 'narrative works . . . resist traditional genre categories. They partake instead of a generic hybridity dictated by the ambitious scope of Sebald's project, which involves an exploration of man's historical relationship to his environment, the connection between individual, familial, and collective memory, and the means by which such memory is passed on from one generation to the next' (2003: 117). The topic of memory in Sebald studies is always also on one level a discussion of genre.[18] Through close analysis of Sebald's own copies of Nietzsche's 'Vom Nutzen und Nachtheil der Historie für das Leben' and *Zur Genealogie der Moral*, Ben Hutchinson deepens our understanding of Sebald's engagement with the central questions of modernity by showing that Sebald's poetics of memory is dependent upon 'the importance – and paradoxically the impossibility – of forgetting', and that his famous melancholy is therefore in large part the product of the failure of the desire to forget (2009a: 325).[19]

In one of the first collections commemorating Sebald's death in 2001, Martin Swales describes his prose output as 'a matchless set of reflections ... on the narratively mediated demands of postmemory' (2003: 83), helping to initiate the study of Sebald as writer of 'postmemorial' fiction whose status as a kind of subgenre of Holocaust literature is still debated.[20] According to Stewart Martin, 'Sebald is perhaps less a "holocaust writer" than a writer of destruction, or, to use some of his own words, a writer of the natural history of destruction who takes the whole passage of European history as his subject matter' (2005: 18).[21] Sebald's 'Europeanness' is addressed in a set of essays covering his reception in Spain and France. Ruth Vogel-Klein (France) identifies Sebald as not a German but as a 'European' writer in exile (2005: 134), which links him, on a metaphorical level at least, to a literary type elaborated by Susan Sontag (to be discussed below). Scott Denham similarly surveys Sebald's reception in the English-speaking world (Denham and McCulloh 2006), but not in terms of how his texts have been received as specific examples of this or that literary genre. Like other contemporary European authors, Sebald's relative commercial success has depended not only on how he has been perceived as national or trans-national writer, but also on how his works have been received in generic terms.[22]

Going beyond the notion of 'generic hybridity', J. J. Long and Anne Whitehead assert that Sebald 'is far removed from the kind of ludic textual experimentation associated with certain strands of postmodernism'.[23] 'On the contrary, Sebald's works are informed by a profound ethical and political seriousness. They evince an almost encyclopaedic knowledge of European cultural, social and political history – particularly the history of colonialism – and an enduring concern with what is arguably the defining historical event of recent times: the Holocaust' (Long and Whitehead 2004: 4). Here we see identified two of the salient features of Sebald's prose: its extraordinary intertextuality, and its deeply ethical and self-conscious approach to the representation of the historical past via fictional narrative. Lilian R. Furst emphasizes the 'historiographic' qualities of Sebald's prose works, arguing that a text like 'Max Ferber' (in *The Emigrants*) belongs to the subgenre of 'typically postmodern historical novels', fusing '*microstoria* with *macrostoria*, the stories of ordinary, private figures with events of public record ... [...] By switching the viewpoint from the public to the private, the postmodern historical novel "explicitly lays out contrasting portraits of the world-making events" underlying the narrative' (2007: 550–1). For all its shortcomings as a generic term, 'postmodern historical novel' has the virtue of deepening the meaning of 'postmodern' while inflecting the 'historical' component in Sebald's prose works in the direction of the 'microhistorical' as a sort of backstairs entry into cultural memory. More broadly, James Chandler frames Sebald's self-reflexive approach to the representation of history in terms of the problem faced by Austerlitz's teacher, Hilary: 'if history is necessary to the purposes of human memory, and history needs a form, and if its forms have degenerated into cliché, then the forms of historiography as we know it must be revitalized by rhetorical genre crossing' (Chandler 2003: 258).[24] Complicating Furst's (actually James E. Lang's) 'postmodern historical novel', Lynn Wolff argues that 'Sebald's texts trouble the fundamental distinction between the historian or historiographer and the poet, as famously described by Aristotle in book nine of his *Poetics* ... "The poet and the historian differ not by writing in verse or in prose. [...] The true difference is that one relates what has happened, the other what may happen" ' (2009: 319). Unaccounted for in this ancient binary is the fact that Sebald, like any writer of post-memorial 'factions', also relates what *may have* happened.[25]

Travel was identified early on by Sontag, John Zilcosky and others as a significant generic mode.[26] Christopher C. Gregory-Guider coins the hybrid genre of 'autobiogeography' to capture what he calls 'a unique subgenre of life-writing in which the story of a person is refracted through the story of place' (Patt 2007: 516), crystallizing in a single term Sebald's transformation of the genre of travel narrative (Patt 2007: 516).[27] Simon Cooke's compelling suggestion that what is new about this kind of travel writing – 'rather than being a marginal or even extra-literary form of writing [the travelogue] has now evidently become increasingly attractive to writers seeking ... literary innovation' (2009: 21) – is tempered, however, by Sebald's avowed opposition in the Zürich lectures to overt 'aesthetic effects' (2003d: 53).[28] Concerning *The Rings of Saturn* specifically, Judith Ryan points out that 'the phrase "an English pilgrimage" [the subtitle of the German original[29]] is not only a thematic description of the text but, in some sense, also a genre designation' (2009: 45).[30] For Ryan, *The Rings of Saturn* is a highly modified species of pilgrimage narrative for an extraterritorialized post-secular late modern mindset (2009: 47–8).[31]

Putting aside the often banal authenticity of the settings through which his characters move, realism in Sebald is inherently complex and problematic. The modern novel's origins in class difference still make themselves felt in the genre's postmodern apotheosis, bourgeois realism long since epitomized in the novel as the quintessential modern genre. For Sebald, therefore, 'an attempt to write a literary account of collective catastrophes inevitably, if it is to claim validity, breaks out of the novel form that owes its allegiance to bourgeois concepts' (2005d: 84). At the centre of this debate is the relation in the prose texts of non-fiction to fiction, or of realism to something like anti- or post-realism. Jens Brockmeier states that 'Sebald's writing not only undermines traditional boundaries between genres and styles ... Rather, it explicitly rejects the distinction between fiction and non-fiction' (2008: 350). As Ruth Franklin reminds us, however, Sebald's

> work has often been described as 'documentary fiction', in that it springs from the roots of actual documents – postcards, letters, diaries – but blossoms into its own creation, in which the original source might recognize itself, as Sebald once put it, as if 'through a dark mirror'. Many critics have argued that it makes no difference whether Sebald's stories are mostly factual, mostly fictional, or anywhere in between: the books present themselves as deliberately ambiguous facsimiles of reality, and they should be understood as such. To parse the difference is 'tiresome', as Sebald himself remarked of critics' emphasis on the realism in [Jan Peter] Tripp's work, the focus on which (in his view) obscures the painter's true accomplishment. (Franklin 2011: 249)[32]

Sebald's deliberate engagement with other media forms justifies the sustained attention to intermediality that his works encourage. This presupposes the older question of intertextuality, which is invoked here in the broadest post-Kristevan sense as another name for cultural memory in material form, never completely determined by authorial agency, without forgetting that 'intertextuality' is Kristeva's translation of Bakhtin's dialogism. Contemporary cultural theory has by and large bought into a distortion of what Bakhtin meant by 'speech', 'word' or 'discourse' at the root of every 'utterance' (Stam 2000: 201) – the discursive practices of a specific national, cultural, or other group, and the aesthetic styliza-tion of these practices by the novelist or other artist.[33] Although intertextuality in itself may not exhaust Sebald's poetics, or rather prosaics, it remains unavoidable in any consideration of Sebald's contribution to genre.[34] According to Duff: 'It is probable ... that the concept of genre will continue to be put in question by more open-ended models of textuality', including 'those that emphasize the potentially unlimited scope of intertextuality (genre is, in effect, a *restrictive* model of intertex-tuality)' (2000: 16–17). For Ann Pearson, Sebald's prose is essentially the product of a learned and complex intertextuality; one which is 'neither misappropriation nor literary exhibitionism but a fertile engagement with earlier texts that contributes to the historical layering of his narratives' (2008: 262). While careful to parse out the intertextual and semantic differences among the various discursive layers typical of the prose works, Pearson (quoting Manfred Pfister) also queries:

> the broader significance of Sebald's intertextual practice. Is it, as [Stewart] Martin suggests, ultimately conservative – in the mode of Eliot's 'fragments shored against

[the] ruins' – a form of homage to models and predecessors that inserts Sebald's own writing within a chosen tradition or lineage? Or is Sebald engaging in a 'playgiarism' ... that recognizes the inescapability of repetition in an era saturated with texts 'in which originality will only survive in the form of sophisticated games with extant texts and traditional structures'? (2008: 262)

Pearson acknowledges that 'the answer to these questions may depend in part on which of his books is under consideration' (2008: 262), and suggests, more positively than Strathausen, that, '[p]aradoxically, it is perhaps in this intertextual polyphony that the true originality of Sebald's writing is to be found – his extraordinary ability to create something unmistakably his own out of the fragments he borrows from other writers and reworks in a context always productive of new meaning even as it draws attention to the continuing resonance of the past' (2008: 277). At the same time, as Long points out, Sebald's postmodern intertextuality takes the special, second-order form of 'an allusiveness aimed at academics and designed to ensure the works' canonicity' (2007: 7), a point related to what I argue here is their status as works of aestheticized genre theory.

To Long's categorical claim that 'intertextuality is the final major field of Sebald research" (2007: 7) I would add that, in some of the prose works, Sebald's intertextual embedding or appropriation amounts to a work of *adaptation* of the source text. What often goes unacknowledged in intertextual studies is that any consideration of a given text's intertextual dimension leads inevitably to the quasi-synonymous question of adaptation.[35] To predicate our approach to adaptation upon a dialogic intertextuality (as opposed to one based in the trope of fidelity, for instance) 'explicitly places the adaptation into its larger cultural-historical context, taking into account its reception by specific or general audience(s) (readers, viewers), as well as the broader political-ethical-ideological implications of a given instance of adaptation' (Naremore 2000: 46). In *Unrecounted*, Sebald writes of a painting by Jan Peter Tripp: 'Time lost, the pain of remembering and the figure of death have there been assembled in a memorial shrine as quotations from the painter's own life. Remembrance, after all ... is nothing other than a quotation. And the quotation incorporated in a text (or painting) by montage compels us ... to probe our knowledge of other texts and pictures and our knowledge of the world. This, in turn, takes time. By spending it, we enter into time recounted and into the time of culture' (Sebald and Tripp 2005: 90). For Sebald, in short, the 'unrecounted' only awaits recounting – although this may bring neither closure nor redemption.[36] And, in this view, adaptation or remediation can be seen as a vital contemporary modality of prosthetic memory: 'Remembrance ... is nothing other than a quotation.' In Sebald, memory never avoids an acute self-awareness of its own limitations; not least those produced by modern memory's irreducible reliance upon pre-existing cultural forms and technologies of meaning production, including genre, which Bakhtin describes as a mode of thinking (Morson and Emerson 1990: 280).

By 2007 an interesting new line of approach had emerged in Sebald studies, based in visual cultural practice and theory focusing on his texts' marked intermediality.[37] In her encyclopaedic introduction to *Searching for Sebald*, Lise Patt describes the author as having '"[come] into view" for a group of artists and art writers, who were already laying the foundation for a genre that included his "post-medium" practices' (2007: 87). 'Today', she concludes, '"Sebaldian" continues to reverberate through art, drawing loose alliances with "medium" and "genre" ' (2007: 93). In terms of Sebald's use of photography in his prose works, literary scholars (e.g. Harris 2001; Long 2003; Crownshaw 2004) have prepared the ground for everyone else (Patt 2007: 84 n. 216).[38] Matthias Frey examines Sebald's relation to cinema, a medium that has so far received much less attention than photography, and of which a great deal still remains to be said in terms of its significance for his work and for late twentieth and early twenty-first-century literature generally.[39] Where, in an early essay I emphasized Sebald's subtle incorporation of filmic allusions as part of his poetics of memory as an 'exteriorized, visually constituted phenomenon' (Kilbourn 2004: 140),[40] Frey focuses on Sebald's 'blurred notion of genre and intellectually rigorous inventory of quotation' (Patt 2007: 232). Moreover, what Frey calls Sebald's literary technique of 'montage', in direct analogy with cinematic montage, 'unleashes pent-up semiosis by destabilizing genre boundaries, subverting a "realistic" ontology of photographic images, and by fundamentally calling into question the aesthetic unity of time/space, image/text' (Frey in Patt 2007: 236).[41] This reading is bolstered by Sebald's use of the same term in the above-mentioned essay on Tripp, where he describes 'the quotation incorporated in a text (or painting) by montage' (Sebald 2005d: 90).

It is clear that Sebald's prose works intertextualize (and thereby privilege) certain exemplars of the post-war European art film tradition.[42] After all, Sebald came of age in post-war Germany at the same time as the young filmmakers (e.g. Fassbinder, Kluge, Herzog, Wenders) who would go on to form the New German Cinema. Although he remained too deeply influenced by the Frankfurt School, perhaps, to be turned on to radical countercultural politics, the indirect impact of 1968 nevertheless can be detected when one looks at Sebald's writings in light of their cinematic, as opposed to their exclusively literary, intertexts.[43] The former reveal a writer far less mired in epigonal melancholia than deeply preoccupied with questions of memory and representation in a late capitalist culture whose historical and political imaginaries alike exist on the cinema screen, available for mass consumption. And, as with his complex engagement with literature (as both writer and critical reader), Sebald's imaginative investment in film also manifests the deeply ethical tendency that grounds any claim to a 'literature of restitution'. As I have argued elsewhere: Sebald's critical work on literary subjects represents a relatively conservative, modernist-humanist frame of reference. His fictional texts, on the other hand, bear witness on the conceptual and even formal levels to a metadiscursive, auto-critical tendency that can be called 'postmodern', and that is radical, for example, in the sense of a return to the origins of the novel form.[44] Sebald's prose works therefore both reflect upon and exemplify the cultural and political status of the novel in what is now the post-cinematic era – the tail end of modernity, during which (to quote Jeffrey Pence) 'cinema carried the burden of memory' (Grainge 2003: 237).

The question of identity is never far from any consideration of form in Sebald. Even allowing for the fictional element, Sebald's writing is unapologetically gendered;[45] one cannot read his books without negotiating a relationship with the 'typical' Sebaldian narrator-protagonist,[46] whose ontological difference from the actual author much early criticism tended to collapse.[47] Genre in Sebald (as everywhere) is most helpfully theorized within the lexical paradigm constituted by genus, genesis, genetics, generation, genocide, gender, etc. – especially the latter: in French, 'genre and gender . . . are "one and the same word" ' (Duff 2000: 16). Hence Derrida: gender is a 'biological *genre* . . . the human *genre*, a *genre* of all that is general' (1992: 224). After all, the markedly gendered quality of Sebald's prose fictions seems to have something to do with their origins – and an abiding fascination with Sebald the man continues to manifest in the critical literature,[48] despite the obvious limitations of intentionalist or biographically based interpretations. For, if poststructuralism has taught us anything, it is that we should read people as texts, and not the other way around.[49] In his copy of Susan Sontag's *Under the Sign of Saturn*[50] (and this in no sense contradicts the previous point), Sebald notes this passage in the essay 'Mind as Passion' on Canetti: 'Portraits drawn from the inside, with or without the poignant inflections of exile, have made familiar the model of itinerant intellectual. He (for the type is male, of course) is a Jew, or like a Jew; polycultural, restless, misogynistic; a collector; dedicated to self-transcendence, despising the instincts; weighed down by books and buoyed up by the euphoria of knowledge' (Sontag 1983: 185). It is not difficult to see the attractions of this type for a writer such as Sebald; or rather for the typical Sebaldian narrator persona (since only those who knew 'Max' intimately could say for sure) – not to speak of a character such as Austerlitz, so tempting to identify with the author who seems to share in a number of these traits. That these do not include Jewishness is a highly significant difference when considering the prose works under the rubric of post-memorial, post-Holocaust literature.[51]

The bilingual collection *W. G. Sebald: Schreiben ex patria/Expatriate Writing* (Fischer ed. 2009), explores the premise of Sebald as writer of Heimat literature even as it extends the investigation of his work within the context of 'cultural memory'[52] and of the author as ideological construct. 'On the one hand', according to Gerhard Fischer's Introduction:

Sebald is not unlike the post-modern, uprooted expatriate in the age of global exchange and communication; but his work is, on the other hand, very much committed to the exploration and the preservation of a cultural sphere which is distinctively the 'old' Europe. The contemporary presence of what is left of this Europe and its special quality as an historical, literary and cultural construct, is ... traced by Sebald in much of his work, sometimes in a seemingly anachronistic and even nostalgic mode, but always as a vital effort to preserve a precious and, in view of current developments towards a homogenizing global cultural market, a potentially emancipatory cultural memory that resists the push and pull of a single, hegemonic world culture (2009: 21).[53]

While 'expatriate' may sound like a sub-genre unto itself (Fischer 2009: 16), it is Sebald's 'perspective as an expatriate German writer which accounts for his own, unique approach to the experience of the Holocaust' (Fischer 2009: 20). How does this square with Sebald's literary postmodernism? According to Duff, 'the modern period has been ... typically characterized by a steady erosion of the perception of genre, and by the emergence of aesthetic programmes which have sought to dispense altogether with the doctrine of literary kinds or genres' (2000: 1); hence the recurring definition of postmodern fictional narrative as open to, or indeed obsessed with, play with pre-established genre forms. 'This may have something to do with the elevation of popular culture which is so conspicuous a feature of Postmodernism, involving as it does a recognition that a much more favourable estimate of the value of genre has always prevailed in the popular sphere, despite the apparent rejection of the concept by the literary avant-garde' (Duff 2000: 2). Duff's insight illuminates our understanding of Sebald, positioned so complexly between modernist nostalgia for past forms and practices (not least of which is the novel itself, notwithstanding Sebald's own disavowals) and, inevitably, something more self-reflexively innovative, even radically so – in terms of content, style, form and structure. In Peter Morgan's estimation, Sebald 'cannot work with traditional genres of closure. He can neither return to his "Heimat" after what has happened, nor can he articulate his relationship to his national history in active terms, whether tragic or otherwise' (Morgan 2005: 82). Sebald's modernism, in other words, conditions his relation to the Holocaust; i.e. to Holocaust literature – just as the opposite is also true: his relation to writing about the Holocaust inflects his modernism in a radical, postmodern direction, from memory to a kind of post-memory. At the same time, his prose narratives' characteristic self-awareness signals a shift in status from belonging to this or that genre per se to works of aestheticized genre theory.

John Zilcosky offers one of the few essays that takes the problem of genre in Sebald as its focus, reading *Austerlitz* in particular against the prevailing positive reception as an instance of what he calls 'Holocaust melodrama' (2006: 691). Zilcosky's premise is that the book betrays elements of not merely genre in the neutral sense of a 'recurring type or category of text, as defined by structural, thematic and/or functional criteria' (Duff 2000: xiii), but also in the potentially pejorative sense of 'genre fiction': 'types of popular fiction in which a high degree of standardization is apparent ... as distinct from more "serious" highbrow fiction' (Duff 2000: xiii). '[S]cholars tend to group all of Sebald's fictions together under the author-function "Sebald"' (Zilcosky 2006: 684), but for Zilcosky *Austerlitz* is Sebald's most 'novelistic' work:

> Despite the long sentences, the lack of paragraph and section breaks, the persistent digressions, and the concentric narration, *Austerlitz* was more easily identifiable as a novel than the earlier three fictions, which all wandered along the borders between travel diary, memoir, collage, and short story. What makes *Austerlitz* more like a 'real novel'? The major factor is *Austerlitz's* de-emphasis of the peculiarly Sebaldian confusion between memoir and fiction, so central to the earlier works. (2006: 685–7)

While acknowledging that, according to Jaggi, 'Sebald loathes the term "Holocaust literature" ("it's a dreadful idea that you can have a sub-genre and make a specialty out of it; it's grotesque")' (2001: 8),[54] in Zilcosky's reading *Austerlitz* is also Sebald's first 'Holocaust novel' (2006: 693). Citing Bryan Cheyette, Franklin argues that 'Sebald's concern is not the actual events [of the Holocaust] so much as their aftereffects ... It would be more accurate to think of Sebald as a "post-Holocaust writer" ... except that such a phrase implies that there is such a thing as the "post-Holocaust", which Sebald, like Imre Kertész, would likely have adamantly denied' (2011: 186).[55] Such protestations aside, Zilcosky argues that 'Sebald comes perilously close here to the melodramatic "impulse toward dramatization" and "desire to express all" that he had scrupulously avoided in the earlier fictions and, what is more, had criticized in other Holocaust representations such as *Schindler's List*' (2006: 694).[56] Citing the rehabilitative efforts of Peter Brooks and Thomas Elsaesser, Zilcosky acknowledges melodrama's status as a dominant mode in contemporary popular culture[57] (2006: 697). The problem, of course, is that books like *Austerlitz* are not popular cultural objects but the product of a more serious artistic endeavour and 'highbrow' marketing campaign. Moreover, for Sebald, as for Jean-Luc Godard in cinema, coming after Adorno's famous dictum about the barbarity of 'poetry' after Auschwitz, it is a question of the appropriate language or style, the proper perspective upon or approach to representing the Holocaust, rather than its absolute unrepresentability or ineffability, a position which Holocaust Studies has had to move beyond.[58] And cinema is relevant here for many reasons, not least of which is what one imagines as Sebald's tacit agreement with Godard on the 'obscenity' of films like *Schindler's List* (1993).[59] Sebald's opposition to the 'Spielberg style of history' takes the same form as Godard's (Sturken 2008: 75): according to Jaggi, the author mistrusts 'recreations' (such as *Schindler's List*), leaving the door open to other, subtler, more indirect approaches.

Zilcosky also criticizes *Austerlitz* for displaying what Brooks identifies as 'a melodramatic desire for "total expressivity" related precisely to the "ineffability" of his subject matter' (Zilcosky 2006: 695). This critique is elaborated in terms of *Austerlitz*'s famous Bernhardian 'periscopic' narrative structure, in which one speaker's words are framed within as many as three others' ('I remembered what Věra had said about my father's account of the National Socialist Party rally of 1936 ... said Austerlitz' (Sebald 2001g: 222)), with the nameless Sebaldian narrator at the outermost narrative layer, as it were 'closest' to the reader's extra-diegetic position. Zilcosky asks whether the melodramatic impact of specific moments in the narrative is mitigated by this multi-layered, dialogic style (2006: 695) – a key question, framing fundamental concerns about representing the Holocaust within more general ethical-aesthetic questions about the representation of alterity, what Sebald calls 'the usurpation of another person's life' (quoted in Franklin 2011: 193). Does the text express an ethical relation to the other – respecting the other in her or his otherness, as Levinas or Derrida might say, over there, outside of us[60] – by 'periscopically' placing an account of an untranslatable experience into the mouth of a character several times removed from the narratorial-authorial, and by extension readerly, 'self'?[61]

It seems more fruitful to consider Sebald's 'transgressions' (whether melodramatic or otherwise) against generic decorum from the perspective of Marianne Hirsch's notion of post-memory, as several critics have done before (e.g. Long 2003; Crownshaw 2004), and as I do in a qualified way throughout this study. For these so-called melodramatic touches are also the result of Sebald's imaginative labour on the part of the other, the victim or victim's child or grandchild; a Jewish subject whose experience, voice and/or point of view, whether first or second hand, Sebald the historical personage clearly does not share, but which the author imaginatively appropriates.[62] In other words, the 'sin' here is succumbing not so much to melodrama as to the (neo-colonialist) arrogance of the (in this case) male writer, creatively imagining himself into situations, times, experiences, memories and subjectivities not properly his own. In this light, Lynn Wolff reads *Austerlitz* as 'first and foremost' a fictional biography, and argues that in this micro-historical approach Sebald in fact succeeds in representing the underside of history, 'especially with regard to the problem of representing the Holocaust. *Austerlitz*, by focusing on one individual, demonstrates Sebald's ... assertion that only in literature is any attempt at restitution possible' (Wolff 2009: 329).

In contrast to the generally accepted view of Sebald as post-memorial writer, however, Kathy Behrendt usefully cautions that he does not qualify as someone engaged in 'cultural postmemory work' in Marianne Hirsch's sense of the term (Behrendt 2011: 5). The danger, for Behrendt, is to overlook the meaningfully pessimistic dimension of Sebald's prose works (which resonates with the *Fortschrittskritik* of the Frankfurt School):[63] the fact that, in *Austerlitz* for example, the protagonist never finds the definitive answers to his questions, never completes his quest to determine his mother's fate even as he heads off in search of his father's traces. For Behrendt, Sebald's representation or appropriation of a Jewish perspective is deliberately characterized by a lack of the 'precision' and clear-eyed witnessing, which for Hirsch are prerequisites of post-memory (Behrendt 2011: 4–5). Behrendt is right to point out that Austerlitz quite simply never acquires the 'epistemic authority' to know what became of his parents, a lack which effectively excludes him from the ranks of post-memorial witnesses (2011: 5): 'one cannot bear witness to a truth that is largely inaccessible or obscured' (2011: 6).[64] This reading complements Long's point that a character like Austerlitz is a representative instance of the modern 'archival subject': one who 'compensate[s] for his lack of memory by substituting the archive for interiority' (2007: 162). (In place of repressed memories of being sent as a small child from Prague to England to escape the Holocaust, Austerlitz fills his mind with the history of the outsized architecture of nineteenth-century colonialist Europe.) But what of Sebald? Which is to say, what is the post-memorial status of the prose narratives, the texts themselves?

CONCLUSION: TOWARDS A LITERATURE OF RESTITUTION

In *On the Natural History of Destruction* Sebald remarks that 'the accounts of individual eyewitnesses … are of only qualified value, and need to be supplemented by what a synoptic and artificial view reveals' (2003d: 25–6).[65] A potential problem, as Julia Hell points out, is the highly gendered nature of this gaze,[66] which in her persuasive reading becomes emblematic of a cultural discourse that transcends 'personal trauma' in order to write 'postwar history … as a melo-traumatic story of German non-Jewish authorship' (Hell 2003: 35). But, as the example of *Austerlitz* makes clear, Sebald's formulation of the 'synoptic view' is thoroughly conscious of its own paradoxical, non-transcendent, discursively 'embodied' status ('for the type is male, of course').[67] After Bakhtin we can say that it is genre itself as an 'organ of memory' that conditions the texts' dialogic relation to representing the other; in this sense even a so-to-speak generic genre like melodrama allows the other's voice to be heard, especially when it is couched in a prose narrative that is on one level a self-reflexive reflection upon the question of genre. The uniqueness of Sebald's memory work can be summed up, perhaps, as the self-conscious *failure* of what Martin Klebes has called 'mnemonic restitution' (2003). This is in effect a constitutional and therefore necessary 'failure', insofar as Sebald writes, in Corngold's words (and in line with Richard Crownshaw's work on photography and trauma in Sebald)[68], 'to bear witness to the complexity of bearing witness' (Corngold 2008: 222). This is the very purpose of post-memory, in a sense beyond Hirsch's original formulation, as a function of the irreducible distance necessitated by the always already second-order perspective of the non-Jewish, second (or later) generation German writer;[69] in bearing witness in this second-order way, it struggles directly with the paradox of making good what cannot be restored, returning what has been irrecoverably lost. In Arthur Williams's words, Sebald sought to 'lend his voice to the silenced victims of history and to uncover the nature of the hegemonic systems that spawned inhumanity [leading] him to reject specific genre attributions for his works' (Williams 2007b: 51). Therefore, from the perspective of the second (and now third) generation of German writers after the war, it is not a question of subject-victim or even spectator assuming the task of representing collective catastrophe,[70] but of a third-party observer whose labour therefore will be largely imaginative, a labour of prosthetic memory interacting dialectically with what Hutchinson identifies as the melancholic inability to forget (2009a: 325).[71] Can we apply the same logic to any writer who lives outside of the place or after the events s/he chooses to explore in a prose narrative? Is it 'permissible', so to speak, to take the Holocaust as a particular model for the writing of post-memorial texts in general?

I follow Franklin (and several others[72]) therefore in citing here Sebald's last public speech, 'on the occasion of the opening of a new Literaturhaus in Stuttgart', 'An Attempt at Restitution' ('Ein Versuch zur Restitution'): 'So what is literature good for? [...] The synoptic view across the barrier of death ... is both overshadowed and illuminated ... by the memory of those to whom the greatest injustice was done. There are many forms of writing; only in literature, however, can there be an attempt at restitution" (2005d: 204–5) [translation altered]. Is it possible to see in Sebald's prose texts the representatives of a new genre *in nuce*: the 'literature of restitution'? As Franklin explains, '[t]he German word, like its English cognate, encompasses multiple meanings, including the restoration of art (which often involves cleaning off the layers of dust left by the passage of time) and the return of anything to its rightful owner. But it also has a specific legal meaning: the restoration of not only property but also of a person's legal status, taken away in violation of international law' (2011: 194). For this study, restitution is a secular alternative to the more loaded concept of redemption, which it complements, to a degree. By the same token, restitution stands in opposition to a term like retribution, which in this context bears only pejorative connotations. For, if retribution implies the adding of violence to violence, in a (usually vain) attempt at restoring a semblance of order, in the process reducing the other to less than one's self, then restitution here signifies the preliminary – and purely imaginative – restoring to the other of what is most proper to it: the radical otherness of that which would otherwise remain forgotten.[73] Is it justifiable or even possible to speak of the restorative or compensatory dimension of the literary mimesis or representation of the past, of history or of memory?[74] Of literature's arrogating to itself at such a late date the burden of history, of memory, of commemorating and remembering, as much as constructively forgetting, rewriting, or imagining outright? Inextricably linked to the question of genre, these questions must for now remain open, any final answers – any closure – still awaiting us, in our post-Sebaldian future.

NOTES

1 Cf. Lubow (2007: 161).

2 See also pp. xx and xxi. Cf. Madden (2008).

3 Cf. Sheppard (2009: 103 n. 33); Dubow (2007: 829); Mack (2009: 234); Chandler (2003: 251); Williams (2007b: 52); Zilcosky (2006: 684); Brockmeier (2008: 368 n. 3).

4 See Sheppard (2005: 433, 443); Corngold (2008: 4). Cf. Franklin (2011: 260 n. 1).

5 Cf. Derrida (1992: 224, 230).

6 On Sebald's appreciation of Bakhtin, see Sheppard (2005: 455 n. 33). On 'genre memory' see e.g. Grainge (2003: 9); Sereda (2010: 10).

7 See Duff (2000: 16). On Sebald as 'post-Romantic' see Chandler (2003: 240–1).

8 See also Gumz (2004: 85).

9 See Franklin (2011: 248); MacCabe (1986).

10 See Long (2007: 1–8). Cf. Bakhtin (1981: 11).

11 See Duff (2000: 10).

12 In the jacket blurb for *The Emigrants* Sontag speaks of 'the non-existent genre to which Sebald's masterpiece belongs' (Sebald 1996).

13 See Bolter and Grusin (1999); Hutcheon (2006: 16–17).

14 See e.g. Long on the 'archival subject' of modernity (2007: 1–8).

15 See Raymond Williams (1973: 12).

16 Cf. Scherpe (2009: 297).

17 See Jaggi (2001: 1); Harris (2001: 380–1). 'At a time when everything is classified and marketed cynically, Sebald defies all genres' (Bryan Cheyette, quoted in Jaggi 2001: 2).

18 See Brockmeier (2008: 347–8).

19 See also Hutchinson (2009b).

20 Originated by Hirsch (1997), '[p]ostmemory can be defined as the highly mediated memories of those who did not witness the traumatic event but who have inherited, by way of a cultural affiliation or familial legacy (even though that traumatic inheritance may be one of silence and the failure of witnessing), memories so affective they feel as they have originated in the postmemorial generation' (Crownshaw 2009: 20).

21 See Anderson (2003: 104–5).

22 See also Denham (2006); Fuchs and Long (2007); etc.

23 On Sebald as modernist and not postmodernist, see also Zilcosky (2004: 102–3). On Sebald as 'postmodern' writer see e.g. Williams, A. (1998 and 2001). See also Kilbourn (2006: 35; 2007: 139).

24 Cf. Wolff (2009: 318).

25 Long concludes his 'Roundup' circa 2007 by remarking the 'predictable' and 'repetitive' nature of much recent Sebald criticism – nowhere more in evidence than from the perspective of genre.

26 Sontag (2002: 43); Zilcosky (2004: 102–4). See also Leone (2004: 100); Zilcosky (2006: 679); Cooke (2009: 16); Gray (2009: 27). See also Zisselsberger (2010), which appeared when this article was already complete.

27 This genre could usefully include other hard-to-categorize twentieth-century prose works, such as Claudio Magris's *Danubio* (1988) (*Danube*).

28 See Corngold (2008: 4).

29 'Eine Englische Wallfahrt'.

30 Cf. Gray (2009: 27); Long (2009: 61). Cf. Cooke (2009: 15).

31 Like Strathausen, Ryan adopts a Deleuzian approach to reading *The Rings of Saturn*, which makes sense in terms of the Kafkan intertext (Patt 2007: 478). See Deleuze and Guattari (1986).

32 See Sebald and Tripp (2005: 80). Franklin concludes provisionally that 'Sebald's inherently destabilizing writing, like Tripp's paintings, can also be seen as a form of hyperrealism, in which the documentary evidence presented by his texts – particularly the often-ambiguous photographs – simultaneously supports and undermines the works' authority' (2011: 188).

33 See e.g. 'Discourse in the Novel' (written in the early 1930s) (1981: 300).

34 On 'prosaics' see Morson and Emerson (1990). Cf. Long (2007a: 25 n. 15).

35 See e.g. Stam (2005: 3–5); Hutcheon (2006: 21–2); Sanders (2006: 1–3).

36 On this passage cf. Franklin (2011: 263).

37 See Fuchs (2004).

38 For a detailed discussion of photography in Sebald see Long (2007: 46–70). See also Sears (2007: 208).

39 See e.g. Sheppard (2005: 443–4).

40 Re. historiography as 'historioscopy' see Kilbourn (2007: 139).

41 See also Long (2007: 112). On 'montage' in Sebald cf. Schalk (2007). On Sebald and the visual arts more generally see Arthur Williams (2007b).

42 See Kilbourn (2004: 141). See also Sheppard (2005: 443–4). Cf. Sebald's essay 'Kafka Goes to the Movies' (2005d: 151–68).

43 For a discussion of Sebald's response to the events of 1968, see Puw Davies (2011); for a discussion of his relationship to the Frankfurt School, see Hutchinson (2011).

44 See Fuchs and Long (2007: 139).

45 On gender (esp. masculinity) in Sebald, see Hell (2003); Barzilai (2004).

46 See Kilbourn (2007: 139).

47 See e.g. Williams, A. (2001: 68).

48 See e.g. Sheppard (2005); Pearson (2008); etc.

49 On Sebald's knowledge of poststructuralist theory, see Albes (2002: 295–6).

50 Part of the collection at the *Deutsches Literaturarchiv* in Marbach, Germany.

51 Cf. Crownshaw (2009: 15).

52 As in Cooke (2009: 15); Crownshaw (2009); etc.

53 See also Fischer (2009: 23).

54 Notice that Sebald focuses on the Holocaust's significance for literary categorization rather than the event in itself. See Zilcosky (2006: 693–5).

55 Cf. Newton (2004: 422).

56 See Anderson (2003: 110).

57 See Linda Williams (2001: 10–44).

58 These images [of concentration camps, etc.] militate against our capacity for discursive thinking ... and paralyze our moral capacity, and the only way we can approach these things is *obliquely*' (Silverblatt 2007: 80; my emphasis).

59 Cf. Jaggi (2001). See also Franklin (2011: 245).

60 For a persuasive Levinasian reading of Sebald, see Ribó (2009: 237).

61 See Zilcosky (2006: 695). Cf. Long (2007: 8, 19).

62 See Zilcosky (2006: 696).

63 See Hutchinson (2009b).

64 On this point see Kilbourn (2004) for an apophatic reading of Austerlitz's willful divestment of memory via memory-objects.

65 See also Sebald (2003d: 67–8). Cf. Hell (2004: 6); Presner (2004).

66 Cf. Barzilai's fascinating analysis of Sebald's gendered representation of a relationship with the Jewish-German past in terms of that between 'a living male character' haunted by 'the image of an absent, dead or ghostly woman' (2004: 212).

67 See Kilbourn (2007: 145). See also Anderson (2003: 119).

68 'Unmoored, trauma demands a new kind of witnessing: the witnessing of the witness who conveys trauma to those who listen. [...] Trauma has departed from its origins and arrived in the cultural memory of events not directly witnessed' (Corngold 2008: 12–13) – i.e. post-memory.

69 See Anderson (2003: 104).

70 I omit the category of perpetrator, recently explored in extraordinary depth by Jonathan Littell in *Les Bienveillantes* (2006) (*The Kindly Ones*).

71 I invoke Alison Landsberg's term 'prosthetic memory' somewhat out of its original context. See e.g. Landsberg (2004).

72 Cf. Sheppard (2005: 424). See also Lubow (2007); Williams (2007b: 55 n. 12).

73 Andreas Huyssen refers to the Sebaldian prose text as 'a unique style of memory narrative, located at the breaking point between documentary and fiction [...] As a German of the postwar generation, he accepts his responsibility to remember while fully acknowledging the difficulty of such remembering across an abyss of violence and pain' (2003: 260–1).

74 As Franklin remarks of Sebald, 'there is also something deeply consoling about his vision of art as capable of offering some sort of recompense' (2011: 257).

REFERENCES

Adler, H. G. 1960. *Theresienstadt 1941–1945: Das Antlitz einer Zwangsgemeinschaft*. 2nd ed. (Tübingen: J. C. B. Mohr).

———. 1989. *Die unsichtbare Wand* (Vienna: Zsolnay Verlag).

———. 1998. *Der Wahrheit verpflichtet*, ed. Jeremy Adler (Gerlingen: Bleicher Verlag).

———. 2008. *The Journey*, trans. Peter Filkins (New York: Random House).

———. 2011. *Panorama*, trans Peter Filkins (New York: Random House).

Adorno, Theodor W. 1964. *Minima Moralia: Reflections from Damaged Life*, trans. E. F. N. Jephcott (London: NLB).

———. 1973. *Negative Dialectics*, trans. E. B. Ashton (London: Routledge & Kegan Paul).

———. 1980. *Minima Moralia: Reflexionen aus dem beschädigten Leben*, vol. 4 of *Gesammelte Schriften*, ed. Rolf Tiedemann (Frankfurt am Main: Suhrkamp).

———. 1981. 'Notes on Kafka', in *Prisms*, trans. Samuel and Shierry Weber (Cambridge, Mass.: The MIT Press): 243–71.

———. 1997. *Aesthetic Theory*, ed. Gretel Adorno and Rolf Tiedemann, trans. Robert Hullot-Kentor (London: Athlone).

Albes, Claudia. 2002. 'Die Erkundung der Leere: Anmerkungen zu W. G. Sebalds 'englischer Wallfahrt'', in *Die Ringe des Saturn*', *Jahrbuch der deutschen Schillergesellschaft* 46: 279–305.

Aliaga-Buchenau, Ana-Isabel. 2006. '"A Time He Could not Bear to Say Anymore about": Presence and Absence of the Narrator in W. G. Sebald's *The Emigrants*', in *History, Memory, Trauma*, ed. Scott Denham and Mark McCulloh (Berlin and New York: Walter de Gruyter): 142–55.

Améry, Jean. 2002. *Jenseits von Schuld und Sühne*, in *Werke* vol. 2, ed. Gerhart Scheit (Stuttgart: Klett-Cotta).

Anderson, Mark M. 2003. 'The Edge of Darkness: On W. G. Sebald', *October* 106 (Fall 2003): 102–21.

———. 2008. 'Documents, Photography, Postmemory: Alexander Kluge, W. G. Sebald, and the German Family', *Poetics Today* 29.1: 129–53.

Angier, Carole. 1997. 'Wer ist W. G. Sebald? Ein Besuch beim Autor der

"Ausgewanderten"', in *W. G. Sebald*, ed. Franz Loquai (Eggingen: Edition Klaus Isele, 1997): 43–50.

——. 2007. 'Who is W. G. Sebald?', in *The Emergence of Memory: Conversations with W. G. Sebald*, ed. Lynne Sharon Schwartz (New York and London: Seven Stories Press): 63–75.

Arnds, Peter. 2010. 'While the Hidden Horrors of History are Briefly Illuminated: The Poetics of Wandering in *Austerlitz* and *Die Ringe des Saturn*', in *The Undiscover'd Country. W. G. Sebald and the Poetics of Travel*, ed. Markus Zisselsberger (Rochester, NY: Camden House): 322–44.

Arnold-de Simine, Silke. 2006. 'Remembering the Future: Utopian and Dystopian Aspects of Glass and Iron Architecture in Walter Benjamin, Paul Scheerbarth, and W. G. Sebald', in *Imagining the City, Volume 1: The Art of Urban Living*, ed. Christian Emden, Catherine Keen, and David Midgley (Oxford: Peter Lang): 149–69.

Atze, Marcel. 2004. 'Wie Adler berichtet': Das Werk H. G. Adlers als Gedächtnisspeicher für die Literatur', in *Text + Kritik, 163*, VII, ed. Heinz Ludwig Arnold (Munich: edition text + kritik): 17–30.

——. 2005. 'W. G. Sebald und H. G. Adler: Eine Begegnung in Texten', in *W. G. Sebald. Mémoire. Transferts. Images/Erinnerung. Übertragungen. Bilder. Recherches germaniques. Hors série no. 2*, ed. Ruth Vogel-Klein (Strasbourg: Université Marc Bloch): 87–97.

Atze, Marcel and Franz Loquai (eds). 2005. *Sebald. Lektüren* (Eggingen: Edition Isele).

Baer, Ulrich. 2002. *Spectral Evidence: The Photography of Trauma* (Cambridge, Mass.: MIT Press).

Bailes, Sara-Jane. 2001. Goat Island website, www.goatislandperformance.org.

Bakhtin, M. M. 1981. 'Epic and Novel', in *The Dialogic Imagination*, ed. Michael Holquist, trans. Caryl Emerson and Michael Holquist (Austin Tex.: University of Austin): 3–40.

Barnstone, Willis. 1993. *The Poetics of Translation: History, Theory, Practice* (New Haven and London: Yale University Press).

Barthes, Roland. 1984. *Camera Lucida: Reflections on Photography*, trans. Richard Howard (London: Fontana).

Barzilai, Maya. 2004. 'Facing the Past and the Female Spectre in W. G. Sebald's *The Emigrants?*', in *W. G. Sebald – A Critical Companion*, ed. J. J. Long and Anne Whitehead (Edinburgh: Edinburgh University Press; Seattle: University of Washington Press): 203–16.

——. 2006. 'On Exposure: Photography and Uncanny Memory in W. G. Sebald's *Die Ausgewanderten* and *Austerlitz*', in *W. G. Sebald: History, Memory, Trauma*, ed. Scott Denham and Mark McCulloh (Berlin: Walter de Gruyter): 205–18.

Bataille, Georges. 1994a. *The Absence of Myth: Writings on Surrealism*, trans. Michael Richardson (London: Verso).

——. 1994b (1939). 'The College of Sociology', in *Visions of Excess: Selected Writings, 1927–1939*, ed. Allan Stoekl, trans. Allan Stoekl with Carl R. Lovitt and Donald M. Leslie, Jr (Minneapolis: University of Minnesota Press): 246–53.

——. 1994c (1936). 'The Labyrinth', in *Visions of Excess: Selected Writings, 1927–1939*, ed. Allan Stoekl, trans. Allan Stoekl with Carl R. Lovitt and Donald M. Leslie, Jr. (Minneapolis: University of Minnesota Press): 171–7.

——. 1994d (1933). 'The Psychological Structure of Fascism', in *Visions of Excess: Selected Writings, 1927–1939*, ed. Allan Stoekl, trans. Allan Stoekl with Carl R. Lovitt and Donald M. Leslie, Jr. (Minneapolis: University of Minnesota Press): 137–60.

——. 2001 (1928). *Story of the Eye*, trans. Joachim Neugroschal (London: Penguin).

Batchem, Geoffrey (ed.). 2009. *Photography Degree Zero: Reflections on Roland Barthes's 'Camera Lucida'* (Cambridge, Mass.: MIT Press).

Beck, John. 2004. 'Reading Room: Erosion and Sedimentation in Sebald's Suffolk', in *W. G. Sebald: A Critical Companion*, ed. J. J. Long and Anne Whitehead (Edinburgh: Edinburgh University Press): 75–88.

Beckett, Samuel. 2009a. *The Letters of Samuel Beckett*, vol. 1: *1929–1940*, ed. Martha Dow Fehsenfeld and Lois More Overbeck (New York: Cambridge University Press).

——. 2009b. *Molloy*, ed. Shane Weller (London: Faber & Faber).

Behrendt, Kathy. 2011. 'Postamnesia', unpublished essay.

Benjamin, Walter. 1974. 'Über den Begriff der Geschichte', in vol. 1 of *Gesammelte Schriften*, ed. Rolf Tiedemann and Hermann Schweppenhäuser (Frankfurt am Main: Suhrkamp): 691–704.

——. 1979 (1929). 'Surrealism: The Last Snapshot of the European Intelligentsia', in *One Way Street and Other Writings*, trans. Edmund Jephcott and Kingsley Shorter (London: NLB).

——. 1982. *Das Passagen-Werk*, in vol. 5 of *Gesammelte Schriften*, ed. Rolf Tiedemann (Frankfurt am Main: Suhrkamp).

——. 1985. 'Berliner Chronik', in vol. 6 of *Gesammelte Schriften*, ed. Rolf Tiedemann and Hermann Schweppenhäuser (Frankfurt am Main: Suhrkamp): 465–519.

——. 1996. *Selected Writings Volume 1. 1913–26* (Cambridge, Mass.: Belknap Press of Harvard University Press).

——. 1999a. *The Arcades Project*, trans. Howard Eiland and Kevin McLaughlin (Cambridge, Mass.: Belknap Press of Harvard University Press).

——. 1999b. 'A Berlin Chronicle', trans. Edmond Jephcott, in vol. 2 of *Selected Writings*, ed. Michael W. Jennings, Howard Eiland and Gary Smith (Cambridge, Mass.: Belknap Press of Harvard University Press): 595–637.

——. 1999c. *Selected Writings Volume 2. 1927–34* (Cambridge, Mass.: Belknap Press of Harvard University Press).

——. 2002. *Selected Writings Volume 3. 1935–38* (Cambridge, Mass.: Belknap Press of Harvard University Press).

——. 2003a. 'On the Concept of History', trans. Harry Zohn, in vol. 4 of *Selected Writings*, ed. Marcus Bullock, Howard Eiland, and Gary Smith (Cambridge, Mass.: Belknap Press of Harvard University Press): 389–400.

——. 2003b. *Selected Writings Volume 4. 1938–40* (Cambridge, Mass.: Belknap Press of Harvard University Press).

Berger, John. 1980. 'Why Look at Animals?', in *About Looking* (London: Writers and Readers): 1–26.

Binczek, Natalie. 2008. 'Ein Wurzelwerk der Zeit: Photographische Medienreflexion der Literatur in W. G. Sebalds *Austerlitz*', in *Durchquerungen*, ed. Iris Hermann and Anne Maximiliane Jäger-Gogoll (Heidelberg: Winter): 13–30.

Blackler, Deane. 2007a. *Reading W. G. Sebald: Adventure and Disobedience* (Rochester, N.Y.: Camden House).

——. 2007b. *Reading W. G. Sebald: Adventure and Disobedience* (Woodbridge: Boydell and Brewer).

Boehncke, Heiner. 2003. 'Clair obscur: W. G. Sebalds Bilder', *Text + Kritik*, 158: 43–62.

Böll, Heinrich. 1957. *Irisches Tagebuch* (Köln: Kiepenheuer & Witsch).

——. 1985. 'Das wahre Wie, das wahre Was' (1966), in *Heimat und keine. Schriften und Reden 1964–1968* (Munich: dtv): 187–92.

Bolter, Jay and Richard Grusin. 1999. *Remediation: Understanding New Media* (Cambridge, Mass.: MIT Press).

Bond, Greg. 2004. 'On the Misery of Nature and the Nature of Misery: W. G. Sebald's Landscapes', in *W. G. Sebald – A Critical Companion*, ed. J. J. Long and Anne Whitehead (Edinburgh: Edinburgh University Press): 31–44.

Borges, Jose Luis. 1998. 'The Theme of the Traitor and the Hero', in *Collected Fictions*, tr. Andrew Hurley (New York: Penguin).

Bottoms, Stephen and Goulish, Matthew (eds). 2007. *Small Acts of Repair* (London and New York: Routledge).

Boyce, David George and O'Day Alan (eds). 1996. *The Making of Modern Irish History: Revisionism and the Revisionist Controversy* (London: Routledge, 1996).

Boyle, Nicholas. 2009. *A Very Short Introduction to German Literature* (Oxford: Oxford University Press).

Breton, André. 1987 (1937). *Mad Love*, trans. Mary Anne Caws (Lincoln and London: University of Nebraska Press).

——. 2007 (1930). 'Second Manifesto of Surrealism', in *Manifestoes of Surrealism*, trans. Richard Seaver and Helen Lane (Ann Arbor: University of Michigan Press).

Brockmeier, Jens. 2008. 'Austerlitz's Memory', *Partial Answers: Journal of Literature and the History of Ideas* 6.2 (June): 347–67.

Bryson, Norman. 1990. *Looking at the Overlooked: Four Essays on Still Life Painting* (London: Reaktion Books).

Buch, Robert. 2010. 'Schlachtgemälde und Schlachtbeschreibung bei W. G. Sebald und Claude Simon', *Weimarer Beiträge: Zeitschrift für Literaturwissenschaft, Ästhetik und Kulturwissenschaft*, 56.1: 30–46.

Caillois, Roger. 2001 (1958). *Man, Play and Games*, trans. Meyer Barash (Urbana and Chicago: Illinois Press).

Calvino, Italo. 2009. *Six Memos for the New Millennium* (London: Penguin Modern Classics).

Catling, Jo and Hibbitt, Richard (eds). 2011. *Saturn's Moons: W. G. Sebald – A Handbook* (Oxford: Legenda).

Ceuppens, Jan. 2004. 'Seeing Things: Spectres and Angels in W.G. Sebald's Prose Fiction', in *W. G. Sebald: A Critical Companion*, ed. J. J. Long and Anne Whitehead (Edinburgh: Edinburgh University Press): 190–202.

——. 2006. 'Transcripts: An Ethics of Representation in *The Emigrants*', in *History, Memory, Trauma*, ed. Scott Denham and Mark McCulloh (Berlin and New York: Walter de Gruyter): 251–63.

——. 2007. 'Tracing the Witness in W. G. Sebald', in *W. G. Sebald and the Writing of History*, ed. Anne Fuchs and J. J. Long (Würzburg: Königshausen & Neumann): 59–72.

Chandler, James. 2003. 'About Loss: W. G. Sebald's Romantic Art of Memory', *The South Atlantic Quarterly* 102.1 (Winter): 235–62.

Chaplin, Elizabeth. 2006. 'The Convention of Captioning: W. G. Sebald and the Release of the Captive Image', *Visual Studies*, 21.1: 42–53.

Clarke, Graham (ed.). 1992. *The Portrait in Photography* (London: Reaktion Books).

Cooke, Simon. 2009. 'Cultural Memory on the Move in Contemporary Travel Writing', *Mediation, Remediation, and the Dynamics of Cultural Memory*, ed. Astrid Erll and Ann Rigney (Berlin and New York: Walter de Gruyter): 15–30.

Corkhill, Alan. 2009. 'Angles of Vision in Sebald's *After Nature* and *Unrecounted*', in *W. G. Sebald: Schreiben in ex patria/Expatriate Writing*, ed. Gerhard Fischer (Amsterdamer Beiträge zur neueren Literatur), 72: 347–67.

Corngold, Stanley. 2008. 'Sebald's Tragedy', in *Rethinking Tragedy*, ed. Rita Felski (Baltimore, Md.: Johns Hopkins University Press): 218–40.

Crownshaw, Richard. 2004. 'Reconsidering Postmemory: Photography, the Archive, and Post-Holocaust Memory in W. G. Sebald's *Austerlitz*', *Mosaic* 37.4 (Special Issue on the Photograph): 215–36.

——. 2009. 'On Reading Sebald Criticism: Witnessing the Text', *Journal of Romance Studies* 9.3 (Winter): 10–22.

Cuomo, Joseph. 2007. 'Conversation with W. G. Sebald', in *The Emergence of Memory: Conversations with W. G. Sebald*, ed. Lynne Sharon Schwartz (New York and London: Seven Stories Press): 93–117.

Darby, David. 2006. 'Landscape and Memory: Sebald's Redemption of History', in *W. G. Sebald: History, Memory, Trauma*, ed. Scott Denham and Mark McCulloch (Berlin: Walter de Gruyter): 265–78.

de Breza, Eugène. 1845. *Monsieur le Marquis de Custine en 1844* (Leipzig: Librarie Etrangère).

de Polnay, Peter. 1950. *Into an Old Room – The Paradox of Edward Fitzgerald* (London: Secker & Warburg).

de Vere White, Terence. 1972. *The Anglo-Irish* (London: Gollancz).

Deleuze, Gilles and Félix Guattari. 1986. *Kafka: Toward a Minor Literature* (Minneapolis: University of Minnesota Press).

Denham, Scott. 2006. 'Foreword: The Sebald Phenomenon', in *W. G. Sebald: History, Memory, Trauma*, ed. Scott Denham and Mark McCulloh (Berlin and New York: Walter de Gruyter): 1–6.

Denham, Scott and McCulloh, Mark (eds). 2006. *W. G. Sebald: History, Memory, Trauma* (Berlin and New York: Walter de Gruyter).

Denneler, Iris. 2001. *Von Namen und Dingen* (Würzburg: Königshausen & Neumann).

Derrida, Jacques. 1992. *Acts of Literature*, ed. Derek Attridge (New York and London: Routledge).

——. 1993. *Memoirs of the Blind: The Self-Portrait and Other Ruins*, trans. Pascale-Anne Brault and Michael Naas (Chicago: University of Chicago Press).

——. 1997. Aufzeichnungen eines Blinden: das Selbstporträt und andere Ruine, ed. Michael Wetzel (Munich: Fink).

Dooley, Terence. 2001. *The Decline of the Big House in Ireland: A Study of Irish Landed Families, 1860–1960* (Dublin: Wolfhound Press).

Dubow, Jessica. 2007. 'Case Interrupted: Benjamin, Sebald, and the Dialectical Image', *Critical Inquiry* 33 (Summer): 820–36.

Duff, David (ed.). 2000. *Modern Genre Theory* (Essex: Longman).

Duttlinger, Carolin. 2004. 'Traumatic Photographs: Remembrance and the Technical Media in W. G. Sebald's *Austerlitz*', in *W. G. Sebald: A Critical Companion*, ed. J. J. Long and Anne Whitehead (Edinburgh: Edinburgh University Press): 155–71.

——. 2010. 'A Wrong Turn of the Wheel: Sebald's Journeys of (In)Attention', in *The Undiscover'd Country. W. G. Sebald and the Poetics of Travel*, ed. Markus Zisselsberger (Rochester, NY: Camden House): 92–120.

Eagleton, Terry. 1995. *Heathcliff and the Great Hunger: Studies in Irish Culture* (London: Verso).

Ebert-Schifferer, Sibylle (ed.). 2002. *Deceptions and Illusions: Five Centuries of Trompe-l'Œil Painting* (Washington: National Gallery of Art, in assoc. with Lund Humphries).

Elias, Norbert. 1994. *The Civilising Process* (Oxford: Blackwell).

Eshel, Amir. 2003. 'Against the Power of Time: The Poetics of Suspension in W. G. Sebald's *Austerlitz*', *New German Critique* 88 (Winter): 71–96.

Etchells, Tim. 1999. *Certain Fragments* (London and New York: Routledge).

Ferenczi, Sándor. 1998. *The Clinical Diary of Sándor Ferenczi*, ed. Judith Dupont, trans. Michael Balint and Nicola Zarday Jackson (Cambridge, MA: Harvard University Press).

Finian, Robert. 2010. 'Borges on Location: Duplicitous Narration and Historical Truths in "Tema del traidor y del héroe"', *Modern Language Review* 105: 743–60.

Finke, Susanne. 1997. 'W. G. Sebald – der fünfte Ausgewanderte', in *W. G. Sebald: Porträt*, ed. Franz Loquai (Eggingen: Edition Isele): 214–27.

Fischer, Gerhard (ed.). 2009. *W. G. Sebald: Schreiben ex patria/Expatriate Writing* (Amsterdam and New York: Rodopi).

Foster, Hal. 1993. *Compulsive Beauty* (Cambridge, Mass.: MIT Press).

Fowler, Alistair. 2000. 'Transformations of Genre', in *Modern Genre Theory*, ed. David Duff (Essex: Longman): 232–49.

Franklin, Ruth. 2007. 'Rings of Smoke', in *The Emergence of Memory: Conversations with W. G. Sebald*, ed. Lynne Sharon Schwartz (New York: Seven Stories Press): 119–44.

——. 2011. *A Thousand Darknesses: Lies and Truth in Holocaust Fiction* (Oxford and New York: Oxford University Press).

Freud, Sigmund. 1955. 'The Uncanny', in *The Standard Edition of the Complete Psychological Works of Sigmund Freud*, Vol. 17, trans. and ed. James Strachey (London: Hogarth Press): 217–52.

Frey, Matthias. 2007. 'Theorizing Cinema in Sebald and Sebald with Cinema', in *Searching for Sebald: Photography after W. G. Sebald*, ed. Lise Patt with Christel Dillbohner (Los Angeles: The Institute of Cultural Inquiry): 226–41.

Friedrichsmeyer, Sara. 2006. 'Sebald's Elective and Other Affinities', in *W. G. Sebald: History, Memory, Trauma*, ed. Scott Denham and Mark McCulloh (Berlin: Walter de Gruyter): 77–90.

Fritzsche, Peter. 'W. G. Sebald's Twentieth-century Histories', in *W. G. Sebald: History, Memory, Trauma*, ed. Scott Denham and Mark McCulloh (Berlin: Walter de Gruyter): 291–300.

Fuchs, Anne. 2004. *Die Schmerzensspuren der Geschichte. Zur Poetik der Erinnerung in W. G. Sebalds Prosa* (Vienna and Cologne: Böhlau).

——. 2006. 'W. G. Sebald's Painters: The Function of Fine Art in His Prose Works', *Modern Language Review* 101.1: 167–83.

Fuchs, Anne and J. J. Long (eds). 2007. *W. G. Sebald and the Writing of History* (Würzburg: Königshausen and Neumann).

Furst, Lilian R. 2006. 'Realism, Photography, and Degrees of Uncertainty', in *W. G. Sebald: History, Memory, Trauma*, ed. Scott Denham and Mark McCulloh (Berlin: Walter de Gruyter), 219–29.

——. 2007. 'Memory's Fragile Power in Kazuo Ishiguro's *Remains of the Day* and W. G. Sebald's "Max Ferber"', *Contemporary Literature* 48.4 (Winter): 530–53.

Gadamer, Hans-Georg. 1991. *Truth and Method*, trans. Joel Weinsheimer and Donald G. Marshall (New York: Crossroad).

Garloff, Katja. 2004. 'The Emigrant as Witness: W. G. Sebald's *Die Ausgewanderten*', *German Quarterly*, 77: 76–93.

Garrigues, Emmanuel. 2000. *L'Écriture photographique: essai de sociologie visuelle* (Paris: L'Harmattan).

Gnam, Andrea. 2007. 'Fotografie und Film in W. G. Sebalds Erzahlung "Ambros Adelwarth" und seinem Roman *Austerlitz*', in *Verschiebebahnhöfe der Erinnerung: Zum Werk W. G. Sebalds*, ed. Sigurd Martin and Ingo Wintermeyer (Würzburg: Konigshausen & Neumann): 27–47.

Godard, Jean-Luc (dir.). 2001. *Eloge de l'amour*, Avventura Films.

Gomez Garcia, Carmen. 2005. '"Ruinen der Gerechtigkeit": zur Rezeption W. G. Sebalds in Spanien', in *Sebald. Lektüren*, ed. Marcel Atze and Franz Loquai (Eggingen: Edition Isele).

Görner, Rüdiger (ed.). 2003. *The Anatomist of Melancholy. Essays in Memory of W. G. Sebald* (Munich: Iudicium Verlag).

Goulish, Matthew. 2000. *39 Microlectures: in proximity of performance* (London and New York: Routledge).

——. 2004. 'Eight Memos on the Creation Process of Goat Island's *When Will the September Roses Bloom? Last Night Was only a Comedy*', *Frakcija/Goat Island*, Part 1, No. 32 (Zagreb: Centre for Dramatic Art).

Grainge, Paul. 2003. 'Introduction: Memory and Popular Film', in *Memory and Popular Film*, ed. Paul Grainge (New York: Manchester University Press): 1–20.

Gray, Richard T. 2009. 'Sebald's Segues: Performing Narrative Contingency in *The Rings of Saturn*', *The Germanic Review* 84.1 (Winter): 26–58.

Gregory-Guider, Christopher. 2005a. 'Memorial Sights/Sites: Sebald, Photography, and the Art of Autobiogeography in *The Emigrants*', *Contemporary Literature* 46.3 (Fall): 516–41.

——. 2005b. 'The "Sixth Emigrant": Traveling Places in the Works of W. G. Sebald', *Contemporary Literature* 46: 422–49.

Gumz, Alexander. 2004. 'The Novel as the City's Body: George Klein's *Libidissi*', in *Cityscapes and Countryside in Contemporary German Literature*, ed. Julian Preece and Osman Durrani (Bern: Peter Lang): 85–106.

Gunther, Stefan. 2006. 'The Holocaust as the still Point of the World in W. G. Sebald's *The Emigrants*', in *History, Memory, Trauma*, ed. Scott Denham and Mark McCulloh (Berlin: Walter de Gruyter, 2006): 279–90.

Hall, John. 2007. *Thirteen Ways of Talking about Performance Writing* (Plymouth: Plymouth College of Art Press).

Harris, Stefanie. 2001. 'The Return of the Dead: Memory and Photography in W. G. Sebald's *Die Ausgewanderten*', *The German Quarterly*, 74.4: 379–91.

Heddon, Deirdre. 2008. *Autobiography and Performance* (London: Palgrave Macmillan).

Heddon, Deirdre and Jane Milling. 2006. *Devising Performance: A Critical History* (London: Palgrave Macmillan).

Heddon, Deirdre, Carl Lavery and Phil Smith. 2009. *Walking, Writing and Performance* (Bristol: Intellect Books).

Hell, Julia. 2003. 'Eyes Wide Shut, or German Post-Holocaust Authorship', *New German Critique* 88 (Winter): 9–36.

——. 2004. 'The Angel's Enigmatic Eyes, or the Gothic Beauty of Catastrophic History in W. G. Sebald's *Air War and Literature*', *Criticism* 46.3 (Summer): 361–92.

Hirsch, Edward. 1991. 'The Imaginary Irish Peasant', *PMLA* 106.5: 1116–33.

Hirsch, Marianne. 1997. *Family Frames – Photography, Narrative and Postmemory* (Cambridge. Mass.: Harvard University Press).

——. 2008. 'The Generation of Postmemory', *Poetics Today* 28: 103–28.

— (ed.). 2004. *Teaching the Representation of the Holocaust* (New York: Modern Language Association of America).

Hofmannsthal, Hugo von. 1979. *Erzählungen, erfundene Gespräche und Briefe, Reisen* (Frankfurt am Main: Fischer Taschenbuch).

——. 1995. *The Lord Chandos Letter*, trans. Michael Hofmann (Harmondsworth: Penguin).

Hollier, Denis (ed.). 1988. *The College of Sociology (1937–39)*, trans. Betsy Wing (Minneapolis: University of Minnesota Press).

Horkheimer, Max, and Theodor W. Adorno. 1997. *Dialectic of Enlightenment*, trans. John Cumming (New York: Continuum).

Horstkotte, Silke. 2005. 'Fantastic Gaps: Photography Inserted into Narrative in W. G. Sebald's *Austerlitz*', in *Science, Technology and the German Cultural Imagination*, ed. Christian Emden and David Midgley (Berlin: Peter Lang): 269–86.

——. 2006. 'Visual Memory and Ekphrasis in W. G. Sebald's *The Rings of Saturn*', *English Language Notes* 44: 117–30.

——. 2009. *Nachbilder: Fotografie und Gedächtnis in der deutschen Gegenwartsliteratur* (Köln: Böhlau Verlag).

Hui, Barbara. 2010. 'Mapping Historical Networks in *Die Ringe des Saturn*', in *The Undiscover'd Country. W. G. Sebald and the Poetics of Travel*, ed. Marcus Zisselsberger (Rochester, N.Y.: Camden House): 277–98.

Hulse, Michael. 2011. 'Englishing Max', in *Saturn's Moons: W. G. Sebald – A Handbook*, ed. Jo Catling and Richard Hibbitt (Oxford: Legenda, 2011): 192–205.

Hutcheon, Linda. 2006. *A Theory of Adaptation* (London: Routledge).

Hutchinson, Ben. 2006. '"Egg Boxes Stacked in a Crate": Narrative Status and Its Implications', in *W. G. Sebald: History, Memory, Trauma*, ed. Scott Denham and Mark McCulloh (Berlin: Walter de Gruyter):171–82.

——. 2007. 'Der Erzähler als Schutzengel? W. G. Sebald's Reading of Giorgio Bassani', *Gegenwartsliteratur* 6: 69–91.

——. 2009a. '"Ein Penelopewerk des Vergessens?" W. G. Sebald's Nietzschean

Poetics of Forgetting', *Forum for Modern Language Studies* 45.3: 325–36.

——. 2009b. *W. G. Sebald – Die Dialektische Imagination* (Berlin and New York: Walter de Gruyter).

——. 2011. '"The Shadow of Resistance": W. G. Sebald and the Frankfurt School', *Journal of European Studies* 41.3–4, special issue ed. Richard Sheppard, 267–84.

Huyssen, Andreas. 2003. *Present Pasts: Urban Palimpsests and the Politics of Memory* (Stanford: Stanford University Press).

Ilsemann, Mark. 2006. 'Going Astray: Melancholy, Natural History and the Image of Exile in W. G. Sebald's *Austerlitz*', in *W. G. Sebald: History, Memory, Trauma*, ed. Scott Denham and Mark McCulloh (Berlin: Walter de Gruyter Verlag): 301–14.

Jaggi, Maya. 2001. 'Recovered Memories [Interview]', *Guardian* (22 September), www.guardian.co.uk/books/2001/sep/22/artsandhumanities.highereducation. Accessed 7 January 2011.

Johnson, Galen A. (ed.). 1993. *The Merleau-Ponty Aesthetics Reader: Philosophy and Painting* ed. and trans. Michael B. Smith (Evanston, Ill.: Northwestern University Press).

Josephs, Jeremy, with Susi Bechhöfer. 1996. *Rosa's Child. The True Story of One Woman's Quest for a Lost Mother and a Vanished Past* (London: I. B. Tauris).

Kafka, Franz. 1964. *The Diaries of Franz Kafka, 1910–23*, ed. Max Brod (Harmondsworth: Penguin).

——. 1990. *Tagebücher in der Fassung der Handschrift*, ed. Hans-Gerd Koch, Michael Müller, and Malcolm Pasley (Frankfurt am Main: S. Fischer).

——. 1994. *Drucke zu Lebzeiten*, ed. Hans-Gerd Koch, Wolf Kittler and Gerhard Neumann (Frankfurt am Main: S. Fischer).

Kambas, Chryssoula. 1983. *Walter Benjamin im Exil: Zum Verhältnis von Literaturpolitik und Ästhetik* (Tübingen: Niemeyer).

Kantor, Tadeusz. 1993. *A Journey through Other Spaces: Essays and Manifestoes, 1944 – 1990* (Los Angeles: University of California Press).

Kantor, Tadeusz and Krzysztof Miklaszewski. 2005. *Encounters with Tadeusz Kantor* (London and New York: Routledge).

Kastura, Thomas. 1996. 'Geheimnisvolle Fähigkeit zur Transmigration: W. G. Sebalds interkulturelle Wallfahrten in die Leere', *Arcadia* 31: 197–216.

Kempinski, Avi. 2007. '"Quel Roman!": Sebald, Barthes, and the Pursuit of the Mother-Image', in *Searching for Sebald: Photography after W. G. Sebald*, ed. Lisa Patt with Christel Dillbohner (Los Angeles: Institute of Cultural Inquiry): 456–71.

Kiberd, Declan. 1995. *Inventing Ireland: The Literature of the Modern Nation* (Verso: London).

Kilbourn, Russell J. A. 2004. 'Architecture and Cinema: The Representation of Memory in W. G. Sebald's *Austerlitz*', in *W. G. Sebald: A Critical Companion*, ed. J. J. Long and Anne Whitehead (Edinburgh: Edinburgh University Press): 140–54.

——. 2006. 'Kafka, Nabokov … Sebald: Intertextuality and Narratives of

Redemption in *Vertigo* and *The Emigrants*', in *W. G. Sebald: History, Memory, Trauma*, ed. Scott Denham and Mark McCulloh (Berlin and New York: Walter de Gruyter): 33–63.

——. 2007. '"Catastrophe with Spectator": Subjectivity, Intertextuality and the Representation of History in *Die Ringe des Saturns*', in *W. G. Sebald: History, Memory, Trauma*, ed. Scott Denham and Mark McCulloh (Berlin and New York: Walter de Gruyter): 139–62.

——. 2010. *Cinema, Memory, Modernity: The Representation of Memory from the Art Film to Transnational Cinema* (New York: Routledge).

King, Alisdair. 2007. *Hans Magnus Enzensberger: Writing, Media, Democracy* (Bern: Peter. Lang).

Klebes, Martin. 2003. 'Remembering Failure: Philosophy and the Form of the Novel' (Ph.D. dissertation, Northwestern University).

——. 2006. *Wittgenstein's Novels* (New York: Routledge).

Kovács, András Bálint. 2007. *Screening Modernism: European Art Cinema, 1950–1980* (Chicago: University of Chicago Press).

Kouvaros, George. 2005. 'Images that Remember Us: Photography and Memory in *Austerlitz*', *Textual Practice*, 19.1: 173–93.

Kracauer, Siegfried. 1947. *From Caligari to Hitler. A Psychological History of the German Film* (Princeton, N.J.: Princeton University Press).

Lacan, Jacques. 1998. *The Four Fundamental Concepts of Psycho-analysis*, ed. Jacques Alain Miller, trans. Alan Sheridan (London: Vintage).

LaCapra, Dominick. 2001. *Writing History, Writing Trauma* (Baltimore, Md.: Johns Hopkins University Press).

Landsberg, Alison. 2004. *Prosthetic Memory: The Transformation of American Remembrance in the Age of Mass Culture* (New York: Columbia University Press).

Lehmann, Hans-Thies. 2006. *Postdramatic Theatre* (London and New York: Routledge).

Lenz, Jakob Michael Reinhold. 1987. 'Catharina von Siena: Dritte Bearbeitung', in *Lenz: Werke und Briefe. Band 1*, ed. Sigrid Damm (Munich: Carl Hanser Verlag): 438–48.

Leone, Massimo. 2004. 'Textual Wanderings: A Vertiginous Reading of W. G. Sebald', in *W. G. Sebald – A Critical Companion*, ed. J. J. Long and Anne Whitehead (Edinburgh: Edinburgh University Press): 89–101.

Lerm Hayes, Christa-Maria. 2007. 'Post-War Germany and "Objective Chance": W. G. Sebald, Joseph Beuys, and Tacita Dean', in *Searching for Sebald. Photography after Sebald*, ed. Lise Patt (Los Angeles: Institute of Cultural Inquiry): 412–39.

Levi, Primo. 1988. *The Drowned and the Saved*, trans. Raymond Rosenthal (New York: Summit).

Levinas, Emmanuel. 1985. *Ethics and Infinity: Conversations with Philippe Nemo*, trans. Richard A. Cohen (Pittsburgh: Duquesne University Press).

Lewy, Guenter. 2000. *The Nazi Persecution of the Gypsies* (New York: Oxford University Press).

Literator, The. 2008. 'Cover Stories: Book-lovers' Dating Agency; Celebrating Sebald', *Independent* (29 August). www.independent.co.uk/arts-entertainment/books/features/cover-stories-booklovers-dating-agency-celebrating-sebald-911844.html. Accessed 5 January 2011.

Littell, Jonathan. 2010. *The Kindly Ones* (Toronto: McClelland and Stewart).

Lloyd, Rosemary. 2005. *Shimmering in a Transformed Light: Writing the Still Life* (Ithaca, N.Y.: Cornell University Press).

Loewy, Hanno. 1997. '". . . without Masks": Jews through the Lens of "German Photography" 1933–1945', in *German Photography 1870–1970: Power of a Medium*, ed. Klaus Honnef, Rolf Sachsse and Karin Thomas (Cologne: Dumont): 100–14.

Loewy, Hanno and Gerhard Schoenberner. 1990. *"Unser einziger Weg ist Arbeit"*: das Getto in Łódź, 1940–1944; eine Ausstellung des Jüdischen Museums Frankfurt am Main / in Zusammenarbeit mit Yad Vashem (Vienna: Löcker).

Lomas, David. 2000. *The Haunted Self: Surrealism, Psychoanalysis, Subjectivity* (New Haven and London: Yale University Press).

——. 2006. 'Labyrinth and Vertigo: On Some Motifs in André Masson and Their Meaning', in *Surrealism: Crossings/Frontiers*, ed. Elza Adamowicz (Bern: Peter Lang): 83–108.

Long, J. J. 2003. 'History, Narrative, and Photography in W. G. Sebald's *Die Ausgewanderten*', *Modern Language Review* 98.1: 117–37.

——. 2006. 'Disziplin und Geständnis: Ansätze zu einer Foucaultschen Sebald-Lektüre', in *W. G. Sebald: politische Archäologie und melancholische Bastelei*, ed. Claudia Öhlschäger and Michael Niehaus (Berlin: Erich Schmidt): 217–37.

——. 2007. *W. G. Sebald: Image, Archive, Modernity* (Edinburgh: Edinburgh University Press; New York: Columbia University Press).

——. 2007a. 'W. G. Sebald: A Bibiliographical Essay on Current Research', in *W. G. Sebald and the Writing of History*, ed. Anne Fuchs and J. J. Long (Würzburg: Königshausen and Neumann): 11–30.

——. 2009. 'W. G. Sebald: The Ambulatory Narrative and the Poetics of Digression', in *W. G. Sebald: Schreiben ex patria/Expatriate Writing*, ed. Gerhardt Fischer (Amsterdam: Rodopi): 61–71.

——. 2010. 'W. G. Sebald: The Anti-Tourist', in *The Undiscover'd Country: W. G. Sebald and the Poetics of Travel*, ed. Markus Zisselsberger (Rochester, N.Y.: Camden House): 63–91.

Long, J. J. and Anne Whitehead (eds). 2004. *W. G. Sebald – A Critical Companion* (Edinburgh: Edinburgh University Press).

Loquai, Franz. 2005. 'Max und Marcel: Eine Betrachtung über die Erinnerungskünstler Sebald und Proust', in *Sebald: Lektüren*, ed. Marcel Atze and Franz Loquai (Eggingen: Edition Isele): 212–27.

Lubow, Arthur. 2007. 'Crossing Boundaries', in *The Emergence of Memory: Conversations with W. G. Sebald*, ed. Lynne Sharon Schwartz (New York and London: Seven Stories Press): 159–73.

McBurney, Simon. 1999. 'Interview', in *On Directing*, ed. G. Giannachi and M. Luckhurst (London: Faber & Faber).

MacCabe, Colin. 1986. 'Theory and Film: Principles of Realism and Pleasure'; 'Realism and the Cinema', in *Narrative, Apparatus, Ideology: A Film Theory Reader*, ed. Philip Rosen (New York: Columbia University Press): 179–97.

McCulloh, Mark. 2003. *Understanding Sebald* (Columbia, S.C.: University of South Carolina Press).

Mack, Michael. 2009. 'Between Elias Canetti and Jacques Derrida: Satire and the Role of Fortifications in the Work of W. G. Sebald', in *W. G. Sebald: Schreiben ex patria/Expatriate Writing*, ed. Gerhard Fischer (Amsterdam and New York: Rodopi): 233–56.

Madden, Patrick. 2008. 'W. G. Sebald: Where Essay Meets Fiction', *Fourth Genre* 10.2 (Fall): 169–75.

Magris, Claudio. 2008 (1988). *Danube* (New York: Farrar Straus Giroux).

Martin, Sigurd. 2007. 'Lehren vom Ähnlichen: Mimesis und Entstellung als Werkzeuge der Erinnerung im Werk W. G. Sebalds', in *Verschiebebahnhöfe der Erinnerung: Zum Werk W. G. Sebalds*, ed. Sigurd Martin and Ingo Wintermeyer (Würzburg: Königshausen & Neumann): 81–103.

Martin, Stewart. 2005. 'W. G. Sebald and the Modern Art of Memory', *Radical Philosophy* 132 (July/Aug): 18–30.

Menninghaus, Winfried. 1986. *Schwellenkunde: Walter Benjamins Passage des Mythos* (Frankfurt am Main: Suhrkamp).

Merleau-Ponty, Maurice. 2008. *The World of Perception*, trans. Oliver Davis, intro. Thomas Baldwin (Abingdon: Routledge).

Morgan, Peter. 2005. 'The Sign of Saturn: Melancholy, Homelessness and Apocalypse in W. G. Sebald's Prose Narratives', *German Life and Letters* 58.1 (January): 75–92.

Morson, Gary Saul and Caryl Emerson. 1990. *Mikhail Bakhtin: Creation of a Prosaics* (Stanford: Stanford University Press).

Mosbach, Bettina. 2007. 'Superimposition as a Narrative Strategy in *Austerlitz*', in *Searching for Sebald: Photography after Sebald*, ed. Lise Patt with Christel Dillbohner (Los Angeles: Institute of Cultural Inquiry): 390–411.

——. 2008. *Figurationen der Katastrophe: Ästhetische Verfahren in W. G. Sebalds Die Ringe des Saturn und Austerlitz* (Bielefeld: Aisthesis).

Mulvey, Laura. 2006. *Death 24x a Second: Stillness and the Moving Image* (London: Reaktion Books).

Naremore, James (ed.). 2000. *Film Adaptation* (New Brunswick, N.J.: Rutgers University Press).

Nayhauss, Hans-Christoph Graf v. 2009. 'Adler und Sebald, Lichtenstein und Grass: Vom Umgang mit Dokumentationen bei der literarischen Produktion' in *W. G. Sebald: Schreiben ex patria/Expatriate Writing*, ed. Gerhard Fischer (Amsterdam and New York: Rodopi): 447–57.

Öhlschläger, Claudia. 2006. *Beschädigtes Leben. Erzählte Risse. W. G. Sebalds poetische Ordnung des Unglücks* (Freiburg im Breisgau: Rombach).

Osborne, Dora. 2007. 'Blind Spots: Trauma in W. G. Sebald's *Austerlitz*', *Seminar* 43: 517–33.

Pages, Neil Christian. 2010. 'Tripping: On Sebald's "Stifter"', in *The Undiscover'd Country: W. G. Sebald and the Poetics of Travel*, ed. Markus Zisselsberger (Rochester, N.Y.: Camden House) 213–46.

Pane, Samuel. 2005. 'Trauma Obscura: Photographic Media in W. G. Sebald's *Austerlitz*', *Mosaic*, 38.1: 37–54.

Patt, Lise. 2007. 'Introduction. Searching for Sebald: What I Know for Sure', in *Searching for Sebald: Photography after W. G. Sebald*, ed. Lise Patt with Christel Dillbohner (Los Angeles: Institute of Cultural Inquiry) 16–97.

Patt, Lise with Christel Dillbohner (ed.). 2007. *Searching for Sebald: Photography after W. G. Sebald* (Los Angeles: The Institute of Cultural Inquiry).

Pearson, Ann. 2008. '"Remembrance ... Is Nothing Other than a Quotation": The Intertextual Fictions of W. G. Sebald', *Comparative Literature* 60.3: 261–78.

Pearson, Mike. 1998. 'My Balls/Your Chin', in *Performance Research on Place*, 3/2 (London: Routledge).

——. 2006. *In Comes I* (Exeter: University of Exeter Press).

Pence, Jeffrey. 2003. 'Postcinema/Postmemory', in *Memory and Popular Film*, ed. Paul Grainge (New York: Manchester University Press) 237–56.

Phillips, Adam. 1997. *Terrors and Experts* (London: Faber & Faber).

Poe, Edgar Allan. 1842. Review of Nathaniel Hawthorne's Twice-Told Tales, in *Graham's Magazine* (May): 298–300.

Poltronieri, Marco. 1997. '"Wie kriegen die Deutschen das auf die Reihe?" Ein Gespräch mit W. G. Sebald', in *Porträt. W. G. Sebald*, ed. Franz Loquai (Eggingen: Isele) 138–44.

Prager, Brad. 2005. 'The Good German as Narrator: On W. G. Sebald and the Risks of Holocaust Writing', *New German Critique* 96: 75–102.

Pralle, Uwe. 2001. 'Mit einem kleinen Strandspaten Abschied von Deutschland nehmen', *Süddeutsche Zeitung* 295, 22/23 December.

Presner, Todd Samuel. 2004. '"What a Synoptic and Artificial View Reveals": Extreme History and the Modernism of W. G. Sebald's Realism', *Criticism* 46.3 (Summer): 341–60.

Puw Davies, Mererid. 2011. 'An Uncanny Journey: W. G. Sebald and the Literature of Protest', *Journal of European Studies* 41.3–4, special issue ed. Richard Sheppard: 285–303.

Radisch, Iris. 2001. 'Der Waschbär der falschen Welt', *Die Zeit* (5 April) 55.

Renner, Rolf G. 2009. 'Intermediale Identitätskonstruktion: Zu W. G. Sebalds *Austerlitz*', in *W. G. Sebald: Schreiben ex patria/Expatriate Writing*, ed. Gerhard Fischer (Amsterdam: Rodopi): 333–45.

Ribó, Ignasi. 2009. 'The One-Winged Angel: History and Memory in the Literary Discourse of W. G. Sebald', *Orbis Litterarum* 64.3: 222–62.

Ridout, Nicholas. 2005. 'A Song for Europe', *Frakcija/Goat Island*, Part 2, No. 32 (Zagreb: Centre for Dramatic Art).

Rodchenko, Alexsander. 1988. 'Against the Synthetic Portrait, for the Snapshot 1928', in John E. Bowlt (ed. and trans.), *Russian Art of the Avant-garde: Theory and Criticism 1902–1934*, ed. and trans. John E. Bowlt (London: Thames and Hudson), 250–4.

Rosset, Clément. 2006. *Fantasmagories suivi de le reel, l'imaginaire et l'illusoire* (Paris: Minuit).

Ryan, Judith. 2007. 'Fulgurations: Sebald and Surrealism', *The Germanic Review*, 82, (Summer): 227–249.

——. 2009. '"Lines of Flight": History and Territory in *The Rings of Saturn*', in *W. G. Sebald: Schreiben ex patria/Expatriate Writing*, ed. Gerhard Fischer (Amsterdam and New York: Rodopi): 45–60.

Saltzman, Lisa. 2006. *Making Memory Matter: Strategies of Remembrance in Contemporary Art* (Chicago: University of Chicago Press).

Sanders, Julie. 2006. *Adaptation and Appropriation* (London and New York: Routledge).

Santner, Eric L. 2006. *On Creaturely Life: Rilke/Benjamin/Sebald* (Chicago and London: University of Chicago Press).

Schalk, Alex. 2007. 'Image and Text: W. G. Sebald's Montage Technique', in *New German Literature: Life-Writing and Dialogue with the Arts*, ed. Julian Preece, Frank Finlay and Ruth J. Owen (Bern: Peter Lang): 37–50.

Scherpe, Klaus R. 2009. 'Auszeit des Erzählens – W. G. Sebalds Poetik der Beschreibung', in *W. G. Sebald: Schreiben ex patria/Expatriate Writing*, ed. Gerhard Fischer (Amsterdam: Rodopi): 297–316.

Scholz, Christian. 2007. '"But the Written Word Is not a True Document": A Conversation with W. G. Sebald on Literature and Photography', trans. Markus Zisselsberger, in *Searching for Sebald: Photography after W. G. Sebald*, ed. Lise Patt with Christel Dillbohner (Los Angeles: The Institute of Cultural Inquiry): 104–9.

Schopenhauer, Arthur. 1966. *The World as Will and Representation*, trans. E. F. J. Payne, 2 vols (New York: Dover).

Schwartz, Lynne Sharon (ed.). 2007. *The Emergence of Memory: Conversations with W. G. Sebald* (New York and London: Seven Stories Press).

Scott, C. 1999. *The Spoken Image: Photography and Language* (London: Reaktion Books).

——. 2011. 'Sebald's Photographic Annotations', in *Under Saturn's Moons: W. G. Sebald – A Handbook*, ed. Jo Catling and Richard Hibbitt (Oxford: Legenda), 217–45.

Sears, John. 2007. 'Photographs, Images, and the Space of Literature in Sebald's Prose', in *Searching for Sebald: Photography after W. G. Sebald*, ed. Lise Patt with Christel Dillbohner (Los Angeles: The Institute of Cultural Inquiry): 204–25.

Sebald, W. G. 1969. *Carl Sternheim. Kritiker und Opfer der Wilhelminischen Ära* (Stuttgart: W. Kohlhammer Verlag).

——. 1972. 'The Undiscover'd Country: The Death Motif in Kafka's *Castle*', *Journal of European Studies* 2: 22–34.

——. 1980. *Der Mythus der Zerstörung im Werk Döblins* (Stuttgart: Ernst Klett).

——. 1982. 'Zwischen Geschichte und Naturgeschichte – Versuch über die literarische Beschreibung totaler Zerstörung mit Anmerkungen zu Kasack, Nossack und Kluge'. *Orbis Litterarum*, 37: 345-366. doi: 10.1111/j.1600-0730.1982.tb01046x.

——. 1988a. *A Radical Stage: Theatre in Germany in the 1970s and 1980s* (Oxford: Berg Press).

——. 1988b. 'Verzehret das letzte selbst die Erinnerung nicht?', *Manuskripte*, 28: 150–8.

——. 1990. 'Und manche Nebelflecken löset kein Auge auf', in *Klagenfurter Texte. Ingeborg-Bachmann-Wettbewerb 1990*, ed. Heinz Felsbach and Siegbert Metelko (Munich: Piper): 111–37.

——. 1994a (1993). *Die Ausgewanderten. Vier lange Erzählungen* (Frankfurt am Main: Fischer Taschenbuch).

——. 1994b (1985). *Die Beschreibung des Unglücks. Zur österreichischen Literatur von Stifter bis Handke* (Frankfurt am Main: Fischer Taschenbuch).

——. 1994c. *Max Aurach*, radio play produced and directed by Ulrich Gerhardt (first transmitted *Bayern 2*, 20 May 1994).

——. 1994d (1990). *Schwindel. Gefühle* (Frankfurt am Main: Fischer Taschenbuch).

——. 1995a (1988). *Nach der Natur. Ein Elementargedicht* (Frankfurt am Main: Fischer Taschenbuch).

——. 1995b (1991). *Unheimliche Heimat. Essays zur österreichischen Literatur* (Frankfurt am Main: Fischer Taschenbuch).

——. 1996 (1992). *The Emigrants*, trans. Michael Hulse (New York: New Directions).

——. 1997a (1996). *The Emigrants*, trans. Michael Hulse (London: Harvill).

——. 1997b (1995). *Die Ringe des Saturn. Eine englische Wallfahrt* (Frankfurt am Main: Fischer Taschenbuch).

——. 1998a. *Logis im einem Landhaus. Über Gottfried Keller, Johann Peter Hebel, Robert Walser und andere* (Munich and Vienna: Carl Hanser).

——. 1998b (1995). *The Rings of Saturn*, trans. Michael Hulse (New York: New Directions).

——. 1998c. *The Rings of Saturn*, trans. Michael Hulse (London: Vintage).

——. 1999a. *The Rings of Saturn*, trans. Michael Hulse (London: The Harvill Press).

——. 1999b (1990). *Vertigo*, trans. Michael Hulse (London: The Harvill Press).

——. 1999c. *Vertigo*, trans. Michael Hulse (London: Vintage).

——. 1999d (1990). *Vertigo*, trans. Michael Hulse (New York: New Directions).

——. 1999e. *Luftkrieg und Literatur: Mit einem Essay über Alfred Andersch* (Munich: Hanser).

——. 2000a (1998). *Logis in einem Landhaus. Über Gottfried Keller, Johann Peter Hebel, Robert Walser und andere* (Frankfurt am Main: Fischer Taschenbuch).

——. 2000b. *Vertigo*, trans. Michael Hulse (New York: New Directions).

——. 2001a (1992). *Die Ausgewanderten: Vier lange Erzählungen* (Frankfurt am Main: Eichborn).

——. 2001b. *Austerlitz* (Munich and Vienna: Carl Hanser).

——. 2001c. *Austerlitz*, trans. Anthea Bell (London: Hamish Hamilton).

——. 2001d. *Austerlitz*, trans. Anthea Bell (London: Penguin).

——. 2001e. *Austerlitz*, trans. Anthea Bell (New York: Random House).

——. 2001f. *Austerlitz*, trans. Anthea Bell (New York: Modern Library).

——. 2001g. *Austerlitz*, trans. Anthea Bell (Toronto and New York: Knopf).

——. 2001h. *For Years Now: Poems by W. G. Sebald Images by Tess Jaray* (London: Short Books).

——. 2001i. 'Ich fürchte das Melodramatische', *Der Spiegel* [*Spiegel*-Gespräch with editors Martin Doerry and Volker Hage] 11/2001 (12 March): 228–34.

——. 2001j. KCRW Radio Interview with Sebald (6 December), Host: Michael Silverblatt, www.kcrw.com/etc/programs/bw/bw011206w_g_sebald. Accessed: 15 November 2006.

——. 2001k (1995). *Die Ringe des Saturn. Eine englische Wallfahrt* (Frankfurt am Main: Eichborn).

——. 2001l (1990). *Schwindel. Gefühle* (Frankfurt am Main: Eichborn).

——. 2002a. *After Nature*, trans. Michael Hamburger (New York: Modern Library).

——. 2002b. *After Nature*, trans. Michael Hamburger (London: Hamish Hamilton).

——. 2002c (2001). *Austerlitz*, trans. Anthea Bell (Harmondsworth: Penguin).

——. 2002d (2001). *Austerlitz*, trans. Anthea Bell (London: Penguin).

——. 2002e (1996). *The Emigrants*, trans. Michael Hulse (London: Vintage).

——. 2002f (1998). *The Rings of Saturn*, trans. Michael Hulse (London: Vintage).

——. 2002g (1999). *Vertigo*, trans. Michael Hulse (London: Vintage).

——. 2003a (2002). *After Nature*, trans. Michael Hamburger (New York: Modern Library).

——. 2003b. *Campo Santo*, ed. Sven Meyer (Munich and Vienna: Carl Hanser).

——. 2003c. *On the Natural History of Destruction*, trans. Anthea Bell (London: Hamish Hamilton).

——. 2003d. *On the Natural History of Destruction*, trans. Anthea Bell (New York: Random House).

——. 2004a. 'Against the Irreversible: On Jean Améry', in *On the Natural History of Destruction*, trans. Anthea Bell (New York: The Modern Library): 143–67.

——. 2004b (1999). *On the Natural History of Destruction*, trans. Anthea Bell (New York: The Modern Library).

——. 2005a. *Campo Santo*, ed. Sven Meyer, trans. Anthea Bell (London: Hamish Hamilton).

——. 2005b (2003). *Campo Santo*, trans. Anthea Bell (London: Penguin).

——. 2005c. *Campo Santo*, trans. Anthea Bell (New York: The Modern Library).

——. 2005d. *Campo Santo*, trans. Anthea Bell (New York: Random House).

——. 2006a (2005). *Campo Santo*, ed. Sven Meyer, trans. Anthea Bell (Harmondsworth: Penguin).

——. 2006b (1985). 'Der Mann mit dem Mantel: Gerhard Roths *Winterreise*', in *Die Beschreibung des Unglücks. Zur österreichischen Literatur von Stifter bis Handke* (Frankfurt am Main: Fischer Taschenbuch): 149–164.

——. 2008a. 'Aufzeichnungen aus Korsika. Zur Natur- und Menschenkunde', ed. Ulrich von Bülow. In *Wandernde Schatten. W. G. Sebalds Unterwelt*, ed. Ulrich von Bülow, Heike Gfrereis, and Ellen Strittmatter (Marbach am Neckar: Deutsche Schillergesellschaft): 128–209.

——. 2008b (1993). *Die Ausgewanderten: Vier lange Erzählungen* (Frankfurt: Fischer).

——. 2008c (1992). *Nach der Natur: Ein Elementargedicht* (Frankfurt: Fischer).

——. 2008d. *Wandernde Schatten. W. G. Sebalds Unterwelt*, ed. Ulrich von Bülow, Heike Gfereis and Ellen Strittmatter (Marbach am Neckar: Deutsche Schillergesellschaft).

——. 2008e. *Über das Land und das Wasser. Ausgewählte Gedichte 1964–2001*(Munich: Hanser).

——. 2009 (1990). *Schwindel. Gefühle* (Frankfurt am Main: Fischer Taschenbuch).

Sebald, W. G. and Jan Peter Tripp. 2003. *»Unerzählt«. 33 Texte und 33 Radierungen. Mit einem Gedicht von Hans Magnus Enzensberger und einem Nachwort von Andrea Köhler* (Munich and Vienna: Carl Hanser).

—— and ——. 2004a. *Unrecounted*, trans. Michael Hamburger (London: Hamish Hamilton).

—— and ——. 2004b. *Unrecounted*, trans. Michael Hamburger (New York: New Directions).

—— and ——. 2005. *Unrecounted*, trans. Michael Hamburger (London: Penguin).

Sereda, Stefan. 2010. 'History and Popular Memory from the Nostalgia Film to the Cinema of Simulation' (Unpublished paper).

Serke, Jürgen. 1987. *Böhmische Dörfer. Wanderungen durch eine verlassene literarische Landschaft* (Vienna: Zsolnay Verlag).

Shaffer, Elinor. 2003. 'W. G. Sebald's Photographic Narrative', in *The Anatomist of Melancholy: Essays in Memory of W. G. Sebald*, ed. Rüdiger Görner (Munich: Iudicium), 51–62.

Sheehan, Rebecca. 2009. 'Competing with "the Barbarous Clangour of a Gong": Why "Theme of the Traitor and the Hero" begins in "Nineteen Hundred and Nineteen"', *Journal of Modern Literature* 32.3: 22–38.

Sheppard, Richard. 2005. 'Dexter – Sinister: Some Observations on Decrypting the Mors [sic] Code in the Work of W. G. Sebald', *Journal of European Studies* 35.4: 419–63.

——. 2009. '"Woods, Trees, and the Spaces in Between": A Report on Work Published on W. G. Sebald 2005–8', *Journal of European Studies* 39.1: 79–128.

——. 2011. 'An Analytical Bibliography of the Works of W. G. Sebald', in *Saturn's Moons: W. G. Sebald – A Handbook*, ed. Jo Catling and Richard Hibbitt (Oxford: Legenda, 2011), pp. 446–96.

Siedenberg, Sven. 1997. 'Anatomie der Schwermut: Interview mit W. G. Sebald', in *Porträt: W. G. Sebald*, ed. Franz Loquai (Eggingen: Edition Isele): 141–3.

Silverblatt, Michael. 2007. 'A Poem of an Invisible Subject (interview)', in *The Emergence of Memory: Conversations with W. G. Sebald*, ed. Lynne Sharon Schwartz (New York and London: Seven Stories Press): 77–86.

Sontag, Susan. 1978. *On Photography* (London: Allen Lane).

——. 1983. *Under the Sign of Saturn* (London: Writers and Readers).

——. 2002. 'A Mind in Mourning', in *Where the Stress Falls* (London: Jonathan Cape): 41–8.

Soulages, François. 1998. *Esthétique de la photographie: la perte et le reste* (Paris: Nathan).

Spiteri, R. and D. LaCoss (eds). 2003. 'Surrealism, Politics and Culture'. *Studies in European Cultural Transmission* 16 (Aldershot and Burlington: Ashgate Publishing).

Stam, Robert. 2000. *Film Theory: An Introduction* (Oxford: Blackwell).

——. 2005. *Literature through Film: Realism, Magic and the Art of Adaptation* (Malden, Mass.: Blackwell).

Strathausen, Carsten. 2007. 'Going Nowhere: Sebald's Rhizomatic Travels', in *Searching for Sebald: Photography after W. G. Sebald*, ed. Lise Patt with Christel Dillbohner (Los Angeles: The Institute of Cultural Inquiry): 472–91.

Struk, Janina. 2004. *Photographing the Holocaust: Interpretations of the Evidence* (London: I. B. Tauris).

Sturken, Marita. 2008. 'Memory, Consumerism, and Media: Reflections on the Emergence of the Field', *Memory Studies* 1.1: 73–8.

Swales, Martin. 2003. 'Intertextuality, Authenticity, Metonymy? On Reading W. G. Sebald', in *The Anatomist of Melancholy: Essays in Memory of W. G. Sebald*, ed. Rudiger Görner (Munich: Iudicium): 81–7.

——. 2004. 'Theoretical Reflections on the Work of W. G. Sebald', in *W. G. Sebald – A Critical Companion*, ed. J. J. Long and Anne Whitehead (Seattle: University of Washington Press): 23–8.

Taberner, Stuart. 2004. 'German Nostalgia? Remembering German-Jewish Life in W. G. Sebald's *Ausgewanderten* and *Austerlitz*', *Germanic Review* 79: 181–202.

Taylor, John. 2010. *Into the Heart of European Poetry* (New Brunswick, N.J.: Transaction Publishers, paperback edn).

Terentowicz-Fotyga, Urszula. 2009. 'Unreal City to City of Referents: Urban Space in Contemporary London Novels', *Journal of Narrative Theory* 39: 305–29.

Tischel, Alexandra. 2006. 'Aus der Dunkelkammer der Geschichte: Zum Zusammenhang von Photographie und Erinnerung in W. G. Sebalds *Austerlitz*', in *W. G. Sebald: politische Archäologie und melancholische Bastelei*, ed. Claudia Öhlschäger and Michael Niehaus (Berlin: Erich Schmidt): 31–45.

Théâtre de Complicité. 1999. *Street of Crocodiles* (London: Methuen).

Tóibín, Colm. 2004. 'The Tragedy of Roger Casement', *The New York Review of Books*, 51: 9 (27 May), www.nybooks.com/articles/17136. Accessed 24 March 2011.

Turim, Maureen. 1989. *Flashbacks in Film: Memory and History* (New York: Routledge).

Turner, Victor. 1974. *Dramas, Fields, and Metaphors: Symbolic Action in Human Society* (Ithaca, N.Y.: Cornell University Press).

——. 1987. 'Betwixt and Between: The Liminal Period in Rites of Passage', in *Betwixt and Between: Patterns of Masculine and Feminine Initiation*, ed. Louise Carus Mahdi, Steven Foster, and Meredith Little (La Salle, Illinois: Open Court): 3–19.

Tythacott, Louise. 2003. *Surrealism and the Exotic* (London: Routledge)

Van Gennep, Arnold. 1909. *Les Rites de Passage* (Paris: Dunod).

Vogel-Klein, Ruth. 2005. '"Stendhal nach Auschwitz": zur Rezeption W. G. Sebalds in Frankreich', in *Sebald. Lektüren*, ed. Marcel Atze and Franz Loquai (Eggingen: Edition Isele): 133–42.

——. 2005a. 'Sebald in seinem Werk die Rückkehr der Toten durch eine "Gegen-zeitigkeit" ermöglicht', in *Mémoire. Transferts. Images. Erinnerung. Übertragungen. Bilder. Recherches germaniques. Hors série no. 2.* (Strasbourg: Université Marc Bloch): 115.

von Bülow, Ulrich. 2011. 'The Disappearance of the Author in the Work', in *Saturn's Moons: W. G. Sebald – A Handbook*, ed. Jo Catling and Richard Hibbitt (Oxford: Legenda, 2011): 247–63.

Wachtel, Eleanor. 2007. 'Ghost Hunter', in *The Emergence of Memory: Conversations with W. G. Sebald*, ed. Lynne Sharon Schwartz (New York and London: Seven Stories Press): 37–61.

Ward, Simon. 2004. 'Ruins and Poetics in the Works of W. G. Sebald', in *W. G. Sebald: A Critical Companion*, ed. J. J. Long and Anne Whitehead (Seattle: University of Washington Press): 58–71.

——. 2006. 'Responsible Ruins? W. G. Sebald and the Responsibility of the German Writer', *Forum for Modern Language Studies* 2.2: 183–99.

Weber, Markus R. 2003. 'Die fantastische befragt die pedantische Genauigkeit: Zu den Abbildungen in W. G. Sebalds Werken', *Text + Kritik*, 158: 63–74.

Weber, Samuel. 2003. '"Streets, Squares, Theaters": A City on the Move – Walter Benjamin's Paris', *Boundary 2*, 30: 17–30.

Wellbery, David (ed.). 2004. *A New History of German Literature* (London: Harvard University Press).

Williams, Arthur. 1998. 'The Elusive First-person Plural: Real Absences in Reiner Kunze, Bernd-Dieter Hüge, and W. G. Sebald', in *'Whose story?' – Continuities in Contemporary German-language Literature*, ed. Arthur Williams, Stuart Parkes and Julian Preece (Bern: Peter Lang): 85–113.

——. 2000. 'W. G. Sebald: A Holistic Approach to Borders, Texts and Perspectives', in *German-language Literature Today: International and Popular?*, ed. Arthur Williams, Stuart Parkes and Julian Preece (Bern: Peter Lang): 99–118.

——. 2001. '"Das korsakowsche Syndrom": Remembrance and Responsibility in W. G. Sebald', in *German Culture and the Uncomfortable Past: Representations of National Socialism in Contemporary Germanic Literature*, ed. Helmut Schmitz (Aldershot and Burlington: Ashgate): 65–86.

——. 2003. 'W. G. Sebald: weit ausholende Annäherungen an ein problematisches Vaterland', in *Deutschsprachige Erzählprosa seit 1990 im europäischen Kontext. Interpretationen, Intertextualität, Rezeption*, ed. Volker Wehdeking and Anne-Marie Corbin (Trier: Wissenschaftlicher Verlag): 179–97.

——. 2004a. '"Immer weiter ostwärts und immer weiter zurück in der Zeit": Exploring the Extended Kith and Kin of W. G. Sebald's *Austerlitz*', in *Strangers and Neighbours: East Europe in Contemporary German-Language Literature*, ed. Ian Foster and Juliet Wigmore (Amsterdam: Rodopi): 121–41.

——. 2004b. 'W. G. Sebald: Probing the Outer Edges of Nature', in *Cityscapes and Countryside in Contemporary German Literature*, ed. Julian Preece and Osman Durrani (Bern: Peter Lang): 179–96.

——. 2007a. 'Modes of Restitution: Schreber as Countermodel for Sebald', in *The Worlds of Elias Canetti. Centenary Essays*, ed. William Collins Donahue and Julian Preece (Newcastle: Cambridge Scholars Publishing): 224–45.

——. 2007b. 'Some Thoughts on W. G. Sebald, Drawing, Painting, and Music', in *New German Literature. Life-Writing and Dialogue within the Arts*, ed. Julian Preece, Frank Finlay and Ruth J. Owen (Bern: Peter Lang): 51–74.

Williams, David. 2010. 'Geographies of Requiredness: Notes on the Dramaturg in Collaborative Devising', in *Contemporary Theatre Review* 20.2 (London: Routledge).

Williams, Linda. 2001. *Playing the Race Card: Melodramas of Black and White from Uncle Tom's Cabin to O. J. Simpson* (Princeton, N.J.: Princeton University Press).

Williams, Raymond. 1973. *The Country and the City* (New York: Oxford University Press).

———. 1977. *Marxism and Literature* (Oxford: Oxford University Press).

Wilton-Ely, John. 1994. *Giovanni Battista Piranesi: The Complete Etchings*, 2 vols (San Francisco: Alan Wolfsy Fine Arts).

Witte, Bernd. 1997. *Walter Benjamin: An Intellectual Biography*, trans. James Rolleston (Detroit, MI: Wayne State University Press).

Wohlfarth, Irving. 2008. 'Anachronie: Interferenzen zwischen Walter Benjamin und W. G. Sebald', *Internationales Archiv für Sozialgeschichte der deutschen Literatur* 33.2: 184–242.

Wohlleben, Doren. 2007. 'Maske – Gesicht – Antlitz: Porträts bei W. G. Sebald in Bild und Text', *Gegenwartsliteratur. Ein germanistisches Jahrbuch* 6: 1–20.

Wolff, Lynn. 2009. 'Literary Historiography: W. G. Sebald's Fiction', *W. G. Sebald: Schreiben ex patria / Expatriate Writing*, ed. Gerhard Fischer (Amsterdam: Rodopi): 317–32.

Wood, James. 1998. 'The Right Thread', *The New Republic* 219.1 (July 16): 38–42.

Zilcosky, John. 2004. 'Sebald's Uncanny Travels', in *W. G. Sebald – A Critical Companion*, ed. J. J. Long and Anne Whitehead (Edinburgh: Edinburgh University Press): 102–20.

———. 2006. 'Lost and Found: Disorientation, Nostalgia, and Holocaust Melodrama in Sebald's *Austerlitz*', *Modern Language Notes* 121: 679–98.

Zisselsberger, Markus (ed.). 2010. *The Undiscover'd Country: W. G. Sebald and The Poetics of Travel* (Rochester, N.Y.: Camden House).

INTERNET SOURCES

Cupola Bobber: www.cupolabobber.com
Goat Island Website: www.goatislandperformance.org.
Lone Twin: www.lonetwin.com.
Platform: www.platformlondon.org.
Volcano Theatre Company: www.volcanotheatre.co.uk.

INDEX

Note: 'n.' following a page reference indicates the number of a note on that page.

Lightning Source UK Ltd.
Milton Keynes UK
UKOW07f2133250316

270913UK00004B/49/P